LEARNING to pass

ECDL

for Office 2000

LEARNING to pass

ECDL

for Office 2000

Angela Bessant

Heinemann Educational Publishers,
Halley Court, Jordan Hill, Oxford OX2 8EJ
A division of Harcourt Education Ltd

Heinemann is a registered trademark of Harcourt Education Limited

OXFORD MELBOURNE AUCKLAND JOHANNESBURG BLANTYRE GABORONE IBADAN
PORTSMOUTH NH (USA) CHICAGO

First published 2000
New edition 2002
06 05 04 03 02
6 5 4 3 2 1

A catalogue record for this book is available from the British Library on request.

ISBN 0 435 45578 8

Cover designed by Sarah Garbett

Pages designed by Paul Davies and Associates

Typeset by TechType, Abingdon, Oxon

Printed and bound in Great Britain by Thomson Litho Ltd, East Kilbride, Scotland

Acknowledgements
I would like to thank all those who helped in the preparation of this book, particularly, Rosalyn Bass,
Margaret Berriman, Gillian Burrell and Pen Gresford at Heinemann Educational. I would like to thank
all past and present students and colleagues who have been uncomplaining when I have tried out
course materials on them. Special thanks must go to my family; my mother and Conrad for their
constant encouragement, Gemma for trialling and proofreading and Mike for his untiring support and
patience.

Dedicated to my father.

Screen shots reprinted with permission from Microsoft Corporation, Yahoo! Inc, AltaVista and the
Natural History Museum, London.

Limit of liability/disclaimer of warranty
The accuracy and completeness of the information provided herein and the opinions stated herein
are not guaranteed or warranted to produce any particular results, and the advice and strategies
contained herein may not be suitable for every individual.

Tel: 01865 888058 www.heinemann.co.uk

Contents

Heinemann is an independent entity from the European Computer Driving Licence Limited, not affiliated with the European Computer Driving Licence Foundation Limited in any manner. This book may be used in assisting students to prepare for the European Computer Driving Licence. Neither the European Computer Driving Licence Foundation Limited ('ECDL-F') nor Heinemann warrants that the use of this book will ensure passing the relevant Examination. Use of the EDCL-F approved Courseware Logo on this product signifies that it has been independently reviewed and approved in complying with the following standards:

- ECDL-F does not review courseware material for technical accuracy and does not guarantee that the end user will pass the associated ECDL Examinations. Any and all assessment tests and/or performance based exercise contained in this book relate solely to this book and do not constitute, or imply, certification by the European Driving Licence Foundation in respect of any ECDL Examination. For details on sitting ECDL Examinations in your country please contact the local ECDL Licensee or visit the European Computer Driving Licence Foundation Limited web site at http://www.ecdl.com.

- ECDL Candidates using this courseware material should have a valid ECDL/ICDL Skills Card/Log book. Without such as a skills card/Log book no ECDL/ICDL tests can be taken and no ECDL/ICDL certificate, nor any other form of recognition can be given to the candidate.

- ECDL/ICDL Skills Cards may be obtained from any accredited ECDL/ICDL Test Centre or from your country's National ECDL/ICDL designated Licensee.

- References to the European Computer Driving Licence (ECDL) include the International Computer Driving Licence (ICDL). The ECDL Syllabus is published as the official syllabus for use within the European Computer Driving Licence (ECDL) and International Computer Driving Licence (ICDL) certification programme.

Introduction

In order to become proficient in using a computer, it is necessary to practise. This book enables you to do that, leading you through Microsoft Office 2000 applications step by step so that you can build up confidence. With the aid of the quick reference guides at the end of each chapter, and referring back through the sections for points you are unsure of, there is ample practice material for you to attempt. In this way, you will consolidate your understanding of the methods used. Sample answers to exercises (where appropriate) are provided. Other useful information appears in the Appendix and Glossary.

This book assumes no prior computer knowledge. It covers all seven modules (listed below) for Version 3 of the European Computer Driving Licence (ECDL) syllabus. However, it is so packed with information and advice that it would be equally suitable for anyone wanting to learn or brush up their skills in Office 2000.

There are many ways of performing tasks in Windows 98 (Windows 98 is used in this book) and Office 2000 applications, for example via the keyboard, using the mouse or using the menus. For simplicity, the practical exercises demonstrated usually show one method. There are however, instructions given for other methods at the end of the chapters or in the Appendix. You will then be able to decide which is the best method for you.

ECDL modules

Module 1   Basic Concepts of Information Technology

Module 2   Using the Computer and Managing Files (using Windows 98 and Windows Explorer)

Module 3   Word Processing (using Word)

Module 4   Spreadsheets (using Excel)

Module 5   Databases/Filing Systems (using Access)

Module 6   Presentation (using PowerPoint)

Module 7   Information and Communication (using Internet Explorer and Outlook Express)

If you want to find out more about the ECDL syllabus, ECDL tests and test centres, the web address is:

http://www.ecdl.com

Contact:

ECDL
The British Computer Society
1 Sandford Street
Swindon
Wiltshire SN1 1HJ

Basic Concepts of Information Technology

Section 1 Getting started

1.1 Information Technology

Information Technology (IT) is the term commonly used to cover the range of computer and telecommunications technologies involved in the transfer and processing of information.

There has always been a need for accurate up-to-date information, even before the advent of computer technologies, but it used to be a time-consuming process to gather and process relevant information. The advent of very large *mainframe* computers, relying on specialised staff to operate them, brought a change in the ways that big business handled information. Increasingly over the past decades, as the cost and size of computers have decreased, many tasks are now undertaken by powerful, inexpensive desktop PCs (personal computers) on a vast scale. Linking these computers together via the *Internet* has resulted in an explosion in the amount of data being manipulated every day. Today, almost all aspects of everyday life rely on information technology and this has generated an ever-increasing demand for IT skills.

The computer system – an overview

A computer is a machine that processes data following a set of instructions. The computer system consists of *hardware* and *software*. Computer equipment that you can touch and handle is called hardware. It is the name given to all the physical devices that make up the computer system. These devices include the input devices (how we get the information into the computer), such as a keyboard or mouse. It also includes the *central processing unit* – the 'brain' of the system that carries out all the instructions received from the operator or the program – and the memory devices that store information. Finally, it includes the output devices (how we get the information out of the computer), such as monitors and printers. Input and output devices are known as *peripherals*.

Software is the name given to the programs, each made up of a series of instructions that tell the computer what to do, allowing the hardware to do a useful job. Without software, hardware is useless. Applications packages such as word processing, spreadsheet, database and drawing programs are all examples of software. Microsoft Office 2000 is software.

Types of computer

Computers vary in size and cost. They range from something that can fit in your pocket costing a few hundred pounds to those that fill a room and cost millions of pounds. They all have the common characteristics that they can store information and carry out stored instructions of tasks (programs) automatically using a *digital* data processor to make information meaningful. In contrast to humans, they can do this repeatedly, accurately and with great speed.

The main types of computers are classed to differentiate between them as follows:

Mainframe

A mainframe (now often referred to as a 'large server') offers the ultimate in processing power and storage capabilities. A mainframe is any powerful general-purpose expensive computer system. It typically has many *dumb* terminals connected to it although these are increasingly being replaced by PCs. Dumb terminals consist of only a keyboard and display unit usually with no disk drives or their own processor so that they cannot work when not connected to the mainframe. Mainframes are used by large commercial organisations such as banks and insurance companies. Mainframes used to fill whole rooms and require specialised staff and air-conditioned clean environments, but these days they are more robust and take up much less space. They have vast storage capacity (hundreds of megabytes of main memory and terabytes (trillions of bytes) of disk storage). It is interesting to note that the computing power of an average home computer now exceeds that of the typical 1970s mainframe.

Minicomputer

With advances in technology, a family of smaller and cheaper computers called minicomputers were introduced. The term 'minicomputer' is not used very often nowadays and they have evolved into 'mid-range servers' that are part of a network. Originally they were typically installed in smaller businesses and research establishments. The processing and storage capacity of the minicomputer is midway between the mainframe and the PC (see below).

Network Computer

Computer systems can be stand-alone (not connected to any other computer) or they can be connected together to form a network for data transfer, communications and backups. When computers are connected together, they are known as networked computers. Networked computers do not have to be in the same building. Using telecommunications, a computer can be linked to another computer anywhere in the world. PCs (see below) can be connected to a network for the processes of sharing information but they also operate when not connected to the network. There are advantages and savings in that they can share peripherals such as printers. They can be used as intelligent terminals. Networked computers are used in medium to large-sized organisations including schools.

Personal Computer

This is a computer that is small enough to fit on a desktop and inexpensive enough to be bought by an individual for personal use. There are two commonly used personal computers. The most widespread of the two is the computer based on the original IBM PC, and all clones of this machine are referred to as PCs. The PC is predominant in business and industry. The other common computer is the Apple Macintosh, known as the Mac, which is predominant in creative fields such as publishing and design. Personal computers vary in price, performance and storage capacity and can be chosen to suit requirements. Typically they range from £500 to several thousands of pounds. The price reflects the performance and storage capacity.

Laptop computer

The laptop computer is a small-sized PC that can use battery power and be carried around. It is used by people on the move, such as sales representatives and business travellers. As with the 'desktop' PC, it can be chosen to suit your personal requirements. Laptops are more expensive than desktop PCs with the same specification due to their components needing to be light, small and able to operate on low power consumption. They have flat-screen displays.

1.2 Hardware

Central Processing Unit (CPU)

The *Central Processing Unit* (CPU) or processor is the processing part of the computer. It carries out all arithmetical and logical operations. It is made up of the *Arithmetic Logic Unit* (ALU) that carries out high-speed data manipulation – calculating and comparing. It also contains the *control unit* that controls the passage of data to and from the ALU by locating, analysing and carrying out instructions and sending information to be temporarily stored in high-speed memory. In a PC the CPU is a single microchip that looks like a thin wafer with legs. In a minicomputer, the CPU is usually contained on a printed circuit board. A mainframe CPU may take up several circuit boards. The speed of the CPU is called the clock speed or clock rate and is measured in megahertz (MHz). It is one of the crucial factors when determining a computer's overall performance. Currently, a typical clock speed for a PC is 500 MHz.

Input devices

There are many ways of feeding information into the computer and this is done using input devices. There are many different input devices including the following.

Keyboard
A keyboard consists of input keys. In the UK, computer keyboards are based on the standard typewriter layout *QWERTY.* They have additional keys, such as function keys programmed to perform frequently used tasks, arrow keys, the Control (Ctrl) key used in conjunction with other keys to perform specific tasks, and often keys used for power saving.

Mouse
The mouse is a pointing device that enables you to interact with (e.g. select and move) items on the screen. The mouse's movements are tracked by a rotating ball and sensors in its base. When you move the mouse on your desk, the mouse pointer moves on the screen in the same direction. The mouse pointer changes depending on where it is and what it is doing. Mice have buttons that can be used to select and choose options.

Trackball
A trackball operates in a similar way to a mouse but is a stationary unit. Unlike a mouse, it has the rotating ball on top instead of underneath and is manipulated with the fingers or palm of the hand. Trackballs are commonly integrated into laptop computers since they are easier to operate in limited spaces.

Touchpad
A touchpad is another alternative to a mouse in that it is a device for interacting with a computer screen. A touchpad is also common on laptop computers for the same reasons as the trackball. It is a flat pad that works by sensing finger movements and downward pressure.

Scanner
A scanner can convert physical printed text or images into electrical signals that the computer can understand. Scanners can be *flatbed* – able to scan a whole page of text or images at a time – or *handheld*.

Light pen

This is a light-sensitive detector in the shape of a pen. It enables the user to draw, and change pictures by moving the pen across the screen. It is normally only used in specialised applications.

Joystick

A joystick is able to interact with a computer program – for example, control the movement of a shape on the screen. It has a stick that moves to effect corresponding movements on screen. Joysticks are usually used with games.

Output devices

There are many ways of getting information out of the computer. Some common output devices include the following.

Monitor

A monitor is the name given to any device that displays information on a screen (soft copy) and is normally separate from other parts of the computer. Laptop computers do not have separate monitors because the display is integrated in one unit. Monitors can be monochrome or colour. A VGA monitor can display up to 256 colours at one time and has a maximum definition of 640 x 480 pixels (pixel is an abbreviation for **picture element** – pixels are the tiny dots on screen that form an image). A Super VGA (SVGA) monitor has a higher definition with 800 x 600 pixels. Performance is improving at a rapid rate. Desktop monitors tend to have cathode ray tube (CRT – a vacuum tube used in televisions) technology. Laptops generally have LCD (Liquid Crystal Display) displays because they are lighter and use less power and less space. However LCD displays are more expensive.

Visual Display Unit (VDU)

This is another device that displays computer output on a screen. It is very similar to a monitor except that it is usually associated with a keyboard and is often used as a terminal to a mainframe computer.

Screen

A screen is the display area of a monitor.

Printers

A printer provides printed (hard copy) output. There are three commonly used types of printer: *dot matrix*, *inkjet* and *laser*.

The *dot matrix* printer is a low-cost printer but is being superseded by newer technologies. It is an impact printer and produces its characters from patterns of individual dots striking the paper via a ribbon (usually) a line at a time. Dot matrix printers are noisy in operation and the print quality is not particularly good but they are cheap to run.

Both *inkjets* and *lasers* are quiet in operation and print to a higher quality. They are both non-impact printers. The inkjet sprays ink on to the paper from an ink cartridge. Laser printers use laser beams reflected from a mirror to attract ink (called toner) to selected paper areas as the paper is fed over a drum. Laser printers are generally quicker and produce the highest quality output. All types have models available to print in black and white, and/or colour. Printers come with a recommendation for types of paper, since the quality of paper used has an effect on the quality of output produced. The resolution (clarity) of the printout is usually measured in dots per inch (dpi). The Epson laser printer (EPL-5800), for example, has a resolution of 1200dpi and a speed of ten pages per minute. Printers range greatly in price depending on the quality of output and speed of print required. Most printers have a built-in local memory in order to speed up the print process.

Plotter

A plotter uses pens to produce drawings. The computer gives the instructions so that the plotter knows which pen to use and where to draw. Plotters are normally used in engineering applications.

Speakers

Speakers produce output in audio format. They are used in music, games and speech.

Speech synthesizers

Speech synthesizers turn text into spoken words and vice versa. They can be used by the visually impaired.

1.3 Storage

Types of memory

Computer memory is the place where instructions and data are stored. A computer has two types of memory, *RAM* (**R**andom **A**ccess **M**emory) and *ROM* (**R**ead **O**nly **M**emory). RAM is the computer's fast short-term memory. It needs electricity to retain information and anything stored in RAM will be lost when the power is turned off. When the computer is running, the greater capacity it has to temporarily store instructions and data, the quicker larger programs will function. ROM permanently stores instructions and data. Its contents are stored when the computer is made and cannot be altered. RAM is faster than ROM and both are faster than disk. Access time to RAM is usually measured in nanoseconds (billionths of a second) whereas access time to a hard disk (see below) or CD-ROM is usually measured in milliseconds (thousandths of a second).

Measuring memory

The binary system is the principle behind digital computers. Binary means two and data is represented by the two digits 0 and 1 (0 is the off state and 1 the on state of the computer's memory cells). Eight *bits* make up one byte. A bit is short for **b**inary dig**it**. It is the smallest element of computer storage. Computer memory is measured in *bytes*. A byte holds the equivalent of a single character – e.g. the letter A or a full stop. Because a byte is such a small unit of storage, computer memory is more commonly measured in terms of thousands of bytes – *kilobyte* or KB (actually 1024 bytes) – or millions of bytes – *megabyte* or MB (1024KB) – and even thousands of millions of bytes – *gigabyte* or GB. A word processor *file* (a document is called a file when it is saved) of 1000 words will use approximately 15KB. A full-screen colour picture will take up approximately 300KB. A *field* is a unit of data that is more than one byte in size. A collection of fields make up a *record* – for example, a person's name, address, etc. on a mailing list makes up one record; each individual part is a field.

Memory storage devices

If you want to store information so that you can re-use it at a later date or just keep it safe, you would need to store it on one of the following non-volatile storage devices.

Hard disk

Most computers have hard disks installed. A hard disk is a fixed disk consisting of magnetic storage plates encased in a drive unit positioned inside the computer. A hard disk is used as the main permanent store of programs that have been loaded on to the computer so that they are always available. If connected to a network, the computer is sometimes able to access other hard disks on other computers. External hard disks are also available. Hard disks provide fast retrieval of information compared with floppy disks. Because hard disk capacity is large, it is measured in MB or GB.

Floppy disk (diskette)

A floppy disk is a removable storage medium used in drive A or B. The $3^1/_2$" floppy disk has become the norm. It provides a cheap way of backing up small amounts of data. It has a hard plastic case (protecting its floppy interior) with a metal cover which slides back when the disk is placed in the disk drive. The amount that can be stored on a floppy disk depends on whether it is single or double sided and whether it is single, double or high density. A double density floppy disk stores approximately 720KB and a high density disk approximately 1.44MB. Some disks come ready formatted, but if not, the first time you use a new floppy disk, you must *format* it so that it is configured for your particular system.

Floppy disks have a notch, called the write-protect notch, which will stop you deleting or altering a disk's contents. On $3^1/_2$" disks there is a small tab in one corner that slides across to write-protect it.

To ensure floppy disks are not damaged, you should do the following:

- always store disks carefully
- keep the disks away from anything magnetic
- keep the disks away from direct heat – e.g. radiators or sunlight
- do not touch the exposed recording surface.

Zip disk

A zip disk is a removable disk similar to a floppy disk but can store 100MB or 250MB of information and is much faster. As with other disk drives, zip drives can be internal or external. Zip disks are useful for storing unusually large files or putting your system on to another computer – e.g. a laptop.

CD-ROM

A CD-ROM (**C**ompact **D**isc **R**ead **O**nly **M**emory) disk is a round and flat optical device (uses a narrow laser beam to read the data, which has been etched on to the surface to form minute patterns). It is usually used in drive D. It can hold in excess of 600MB, equivalent to about 250,000 pages of text or 500 floppy disks. It has fast data retrieval. As the size of software has increased, it is now usually distributed on CD-ROMs instead of floppy disks. A *CD-R* is a recordable CD that can be recorded on once only. A *CD-RW* is recordable and can be used many times. A *CD-WORM* (**W**rite-**O**nce **R**ead-**M**any) is an optical disk that allows the user to write data onto it once only.

Data cartridges

Data cartridges use magnetic tape technology and are often used for backing up data in large organisations. They are slower and cheaper than other storage devices because they have sequential access (scanning information starting at the beginning and working through until it finds the required information) rather than random access (accessing information without having to read everything that comes before it).

Computer performance

Computer performance can be determined by the following factors.

Speed of the CPU

There are different types of processor – e.g. Pentium, PowerPC. The speed at which they perform is measured in megahertz (MHz). The greater the number of MHz, the better the performance.

Amount of RAM

Most desktop and notebook computers sold today include at least 32MB of RAM, and can normally be upgraded to 128MB. The more RAM you have, the less frequently the computer has to access instructions and data from the more slowly accessed hard disk.

Hard disk speed and capacity

Hard disk speeds vary. It is always a good idea to buy a large hard disk so that you will not run out of storage space and have to rely on using slower floppy disks or have to delete items stored on the hard disk to make room.

1.4 Software

Types of software

There are two main categories of software, *systems* software and *applications* software. Systems software includes the control programs, such as the operating system. Application software is any program that processes information for the user – e.g. word processor, spreadsheet, payroll.

Operating system software

The operating system (OS) is the software that controls the hardware and runs the programs. It is the first program run when the computer is turned on. Common operating systems include MS-DOS, Windows, Linux, Mac OS and UNIX. Windows is an example of a *Graphical User Interface* (GUI) because it uses icons (small pictures), menus and a mouse. These make the software more user-friendly since it is intuitive and you don't have to remember complicated commands. The Apple Macintosh also has a GUI.

Applications software

Common applications software includes:

- *Word processing.* A word processing program allows you to enter and manipulate text on screen. The text can be saved as a file and then printed. It is the most commonly used application. Once the basics have been learnt, it is easy to produce professional-looking documents. These documents can be stored on disk so that they can be recalled and altered at a later date. Microsoft Word is a word processing program.

- *Spreadsheet.* This program has some aspects of a filing system and some of a calculator. It consists of a large area, or grid, in which you enter data and text and work out sums. The program will do the calculations as instructed by you. When changes are made, the spreadsheet automatically recalculates new values. It is very fast, accurate and flexible. You can save the spreadsheets to disk and print them. It is used in accounting to produce budgets, balance sheets, payrolls and in scientific modelling and 'what if' analyses. Microsoft Excel is a spreadsheet program.

- *Database.* This is a program that allows you to store data in an organised record format. It is sometimes known as an 'electronic filing system'. It is structured so that it can be used to retrieve, sort and search for data quickly and in many different ways. Databases can be saved to disk and can be printed. It is much faster than using a paper database, where filing cards are stored in a manual card-index system, and has a much greater storage capacity. Databases are extensively used in all types of business and commerce. Microsoft Access is a database program.

- *Payroll.* There are many specialised programs available for payroll tasks. Spreadsheet packages are capable enough to carry out payroll tasks for small companies.

- *Presentation.* Presentation software allows you to create, organise and design effective presentations. These can produce overhead transparencies, 35mm slides or automated presentations on the computer. Microsoft PowerPoint is a presentation program.

- *Desktop publishing.* Desktop publishing (DTP) software allows you to create professional-looking manuals and brochures. Microsoft Publisher is a DTP program.

- *Multimedia.* There are many programs available to use with multimedia – i.e. combining graphics, text, sound, video and user interaction. Paintshop Pro (image manipulation) and programs for music generation are popular.

Systems development

Computer systems development employs a number of specialised staff – e.g. systems analysts, programmers – that work together at different stages. It has a life cycle as follows:

Research, analysis and design
This includes a feasibility study, the overall general design, prototyping, the detail design and the functionality requirement specifications.

Programming
This includes the design and coding of the system.

Testing
The system then needs to be tested to ensure that it will perform correctly.

Implementation
This includes training of staff, converting from the old system and installation of the new one.

User acceptance
The user will accept the system once it has been fully implemented and tested.

Section 2 Information networks

2.1 Network systems

LAN and WAN

There are two distinct types of information network:

- *LAN* (**L**ocal **A**rea **N**etwork). This is a network that connects computers within a local confined geographical area – e.g. a single office, building or across a site.

- *WAN* (**W**ide **A**rea **N**etwork). This connects computers over a wide area and across countries.

There are many advantages in working on a network. It is easy to share files and resources and to group-work on specific tasks because of this. It is easy to communicate via e-mail. Software programs can be installed centrally from one powerful server computer. Resources such as printers and scanners can be shared, thus keeping equipment costs down.

The telephone network in computing

LANs usually have cables that connect the computers on the network. However WANs often use the national and international telephone systems that rely on the Public Switched Data Network (PSDN), the Integrated Service Digital Network (ISDN) and satellite communications. The purpose of these is to ensure that people and computers can communicate over standardised connection facilities using common protocols.

When a computer needs to send information to another computer using the telephone system it must have a means of converting the digital signals (that have two distinct states) from the computer, into analogue signals (not absolute values but ones that constantly change – e.g. audio tones) used by the phone line, and vice versa for incoming information. (It must **mo**dulate and **dem**odulate.) The hardware that enables this is called a *modem*. The rate of signal changes when transmitting/receiving data is known as the *baud*. At very low speeds the baud rate is equal to bits per second (bps) – e.g. 300 baud is the same as 300bps. Beyond this one baud can be made to represent more than one bit. Currently the maximum rate over the public telephone network is 56 Kbaud.

Fax and telex machines also use the phone system. Fax machines communicate a printed page between remote locations. A stand-alone fax machine is made up of a scanner, printer and modem with fax signalling, but electronic fax/modems are available that can be attached to a computer either internally or externally. Telex machines were the first worldwide real-time data communications service to use terminals for transmitting and receiving messages. Telex messaging is now in decline.

Electronic mail

Electronic mail (e-mail) is a method of sending messages from one computer to another. You can send and receive the electronic equivalent of letters, faxes, pictures and sound. Some organisations have their own internal e-mail systems. Others are connected to the *Internet* in order to send and receive e-mail locally and internationally. It is a quick and efficient means of communication. It has the advantage that you can send and receive your messages when you choose (unlike telephone communication) and is cheaper because calls are charged at local rates (and sometimes even free!). In addition, you will usually be informed if your message has failed to reach its destination. E-mail messages (and any files transmitted with them) can be saved and edited by the recipient, whether text or graphics.

In order to send/receive e-mail over the Internet you will need:

*   a telephone system to connect to, either dial-up (temporary) or a leased line (permanent) connection

*   a modem

*   communications software

*   an account with an Internet Service Provider (ISP) who will register your unique e-mail address.

The Internet

The Internet is made up of interconnected networks all over the world that send, receive and store information. Originally developed by the military, it became widely used for research work in academia and commerce. It is now widely used throughout all walks of life for work and leisure pursuits. Access is provided, (for individuals) through ISPs. The World Wide Web (WWW) is a part of this network. It contains millions of pages of words, pictures, sounds and graphics, stored on computers connected to the Internet. It has been called an 'information superhighway'. It provides information on almost every subject. Each document on the WWW is written in HTML (Hypertext Markup Language). This commonality of language makes it easy for a *web browser* (software that lets you select and view web pages) to display web pages. The two most common web browsers are *Internet Explorer* and *Netscape Navigator*. The web uses the Hypertext Transfer Protocol (HTTP) to download web pages to the browser and TCP/IP (Transmission Control Protocol/Internet Protocol) allowing information to travel between networks. Web pages can contain hyperlinks – addresses, known as URLs (Uniform Resource Locators) – to other web pages so that users can plot their own routes through the web pages depending on their area of interest. The WWW is now used for business, commerce and education as well as recreational pursuits.

When looking for specific information on the web, if you do not know an address where you can find it, you can use a search engine. A search engine will look through its database of sites that contain the 'Key word(s)' that you are looking for and will return a list of possible suitable sites. There are also search directories that set out information in subject categories.

Section 3 Computers in everyday life

3.1 The use of computers

With the advent of microchip technology, computers have become smaller, faster, more reliable, easier to use and cheaper. Since the late 70s when personal computers first became available, there has been an ever-increasing growth in their popularity that shows no signs of slowing down.

Computers in the home

An increasing number of households now have a computer, many with Internet access. It is used for various activities by all family members including:

- working from home (teleworking)
- sending e-mails
- accessing the internet to find information for various activities – e.g. homework, projects, hobbies
- keeping household accounts and Income Tax submissions
- shopping, banking, booking tickets
- playing games.

Computers at work or in education

Business, industry, government and educational establishments have a great need for computers since they have a great deal of data that needs calculating and analysing. They may have special systems known as IMS (Information Management Systems) or DMS (Database Management Systems). Even the smallest office has now come to rely on computers. However, in some situations, person skills cannot be replaced (such as in the caring professions – e.g. nursing and counselling – and anywhere where innovation, thinking and communication is vital). Typical computer uses include:

- keeping databases of names and addresses (database applications) e.g. for mailshots, employee information and in government offices, large scale databases are required for tasks such as registering births, marriages and deaths, tax and census data.
- account information (spreadsheet and database applications)
- stock control and sales analysis (spreadsheet and database applications)
- marketing, including advertising and selling via websites (using e-mail and the Internet and web browser software)
- payroll (using spreadsheets or customised software) and Electronic Funds Transfer (EFT) – i.e. moving money from one account to another – e.g. wages
- student grades and project work (using database and spreadsheet applications and other specialised software for projects – e.g. Drawing software for Art and Design, Language software
- producing all paperwork: letters, memos, brochures, etc. (word processing, DTP and integrated office suites)
- designing products (Computer Aided Design (CAD) software)
- automating industrial processes (specialised software), robotics

- traffic lights, which have sensors to detect traffic and send messages to a controlling computer, which maintains regulated traffic flow
- Computer Based Training (CBT) – many specialised software packages are now available to assist with all types of training and for all age groups; people can work at their own pace and at a time that suits them.

Computers in daily life

In fact, computers are everywhere. Some common places they are used include:

- supermarkets, where bar codes are scanned and product and (sometimes) customer information is stored. This is known as Electronic Point of Sale (EPOS). Using such methods stock levels can be managed. Bank cards are swiped and payment is taken directly for goods. This is termed Electronic Funds Transfer at Point of Sales (EFTPOS)
- libraries where books are kept track of using database facilities and books are scanned when taken out and returned
- doctors' surgeries, where patient records are computerised
- bank/building society cash machines (known as Automated Teller machines or ATMs) where cards are used to identify the customer by reading the magnetic strip and checking the user's PIN (Personal Identification Number).

3.2 IT and society

A changing world

Information society

The society that we live in today relies on computers to enable us to gather and disseminate information quickly and easily. Because of this it has become known as the 'Information Society'. Some people feel uneasy about so much reliance on computers and wonder where it is leading us. Some people feel threatened by it. Some people feel empowered by it. You will have your own views. In situations where you see computers being used it is worth asking 'Is this a job for a computer or would a human interface be better?' Sometimes there are no clear-cut answers and much depends upon your general values.

Information superhighway

This is another name given to the Internet – the telecommunications infrastructure that allows access to a never-ending source of information across the world. It is changing the way we live and work at an ever-increasing rate. Only our imagination can limit its usefulness.

Year 2000 issue

This issue affected computers that only used '00' and not '1900' in the year field, so 1988 was 88 and 1996 96 and so on. With memory being in short supply with some of the earlier computers, it had seemed prudent to try and save two bytes (the first two digits of the year). There were fears that the computer would understand year '00' as being '1900' and not 2000. Programmers needed to work on systems before the year 2000 arrived so that computers were not affected. Although the Year 2000 bug created few problems there were predictions that it could have been much worse.

Electronic commerce

Electronic commerce (e-commerce) means doing business on-line. If you advertise a service or product; order a book, your groceries or your holiday using the Internet, you are participating in e-commerce.

A good workspace

When you are using a computer it is important that you make yourself comfortable otherwise you may easily become fatigued, ill or injured. Repetitive strain injury (RSI), an injury arising from making awkward movements or the prolonged use of particular muscles, is a recognised condition. It can affect the hands, neck, back and eyes due to incorrect computer use. Be aware of the following:

Positioning of the screen
All screens should be adjustable so that you can set them up for your requirements so that you avoid muscle strain in the neck and shoulders. The screen should be directly in front of you, roughly at arm's length. The top of the screen display should be just above eye level.

Positioning of documents
To prevent visual fatigue and muscle tension and to minimise refocusing and twisting the neck, these should be near to the screen, at the same height and distance.

Positioning of keyboard
If your keyboard is not comfortable – i.e. it is placed too near to the edge of the desk so that there is nowhere to rest your wrists – you could put unnecessary strain on the wrists causing RSI.

Type of chair
An adjustable chair is essential. Your back should be straight and your feet should rest on the floor. Your forearms should be roughly horizontal when using the keyboard.

Lighting
Screen glare should be avoided by adjusting background lighting and using window blinds or positioning the screen so that it is unaffected. Anti-glare filters are available.

Ventilation
Adequately ventilated working areas should be provided.

Frequent breaks
It is important to take frequent breaks and rest your eyes by focusing them on something in the distance and walking around.

Health and safety

There is legislation, administered by the Health and Safety Executive, covering computing environments. Some of the issues have been covered in the preceding paragraph. It is also important to ensure that equipment is safe. Power cables should be secured so that they cannot be tripped over and power sockets should not be overloaded.

Section 4 Security, copyright and the law

4.1 Security

For security reasons it is always a good idea to produce a backup (exact copies) of your data (data is the information that you put into the computer) on a regular basis. Then if anything goes wrong with your computer or the data becomes corrupted (damaged), you will be able to revert to the safely stored version. Various backup programs are available which use removable disks or tapes. It is best to store the backups in a safe and separate place away from your computer.

If there is a power cut when you are using your computer, the documents and information that you have not saved to disk will be lost. It is important that you save your work regularly so that you will minimise the amount of effort required to re-do the work in such situations. Sometimes the computer may just crash – i.e. cease to function – either because there is a program error or a more serious system problem. If it is a program problem, restart the program. If it is a system problem, restart the computer by pressing the keys **Ctrl**, **Alt** and **Delete** at the same time. If this doesn't have any effect, turn the computer off and then restart it.

Computers can be password protected so that only the user can access the data on them. In some organisations several passwords are needed to access strictly confidential data giving added security. Document files can also be password protected. It is always good practice to use a password that is not easy for anyone to guess and it must not be divulged to anyone.

Data can also be encrypted – i.e. turned into a special sort of code. A key to this code is required to make the data readable again.

4.2 Computer viruses

A computer virus is a destructive program that is buried within an existing program. They are written by people with programming skills who want to cause widespread problems for computer users. Once the infected program is run, the virus coding is activated and attaches copies of itself to other programs. Infected programs copy the virus to other programs. In this way it can quickly spread causing severe damage to computers and networks. A virus cannot attach itself to data. To protect against viruses, always know the source of your software. When downloading software from the Internet always save it and virus check it before running it. Antivirus utilities are available and are a good 'insurance' investment. If you are unfortunate enough to have a virus on your computer – close down the computer and restart it using a write-protected floppy boot disk and then run a virus utility.

4.3 Copyright

When you buy a software package – e.g. MS Office – you have an agreement (a user licence) with the manufacturer that you will only use it for personal use – i.e. that you will not duplicate it or lend it to someone else for them to use. Copying licensed software can be quite easy to do but it is illegal. It is also a good way of allowing viruses to enter your system, since shared resources like floppy disks or e-mail files could be infected. You should only purchase software from reputable sources so that you know that your software is not 'pirated' – copied illegally.

Freeware

Freeware is software that you can use free of charge. Often it is given away with computer magazines or it can be downloaded from the Internet.

Shareware

Shareware software can also be downloaded from the Internet and is distributed with computer magazines. The idea is that if you try it and would like to keep using it, you should register and pay for it.

4.4 Data Protection Act

In the UK, the Data Protection Act was passed in 1984 and was updated on March 1 2000. It sets rules for processing personal information on computers (and on some paper records). It gives individuals the right to know about the information that is held about them (exceptions being police and sometimes medical records). All organisations that hold computerised data on individuals must register with the Data Protection Registrar as a data user. Personal data is kept for many reasons – e.g. by tax offices, personnel departments, banks, hospitals. There are eight principles to ensure that information is handled properly. The data must be:

- fairly and lawfully processed
- processed for limited purposes
- adequate, relevant and not excessive
- accurate
- not kept for longer than necessary
- processed in line with your rights
- secure
- not transferred to other countries without adequate protection.

Module 1 practice tasks

1 List the main items that make up a computer.

2 Explain the differences between RAM and ROM.

3 What are the main factors affecting a computer's performance?

4 What is the CPU?

5 What unit is the CPU speed measured in?

6 What is an operating system?

7 What is hardware?

8 Name three output devices and three input devices.

9 Explain the terms Bit, Byte and Megabyte.

10 What is a Graphical User Interface? Give some examples of its main advantages.

11 What is needed to send and receive e-mail? Name three advantages of e-mail compared with other methods of communication.

12 What is the Internet?

13 Explain the terms LAN and WAN. What are the advantages of group working?

14 How do you search for information on the World Wide Web?

15 Give three examples of computers in everyday life.

16 Explain the terms Information Society and Information Superhighway.

17 What is RSI? What can you do to prevent it?

18 Why do you need to backup computer files?

19 What precautions should you take to ensure that unauthorised people do not have access to your computer files?

20 What is a computer virus? What effective measures can you take to minimise the risk of infection?

21 Describe the terms of the Data Protection Act? Give three uses of personal data.

Note: This is only a practice test. Successful completion does not imply certification of the module by the ECDL Foundation.

Module 2

Using the Computer and Managing Files

Section 1 Getting started

In this section you will practise and learn how to:

- start the computer
- use the mouse
- recognise parts of the desktop and parts of an application window

- reduce/enlarge, resize, rescale and close a desktop/application window
- move windows on a desktop
- use Help functions
- shut down the computer.

1.1 Windows 98

Windows 98 is an operating system that ensures all parts of the computer system work together. It controls the hardware and starts and operates the software. It provides ways to manage files stored on the computer.

1.2 Starting the computer

 Method

1 Ensure that the computer is plugged into the electricity socket.
2 Press the button on the computer base unit (and on the monitor, if it has a separate button) to switch the power on.

The computer will perform its start-up checks and load Windows 98 and accessories. You will see the Windows 98 desktop displayed. The items that appear on this screen depend on how your computer is set up. It will look something like Figure 2.1.

Note: The small pictures that Windows 98 uses to represent programs, files etc are called icons.

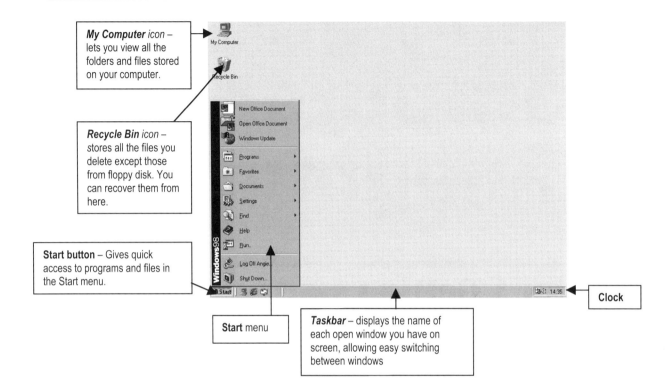

My Computer icon – lets you view all the folders and files stored on your computer.

Recycle Bin icon – stores all the files you delete except those from floppy disk. You can recover them from here.

Start button – Gives quick access to programs and files in the Start menu.

Start menu

Taskbar – displays the name of each open window you have on screen, allowing easy switching between windows

Clock

Figure 2.1 Windows 98 desktop

1.3 The mouse

The mouse lets you select and move items on the screen. When you move the mouse on your desk, the mouse pointer ⯆ moves on the screen in the same direction. You will notice that the mouse pointer changes depending on where it is and what it is doing. The mouse has a left and a right button. These can both be used to select options. In Windows 98, the right mouse button is usually used to access alternative context-sensitive pop-up menus.

Mouse terms

- *Click.* Press and release the mouse button.

- *Double-click.* Quickly press and release the mouse button twice.

- *Drag and drop.* When the mouse pointer is over an object on your screen, press and hold down the left mouse button. Still holding down the button, move to where you want to replace the object. Release the mouse button.

- *Hover.* Place the mouse pointer over an object for a few seconds so that something happens – e.g. another menu appears or a ToolTip.

Practice

An excellent way of practising mouse skills is to play the game of Solitaire that comes with Windows 98.

Using the Start button

To start Solitaire follow the directions given in Figure 2.2.

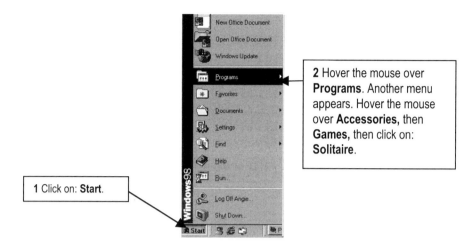

2 Hover the mouse over **Programs**. Another menu appears. Hover the mouse over **Accessories**, then **Games,** then click on: **Solitaire**.

1 Click on: **Start**.

Figure 2.2 Starting Solitaire

Info

If you do not have Solitaire on your computer, load any other Accessories program and practise some of the skills shown below.

The Solitaire window appears (see Figure 2.3). Notice that the taskbar, at the bottom of your screen, now displays a button for Solitaire.

1.4 Parts of a window

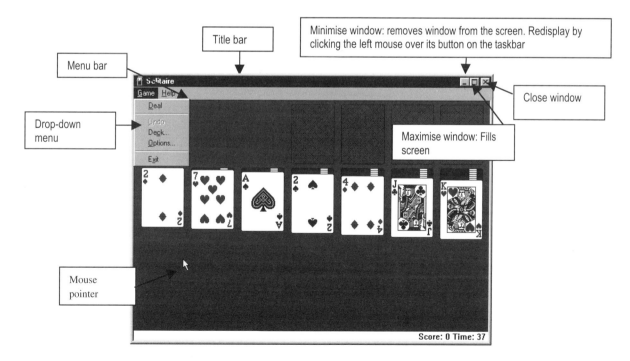

Title bar

Menu bar

Minimise window: removes window from the screen. Redisplay by clicking the left mouse over its button on the taskbar

Close window

Drop-down menu

Maximise window: Fills screen

Mouse pointer

Figure 2.3 Parts of a window

Info

Windows can also contain toolbars. A toolbar is a strip of clickable shortcut buttons, usually along the top of a window (directly below the menu bar). (See Module 3, Section 1 – page 43.)

Play Solitaire

Method

1 On the menu bar, click on: **Help**. A menu appears.
2 Click on: **Help Topics**; the **Solitaire Help** window appears (see Figure 2.4).
3 Click on: the **Contents** tab, if not already selected (on top of **Index** and **Search** tabs).
4 Click on: **Playing Solitaire**.

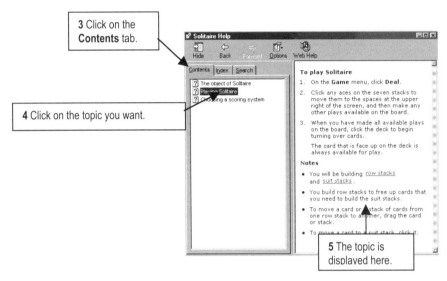

Figure 2.4 Solitaire Help window

5 The rules of the game are displayed in the right-hand window.
6 When you have read the rules, click on the **Close** button (see Figure 2.5).

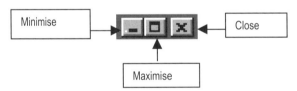

Figure 2.5 The Close button

You are now ready to play Solitaire!

Practise:

• the mouse actions while playing the game

• using the menus to get Help and choose other options for the game

• moving the window by pointing to the title bar and dragging and dropping

• resizing the window by moving the mouse pointer over the edge of the window until a double arrow appears, pressing and holding down the left mouse and dragging to the required shape, then releasing the mouse button.

Note: To keep the same proportions of the window, drag from a corner.

When you have had enough practising, from the **Game** menu, select: **Exit** or click on: the **Close** button.

1.5 Getting Help

You can get Windows 98 Help by clicking on the **Start** button, then on **Help**. The **Windows Help** window appears (see Figure 2.6).

Practise:

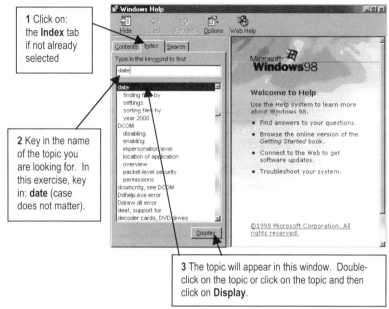

1 Click on: the **Index** tab if not already selected

2 Key in the name of the topic you are looking for. In this exercise, key in: **date** (case does not matter).

3 The topic will appear in this window. Double-click on the topic or click on the topic and then click on **Display**.

Figure 2.6 Windows Help

The Topics Found box appears (see Figure 2.7). A list of date-related topics is given.

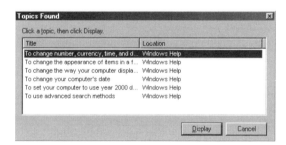

Figure 2.7 Topics Found

Choose a topic by double-clicking on it. I have chosen 'To change your computer's date' and the **Windows Help** appears displaying help in the right-hand pane (see Figure 2.8).

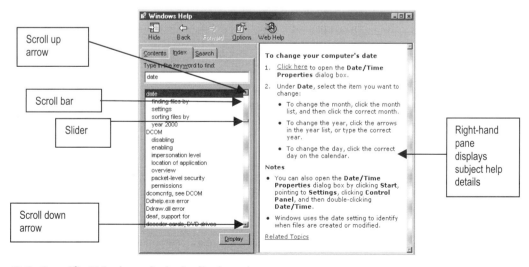

Scroll up arrow

Scroll bar

Slider

Scroll down arrow

Right-hand pane displays subject help details

Figure 2.8 Specific Windows help is displayed

Scroll bars

When a window is not big enough to display all the information in it, scroll bars appear, vertically and/or horizontally (see Figure 2.8).

Practise:
* clicking on the scroll bar arrows to move through the index entries
* dragging the slider along the scroll bar to move more quickly through the entries
* searching for other Help topics.

When you have finished searching for Help topics, close the help window by clicking on the **Close** button.

1.6 Shutting down the computer

From the **Start** menu, select: **Shut Down.** The **Shut Down Windows** dialogue box appears (see Figure 2.9).

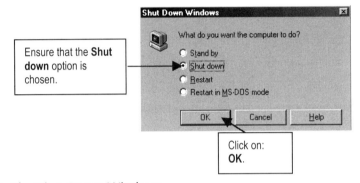

Figure 2.9 Shutting Down Windows

A message: **It's now safe to turn off your computer** is displayed. You can now switch off.

> It is important that you close down Windows correctly when you have finished your work. Sometimes a program will tell you to restart your computer. When this happens you can use the **Restart** option.

Section 1 CHECKLIST

Are you familiar with the following?

Starting the computer
Using the mouse
Recognising parts of the desktop and parts of an application window
Reducing/enlarging a desktop/application window
Resizing, rescaling and closing a window
Moving windows on a desktop
Using Help functions
Shutting down the computer

Section 2 Working with icons

In this section you will practise and learn how to:

- restart the computer
- recognise icons
- view the computer's basic system information – e.g. operating system, processor type, installed RAM etc.
- view the computer's desktop configuration: date and time, volume settings, desktop display options – e.g. background options, screen settings, screen saver etc.
- create a desktop shortcut icon
- select and move desktop icons.

2.1 Recognising icons

1 Restart the computer as in Section 1.2 (page 17).

2 Double-click on: the 🖳 **My Computer** icon. The **My Computer** window appears.

3 Maximise the window, if not already maximised, by clicking on the 🔲 **Maximise** button. The window will look similar to Figure 2.10.

> **Info**
>
> Notice the floppy disk drive icon (drive A:), the hard disk drive icon (drive C:) and the compact disk drive icon (drive D:). Right-clicking on any of these icons will display a pop-up menu; select **Properties** for more information – e.g. free disk space. Try this now, selecting the hard disk drive. In Figure 2.10 notice that there are 'special' folder icons including Printers and Control Panel. The Status bar is at the bottom of the window and will change to reflect current operations.

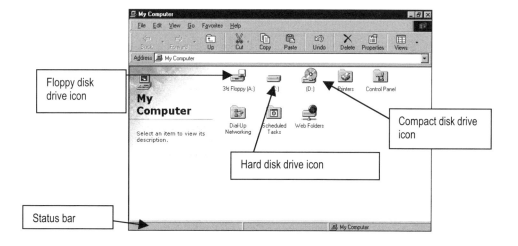

Figure 2.10 My Computer window

2.2 Viewing the computer's basic system information

> **Info**
>
> You can use Control Panel to view and alter numerous settings on your computer.

1 Double-click on: the **Control Panel** folder. The **Control Panel** window and contents are displayed.
2 Double-click on: the 🖥 **System** icon.
3 The **System Properties** window is displayed. With the **General** tab selected, you can view the operating system, processor type and installed RAM.
4 Close the **System Properties** window by clicking on **Cancel**.

2.3 Viewing and customising the computer's desktop configuration

Date and time

1 Double-click on: the 🕒 **Date/Time** icon. The **Date/Time Properties** dialogue box appears (see Figure 2.11).
2 Click in the relevant boxes to change date and time as necessary.
3 Click on: **Apply**.
4 Click on: **OK**.

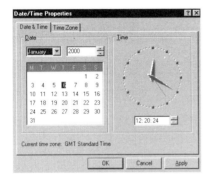

Figure 2.11 Date/Time Properties dialogue box

Display options

Double-click on: the 🖥 Display icon. The **Display Properties** dialogue box appears (see Figure 2.12).

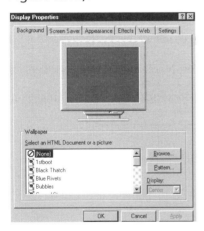

Figure 2.12 Display Properties dialogue box

Background

With the **Background** tab selected, you can change the wallpaper (desktop background). To do this:

1 Make a selection from the list. A preview will display on the screen graphic above.
2 Click on: **Browse** to select a file that you want to use as wallpaper or click on: **Pattern** to select a pattern.
3 In the **Display** box, from the list, select the type of display you want.
4 Click on: **Apply**.

Screen Saver

Click on: the **Screen Saver** tab to apply/change the screen saver. (A screen saver is displayed when you have not interacted with your computer for a while.) Set the time delay before the screen saver is activated. Click on: **Apply**.

By selecting other tabs you can change other desktop settings. Experiment with this now, then close Display Properties (click on: **OK** to save settings) when you have finished. Click on: the **Close** button to close Control Panel.

Sound settings

1 Either:

> Double-click: on the **Volume** icon on the taskbar.

or:

> From the **Start** menu, select: **Programs, Accessories, Entertainment, Volume Control**.

2 The Volume Control window appears. In the **Volume Control** section adjust as required using the sliders.

3 Click on: **OK**.

2.4 Creating a desktop shortcut

> ### i Info
> It is a good idea to create desktop shortcuts for applications that you use often. You can also create shortcuts for folders and files in the same way. This saves having to go through the Start menu. In this example we will create a shortcut for Notepad. This is one of the Accessories applications that is part of Windows 98. It is a simple 'no frills' word processor application.

1 From the **Start** menu, select: **Programs, Windows Explorer**.
2 The Exploring window appears.
3 Click on: the 🗗 **Restore** button so that part of the desktop is visible.

Note: A **Restore** button is displayed instead of the **Maximise** button when a window is already maximised.

4 Select the location of the application that you want to make a shortcut for. In this case, in the **Folders** section, double-click on: the **Windows** folder.
5 In the right-hand section, select: **Notepad** (see Figure 2.13).
6 Hold down the right mouse button and drag **Notepad** on to the desktop.
7 Release the mouse button.
8 A shortcut icon appears on the desktop that looks like this:
9 Close the **Exploring** window.

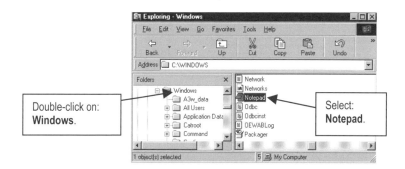

Figure 2.13 The Exploring window

2.5 Recognising more desktop icons

The main types of icons that you see on a normal desktop and that we will be working with are as follows:

- Application/Program shortcut icons such as Notepad, Word, Excel, Access, and PowerPoint, shown below:

- File icons, shown below:

    A Word file   An Access file   An Excel File   A PowerPoint file

- Folder icons that look like this: 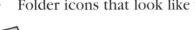.

Info

There is more about files and folders in Section 3 (page 28).

2.6 Arranging desktop icons

You can arrange desktop icons by dragging them to the required position on the desktop. If you right-click on: the desktop, a pop-up menu appears (Figure 2.14).

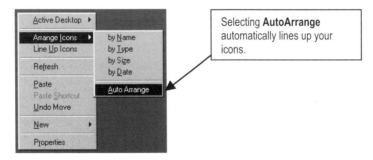

Figure 2.14 Arranging icons on the desktop

Section 2 CHECKLIST

Are you familiar with the following?

Restarting the computer	
Recognising icons	
Viewing the computer's basic system information – e.g. operating system, processor type, installed RAM etc.	
Viewing the computer's desktop configuration: date and time, volume settings, desktop display options – e.g. background options, screen settings, screen saver etc.	
Selecting and moving desktop icons	
Creating a desktop shortcut icon	

Section 3 Working with folders and files

In this section you will practise and learn how to:

- use Windows Explorer
- understand basic directory and folder structure
- examine folders/files
- view folder/file attributes
- recognise most widely used file types
- create a folder and subfolders
- rename folders/files
- delete folders/files
- use the Recycle Bin
- copy/move folders/files
- select an individual file, adjacent files and non-adjacent files
- make backups onto a floppy disk
- format a disk
- use find to locate folders/files.

3.1 Windows Explorer

Windows Explorer is a program that allows you to view all the folders and files on your computer. It can be used for disk and file management.

Starting Explorer

 Method 1

From the **Start** menu, select: **Programs**, then **Windows Explorer**.

 Method 2

1 Right-click on: **Start**.
2 Select: **Explore** from the pop-up menu.

The **Explorer** window appears. In this example (see Figure 2.15), the **3$^{1}/_{2}$ Floppy (A:)** drive is selected in the left pane and the contents of the disk in drive A are displayed in the pane on the right.

> **i Info**
>
> If your window has a different layout, you may be in **Web Page View**. To change this, from the **View** menu, select: as **Web Page** so that there is no tick next to it. Your display may be set to show large icons. To change this, from the **View** menu, select: **Small Icons**.

Spreadsheets

| This is an example of a *folder*. It stores related information. It can contain files and other folders (which can also contain files). Sometimes folders are referred to as *directories*. |

Gem news

| This is an example of a *file*. When you save your work onto a computer disk, it becomes a file. The icon above the filename identifies its type (this is a Word file). |

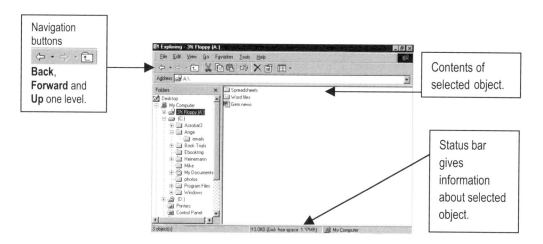

Figure 2.15 Windows Explorer

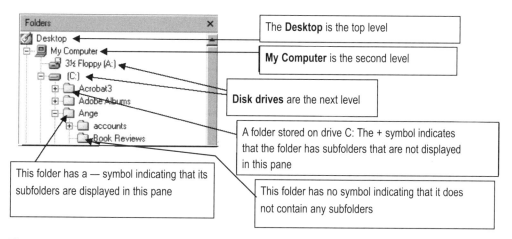

Figure 2.16 Structure of computer storage

Displaying the contents of a folder

Double-click on: the folder.

> **ⓘ Info**
>
> It is better to double-click the icon rather than the text, as sometimes you will not get the action you expect (if you have not double-clicked properly). Instead, a box may appear round the text, waiting for your input. If this happens, press: **Esc** and try again.

> **ⓘ Info**
>
> **Navigating**
>
> At some stages you may get lost. Use the navigation buttons shown in Figure 2.15 and the following:
>
> To return to a previously viewed folder, click on: the **Back** button arrow or select it from the **File** menu.
>
> The **Address bar** list displays a list of other locations when the down arrow is clicked.

3.2 Examining folders and files

To obtain more information about folders/files:

1 Right-click on: the folder/file. A pop-up menu appears (see Figure 2.16).

Figure 2.17 Right-click to display pop-up menu

2 Select: **Properties**. The object's properties are displayed (see Figure 2.17).

Figure 2.18 Displaying properties

3.3 Recognising file types

There are many different types of file and it is useful to be able to recognise those that are most common. Right-clicking on the **Gem news** file and selecting: **Properties** displays the properties shown in Figure 2.18.

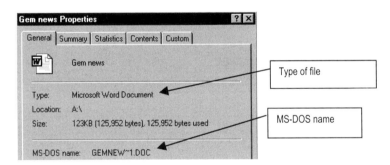

Figure 2.19 File properties

Note: You will not have the file **Gem news** on your computer but this explanation will enable you to look at the properties of files on your computer.

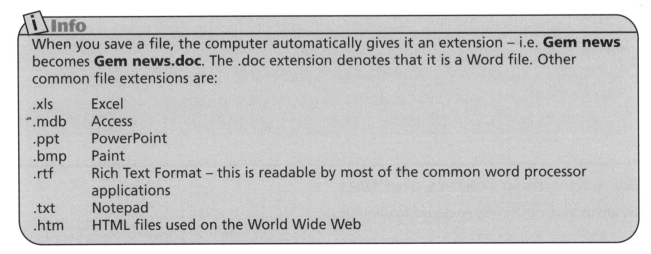

When you save a file, the computer automatically gives it an extension – i.e. **Gem news** becomes **Gem news.doc**. The .doc extension denotes that it is a Word file. Other common file extensions are:

.xls   Excel
.mdb   Access
.ppt   PowerPoint
.bmp   Paint
.rtf   Rich Text Format – this is readable by most of the common word processor
          applications
.txt   Notepad
.htm   HTML files used on the World Wide Web

Other information about the file is available by selecting the other tabs. Figure 2.19 shows the Statistics for the file **Gem news**.

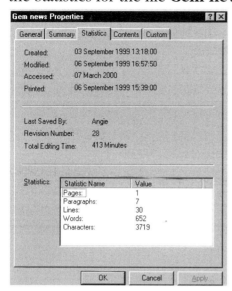

Figure 2.20 Displaying file statistics

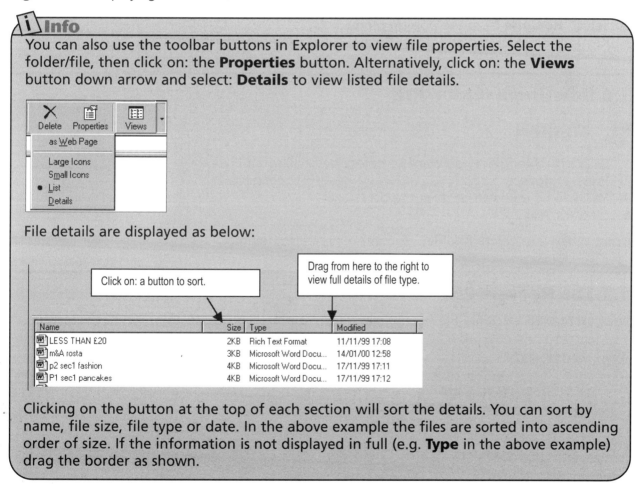

You can also use the toolbar buttons in Explorer to view file properties. Select the folder/file, then click on: the **Properties** button. Alternatively, click on: the **Views** button down arrow and select: **Details** to view listed file details.

File details are displayed as below:

Clicking on the button at the top of each section will sort the details. You can sort by name, file size, file type or date. In the above example the files are sorted into ascending order of size. If the information is not displayed in full (e.g. **Type** in the above example) drag the border as shown.

3.4 Creating a new folder and subfolders

You can create new folders in which to store related documents. This is always good practice as it makes for easier location at a later date.

Example

To create a new folder on the disk in drive A:

Method

1 In the left-hand pane of the **Windows Explorer** window, click on: **3¹/₂ Floppy (A:)**.
2 The contents of the floppy disk in drive A are displayed in the right-hand pane.
3 Right-click in the white space of this section. A menu appears.
4 Select: **New** and then **Folder**.
5 Key in the name for the new folder and press: **Enter**.

To create a subfolder within the newly created folder:

 Method

1 Double-click on: the newly created folder.
2 Carry out steps 3–5 above.

3.5 Renaming a file/folder

 Method

1 Right-click on: the file/folder.
2 Select: **Rename** from the pop-up menu.
3 Key in the new name and press: **Enter**.

3.6 Deleting a folder/file

 Method

1 Select the file/folder you want to delete by clicking on it.
2 Press: **Delete**.
3 You will be asked to confirm the deletion.
4 Click on: **Yes**.

Note: When you delete a folder, its contents are also deleted.

3.7 The Recycle Bin

You can restore a deleted file (*not one deleted from a floppy disk*) from the **Recycle Bin**.

 Method

1 Click on: the **Recycle Bin**.
2 Select: the file you want to restore.
3 From the **File** menu, select: **Restore**.

Emptying the Recycle Bin

It is a good idea to remove files from the Recycle Bin from time to time.

 Method

1 Click on: the **Recycle Bin** to select it.

2 From the **File** menu, select: **Empty Recycle Bin**.

3.8 Copying folders/files

Example

Copy the file **Gem news** so there is a copy in the folder **Word files**.

There are three main ways to copy a file:

 Method 1

1 Select the file **Gem news**.
2 Hold down the left mouse button and, at the same time, hold down the **Ctrl** key.
3 Drag the file to the folder **Word files**.
4 Release the **Ctrl** key and the mouse button.

 Method 2

1 Select the file **Gem news**.
2 Hold down the *right* mouse button and drag the file to the folder **Word files** (it will become highlighted).
3 Release the mouse – a menu appears.
4 Click on: **Copy Here**.

 Method 3

1 Right-click on: the file **Gem news** – a menu appears.
2 Select: **Copy**.
3 Right-click on: the folder **Word files**, select: **Paste**.

> **i Info**
> The third method is sometimes easier when you have numerous files and folders, as they may scroll out of view when you are trying to drag them. Check the quick reference for keyboard shortcuts and toolbar button methods.

You can check that the file **Gem news** is in the **Word files** folder by clicking on it to reveal its contents. *Note:* Folders can be copied in the same way.

3.9 Moving folders/files

Files/folders can be moved following methods 1, 2 and 3 above, except:

 Method 1

Do not hold down the **Ctrl** key when moving files/folders.

 Method 2

Select: **Move Here** instead of **Copy Here**.

 Method 3

Select: **Cut** instead of **Copy**.

3.10 Selecting adjacent folders/files

You can select more than one file to delete, copy or move.

Method

1 Select: the first folder/file in the group.

2 Hold down the **Shift** key on the keyboard and select: the last file you want.

3.11 Selecting non-adjacent folders/files

 Method

1 Select: the first folder/file.

2 Hold down the **Ctrl** key on the keyboard and select: each file in the group.

3.12 Backing up a floppy disk

Backing up a disk means producing an exact copy of the contents of a disk. This is done as a security measure in case anything happens to the original disk.

Produce a backup of a floppy disk

 Method

1 Select: 3½Floppy (A:).
2 Right-click. A menu appears.
3 Click on: **Copy Disk**.
4 Follow the instructions on screen.

 Info

You can also backup your data by selecting **Programs, Accessories, System Tools, Backup** from the **Start** menu and then following the instructions given. You can backup selected files only by copying them to floppy disks (as in Section 3.8 – page 33).

3.13 Formatting a floppy disk

Most new floppy disks are already formatted for use on your computer. If not, you will need to format them before use. Formatting prepares the disk so that it can be recognised by your computer, and information can be quickly and easily stored and accessed on it. A floppy disk only needs to be formatted once. Formatting a disk will erase any information stored on that disk.

Formatting a disk in Drive A

 Method

1 Select: **3½ Floppy (A:)**.
2 Right-click. A menu appears (see Figure 2.20).

Figure 2.21 Formatting a disk

3 Click on: **Format**. The **Format** dialogue box appears (see Figure 2.21).

4 Check the capacity of your disk:

High density – 1.44MB
Double density – 720KB
Choose accordingly.

Note: High-density disks have two holes at the bottom.

5 Click on: the **Full** button.

6 Click on: **Start**.

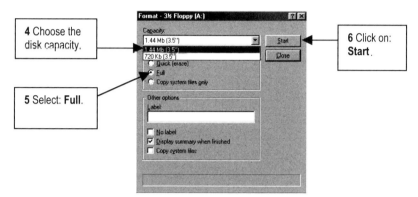

Figure 2.22 The Format dialogue box

You can also carry out file maintenance within an application such as Word. See the Appendix for details.

3.14 Finding files

To find a folder/file use the following method:

 Method

1 In Windows Explorer, select: **Find** from the **File** menu *or* from the **Start** button menu, select: **Find**, then **Files** or **Folders**.

2 The **Find: All Files** dialogue box appears (see Figure 2.22).

Figure 2.23 Finding files/folders

3 With the **Name & Location** tab selected, key in the name of the file you want to find and possible location.

4 Ensure **Include subfolders** is ticked if appropriate for your search.

If you do not know exactly what the file name is, key in just a part of the name e.g. phone will find telephone, phone list, headphones, etc. Use the wildcard * – e.g. *.xls to find all Excel files.

5 Use the **Date** tab to refine your search to an approximate date.

6 Use the **Advanced** tab to refine your search to a specific file type and size.

7 Click on: **Find Now**.

> **⚠️ ℹ️ Info**
>
> In this section we have used Windows Explorer. Windows Explorer gives a bird's-eye view of the system. However, it is possible to carry out most of the tasks using My Computer.
>
> Double-click on: the 🖥️ **My Computer** icon on the Windows desktop. Practise the exercises again using My Computer choosing your own file/folder names.

Section 4 Using and printing from a text editing application

In this section you will practise and learn how to:

- launch a word processing program and create a file
- save the file
- close an edit application
- print from an installed printer
- change default printer
- view a print job's progress from a desktop print manager
- move between open windows.

4.1 Creating a folder for your file

 Exercise 1

Create a folder named **Examples** on Floppy drive A using the methods in section 3.

4.2 Creating a word processed file

Info

For the following exercises we will be using the program **Notepad**.

 Exercise 2

Open Notepad and key in the following text:

This is an example of creating and saving a file.

 Method

1 From the **Start** menu, select: **Programs**, **Accessories**, **Notepad** or double-click on: its shortcut icon.
2 The **Notepad** window appears.
3 Key in the text.

4.3 Saving the file

 Exercise 3

Save the file.

 Method

1 From the **File** menu, select: **Save As**.
2 The **Save As** dialogue box appears see (Figure 2.23).

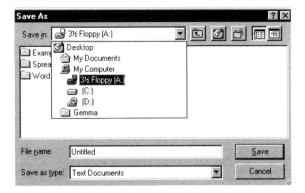

Figure 2.24 Saving the file

3 In the **Save in** box, select **Floppy (A:)** by clicking on the down arrow and selecting it from the list.
4 Open the **Examples** folder by double-clicking on it.
5 In the **File name** box key in the filename (precede the name with your initials, in my case ajb) **ajb testing**.
6 Click on: **Save**.

4.4 Printing the file

 Exercise 4

Print the file saved in 4.3.

 Method

1 Ensure that the printer is loaded with paper.
2 From the **File** menu, select: **Print**.

4.5 Changing the default printer

Sometimes you may need to change from the default printer – e.g. to print in better quality. You can usually change from the default printer within the program you are using.

Method (In Notepad)

1 From the **File** menu, select: **Page Setup**.
2 Click on: **Printer**.
3 In the **Name** section, click on: the down arrow and select another printer from the list.
4 Click on: **OK**.

 Info

You can also change from the default printer for your computer using the following methods:

Using the Start menu
1 From the **Start** menu, select **Settings**, then **Printers**.
2 The Printers box appears. Right-click on: the printer that you want to be the default.
3 Select: **Set as default**.

Using My Computer
1 Open the **Printers** folder.
2 Follow steps 2 and 3 above.

4.6 Viewing a print job's progress

You can view how your print job is progressing by carrying out step 1 in the Info box above. At step 2 double-click on: the printer.

4.7 Moving between open windows

When you are working you may find that you have more than one window open. The open windows will appear (minimised) on the taskbar (see Figure 2.24). In this case the file **Testing** is visible on screen (the button appears pushed in).

Figure 2.25 Open windows appear on the taskbar

It is easy to switch between windows, just click on: the button for the window that you want displayed *or* select it from the **Window** menu.

4.8 Closing a program

To close Notepad:

 Method

From the **File** menu, select: **Exit**.

Using the computer and managing files quick reference guide

Action	Keyboard	Mouse	Right-mouse menu	Menu
Backup a floppy disk			**Copy disk**	
Backup to floppy disk	**Start** menu, **Programs**, **Accessories**, **System Tools**, **Backup**			
Copy file/folder	Select the file/folder			
	Ctrl + C	Click: the 📋 **Copy** button	**Copy**	**Edit**, **Copy**
	Click where you want to copy the file/folder			
	Ctrl + V	Click: the 📋 **Paste** button	Paste	**Edit**, **Paste**
Create a new folder	Select where you want the new folder to be			
			New, **Folder**	**File**, **New**, **Folder**
Create a subfolder	Select the folder in which you want the subfolder to be and follow the steps for creating a new folder.			
Delete a file/folder	Select the file/folder			
	Delete		**Delete**	**File**, **Delete**
Display contents of folder		Double-click: the folder		
Exit Windows Explorer		Click: the ⊠ **Close** button		**File, Close**
Find files/folders	**Start** menu, **Find**, **Files** or **Folders** or in Windows Explorer **File** menu, **Find**			
Format a floppy disk	Select drive			
			Format	
Load Windows Explorer	In Windows 98 desktop			
		Double-click: the **Windows Explorer** shortcut icon		**Start, Programs, Windows Explorer**
Move file/folder	Select the file			
	Ctrl + X	Click: the ✂ **Cut** button	Cut	**Edit, Cut**
	Click where you want to move the file/folder to			
	Ctrl + V	Click: the 📋 **Paste** button	**Paste**	**Edit, Paste**
Notepad, open		Double-click: the **Notepad** shortcut icon		**Start, Programs, Accessories, Notepad**
Notepad, close		Click: the ⊠ **Close** button		**File, Exit**
Notepad, saving a document				**File, Save** or **Save As**
Notepad, print				**File, Print**

Action	Keyboard	Mouse	Right-mouse menu	Menu
Notepad, change default printer				**File**, **Page Setup**, **Printer**
Printer, change default, View print job's progress				**Start**, **Settings**, **Printers**
Recycle Bin, *restore files*	Double-click on the Recycle Bin icon Select the file you want to restore			
			Restore	**File**, **Restore**
Recycle Bin, *empty*			**Empty Recycle Bin**	
Rename file/ folder			**Rename**	**File**, **Rename**
Select files *adjacent* *non-adjacent*	Click: the first file Holding down: **Shift**, click: the last file Click: the first file Holding down: **Ctrl**, click: each file in turn			
Shortcut, creating	In Windows Explorer			
		Drag object to desktop	**Create Shortcut**	**File**, **Create Shortcut**
Shut down the computer	**Start, Shut Down**			
View all file/ folder attributes		Click: the ⊞ ▾ **Views** button arrow, **Details**		
View individual file/folder attributes	Select file/folder	Click: the 🗐 **Properties** button	**Properties**	**File**, **Properties**

Module 2 practice tasks

For this module you will need to have some folders and files already set up. Ask your supervisor or tutor to prepare them for you.

Preparation

1   Create a folder **ECDL Practice** within the **C:/** drive or on a floppy disk.

2   Create some files in the **ECDL Practice** folder with **Tea** as part of the filename – e.g. **Teabag**, **Green Tea**, **Teapot,** etc.

3   Create eight subfolders in the **ECDL Practice** folder. Name them **Sub1**, **Sub2**, **Sub3** etc.

4   Create two subfolders in each Sub folder. Folder names do not matter.

5   Put a selection of files – e.g. types, dates, sizes – into all the folders.

Practice tasks

1   Within the **ECDL Practice** folder, create a folder named **Test** and two subfolders named **Test One** and **Test Two**.

2   Open a text editor program (Notepad). Create an 'Answer' file by keying in your name, the date and the text **ECDL Module 2 Practice test**. The file will be referred to as **Answer** file.

3   Find all files with the extension **.xls** in the **ECDL Practice** folder (include all subfolders) and key in the total number found on the next line of the **Answer** file.

4   How many files are there in the folder (include all subfolders) with 'Tea' in the filename? Key in the number found on the next line of the **Answer** file.

5   How many files in total are there in the **Sub3** folder (include subfolders)? Key in the answer on the next line of the **Answer** file.

6   Copy all the files with the extension **.doc** from ECDL Practice**Sub1** to ECDL Practice**Sub5**.

7   Move the three smallest files from ECDL Practice**Sub2** to ECDL Practice\\Test**Test One**.

8   Copy the two oldest files from ECDL Practice**Sub1** to ECDL Practice\\Test**Test Two**.

9   Rename files starting with **Tea** so that they start with **One** eg **Teapot** becomes **Onepot**.

10   Delete all files in the ECDL Practice**Sub8** folder with the extension **.ppt**.

11   Answer the following questions in the **Answer** file:

   _   What is the procedure for shutting down the computer?
   _   How do you create a desktop shortcut icon?
   _   How can you view the computer's processor type and installed RAM?
   _   How do you change from the default printer in an application?

12   Save and print the **Answer** file.

13   Empty the Recycle Bin.

Note: This is only a practice test. Successful completion does not imply certification of the module by the ECDL Foundation.

Word Processing

Section 1
Basics – getting started

In this section you will practise and learn how to:

- load Word

- understand the parts of the document window

- understand and use the functions available including Help functions

- modify the toolbar display

- create a document: enter text, insert text, delete text

- save a document

- exit Word.

1.1 Loading Word

 Exercise 1

Load Word.

 Method

1 Switch on your computer and log in until the Windows 98 desktop screen appears.
2 Move the mouse pointer over the **Start** button and click the left button – a menu appears.
3 Select: **Programs** by hovering the mouse over it – another menu appears.
4 Select: **Microsoft Word** and click the left button (see Figure 3.1).

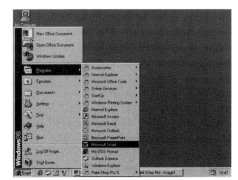

Figure 3.1 Loading Word

The Word Document window will be displayed on screen looking similar to Figure 3.2 showing a blank document with default values – i.e. pre-programmed settings such as line spacing, width of margins, font type. These settings will remain unchanged until you alter them.

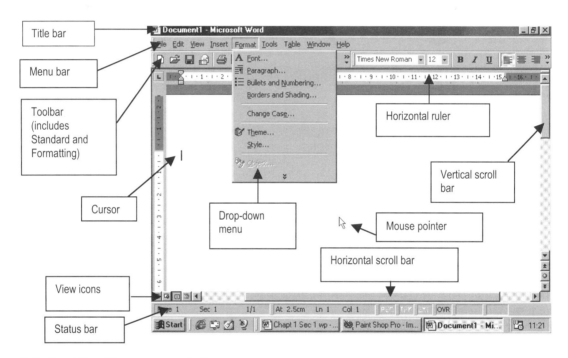

Figure 3.2 The Word Document window

1.2 Parts of the document window – an overview

Title bar. This shows the name of the application being used, Microsoft Word, and the current document name, **Document1** (this is the default name).

Menu bar. This has menu names, which can be selected using the mouse/keyboard. A drop-down menu then gives you options within that menu. This initially displays options used most recently. After a few seconds, the drop-down menu expands to include all available options. These menus will personalise to display your most recently selected options as you progress through your work.

Standard toolbar. This contains shortcut buttons for actions used frequently. For example, to open an existing file, click on: the button shown in Figure 3.3.

Open an existing file

Figure 3.3 Standard toolbar buttons

To quickly find out what each button on the toolbar does, point the mouse over the button and wait for a few seconds. A ToolTip will appear giving a brief explanation of the button. Try this now.

Formatting toolbar. This contains shortcuts for formatting your document, such as underlining text and centring text.

---

i Info

Modifying the toolbar display

By default the Standard and Formatting toolbars are displayed together on the same row. Since these contain frequently used shortcut buttons, it is useful to display both the Standard and Formatting toolbars in full on separate rows (the exercises in this chapter will assume this). To display the Standard and Formatting toolbars in full on separate rows:

1   From the **View** menu, select **Toolbars**, then **Customize**.

2   Click on: the **Options** tab.

3   Click to remove the tick in the **Standard and Formatting toolbars share one row** box.

4   Click on: **Close**.

Note: If you prefer not to alter the default setting and so have more screen area you can still access the remaining options on each toolbar by clicking on the ⏬ **More Buttons** icons.

You can choose to have more toolbars visible by selecting: **Toolbars** from the **View** menu and then selecting the toolbar to display. Ticks appear next to the currently displayed toolbars. The content of your work will dictate which ones are useful to you.

Cursor. The cursor shows where your text will appear.

Horizontal ruler. This shows the position of text and can be displayed in centimetres or inches. (See the Appendix if you want to change the default.)

Mouse pointer. This will move when you move the mouse – use it to select items in the window.

Scroll bars. You can quickly scroll through your document using the scroll bars.

Status bar. This provides information about the position of the cursor and the text displayed on your screen.

View icons. There are different ways of viewing your text. (See section 3.14 – page 79 – for more information on types of View.)

1.3 Getting help

Note: Throughout this book, the Office Assistant facility has been hidden so as not to distract from the main objectives. More information about the Office Assistant can be found in the Appendix.

 Method

From the **Help** menu, select: **Microsoft Word Help** or click on: the 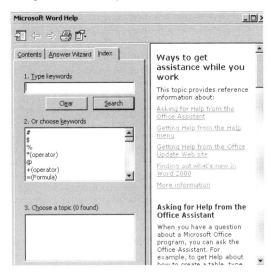 **Microsoft Word Help** button or press: **F1**. The **Microsoft Word Help** window is displayed (see Figure 3.4).

Figure 3.4 Microsoft Word Help

You can select any of the following tabs.

- The **Contents** tab displays a list of help topics. By clicking on a topic, a display of that topic will appear.

- The **Answer Wizard** tab allows you to key in a question and then click on: **Search**. The topic will then be highlighted in the contents list and the topic displayed as above.

- The **Index** tab allows you to key in key words and click on: **Search**. Again, the topic will be highlighted and displayed as above.

ScreenTips

1 From the **Help** menu, select: **What's This?**

2 Click on: the item you want to find out about. A short description appears.

3 Press: **Esc** to remove the ScreenTip.

Accessing help in a dialogue box

To access **Help** in a dialogue box, click on: the ⚇ **Help** button in the dialogue box and then click on: the item you want to find out about.

1.4 Entering text

Exercise 2

With the new Word Document window on your screen, key in the following text:

Picnics can be enjoyed in the early summer when the weather is warm and dry.

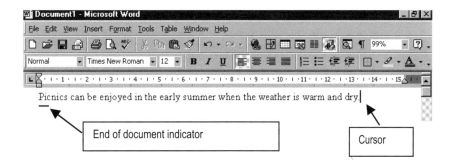

End of document indicator

Cursor

Figure 3.5 The keyed in text will look similar to this

1.5 Moving around your text

Here we will learn three methods to move around the text:

1 Using the arrow keys.
2 Using the mouse.
3 Using two keys together, **Ctrl + Home**, and **Ctrl + End**.

 Method

1 **Moving around your text using the arrow keys**
   The arrow keys →↑ ←↓ ((located at the bottom right of the main keyboard) allow you to move the cursor (a flashing black vertical line) in the direction of the arrows. You can move one space forwards or backwards at a time, or you can move up or down one line at a time. If you keep an arrow key pressed down, the cursor will move quickly through the document. Remember to release the arrow key when you reach the required place.

2 **Moving around your text using the mouse**
   As you move the mouse around the screen, you will notice that the I-beam moves with you. Move it until you have reached the required position, click the left mouse button once and the cursor will appear where you clicked.

3 **Using Ctrl + Home and Ctrl + End**
   Hold down: **Ctrl** at the same time as the **Home** key to move to the top of your text.

   Hold down: **Ctrl** at the same time as the **End** key to move to the bottom of your text.

 Info
There are other ways to move around the document and these are included in the quick reference at the end of this chapter.

1.6 Inserting text

 Exercise 3
Insert the word **usually** between the words **is** and **warm**.

 Method

Position the cursor at the point where you want to insert text (in this case after the space after the word **is**), and then key in **usually** and a space (see Figure 3.6).

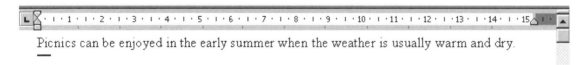

Figure 3.6 Inserting text

Notice how the text to the right of the cursor moves to make room for the new text.

 Info
If your text does not move across but overwrites text already there, check that **OVR** is not displayed on the Status Bar. If it is, press: **Insert** to remove overwrite.

1.7 Deleting text

 Exercise 4

Delete the word **early**.

 Method

Either:

Position the cursor to the left of the first character that you want to delete – i.e. the **e** of **early** – and press: **Delete** until all the letters of **early** (and the space) have been deleted

or:

Position the cursor to the right of the last character you want to delete – i.e. the **y** of **early** – and press: ← **Del** (Backspace) key (top right of main keyboard) until all the letters of **early** (and the space) have been deleted.

 Exercise 5

Now try keying in a larger piece of text.

 Method

1 Click on: the ⬜ **New** button.

2 Key in the following text **LANDMARKS IN LONDON**:

(This should not be in bold lettering and the line endings will not necessarily be in the same place.)

LANDMARKS IN LONDON

St Paul's Cathedral

St Paul's Cathedral is one of London's landmarks and is renowned throughout the world. It is the largest church in the city and was built on the same site and to replace a Norman church that was destroyed by the Great Fire of 1666.

The Whispering Gallery

This famous Renaissance building was designed by Sir Christopher Wren and has many interesting features. One of its most intriguing is the Whispering Gallery which runs round the inside of the great dome. If you speak in this gallery the sound waves of your voice are carried round the entire circumference of the gallery because the waves are prevented from going outwards by the stones lining the circular wall. These acoustic properties enable someone sitting far away on the opposite side of the gallery to hear your voice, even if you are whispering.

Famous people

Many famous people are buried at St Paul's and their tombs can be found either in the church or in the crypt beneath. They include Nelson, Wellington, Turner and Sir Christopher Wren.

1.8 Saving text

Exercise 5

Save the text.

 Method

 Info

Note that the text will now be referred to as a file.

1 From the **File** menu, select: **Save As** (see Figure 3.7).

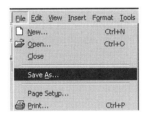

Figure 3.7 Saving a file for the first time using Save As

2 The **Save As** dialogue box is displayed.

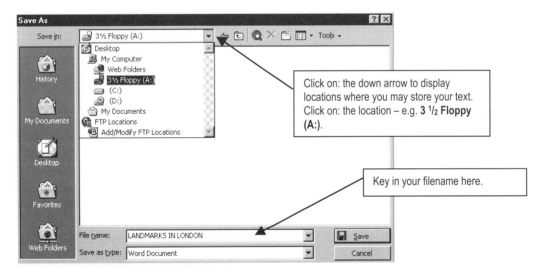

Figure 3.8 The Save As dialogue box

3 Click on: the down arrow as shown in Figure 3.8 and click on: the location where you want to save your text. (If you are saving to a floppy disk, remember to have your disk inserted in the drive.)

4 Click in the **File name** box at the beginning of the name that is already there and delete it by pressing: **Delete**.

5 Key in the filename: **London** (case does not matter).

6 Click on: **Save**.

Info

Notice that the default filename (**Document1**) has been replaced with the new filename (**London**) on the Title bar.

1.9 Closing a file

Exercise 6

Close the file **London**.

 Method

From the **File** menu, select: **Close**.

1.10 Exiting word

Exercise 7

Exit Word.

Click on: the ☒ Close button in the top right-hand corner.

 Info

You will be asked if you want to save the one-sentence practice file. Click on: **Yes** and follow the method above using the filename: **Picnic**.

Section 1 Word Processing practice

Practice 1

1   Load Word, open a new file and enter the following text:

THE WORLD WIDE WEB

Many commercial services are now offered on the WWW. You can order books, arrange a car rental anywhere in the world, and even purchase and download new software direct to your computer. If you live in the right area, you can even order a pizza via the WWW!

It was developed to help scientists share information and has rapidly become a general service for everyone. Using a suitably configured computer, users can access information on the WWW (known as web pages) from anywhere in the world. These pages can be created by anyone, from schoolchildren right up to the world's largest companies.

The ability to combine text, pictures, videos and sound makes the WWW ideal for entertainment pages. Most bands, films and computer games have their own official pages, and there are often many more set up by fans.

Be wary of what you find on the WWW. Always check the source of any information given. Remember that anyone can set up a website and the content authenticity will not always have been scrutinized.

2   Save the text with the filename: **P1 sec1 www**.

3   Close the file and exit Word.

Practice 2

1   Load Word, open a new file and enter the following text:

Thank you for filling in our recent Holiday questionnaire.

We are constantly striving to improve our services for you and to offer the kind of holidays that you will enjoy. Your comments have been noted and we will do our best to exceed your expectations.

Our new brochure features more than 1,100 idyllic cottages, 160 luxury villas with pools (usually available in the summer months only), more than 2,000 hotels and over 40 apartments at holiday villages, with superb on-site facilities. We also offer deluxe camping and mobile homes at 20 wonderful 4-star sites and theme parks including Disneyland, Paris, Parc Asterix and Futuroscope.

We would like to reward you for helping us with our survey. We are delighted to offer you a 10% saving on your next holiday. If you would like to benefit from this offer, please quote code Q2000 when you call.

We look forward to hearing from you soon.

2   Save the text with the filename: **P2 sec1 holiday**.

3   Close the file and exit Word.

Section 2 Basics – editing and printing

In this section you will practise and learn how to:

- open an existing document
- spellcheck and make changes where necessary
- use the grammar tool and make changes where necessary
- resave a previously saved file
- preview and print a document and print part of the document from an installed printer
- insert/delete text
- insert a new paragraph

- use the Undo command
- select character, word, sentence, paragraph or entire document
- replace words with other words
- use the Find command for a word or phrase within a document
- copy/move text within a document and to another document
- open several documents
- insert special characters/symbols
- modify document setup: page orientation, margins, page size, etc.

2.1 Opening an existing document

 Exercise 1

Load Word and open the file **London** saved in Section 1.

 Method

Click on: the 🖿 **Open** button.

Carry out the instructions given in Figure 3.9 that shows the **Open** dialogue box.

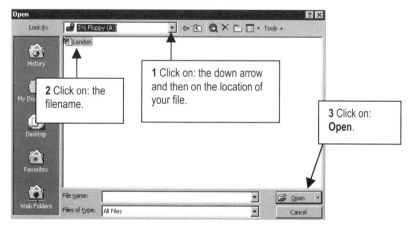

Figure 3.9 Opening a file

Info

Recently opened files appear listed at the bottom of the File menu. Click on: the filename to open it.

2.2 Proofreading and correcting errors

It is important to proofread your work carefully against the hard copy. Correct any errors in the text using the methods described in Section 1.

2.3 Spellchecking

Info

It is always important to use the spellchecker before you print a document as it will pick up most misspelt words and provide you with the chance to correct them. Word provides an option to check spelling and grammar together. It also provides the option to check spelling and grammar as it is being keyed in. For a beginner this can be quite distracting since it places wavy red lines under misspelt words and wavy green lines under possible grammatical errors. Throughout this book I have chosen to turn the **Check spelling as you type** off. To do this:

From the **Tools** menu, select **Options**.

Click on: the **Spelling and Grammar** tab.

In the **Spelling** section, click in the box next to **Check spelling as you type** to remove the tick.

Do the same in the **Grammar** section.

Note: There are limitations to the spellchecker's abilities and it may not pick up wrong usage of words, e.g. where and were, stair and stare. Although these words are spelt correctly they may be used in the wrong context. Similarly, do not rely unquestionably on the grammar checker.

Exercise 2

Run the spellchecker through the document.

Method

1 Position the cursor at the start of the document by pressing: **Ctrl + Home**.
2 Click on: the **Spelling and Grammar** button (see Figure 3.10).

Figure 3.10 The Spelling and Grammar button

3 The Spelling and Grammar dialogue box appears (see Figure 3.11).

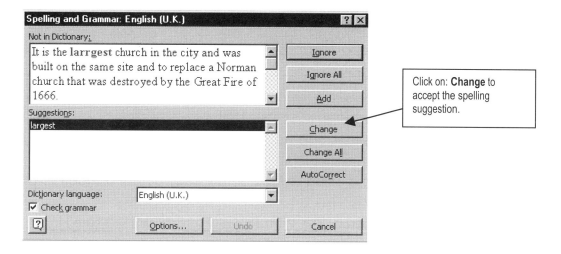

Figure 3.11 Spelling and Grammar dialogue box

The spellchecker will go through your text and match it with the words in its dictionary. It will highlight unrecognisable words and offer suggestions. (You may not have made any spelling errors!) In the example above, it has highlighted the word **larrgest** and it is offering its preferred replacement, **largest**, also highlighted in the lower box. In this case accept the suggestion by clicking on **Change**. If you do not want to accept a suggestion that the spellchecker has made, then click on: **Ignore**. If you want to accept one of the other suggestions that it may have made, click on: it to select it and then click on: **Change**. The spellchecker will repeat this process until it has finished checking all the text. It will then display a message telling you the spellcheck is complete.

2.4 Resaving a previously saved file

 Exercise 3

Resave the file **London**.

 Info

As you have already saved the first draft of this document, you will now be able to do a quick save instead of using **Save As**. This will overwrite your original with the changes you have made, but still keep the same filename **London**.

 Method

Click on: the **Save** button (see Figure 3.12).

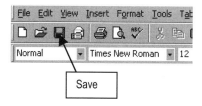

Figure 3.12 The **Save** button

2.5 Previewing a document

Exercise 4

Print Preview your document.

Method

If you want to see how your document is going to look on the page before printing it, you can use Word's Print Preview facility.

1 Click on: the **Print Preview** button. The Print Preview screen appears (see Figure 3.13).

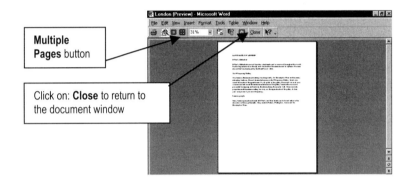

Figure 3.13 The Print Preview screen

Info

The cursor, when placed over the document, appears in the shape of a magnifying glass. You can zoom in to any part of the document by clicking over it with the left mouse button. To zoom out, click again. The **Multiple Pages** button is useful when your document has more than one page.

2 Press: **Esc** *or* click on: **Close** to return to the document window.

2.6 Printing a document

Exercise 5

Print one copy of the document on A4 paper.

Method

1 From the **File** menu, select: **Print** (see Figure 3.14).

Figure 3.14 File menu, Print

2 The **Print** dialogue box appears (see Figure 3.15).

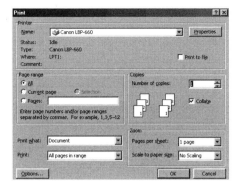

Figure 3.15 The Print dialogue box

3 Check the printer you are using. If it is not the one shown in the **Name** section of the Print dialogue box, click on: the down arrow and select the correct printer so that it appears in the **Name** box. Check that the printer is ready and loaded with paper.

4 There are several other default control options concerning printing (shown in the Print dialogue box – Figure 3.15 and in the Info box below). At this stage, you should not need to change any settings, so just click on: **OK**.

Info

Quick method to print
On the toolbar, click on: the 🖨 **Print** button.

Use this if you know that you do not need to alter anything in the Print dialogue box.

Useful printing options
In the **Page range** section, choose which pages to print.

In the **Copies** section, select the number of copies to print.

In the **Print** section, you can select to print only **Odd** or **Even** pages.

2.7 Inserting text

 Exercise 6

Using the instructions for inserting text in Section 1.6 (page 48) and below, insert the new paragraph (shown below) after the second paragraph ending: …**even if you are whispering.**

Sir Christopher Wren

Over the north door, Wren's epitaph is inscribed in Latin. It is – Si monumentum requiris, circumspice. This translated into English means – If you seek his memorial, look around you.

🔖 **Method**

1 Position the cursor at the beginning of the blank line in between the two paragraphs.
2 Press: **Enter**.
3 Key in the text.
4 Press: **Enter**.

Info

Remember when you insert or delete text, check that the spacing between words, sentences and paragraphs is still consistent. Use the ¶ **Show/Hide** button to check this.

 Exercise 7

In the second sentence of the last paragraph, insert the following after **include** and before **Nelson**:

Roberts, Jellicoe, Beatty,

 Method

Follow the method given in Section 1.6 (page 48).

2.8 Deleting text

We have already learnt how to delete text using the **Delete** or ← Del (backspace) key. However, this is not the quickest method to delete whole sentences or longer portions of text. To do this we need to select the text to be deleted.

 Exercise 8

In the second sentence of the first paragraph, delete the words: **on the same site and.**

 Method

1   Move the cursor to the beginning of the text you want to delete – in this case the **o** of **on** (see Figure 3.16).

> St Paul's Cathedral
>
> St Paul's Cathedral is one of London's landmarks and is renowned throughout the world. It is the largest church in the city and was built |on the same site and to replace a Norman church that was destroyed by the Great Fire of 1666.

Figure 3.16 Positioning the cursor

2   Hold down the left mouse button and drag the I-beam pointer across the words to be deleted (see Figure 3.17).

> St Paul's Cathedral is one of London's landmarks and is renowned throughout the world. It is the largest church in the city and was built on the same site and to replace a Norman church that was destroyed by the Great Fire of 1666.

Figure 3.17 Selecting text

3   Release the mouse button. The highlighting shows the text that is selected. If you need to cancel the selection, then click anywhere on the screen or press any arrow key.
4   Press: **Delete**.
5   Check for consistency of spacing.

2.9 Replacing text

 Exercise 9

The word **church** appears three times in the text. Replace the word **church** with the word **cathedral** each time it appears.

 Method

1   Move your cursor to the top of the document (**Ctrl + Home**).
2   From the **Edit** menu, select: **Replace** (see Figure 3.18).

Figure 3.18 Edit menu, Replace

3   The **Find and Replace** dialogue box appears (Figure 3.19).
4   Click on: the **Replace** tab (if not already selected).
5   Click in the Find what box, key in the word church.

   ***Note:* Do not press Enter yet.**

6   Click in the **Replace with** box, key in the word **cathedral** (lower case).
7   Click on: **Replace All**.

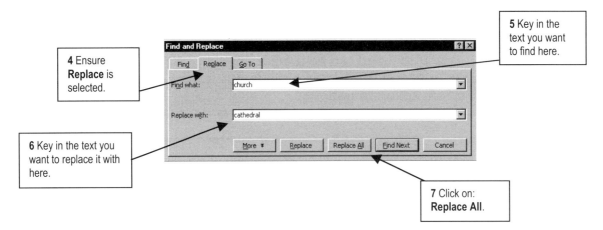

4 Ensure **Replace** is selected.

5 Key in the text you want to find here.

6 Key in the text you want to replace it with here.

7 Click on: **Replace All**.

Figure 3.19 The Find and Replace dialogue box

8 A box appears telling you how many replacements have been made (see Figure 3.20).

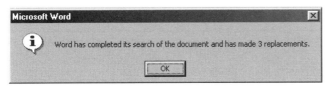

Word has completed its search of the document and has made 3 replacements.

Figure 3.20 You are advised how many replacements have been made

9 Click on: **OK**.

10 Click on: **Close**.

> **Info**
>
> There are options available within Find and Replace. The commonly used option is **Match Case**. Use this if you are replacing a word consisting of capital letters. If you do not use it, the replacement word will also have capital letters (it will not have matched the case you have keyed in). To set Match Case, in the **Find and Replace** dialogue box, click on: **More**, then on **Match Case** and proceed as before.

2.10 Searching for words or phrases

> **Info**
>
> When working with long documents, it is useful to be able to find words or phrases quickly. To do this:
>
> From the **Edit** menu, select: **Find**.
>
> Key in the word or phrase that you want to find and click on: **Find Next**.

2.11 Moving text

> **Exercise 10**
>
> Move the third paragraph and its heading: **Sir Christopher Wren...** so that it then becomes the second paragraph.

Method

1 Select the paragraph as in Section 2.8 (page 58).

2 Click on: the **Cut** button. The text will be saved on to the clipboard (you will not see or be told this).

3 Position the cursor where you want the text to reappear, then click on: the **Paste** button.

Info

Remember to check that spacing is still consistent.

Info

The Clipboard
The clipboard is a memory store. Whenever you cut or copy an object, the computer temporarily stores the copy on the clipboard. It can then quickly retrieve it when you want to paste it somewhere else, even into other Office applications such as Excel or PowerPoint. To view what is on the clipboard, from the **View** menu, select: **Toolbars** and then: **Clipboard**. Office 2000 enables you to store up to 12 items at a time on the clipboard. Items on the clipboard are removed when the computer is turned off.

2.12 Copying text

 Exercise 11

Copy the heading **LANDMARKS IN LONDON** so that it is repeated at the end of the text.

 Method

Follow the method shown in Section 2.11 (page 60) except, at step 2, click on: the **Copy** button instead of the **Cut** button.

2.13 Saving and printing

 Exercise 12

Save your file with the filename, **London1**, (as shown in Section 1.8 – page 50) and print one copy on A4 paper.

2.14 Copy text to another document

Info

By saving your file as **London1**, you will ensure that the original file is not overwritten. When practising working through assignments you will then be able to go back and correct any errors should this be necessary.

Note: It is good practice to get into the habit of saving your work regularly. If you encounter a problem you can always revert back to the most recently saved version of your work.

Exercise 13

Copy the first paragraph beginning **St Paul's Cathedral...** of the document currently open - i.e. **London1** - to a new Word document. Do not include the paragraph heading.

 ## Method

1 Select the text to be copied so that it is highlighted.

2 Click on: the **Copy** button.

3 Open a new Word document by clicking on the **New Blank Document** button. A new document appears.

4 Click on: the **Paste** button.

Info

You will notice that the document **London1**, which you have copied from, is hidden from view. To return to the document **London1**, click on: the shortcut button displaying the filename on the Taskbar or select the document name from the **Window** menu.

 ## Exercise 14

Open the file saved as **Picnic** in Section 1.10 and copy the same piece of text as in Exercise 13 so that it becomes the second paragraph of the document.

 ## Method

1 Open the file **Picnic** following the Method shown in Section 2.1 (page 53).

2 Position the cursor where you want the copied text to appear.

3 The text should already be on the clipboard so click on: the **Paste** button.

Note: You should now have three Word documents open - i.e. **London1**, **Picnic** and **Document1** (which has not yet been given a filename).

 ## Exercise 15

Save and print the documents **Picnic** and **Document1** choosing a suitable filename for **Document1**. Close all three documents.

 ## Method

Use the quick save Method for documents **London1** and **Picnic** as in section 2.4. Save the file **Document1** using the method in Section 1.8 (page 50) so that you can give the document a filename.

Info

Always give your documents meaningful filenames so that it will be easier to recognise them at a later date.

2.15 Inserting special characters

Exercise 16

Load the file **London1** saved in Section 2.14 and insert the following text after and on the same line as **LANDMARKS OF LONDON** at the end of the document:

Walkabouts Company ©

Method

1 Open the file and position the cursor where you want to key in the text.
2 Key in: **Walkabouts Company**.
3 The © symbol does not appear on the keyboard. To insert this special character, ensure that the cursor is positioned where you want the character to appear.
4 From the **Insert** menu, select: **Symbol** (see Figure 3.21).

Figure 3.21 Inserting a special character/symbol

5 The **Symbol** dialogue box appears (see Figure 3.22).

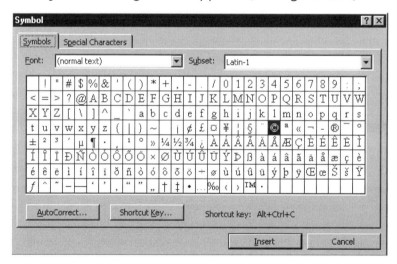

Figure 3.22 The Symbol dialogue box

6 With the **Symbols** tab selected, click on: the special character to insert.
7 Click on: **Insert** and then on **Close**.

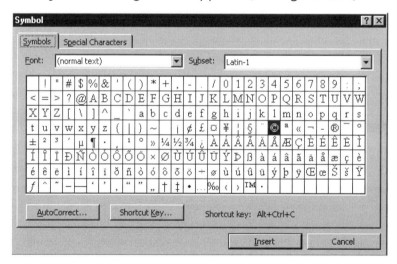
Info

There are some commonly used special characters/symbols to choose from. It is worth taking time to acquaint yourself with some of them. There are other fonts (especially Wingdings and Symbol) that have some useful special characters. Select other fonts from the list in the **Font** box.

2.16 Modifying document setup

Change the document layout to landscape display.

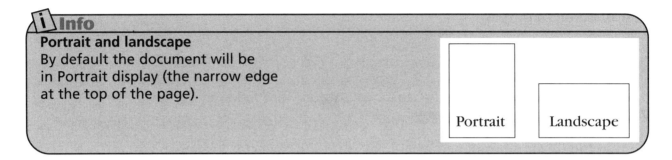

Portrait and landscape
By default the document will be
in Portrait display (the narrow edge
at the top of the page).

Portrait   Landscape

 Method

1 From the **File** menu, select: **Page Setup**.

2 The **Page Setup** dialogue box appears (see Figure 3.23).

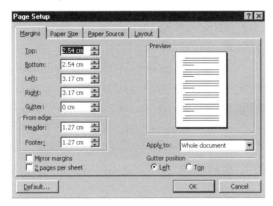

Figure 3.23 Page Setup dialogue box

3 Click on: the **Paper Size** tab (see Figure 3.24).

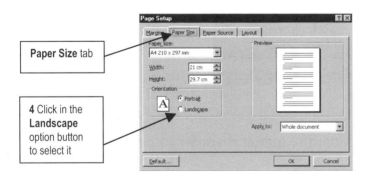

Figure 3.24 Selecting page orientation

4 In the Orientation section, click in the **Landscape** option button to select it.

5 Click on: **OK**.

Note: You can check the new document orientation in Print Preview.

Exercise 18

Inset both the left and right margins by 2 cm.

Method

Changing the margins

1 From the **File** menu, select: **Page Setup**: the **Page Setup** dialogue box appears (see Figure 3.24).

2 Ensure that the **Margins** tab is selected. The default landscape left and right margin width is 2.54 cm. Therefore to inset the margin by 2 cm you will need to add 2 cm to the default width of 2.54 cm. The result is 4.54 cm.

3 Delete 2.54 cm from the **Left** margin box and key in: **4.54 cm**. Repeat in the **Right** margin box.

4 Click on: **OK**.

Note: The default left and right margins in portrait display are 3.17 cm. You will notice that the Page Setup dialogue box allows you to change many of the defaults. Take a look at these now.

2.17 Printing part of a document

Method

1 Select the text to be printed so that it is highlighted (see Figure 3.25).

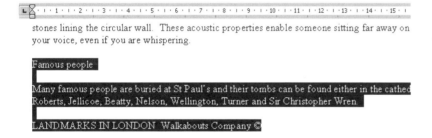

Figure 3.25 Section to be printed is selected

2 Follow the Method in Section 2.6 (page 56) but at Step 4 in the **Page range** section of the Print dialogue box, click in the option button next to **Selection** so that a dot is shown (see Figure 3.26).

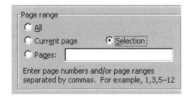

Figure 3.26 Printing part of a document

Info

If a document consists of more than one page, you can print selected pages only by clicking in the **Pages** option button (see Figure 3.26) and keying in the pages to print in the adjacent box.

2.18

Exercise 19

Close the file, save changes and exit Word.

Section 2 Word processing practice

Practice 3

1 Load Word and reload the file **P1 sec1 www** saved in Section 1.

2 Proofread and spellcheck the document, making corrections where necessary.

3 Quick save the document.

4 Print one copy.

5 Insert a new paragraph after the first one ending **...you can even order a pizza via the WWW!**

The possibilities are endless. User groups are growing daily. Who would have thought that people would be doing their weekly grocery shopping using the WWW?

6 In what is now the third paragraph delete the sentence beginning **These pages can be created by anyone...**

7 Replace **WWW** with the word **web** each time it appears.

8 In the first paragraph move the sentence beginning **You can order books...** from being the second sentence so that it becomes the last sentence in the paragraph.

9 Change the page orientation to landscape.

10 Change the left and right margins so that they are both 5.54 cm.

11 Save the document with the filename **P3 sec2 www** and print a copy.

12 Print only the last two paragraphs.

13 Close the file and exit Word.

Practice 4

1 Load Word and reload the file **P2 sec1 holiday** saved in section 1.

2 Proofread and spellcheck the document, making corrections where necessary.

3 Quick save the document.

4 Print one copy.

5 Insert the following sentence in the fourth paragraph after the sentence ending **...saving on your next holiday.**

However, you must act within 28 days.

6 In the second paragraph delete the sentence beginning **Your comments...**

7 Replace the word **constantly** with the word **continually**.

8 Move the fourth paragraph so that it becomes the third paragraph.

9 Find the word **Asterix** and replace the **e** with an accented **e** – i.e. **é**.

10 Inset the left and right margins by 2 cm.

11 Save the document with the filename **P4 sec2 holiday** and print one copy.

12 Close the file and exit Word.

Section 3 Basics – formatting

In this section you will practise and learn how to:

- centre, embolden, italicise and underline text
- format superscript, subscript text
- apply different colours to text
- change line spacing
- control justification/alignment
- control hyphenation
- change font and font size
- copy the formatting from a selected piece of text
- indent text
- create a header and a footer, inserting date, author, page numbers, etc.
- apply basic text format in headers and footers
- change page display modes
- use the page view magnification tool/zoom tool
- use and change pagination.

3.1 Centring text

 Exercise 1

Reload the file **London1**, saved in Section 2 and ensure that it is showing portrait display.

Centre the heading: **LANDMARKS IN LONDON**.

 Info

When the display is changed back to portrait, the changes that were made to the left and right margins in landscape are now applied instead to the top and bottom margins. We do not need to be concerned with this for the following exercises but you will need to be aware for future reference.

 Method

1 Select the text to be centred or position the cursor on the line where the text appears.

2 Click on: the **Centre** button (see Figure 3.27).

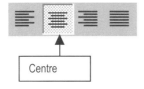

Figure 3.27 The Centre button

3.2 Emboldening text

 Exercise 2

Embolden the heading: **LANDMARKS IN LONDON**.

Method

1 Select the text to be emboldened.

2 Click on: the ◼**B** **Bold** button.

3.3 Italicising text

 Exercise 3

Italicise the Latin text in the second sentence of the second paragraph that reads:

Si monumentum requiris, circumspice.

 Method

Follow the method shown in 3.2 except, at Step 2 click on: the ◻*I* **Italic** button.

3.4 Underlining text

 Exercise 4

At the bottom of the document underline the text **Walkabouts Company**. Do not underline the copyright symbol.

 Method

Follow the method shown in 3.2 except, at Step 2 click on: the ◻**U** **Underline** button.

 Info

Emboldening, italicising or underlining text is a way of giving emphasis to the text. There are also other ways to emphasise text. Practise using some different effects now:

1 Select the text to format.

2 From the **Format** menu, select: **Font**.

3 Choose from the **Effects** section.

Note: Text can be made superscript – e.g. 3^2 – and subscript – e.g. H_2O.

3.5 Applying different colours to text

Exercise 5

Change the colour of the text: **Walkabouts Company** at the bottom of the document.

Method

1 Select the text to be changed.

2 Click on: the down arrow next to the **Font Color** button to display colour choices (see Figure 3.28).

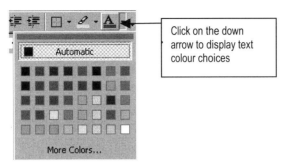

Click on the down arrow to display text colour choices

Figure 3.28 Changing text colour

3 Click on: your selected colour.

Info

If you do not have a colour printer, the selected colours will display in grey shades.

3.6 Changing line spacing

Exercise 6

Change the whole document to double line spacing.

Info

Word lets you apply a variety of line space settings (the distance between individual lines of text). Examples are:

Single line spacing...   this is the default

Double line spacing...   one blank line is left between the lines of text

> This is an example of single line spacing. The default setting is single line spacing where the gap between the lines of text is just over the type size. If the specification for a document is single line spacing, then usually you need do nothing.

> This is an example of double line spacing. There is one blank line left between lines
>
> of text. It is often used when a section needs extra emphasis.

 Method

1 Select all the text using the quick method (Press: **Ctrl + A**).

2 From the **Format** menu, select: **Paragraph**. The **Paragraph** dialogue box is displayed (see Figure 3.29).

3 Ensure the **Indents and Spacing** tab is selected.
4 In the **Spacing** section, **Line spacing** box, click on: the down arrow and click on: **Double**.
5 Click on: **OK**.
6 Click in a white space to remove highlighting.

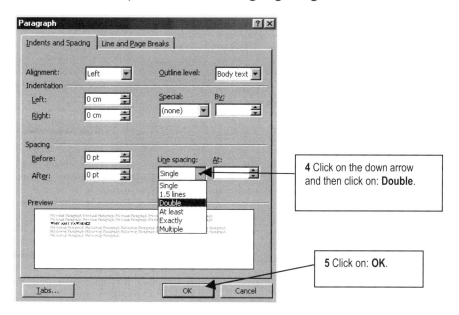

Figure 3.29 The Paragraph dialogue box – selecting double line spacing

Info

At Step 1, you can select a smaller portion of text if necessary and follow the same instructions.

Info

In double line spacing there are usually three lines between paragraphs. If you look on the status bar you will notice that your document now takes up two pages since **2/2** is displayed. When you scroll through your document you will see a dotted line across the page indicating that Word has inserted a page break.

3.7 Control justification/alignment

 Exercise 7

Justify the text at the right and left-hand margins (full justification).

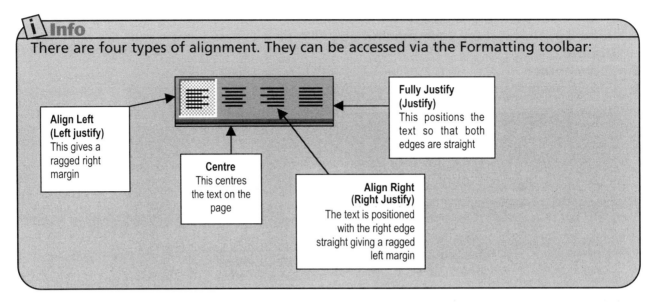

Align Left (Left justify)
This gives a ragged right margin

Centre
This centres the text on the page

Align Right (Right Justify)
The text is positioned with the right edge straight giving a ragged left margin

Fully Justify (Justify)
This positions the text so that both edges are straight

1 Select all of the text (**Ctrl + A**).

2 Click on: the **Justify** button (shown above).

3 Click anywhere to remove the selection.

You will notice that the centred heading **LANDMARKS IN LONDON** has also justified. Recentre it by following the instructions in Section 3.1 (page 68).

3.8 Save the file as **London2**.

3.9 Print one copy on A4 paper.

3.10 Changing font and font size

 Exercise 8

Change the font of the main heading to **Arial** and the size to **16 pt**.

 Method

Changing font type

 Info

Serif and sans serif fonts
The default font in Word is Times New Roman. This is a serif font. Serifs are small lines that stem from the upper and lower ends of characters. Serif fonts have such lines. Sans serif fonts do not have these lines. As a general rule, larger text in a sans serif font and body text in a serif font usually makes for easier reading. Examples:

Times New Roman is a serif font.

Arial is a sans serif font.

1 Select the heading: **LANDMARKS IN LONDON** so that it is highlighted.

2 Click on: the down arrow in the **Font** box (where Times New Roman is displayed, shown in Figure 3.30) to display fonts that are available on your computer.

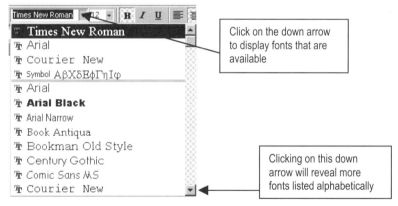

Figure 3.30 Fonts available in Word

3 Click on: **Arial** to select it.

Changing font size
4 With the text still selected, click on: the down arrow in the **Font Size** box (see Figure 3.31).
5 Click on: the size required.

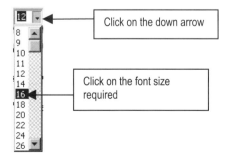

Figure 3.31 Changing font size

3.11 Copying the formatting from a selected piece of text

 Exercise 9

Change all other headings in the document to Arial, size 14 pt.

 Method

1   Follow the method shown in Section 3.10 (page 73) to change the first heading – i.e. **St Paul's Cathedral**.
2   With the changed heading still selected click twice on: the **Format Painter** button.
3   Select the other headings in turn. They will automatically reformat.
4   Press: **Esc** to turn the **Format Painter** off.

3.12 Indenting text

Info

Do not confuse indentation with page margins. An indent is the difference between the margin and the text.

 Exercise 10

Indenting on the left side
Indent the first paragraph on the left side only. Do not include the heading.

 Method

1   Select the text to be indented.

Info

The **Increase Indent** button moves the text in from the margin by 1.27 cm. Click on: it again to increase the indentation further. To remove the indentation, use the ⬅ **Decrease Indent** button.

 Exercise 11

Indenting both the left and right
Indent the second paragraph on both the left and the right by 2 cm.

Info

There are two ways to indent on the right-hand side. If you have good control of the mouse, using the ruler is a quick method.

2   Click on: the ➡ **Increase Indent** button.

Method 1

Indenting using the ruler

1 Select the text to be indented.

2 Click and drag the Left Indent marker (the square block) on the ruler to the right as shown in Figure 3.32. The text will indent accordingly.

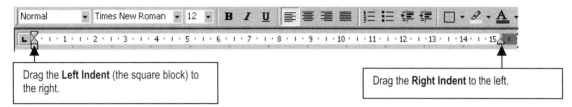

Drag the **Left Indent** (the square block) to the right.

Drag the **Right Indent** to the left.

Figure 3.32 Indenting using the ruler Method

3 Drag the Right Indent marker to the left.

 Info

It is worth making a note of the measurements already showing on the ruler before altering them. Don't forget, you can use the **Undo** button if you make a mistake.

4 Click in a white space to turn the highlighting off.

 ## Method 2

Indenting using the Format menu

1 Select the text to be indented.

2 From the **Format** menu, select: **Paragraph**. The **Paragraph** dialogue box appears (see Figure 3.33).

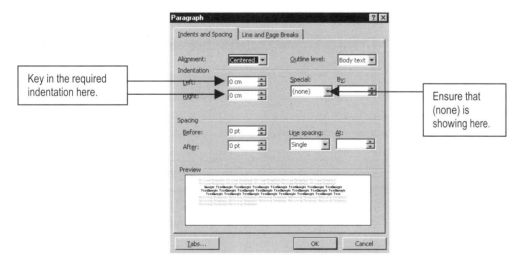

Key in the required indentation here.

Ensure that (none) is showing here.

Figure 3.33 Paragraph dialogue box

3 Ensure the **Indents and Spacing** tab is selected.

4 In the **Indentation** section, click in the **Left** box and key in the measurement you require.

5 Repeat in the **Right** box.

6 In the **Special** box, ensure that **(none)** is displayed.

7 Click on: **OK**.

8 Remove the highlight.

Info

This method can be used if you need a non-standard-sized indent. It can also be used to create special indents by selecting **First line** or **Hanging** in the **Special** box and keying in the size of the indent in the **By** box.

First line indents only the first line of the selection.

Hanging does not indent the first line but indents all the following lines.

Note: These special indents can also be achieved using the ruler. See Word Online Help for more detail.

3.13 Creating headers and footers

Exercise 12

Create a footer in size 8 pt to display **London Information, today's date** and **your name.**

 Method

1 Move the cursor to the start of the document (press: **Ctrl + Home**).

2 From the **View** menu, select: **Header and Footer**. The **Header and Footer** box appears (see Figure 3.34).

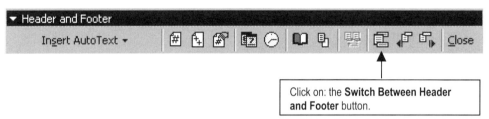

Figure 3.34 Header and Footer box

3 Click on: the **Switch Between Header and Footer** button. The **Footer** section appears (see Figure 3.35).

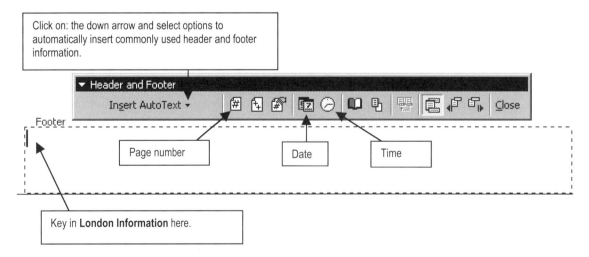

Figure 3.35 Footer section

4 Key in: **London Information** directly into the Footer section.

5 Press: **Tab** (or the spacebar) several times to move the cursor across the page.

6 Click on: the **Date** toolbar button (see Figure 3.35) to automatically insert today's date.

7 Press: **Tab** (or the spacebar) again to move the cursor across and then key in your name. It will look something like Figure 3.36.

London Information   27/01/00   Angela Bessant

Figure 3.36 Text inserted into footer

 Info

Check that the date is correct. The date may not be set up correctly on your computer. If it shows the wrong date, select the date only, then press: **Delete**. Key in the date manually or reset the computer's date.

Formatting the footer text

8 Select the footer text and change the size using the formatting toolbar. You may now want to alter the spacing.

9 Click on: **Close**.

 Info

You will not be able to see the footer if you are in **Normal View** but it will show up on Print Preview. (See Section 3.14 – page 79 – for information on different types of view.)

 Exercise 13

Add page numbers to the top centre of each page.

 Info

There are two ways of adding page numbers.

 Method 1

Using the View menu

1 Follow steps 1 and 2 in Section 3.13 (page 76). The **Header and Footer** box appears.

2 Click on: the **Centre** button so that the page numbers will appear in the centre.

3 Click on: the 🔢 **Insert Page Number** button (see Figure 3.37).

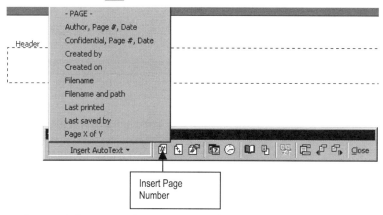

Figure 3.37 Inserting page numbers on a header

Method 2

Using the Insert menu

1 From the Insert menu, select: **Page Numbers**.

2 The **Page Numbers** dialogue box appears (see Figure 3.38).

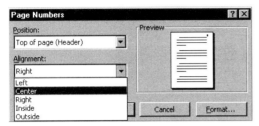

Figure 3.38 Page Numbers box

3 Use the down arrows next to **Position** and **Alignment** to select where you want the numbers to be.

4 Click on: **OK**.

Info

Should you need to adapt page numbers – e.g. start at a number other than 1, click on: the 🖻 **Format Page Number** button in Method 1. For both methods, click on: **Format** if you need to amend further i.e. select a different number format.

Info

Inserting document author's name on header/footer

If you are not the regular user of a computer, it will not be set up to automatically display your name as the author of the document. To display your name:

1 With the document open, from the **File** menu, select: **Properties**.

2 With the **Summary** tab selected, key in your name in the **Author** box.

3 Click on: **OK**.

4 From the **View** menu, select: **Headers and Footers**.

5 Position the cursor where you want your name to display.

6 From the **Insert** menu, select: **Field**.

7 In the **Categories** box, select: **Document Information**.

8 In the **Field names** box, select: **Author**.

9 Click on: **OK**.

3.14 Changing page display modes

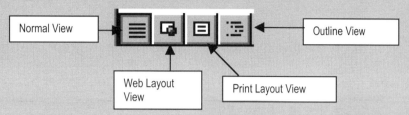

Normal View | Web Layout View | Print Layout View | Outline View

Normal View This is the default. It allows for quick and easy text editing.

Web Layout View Displays the document as it would appear on the web.

Print Layout View This view allows you to see how objects will be positioned on the printed page. It shows margins, headers and footers and graphics.

Outline View This view allows you to see your document in an outline format.

 Exercise 14

Change to Print Layout View and use the Zoom button to magnify the footer text.

 Method

1   Click on: the **Print Layout View** button shown above.

2   The header and footer will now be visible. The text, set at size 8 pt will be small and since header text is greyed out it may be difficult to read. Use the **Zoom** box to enlarge the text on screen as follows:

Using the page view magnification/zoom tool

3   Click on: the down arrow in the **Zoom** toolbar box to reveal default zoom views (see Figure 3.39).

4   Select a zoom greater than 100% (the default) to enlarge text.

5   To revert back, select zoom 100%.

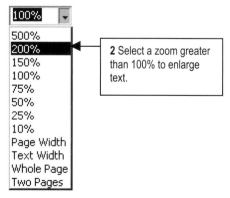

Figure 3.39 Using Zoom

3.15 Using and changing pagination

Exercise 15

Insert a page break after the second paragraph ending **...look around you.**

Method

1 Position the cursor on the line in between the second paragraph and the third paragraph heading.
2 From the **Insert** menu, select: **Break**. The **Break** dialogue box appears (see Figure 3.40).
3 Ensure that the **Page break** option button is selected.
4 Click on: **OK**.

Figure 3.40 The Break dialogue box

Info

It is important to set out the pages so that they are easy to read. Check that the default setting for **Widow/Orphan** control (**Format** menu: **Paragraph, Line and Page Breaks**) is ticked. This ensures that paragraphs are not split so that one stray line of text appears at the bottom or top of a page. Always check that headings are not split from the text to which they refer.

There are soft and hard page breaks. As your text reaches the bottom margin of a page, a soft page break is automatically inserted by Word. This will reposition itself should you add or delete text from the document. A hard page break is inserted by you. Its position will always remain constant until you decide to alter it.

To delete a hard page break
1 Ensure that you are in **Normal** View by selecting it from the bottom left corner of the document window.

2 Position the cursor on the page break (dotted line).
3 Press: **Delete**.

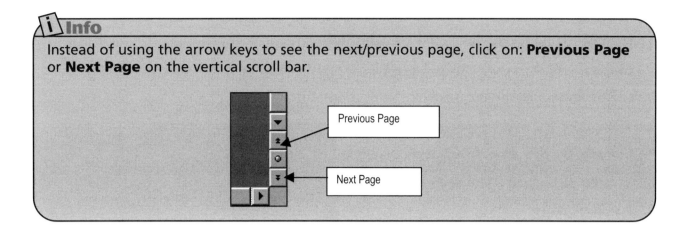

Info

Instead of using the arrow keys to see the next/previous page, click on: **Previous Page** or **Next Page** on the vertical scroll bar.

Previous Page

Next Page

3.16 Save the document as **London3**.

3.17 Print one copy on A4 paper.

3.18 Close the file and exit Word.

Section 3 Word processing practice

Practice 5

1 Load Word and reload the file **P3 sec2 www** saved in Section 2.

2 Centre and embolden the heading: **THE WORLD WIDE WEB**.

3 Inset the whole document by 1.27 cm at the left margin.

4 Set the document in double-line spacing.

5 Change the colour of all the text in the second and fourth paragraph to red.

6 Justify the first and second paragraphs only.

7 Change the font in the final paragraph to Arial 16 pt.

8 Add a header containing the text **World Wide Web** and your name.

9 Format the header to 8 pt.

10 Add page numbers at the bottom right, starting at 3.

11 Insert a page break after the second paragraph.

12 Save the document as **P5 sec3 www**.

13 Print one copy.

14 Close the file and exit Word.

Practice 6

1 Load Word and reload the file **P4 sec2 holiday** saved in section 2.

2 At the top of the document add a heading **Details of your reward** in Arial 16 pt.

3 Centre and underline the heading that you just entered.

4 Except the first and last paragraphs, give each paragraph a hanging paragraph by 1 cm.

5 Increase the font size of the fourth paragraph by 2 pt.

6 Save the document as **P6 sec3 holiday**.

7 Print one copy.

8 Close the file and exit Word.

Section 4 Basics – more formatting

In this section you will practise and learn how to:

- use lists (bulleted and numbered)
- use and set tabs
- add borders to a document
- save an existing document under another file format including saving a document for posting on the web

- apply existing styles to a document
- choose an appropriate document template for use in a specified task
- work within a template on a specified task.

4.1 Using lists (bulleted and numbered)

 Exercise 1

Open a new Word document and key in the following text, perform a spellcheck and save the document with the filename **Volunteers**.

VOLUNTEERS REQUIRED

Do you meet the following criteria?

Age range 16 to 40
Computer literate
Available during the hours of 16.00 and 18.00

We are looking for volunteers to take part in a survey on computer usage. We are able to offer you a small payment and a cup of tea or coffee! If you think that you may be able to help us, we would like to hear from YOU.

We look forward to your call.

 Exercise 2

Make the section starting at **Age range...** and ending at **...18.00** into a bulleted list.

 Method

1 Select the text to be bulleted.
2 Click on: the ▤ **Bullets** button.

Info

Bullets/numbering can be selected before keying in the text, if preferred.

Formatting bullets
Bullets can take many forms:

1   From the **Format** menu, select: **Bullets and Numbering**.

2   Select your preferred option and click on: **OK**.

3   Click on: **Customize** if you require a different bullet type.

Numbered lists
Numbering lists is carried out following the same method except, at Step 2 clicking on the ▤ **Numbering** button. This is useful if lists need to be in a specific order – e.g. a set of instructions. You can format numbers in the following way.

1   Select the list.

2   From the **Format** menu, select: **Bullets and Numbering**. The **Bullets and Numbering** dialogue box is displayed.

3   Click on: **Customize**. The **Customize Numbered List** dialogue box is displayed.

4   Select a format from the **Number style** list. Options include Roman numerals and A, B, C etc.

Turning bullets/numbering off
To turn Bullets and Numbering off, select the bulleted/numbered text, and click on: the relevant **Bullets/Numbering** button.

4.2 Using and setting tabs

 Exercise 3

Using tabs, insert the following before the final sentence beginning **We look forward...**

Please contact one of the following: **Mike**   **ext 4448**
                                             Chris   **ext 4462**
                                             Jane   **ext 4463**

Method

Info

Tabs are used to line up columns and Word offers several types of tab.

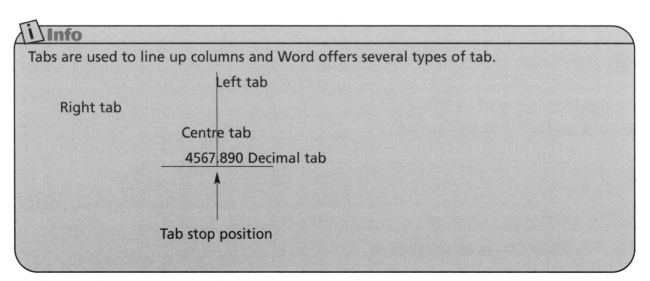

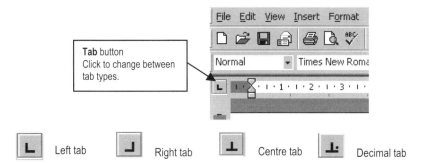

L Left tab   **⅃** Right tab   **⊥** Centre tab   **⊥·** Decimal tab

Note: In Office 2000, the following tabs are also available:

Ⅰ   *Bar tab*. This draws a vertical line on a document

▽   *First Line Indent*. This sets the first line of paragraphs

凵   *Hanging Indent*. This defines the left margin of every line but the first line in a paragraph

Note: It is useful to have the **Show/Hide** on when setting tabs.

Using pre-set tabs

1 Key in the text: **Please contact one of the following**: in the correct position in the document.
2 Press: **Tab** once to move to the preset tab stop and key in **Mike**.
3 Press: **Tab** once and key in **ext 4448**. Press: **Enter** (see Figure 3.41).

¶
Please·contact·one·of·the·following:→Mike→ext·4448¶

Figure 3.41 Using tabs

4 Press: **Tab** a number of times until the cursor is lined up under the **M** of Mike.
5 Key in: **Chris**, press: **Tab** once and key in **ext 4462**. Press: **Enter**.
6 Repeat Steps 4 and 5 for **Jane ext 4463** (see Figure 3.42).

¶
Please·contact·one·of·the·following:→Mike→ext·4448¶
→   →   →   →   →   Chris→ext·4462¶
→   →   →   →   →   Jane→ext·4463¶
¶

Figure 3.42 Text keyed in displaying hidden characters

Exercise 4

Key in and position the name and extension number **Felicity ext 6884**.

Method

1 Enter the name and extension (ext) number using the above method. You will notice that because the name Felicity is longer than the other names, the ext number is not lined up (see Figure 3.43).

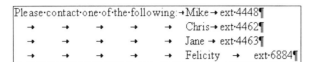

Figure 3.43 ext numbers are not aligned

2 To rectify this, add an extra tab space between **Mike** and **ext**, **Chris** and **ext** and **Jane** and **ext** (see Figure 3.44).

Figure 3.44 Extra tab spaces inserted

3 However, now when you take the Show/Hide off you will notice that the ext numbers are rather a long way from the names. In order to move them closer to the names we will need to set a left tab stop.

4 Select all of the tabulated text.

5 From the **Format** menu, select: **Tabs**. The **Tabs** dialogue box appears (see Figure 3.45).

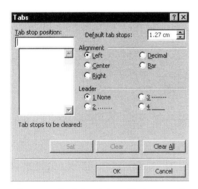

Figure 3.45 Tabs dialogue box

6 In the **Tab stop position** box, key in the first tab stop position (I am using 6.75 cm). Ensure **Alignment** is set to **Left**. Click on: **Set**.

7 Key in the second tab stop position (I am using 8.25 cm). Click on: **Set**.

8 Click on: **OK**.

9 Your text and ruler will now look similar to that in Figure 3.46.

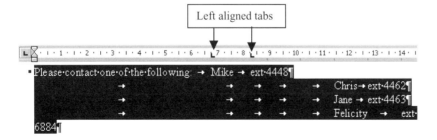

Figure 3.46 Tab set at 6.75 cm and 8.25 cm

10 To realign the text, position the cursor before the **C** in Chris and press: the ← Del (Backspace). Repeat for Jane and Felicity. The text will now be aligned (see Figure 3.47).

11 Remove the highlighting. Turn Show/Hide off.

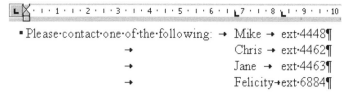

- Please·contact·one·of·the·following: → Mike → ext·4448¶
  → Chris → ext·4462¶
  → Jane → ext·4463¶
  → Felicity→ext·6884¶

Figure 3.47 Text realigned

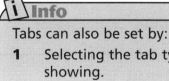

Tabs can also be set by:

1 Selecting the tab type by clicking on the Tab button until the type you require is showing.

2 Click once on the ruler where you want the tab stop to be.

3 Repeat as necessary.

To remove tabs, drag them off the ruler.

Setting leader tabs

Leader tabs have a line for the eye to follow to the tabulated entry – e.g.

Dotted line leader ....tab

Continuous line leader __tab

To set a leader tab:

1 From the **Format** menu, select **Tabs**.

2 In the **Tabs** dialogue box, set the tab as normal.

3 In the **Leader** section, set the format.

4 It is well worth practising setting tabs. It is quite difficult to master.

4.3 Adding borders to a document

Exercise 5

Add a border to the document.

Method

1 From the **Format** menu, select: **Borders and Shading**. The Borders and Shading dialogue box appears (Figure 3.48).

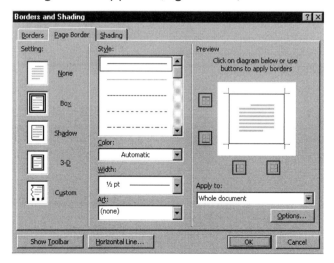

Figure 3.48 Borders and Shading dialogue box

2 Click on: the **Page Border** tab and make selections from the various sections – e.g. Box, Shadow, 3-D.

3 Click on: **OK**.

Info

You can apply borders to individual paragraphs by first selecting the relevant paragraph. Ensure that the **Borders** tab is selected, format as required, make a selection in the **Apply to** section. Click on: **OK**.

4.4 Saving documents under a different file format

Exercise 6

Save the document in the normal way with the filename **Volunteers1**. Also save the file with the filename **Wanted** in a format suitable for posting on the web.

Info

By default Word automatically saves files in the version of Word format that you are using – i.e. WORD 2000 and adds the extension .doc – e.g. Volunteers1.doc. However, it is possible to save documents in other formats.

 Method

1 Save the file with the filename **Volunteers1** in the normal way.

Saving a document in web format

2 From the **File** menu, select: **Save As**. The **Save As** dialogue box appears.

3 In the **Save as type** section, click on: the down arrow to reveal a list. Scroll through to see the formats that the document can be saved as (see Figure 3.49).

4 Select: **Web Page**.

5 Key in the filename **Wanted**. Click on: **Save**.

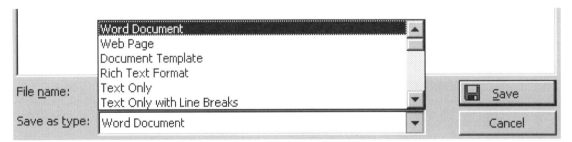

Figure 3.49 File formats available

Note: You can check the file format by selecting: **Properties** from the **File** menu. Figure 3.50 shows the Type as Microsoft HTML Document 5.0 (this is a web format), the MS-DOS name is Wanted.htm instead of Wanted.doc.

File formats available

Being able to save files in different formats is extremely useful. It means that you can share files with others who do not have the same software or version of software that you are using. You can save in a previous version of Word, WordPerfect or Works format (WordPerfect and Works are other common word processors). Other useful formats include:

Text Only – This is a basic no frills, compact text format. It can be opened and read by almost any software on any computer.

Rich Text Format – This format saves text and essential formatting. It can be opened accurately (keeping its layout) by most word processors.

Document template – This will save the style and page layout settings as the basis for another document.

Figure 3.50 File properties

Exercise 7

Print either of the saved files **Volunteers1** *or* **Wanted** and close both of them.

4.5 Working with templates and applying existing styles to a document

Info

Word documents are based on a template called Normal.dot. Templates act as a document model and store settings. Each template has various set styles associated with it. Normal is the default style applied to the default template for Word documents. It has the properties of being left aligned, Times New Roman, 12 pt. Other styles have their own properties, which are given next to the example text. Styles are linked to templates so that Heading1 in one template may be Arial, right-aligned, 16 pt, and in a different template could be Times New Roman, centred, 20 pt. You will notice that not all styles are suitable as they will upset bulleted lists, tab settings etc. Use the **Undo** button to recover original text style.

More styles are available by selecting: **Style** from the **Format** menu. Also from the **Format** menu, you can experiment with **Autoformat** and **Theme**. As you work through a document, styles that you are using will be added to the Style list.

Exercise 8

Open the file: **Volunteers1** and format it using Word's default template existing styles.

 **Method**

1 With the document open on screen, select the heading **VOLUNTEERS REQUIRED**.
2 Click on: the down arrow in the **Style** box.
3 Click on: a suitable style.
4 Format some of the other text within the document in the same way.
5 Resave and close the document.

Exercise 9

Use a suitable Word template to produce a fax using your imagination to fill in the details.

 Method

1 From the **File** menu, select **New**.
2 Click on: the **Letters and Faxes** tab (see Figure 3.51).

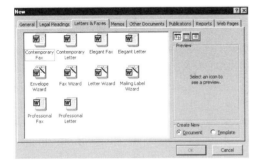

Figure 3.51 Selecting a template

3 Select a suitable template (you will see a preview on the righthand side) and then click on: **OK**.
4 You may need to use Zoom to see all of the document details.
5 Overwrite the text with your own.
6 Save the document and print one copy on A4 paper.

 Info

Templates have fields that are already set up. These fields are marked in grey. If they are not marked in grey, from the **Tools** menu, select: **Options**. With the **View** tab selected, in the **Show** section, ensure that the **Field shading** box is set to **Always**. You can delete fields by selecting them and pressing: **Delete**. Familiarise yourself with the different templates available in Word.

Creating a new template

1 Create the document that you want to become a template.
2 From the **File** menu, select: **Save As**.
3 Key in the filename and in the **Save as type** box, select: **Document Template**.
4 Choosing Document Template automatically takes you to the Templates folder where it will be saved.
5 Click on: **Save** and close the template document.

Opening the new template

1 From the **File** menu, select: **New**. The **New** dialogue box is displayed.

2 With the **General** tab selected, you should be able to see your new template.
3 Click on it and then on **OK**.

4.6 Close the document and exit Word.

Section 4 Word processing practice

Practice 7

Open a new Word document and key in the following text, formatting as shown:

GRAND OPENING
THE COMPUTER SHOP
SATURDAY 25 MARCH 2000

Format the three headings as follows: sans serif font, 26 pt, bold, font colour red, centre across the page.

Many opening bargains including

Computers
Printers
Scanners
Modems
Software

Make into bulleted list. Format the bullets to match the theme of the flyer if possible.

Come and see for yourself

Our prices are keen:
Internal Zip drives from £102.95
Hard drives 20Gb from........£129.99
Scanners from £79.99

Tabulate with decimal tab stops and leader dots.

The first 10 customers will each receive boxed software of their choice up to the value of £50

We look forward to welcoming you!

All other formatting is at your discretion using styles. Add a shadow border around the whole document. Print on A4 paper in portrait display.

Save in a format suitable for posting on the web.

Practice 8

1 Load Word and the Professional Memo template. Insert the following text in the appropriate places:

Company name: THE COMPUTER SHOP
To: Andrea Whitely
From: Paul Hunter

Cc: Gita Meehan
Today's date
Subject: Delivery of laptops
Message: Thank you for the delivery that I received this morning. As you know we are opening next Saturday and you would be most welcome to come and join us then. Please let me know if you can make it.
Best Regards.

2   Save the document as **Fax laptops**.

3   Print one copy on A4 paper.

Section 5 Advanced – tables

In this section you will practise and learn how to:

- create standard tables
- add/remove borders on a table
- change cell attributes: formatting, cell size, colour, etc.
- insert/delete columns/rows
- use the automatic table formatting tool.

5.1 Creating a standard table

 Exercise 1

Open a new Word document and create the following table using the Table facility.

Largest Continents	Largest Countries	Largest Oceans and Seas
Asia	Russian Federation	Pacific
Africa	Canada	Atlantic
North America	China	Indian

 Method

1 With a new document open, position the cursor where you want the top left corner of the table to be.

2 Hold down the left mouse over the ▦ **Insert Table** button: a grid appears.

3 Drag the mouse across and down the grid to result in the number of columns and rows required for the table (3 columns and 5 rows, including a blank row after the headings – see Figure 3.52). Release the mouse button.

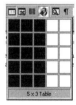

Figure 3.52 Setting cells for a new table

4 The empty table appears in your document.
5 Key in the table's text, pressing: **Tab** to move to the next entry position (or use the arrow keys).

 Info

If you press **Enter** by mistake, a line space will appear. Press: the ← **Del** (Backspace) key to remove the line space.

Working with borders

6 Remove the borders on the table by positioning the cursor anywhere in the table and from the **Table** menu, selecting: **Select**, then: **Table**.

7 From the toolbar, click on: the down arrow next to the **Border** button. Click on: **No Border** as shown in Figure 3.53.

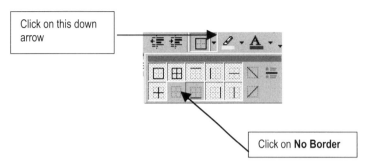

Click on this down arrow

Click on **No Border**

Figure 3.53 Deleting borders

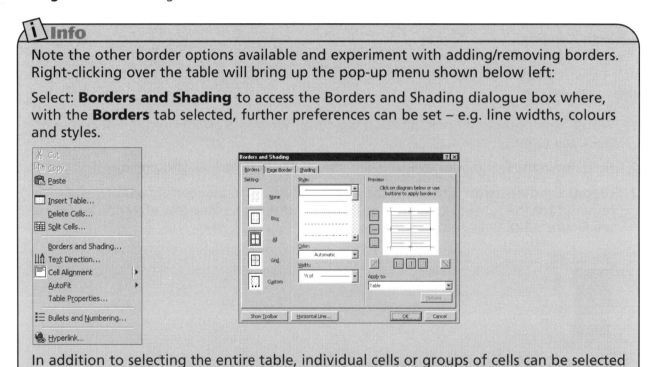
8 Save the document with the filename: **Geography**.

5.2 Inserting/deleting rows/columns

Exercise 2

Adding rows at the end of a table

Add a row at the bottom of the table and key in the following in the relevant places:

Antarctica   **Brazil**   **South China**

Method

1 Position the cursor at the end of the last table entry – i.e. the **n** of **Indian**.
2 Press: **Tab**. A new row is created.
3 Key in the text and resave the document.

Exercise 3

Inserting rows within the table

Insert a row between the one displaying North America and Antarctica and insert the text:

South America   **USA**   **Arctic**

Method

1 Select the row below where you want to insert the new row, by dragging the mouse over it.

2 From the **Table** menu, select: **Insert**, then **Rows Above** (see Figure 3.54).

Figure 3.54 Inserting rows

3 Key in the text.

Exercise 4

Deleting rows

Delete the row containing **Africa**, **Canada** and **Atlantic**.

Method

1 Select the row to be deleted.
2 Right-click over the selection. A pop-up menu appears (see Figure 3.55).
3 Select: **Delete Cells**. The **Delete Cells** box appears (see Figure 3.56).
4 Click next to **Delete entire row**.

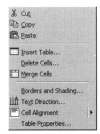
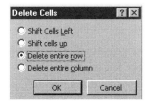

Figure 3.55 Pop-up menu   **Figure 3.56** Deleting a row

Exercise 5

Deleting columns

Delete the middle column.

Method

1 Select the column to delete by hovering over the top of the column. When a thick black arrow appears, click the mouse.

2 Right-click over the selection.

3 From the pop-up menu, select: **Delete Columns** (see Figure 3.57).

Figure 3.57 Deleting columns

Exercise 6

Inserting columns

Re-insert the deleted column (For practice purposes, do not use **Undo**).

Method

1 Select the column to the right of the required position for the new column.
2 Right-click over the selection.
3 From the pop-up menu, select: **Insert Columns**.
4 Key in the text.

Exercise 7

Inserting columns to the right of the last column in a table

Insert a column, which will become the fourth column of the table and enter the following:

Largest Islands

Greenland

Borneo

Madagascar

Baffin

 Method

1 Click just outside the right-hand column.
2 From the **Table** menu, select: **Select**, then **Column**.
3 Right-click over selection, select: **Insert Columns**.

Deleting an entire table
Select the table by clicking anywhere in it and from the **Table** menu, select: **Select**, **Table**. Click on: the **Cut** button. Click on: the **Undo** button to reinstate the table!

5.3 Changing cell attributes

 ## Exercise 8

Change the font in the heading row to Arial, 16 pt size, embolden and centre it.

 Method

1 Select the heading row.
2 Format it in the usual way using the toolbar buttons.

 ## Exercise 9

Change the background of the heading cells to a colour instead of white.

 Method

1 Select the cells and right-click to bring up a pop-up menu.
2 Select: **Borders and Shading**.
3 Ensure the **Shading** tab is selected.
4 Click on: a colour.
5 Click on: **OK**.

Exercise 10

Change the width of the first column so that it is narrower than the other 3.

 Method

1 Select the first column.
2 Drag the right column border to the required position.

 Info

Tables are created with standard cell widths and heights. Change them by selecting them and dragging the borders, as in Exercise 10. You can also use **Autofit**. With the table or cell(s) selected, from the **Table** menu, select: **Autofit, Autofit to contents**.

5.4 Using automatic table formatting

Info

Word has several table formats to select from.

To Autoformat a table:

Position the cursor in the table

From the **Table** menu, select: **Table Autoformat**.

Select from the **Formats** list. (**Contemporary** is a good choice for the table you have just created.)

Experiment with the formats. Notice that some will not suit the table since they have headings in the first column.

5.5 Resave the document and print one copy on A4 paper.

5.6 Close the document and exit Word.

Section 5 Word processing practice

Practice 9

1 Open a Word file.

2 Key in the following:

Earthquake Measurements

The magnitude of earthquakes is measured in units on the Richter Scale and their intensity on the Mercalli Scale.

3 Create the following table:

Mercalli	Richter	Characteristics
1	Less than 3.5	Only detected by seismograph
2	3.5	Only detected by people at rest
3	4.2	Similar to vibrations from HGV
4	4.5	Felt indoors; rocks parked cars
5	4.8	Generally felt; awakens sleepers
12	Greater than 8.1	Total destruction of area

4 Format the headings in bold, centre and make 2 pt larger than the other text.

5 Set the width of the columns so that they are in the same proportions as the columns above.

6 Delete all borders except the outside border and the bottom border of the headings row.

7 Shade the headings row cells in blue.

8 Insert a row after the one containing 5 in the Mercalli column and enter the details:

9 **6.1 Causes general alarm; building walls crack**

10 Save the document with the filename **Earthquakes** and print the table only in landscape display on A4 paper.

Practice 10

1 Load Word and reload the file: **Earthquakes** saved in Practice 9.

2 Delete the **Mercalli** column from the table (ensure that an outside border is maintained).

3 Inset the left and right margins by 3 cm.

4 Change the font throughout the document (except the title) to Times New Roman pt 16.

5 Centre the title and change to 20 pt.

6 Save the file with the filename: **Earthquakes Richter**.

7 Print the file in landscape on A4 paper.

Section 6 Advanced – mail merge

In this section you will practise and learn how to:

- create a data file for use in a mail merge
- merge a data file with a letter document or a label document.

What is mail merge?

Mail merge is the name given to the merging of information (usually names and addresses) with a standard document (usually a letter). The names and addresses are keyed in and stored in a database file and can be used with any standard document without having to laboriously key in the information again. Therefore it saves a lot of work. The end result of a mail merge is that the letter (or document) looks personal since it is impossible to tell that a number of other people have received the same letter.

6.1 Creating/opening a merge letter document

 Exercise 1

Open a new Word document and key in the following letter. Save the document with the filename: **Merge1**.

10 February 2000

Dear

Box Office Film Club

I am pleased to enclose details of our forthcoming film season.

All films will be shown in the Lecture Room on the Hemsley Hall Campus. Ample free parking spaces are available at both sides of the hall. If you are travelling by public transport, the nearest bus stop is in Regent Avenue. May I remind you that guest tickets will be on sale in the Hemsley Bar 20 minutes before each performance.

I look forward to welcoming you this season.

Yours sincerely

Club Secretary

Enc

Method

1 Key in the document, proofread, spellcheck and save it.
2 From the **Tools** menu, select: **Mail Merge**. The **Mail Merge Helper** dialogue box appears (see Figure 3.58).

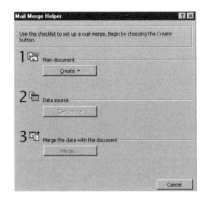

Figure 3.58 Mail Merge Helper dialogue box

3 In the **Main document** section 1, click on: **Create**.
4 Select: **Form Letters** from the menu (see Figure 3.59).

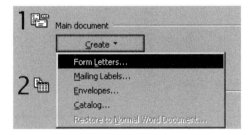

Figure 3.59 Creating form letters

5 When prompted, select: **Active window** (see Figure 3.60).

Figure 3.60 Select Active Window

6 The **Mail Merge Helper** dialogue box appears again (see Figure 3.61). The filename and path of the merge document is now displayed in section 1.
7 In the **Data source** section 2, click on: **Get Data**.

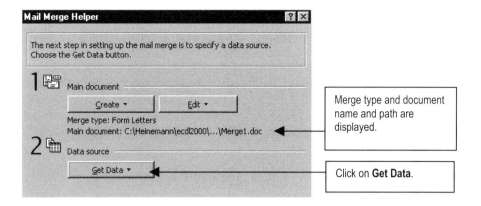

Figure 3.61 Mail Merge Helper dialogue box at Section 2

8   Select: **Create Data Source** from the menu (see Figure 3.62).

Figure 3.62 Creating a data source

9   The **Create Data Source** dialogue box appears (see Figure 3.63).

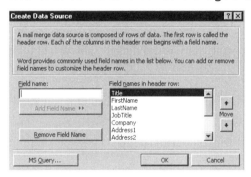

Figure 3.63 Create Data Source dialogue box

i Info

If the data source already existed, you would need to click on: **Open Data Source**.

6.2 Creating a data source

 Exercise 2

Use the following information to create the data source:

Mr Murray Dixon	**Miss Lynne Carter**
63 Harpur Street	**10 Brook End**
Luton	**Bedford**
LU6 1AS	**MK42 7NS**
Mr Jack Hobson	**Mrs Susi Malucci**
18 Ryton Close	**38 Sandhurst Road**
Bedford	**Luton**
MK43 6PZ	**LU5 3JU**

 Method

 Info

In the data source, each field contains the same type of information – e.g in the 'Title' field Mr, Mrs, Miss etc. are acceptable. Each addressee's data is called a record. By examining the data source information, you will see that the data has the following six fields: Title, FirstName, LastName, Address1, Address2 and PostalCode. Word provides commonly used field names, which are displayed in the **Field names in header row** box.

1 With the **Create Data Source** dialogue box displayed (see Figure 3.63) from the **Field names in header row**, delete the fields that are not relevant to our data source. To do this, click on: the first field that is not required and click on: **Remove Field Name**. Repeat for the other fields until the **Field names in header row** look like Figure 3.64.

Info

When a field is not displayed in the **Field names in header row,** you can add it by keying in an appropriate name in the **Field name** dialogue box (no spaces are allowed) and clicking on **Add Field Name**.

2 Click on: **OK**. Save the data source when the **Save As** dialogue box is displayed.

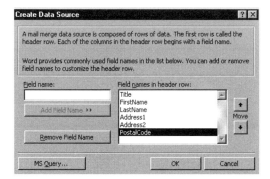

Figure 3.64 Field names in header row altered to reflect our data source

3 Click on: **Edit Data Source** when the prompt box appears (see Figure 3.65).

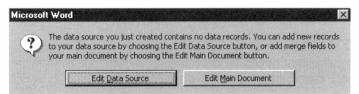

Figure 3.65 Select Edit Data Source to add data

4 The **Data Form** dialogue box appears (see Figure 3.66).
5 Key in the information in the **Title** field, press: **Enter**.
6 Repeat until all the fields for the first name and address have been keyed in.
7 Press: **Enter** to move on to the next name and address.
8 Repeat until all the data has been entered.
9 Click on: **OK**. Remember to press **Enter** after the final entry so that it is included in the data file. The data is saved automatically.

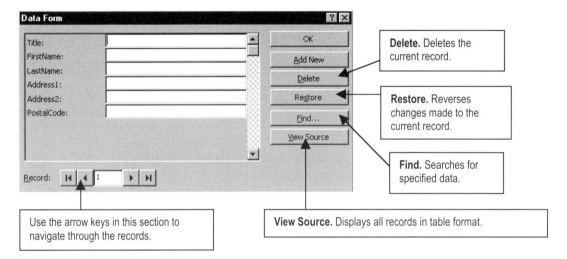

Figure 3.66 Data Form dialogue box

You are now returned to your original form letter. You will notice that the **Mail Merge** toolbar has appeared (see Figure 3.67).

6.3 Entering merge fields

Exercise 3

Insert merge fields into the document.

 Method

 Info

In order for Word to know where you want the data in the data source to be merged, it is necessary to insert merge fields.

1 Position the cursor where you want the first merge field to be – in this case the addressee Title that will need to be placed under the date of the letter (see Figure 3.68).

2 On the **Mail Merge** toolbar, click on: the down arrow of the **Insert Merge Field** button (see Figure 3.67).

3 Select: the field name required – i.e. Title.

4 Repeat until all merge fields have been inserted.

Note: Remember to press the space bar to leave spaces in the relevant places – e.g. between **Title** and **FirstName**.

Figure 3.67 Mail Merge toolbar

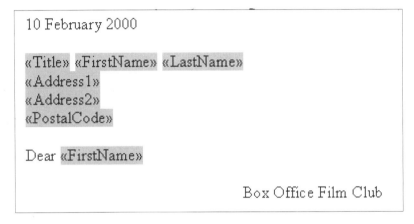

10 February 2000

«Title» «FirstName» «LastName»
«Address1»
«Address2»
«PostalCode»

Dear «FirstName»

Box Office Film Club

Figure 3.68 Merge codes inserted

6.4 Viewing merged document

1 To view the merged document click on: the ⟪⟫ABC **View Merged Data** button on the Mail Merge toolbar.

2 The first merged document is displayed.

3 To view the other three, click on: the ◄◄ ◄ 1 ► ►► arrow buttons on the Mail Merge toolbar.

6.5 Printing the merged file

1 Click on: the 🖳 **Merge to Printer** button on the Mail Merge toolbar.

2 Print in the normal way.

6.6 Save all documents with new filenames where appropriate and exit Word.

> **ℹ️ Info**
>
> You can also use mail merge to produce address labels. To do this, at Step 4 in 6.1, select: **Mailing Labels**. You will need to know what type of labels they are to set up the main merge document. There is a list of standard ones to choose from.

> **ℹ️ Info**
>
> When mail merging, always proofread and spellcheck the main document carefully. One simple mistake has the potential of being duplicated many times!

Section 6 Word processing practice

Practice 11

1 Key in the following letter to be used as a merge letter:

Insert date

Dear

Town and Country Enterprise AGM

Please note that the AGM will take place on Tuesday 20 June at 7.30 pm in the Coleridge Meeting Room. I am enclosing the agenda. Please let me know if you have any further items to add.

Coffee and light snacks will be provided. I look forward to seeing as many of our members as possible.

Yours sincerely

Jenny Jinx
Secretary

Enc

2 Create the data source:

Miss King	Mr Gregory	Dr Walpole
8 Wendover Place	10 George Gardens	118 Exeter Way
Kempston	Silsoe	Harrold
Bedford	Bedford	Bedford
MK32 9TG	BD27 9JU	MK55 2AS

3 Merge the letter with the data source.

4 Save all files.

5 Print the merged letters.

Practice 12

1 Use the data source created in Practice 11 to create mailing labels.

2 Print the labels onto A4 paper.

Section 7 Advanced – pictures, images and other objects

In this section you will practise and learn how to:

- add an image to a document
- add autoshapes to a document: change line colours, change autoshape fill colours
- move images or drawn objects within a document
- resize a graphic
- import an image file, chart or graph into a document
- import a spreadsheet into a document.

7.1 Adding an image to a document

 Exercise 1

Open a new Word document and add an image suitable for a leaflet about a theatre visit.

 Method

1 Open a new Word document.

2 Position the cursor, by double-clicking the mouse, where you want the image to appear.

3 From the **Insert** menu, select: **Picture**, then **ClipArt** (see Figure 3.69).

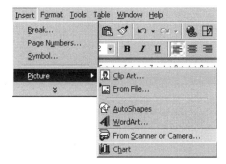

Figure 3.69 Inserting an image

 Info

Notice the other picture options here, notably **From File** (to import an existing picture file) and **Chart**, which are inserted in a similar way. As well as this method, objects including spreadsheets, graphs and graphics can be pasted in from other documents using the **Cut** and **Paste** buttons. When importing using the **Insert File** method, remember to set the file type to that which you are importing. As an example, if the file type is set to the Word document type and you want to insert an Excel file, the Excel file will not be displayed in the files list.

4 The **Insert ClipArt** dialogue box appears (see Figure 3.70).

Figure 3.70 Insert ClipArt dialogue box

5 Select a suitable picture by clicking on a category and then on the ClipArt you have chosen.

6 A pop-up menu appears; click on: **Insert clip** (see Figure 3.71).

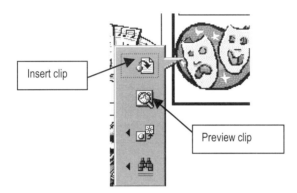

Insert clip

Preview clip

Figure 3.71 Chosen clip has a pop-up menu

7 Close the **Insert ClipArt** dialogue box by clicking on the **Close** button.

8 The chosen image appears in the new document. It may be rather large!

Resizing an image

9 Click on: the image to select it. It will have handles on the corners and at the sides (see Figure 3.72).

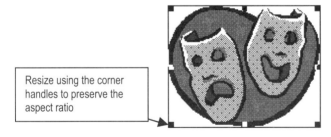

Resize using the corner handles to preserve the aspect ratio

Figure 3.72 A selected image

10 Hover the mouse over a handle until a double-sided arrow appears. Drag a corner handle inwards to reduce the size of the image.

11 Centre the image using the **Centre** button.

> **i** **Info**
>
> To resize to an exact measurement: right-click on the image, from the pop-up menu, select: **Format Picture**, **Size** tab. Insert new measurements. Click on: **OK**.
>
> If you drag from a corner, the graphic will keep its aspect ratio (its original proportions). If you try to resize it from the side handles, it will loose its shape. Try it and see what happens. Use the **Undo** button to revert back to the original proportions.

Exercise 2

Underneath the image enter the following text. Format the text as you want.

Shakespeare Season

ROMEO AND JULIET

All this week at 7 pm in the Drama Studio

Tickets available at the door

7.2 Moving images within a document

Exercise 3

Move the image so that it appears at the bottom of the text.

Method

1 Select the image.
2 Click on: the **Cut** button.
3 Position the cursor where you want the image to appear, then click on: the **Paste** button.

7.3 Adding autoshapes to a document

Exercise 4

Using Word's drawing features, add some autoshapes to the document.

Method

1 From the **View** menu, select: **Toolbars**, then click on: **Drawing**.
2 The **Drawing** toolbar buttons are labelled in Figure 3.73 and are straightforward to use.
3 Practise adding autoshapes, changing line colours and changing autoshape fill colours, as follows:

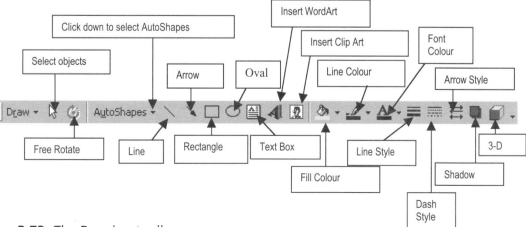

Figure 3.73 The Drawing toolbar

Adding autoshapes

1 Click on: the arrow of the **AutoShapes** button.
2 Select: a category – e.g. Basic Shapes.
3 Click on: the shape you want to use.
4 On the document, click where you want to place the shape.
5 You can move the shape by dragging it with the mouse.

Filling a shape with colour

1 Select the shape to fill.
2 Click the down arrow on the **Fill Colour** button.
3 Click on: the chosen colour.

Filling a shape with a pattern

1 Follow steps 1 and 2 above.
2 Click on: **Fill Effects**. The **Fill Effects** dialogue box appears.
3 Click on: the **Pattern** tab.
4 Click on: the chosen pattern.
5 Click on: **OK**.

Adding a line

1 Click on: the **Line** button.
2 Position the crosshair where you want the line to start.
3 Hold down the left mouse button and drag the mouse to where you want the line to end.
4 Release the mouse button.

Formatting the line

1 Select the line by clicking on it. When it is selected, handles appear at each end.
2 Click on: the **Line Style** button.
3 Click on: the line style that you want.

Changing line colours

1 Select the line or object to change.
2 Click on: the **Line Colour** button.
3 Click on: a colour.

Adding a circle or ellipse

1 Click on: the **Oval** button.
2 Hold down the left mouse button and drag out to the required shape.
3 Release the mouse.

Adding a box

Follow the method for a circle/ellipse, shown above.

 Info

Experiment with the other Drawing toolbar buttons to create some stunning effects. Also worth noting is the 📷 **Insert WordArt** button on the Drawing toolbar. Click on: it to create special text effects.

7.4 Save, print and close the leaflet document and exit Word.

Section 7 Word Processing practice

Practice 13

Note: For this Exercise you will need to have a simple Excel spreadsheet file to import at step 7. (See Module 4.)

1 Open a new Word document.

2 Key in the following text:

Working with imported objects

Possible logo idea

3 Import a piece of ClipArt in between the two headings.

4 Centre the ClipArt within the left and right margins.

5 Keeping its original aspect ratio, resize the ClipArt so that it is approximately 4 cm square.

6 Insert a page break after the ClipArt.

7 At the top of the second page, key in the following text:

Inserting a spreadsheet file

8 Insert a simple spreadsheet file under the text.

9 Under the heading **Possible logo idea**, using Word's drawing features, create a simple design to be used as a logo for a sailing club, **Aquamarine Sailing**.

10 Number the pages at the top centre, starting at 5.

11 Copy the ClipArt and heading only to a new Word document.

12 Key in your name and the date as the first line of the first page of both documents.

13 Save and print both documents.

Note: There is no worked example of this exercise as versions will vary considerably.

Word quick reference guide

Action	Keyboard	Mouse	Right-mouse menu	Menu
Bold text	Select text to embolden			
	Ctrl + B	Click: the **B** **Bold** button	Font	**Format**, **Font**
			Select: **Bold** from the **Font style:** menu	
Borders	Select text			
		Click: the ⊞▾ Borders button		**Format**, **Borders and Shading**
	Select the border options you require			
Capitals (blocked)	Caps Lock Key in the text **Caps Lock** again to remove			Select text to be changed to capitals: **Format**, **Change Case**, **UPPERCASE**
Centre text	Select the text			
	Ctrl + E	Click: the ≡ **Center** button	**Paragraph**	**Format**, **Paragraph**
			Select: **Centered** from the **Alignment:** drop-down menu	
Change case	Select the text to be changed From the **Format** menu, select: **Change Case** Select the appropriate case			
Close a file	**Ctrl + W**	Click: the ✕ **Close Window** icon		**File**, **Close**
Columns		Click: the ▦ **Columns** button and drag the mouse until you have selected the number of columns		**Format**, **Columns** Select the number of columns and options you require
Cut text	Select the text to be cut			
	Ctrl + X	Click: the ✂ **Cut** button	**Cut**	**Edit**, **Cut**
Delete a character	Press: **Delete** to delete the character to the right of the cursor Press: ← (Backspace) to delete the character to the left of the cursor			
Delete a word	Double-click: the word to select it Press: **Delete**			
Delete/cut a block of text	Select the text you want to delete			
	Delete or **Ctrl + X**	Click: the ✂ **Cut** button	**Cut**	**Edit**, **Cut**
Drawing features	To display the **Drawing** toolbar: From the **View** menu, select: **Toolbars**, **Drawing**			
	Select from the toolbar buttons (see Section 7 – page 107)			
Exit Word		Click: the ✕ **Close Window** icon		**File**, **Exit**
Find text	**Ctrl + F**			**Edit**, **Find**

Action	Keyboard	Mouse	Right-mouse menu	Menu
Font size	Select the text you want to change			
		Click: the ▼ down arrow next to the **Font Size** box Select: the font size you require	**Font**	F**o**rmat, **F**ont
			Select: the required size from the **Size:** menu	
Font	Select the text you want to change			
		Click: the ▼ down arrow next to the **Font** box Select: the font you require	**Font**	F**o**rmat, **F**ont
			Select: the required font from the **F**ont: menu	
Formatting, copying	Select text to copy			
	Click: the ✎ **Format Painter** button Double-click to copy to several pieces of text			
Headers and Footers				**V**iew, **H**eader and **Footer**
Help	**F1**			**H**elp, Microsoft Word **H**elp
	Shift + F1			**H**elp, What's **T**his?
Hyphenation				**T**ools, **L**anguage, **H**yphenation
Indenting		Click: the ⧉ **Increase Indent** button	**Paragraph**, **Indents and Spacing**	F**o**rmat, **P**aragraph, **Indents and Spacing**
To remove indent		Click: the ⧉ **Decrease Indent** button	In the **Indentation** section, select your options as appropriate	
Insert image, file, chart, spreadsheet		Use Cut and Paste method		**Insert**, *either* **P**icture, **O**bject, **Fi**le Resize using handles
Insert text	Position the cursor where you want the text to appear Key in the text			
Justified margins	Select the text you want to change			
	Ctrl + J	Click: the ▤ **Justify** icon	**Paragraph**	F**o**rmat, **P**aragraph
			Select **Justified** from the **Alignment:** drop-down menu	
Line length, changing		Use the ruler (see separate table)		**F**ile, **Page Set**u**p**, **Margins** (see separate table)
Line spacing			**Paragraph**	F**o**rmat, **P**aragraph, **Indents and Spacing**
			In the **Spacing** section, select the options you require	

Action	Keyboard	Mouse	Right-mouse menu	Menu
Lists, bulleted and numbered	Click: the [icons] **Numbering** or **Bullets** button		**Bullets and Numbering**	**Format**, **Bullets and Numbering**
Load Word	In Windows 98 desktop			
		Double-click: the **Word** shortcut icon		**Start**, **Programs**, **Microsoft Word**
Mail merge	See separate section			
Margins				**File**, **Page Setup**, **Margins**
Move a block of text	Select: the text to be moved Cut it and paste it where you want it moved to *or* Select: the text to be moved Click and drag: it to the correct position Release the mouse button			
Moving around the document	Use the cursor keys (see separate table for more)	Click: in the required position		
New file, creating	**Ctrl + N**	Click: the ☐ **New** button		**File**, **New**
Open an existing file	**Ctrl + O**	Click: the ☞ **Open** button		**File**, **Open**
	Select the appropriate directory and filename Click: **Open**			
Page break, adding	**Ctrl + Enter**			**Insert**, **Break**, OK
Page break, deleting	In Normal View, place the cursor on the page break Press: **Delete**			
Page display		Click: the appropriate [icons] **View** button		**View**
Page numbering				**Insert**, **Page Numbers** Select the required options
Page Setup				**File**, **Page Setup** (Choose from **Margins**, **Paper Size**, **Paper Source**, **Layout**)
Paper size	(See Page Setup)			

Action	Keyboard	Mouse	Right-mouse menu	Menu
Paragraphs – splitting/joining	Splitting: Move the cursor to the first letter of the new paragraph Press: **Enter** twice Joining: Move the cursor to the first character of the second paragraph Press ← (Backspace) twice (Press the spacebar to insert a space after a full stop)			
Print file	**Ctrl + P** Select the options you need Press: **Enter**	Click: the 🖨 **Print** button		**File**, **Print** Select the options you need and click **OK**
Print preview		Click: the 🔍 **Print Preview** button		**File**, **Print Preview**
Ragged right margin	**Ctrl + L**	Click: the ≡ **Align Left** button	**Paragraph**	**Format**, **Paragraph**
			Select **Left** from the **Alignment:** drop-down menu	
Remove text emphasis	Select text to be changed			
	Ctrl + B (remove bold) **Ctrl + I** (remove italics) **Ctrl + U** (remove underline)	Click: the appropriate button: **B** *I* U	**Font**	**Format**, **Font**
			Select **Regular** from the **Font Style:** menu	
Replace text	**Ctrl + H**			**Edit**, **Replace**
Save	**Ctrl + S**	Click: the 💾 **Save** button		**File**, **Save**
	If you have not already saved the file you will be prompted to specify the directory and to name the file. If you have already done this, then Word will automatically save it.			
Save using a different name or to a different directory	Select the appropriate drive and change the filename if relevant.			
		Click: **Save**		**File**, **Save As**
Save file in a different file format	Save as above, select from **Save as type**			
Special characters/ symbols, inserting				**Insert**, **Symbol**
Spell check	**F7**	Click: the 🔤 **Spelling** button		**Tools**, **Spelling and Grammar**
Styles	Select from the Style box drop-down list [Normal ▼]			**Format**, **Style**

Action	Keyboard	Mouse	Right-mouse menu	Menu
Superscript Subscript			**Font**	**Format**, **Font**
Tables		Click: the ▦ **Insert Table** button		**Table**, **Insert**, **Table**
	See Section 5			
Tabs	See separate information below			
Template, selecting				**File**, **New**, Select a template
Text colour	Select the text to colour			
		Click: the **A** ▾ **Font Color** button	**Font**, **Font color**	**Format**, **Font**, **Font colour**
Toolbar, modify				**View**, **Toolbars**, **Customize**
Undo	**Ctrl + Z**	Click: the ↶ **Undo** button		**Edit**, **Undo Typing**
Widows and Orphans				**Format**, **Paragraph**, **Line and Page Breaks** Select: **Widow/Orphan control**
Zoom	Click: the 100% ▾ **Zoom** button			**View**, **Zoom**

Moving around a document	
Move:	**Keyboard action:**
to top of document	**Ctrl + Home**
to end of document	**Ctrl + End**
left word by word	**Ctrl + ←**
right word by word	**Ctrl + →**
to end of line	**End**
to start of line	**Home**

Selecting text	
Selecting what:	**Action:**
Whole document	**Ctrl + A**
One word	Double-click on: word
One paragraph	Double-click in selection border
Any block of text	Click cursor at start of text, press: Shift. Click cursor at end of text and click.
Deselect text	Click in any white space

See Appendix for keyboard shortcuts.

Line lengths

Line length	Margin width
12.7 cm (5″)	4.15 cm (1.63″)
14 cm (5½″)	3.5 cm (1.38″)
15.3 cm (6″)	2.85 cm (1.13″)
16.5 cm (6½″)	2.25 cm (0.88″)

Indentation using the ruler

Select the text you want to indent. Drag the respective markers (shown below) on the ruler to the location you want.

Hard spaces

It is better not to split some words at line ends – e.g. Mr Brown – Mr and Brown should be on the same line. A hard space keeps the words on either side of it together. To insert a hard space:

Instead of just pressing the spacebar between the words, press: **CTRL + SHIFT + Spacebar**.

Mail merge

Creating and saving the merge document
1   Open a new Word file.
2   Key in the document.
3   Save the file.
4   From the **Tools** menu, select: **Mail Merge, Create, Form Letters** (*or* **Mailing Labels**).
5   Click on: **Active Window**.

Creating and saving the data source
1   Click on: **Get Data, Create Data Source**.
2   Add/Remove Field names as appropriate.
3   Click on: **OK**.
4   Save the Data Source.

Editing the Data Source
1   Click on: **Edit Data Source**.
2   Enter records.
3   Press: Enter after each record.
4   Click on: **OK**.

Entering Merge Fields in merge document
1   Position the cursor where you want the first Merge Field to be.
2   On the Mail Merge toolbar click on: **Insert Merge Field**.
3   Click on the field to insert.
4   Repeat until all Merge Fields are inserted.

Viewing merged document
Click on: **View Merged Data** button on Mail Merge toolbar.

Printing the merged document
Click on: **Merge to Printer** button on the Mail Merge toolbar.

Module 3 practice tasks

For this module you will need to have some files already set up. Ask your supervisor or tutor to prepare them for you.

Preparation

1   Create the following document and save as **Language**.

Sample extract

The people of Europe speak many different languages. English is termed a 'Germanic' language. This is because it is related to languages such as Dutch as well as German. The links are not as easily noticed in modern day English but the relationship is much clearer in Old English.
Old English is the name given to the English language up to c.1150. It was spoken from the fifth century. It has different vocabulary, word meanings and spellings to modern English. It even has letters, such as $\flat$ that are not found in modern English. Its pronunciation and grammar and the ways it was used are also different. So much so in fact that it would be most unlikely that Old English would be understood by the average English speaker today. Although anyone speaking or writing English at the beginning of the 21st century is using a language that dates back to Anglo Saxon times.
There is also the subject of accents and dialects to consider. Accents can be defined as the same language but differing in terms of pronunciation. Dialects differ in terms of grammar and vocabulary as well.
Nearly one billion people speak different varieties of modern-day English. There are mother tongue speakers, second language speakers and those for whom it is a foreign language. The spread of English to different parts of the world and it being used as an 'international' language has caused much debate.

This is just a taster of course content. Please ring for details of courses in French, German, Spanish, Welsh and Italian.

---

2   Create a name and address file and save as **Address**.

Title, Name, Address, Town, Postalcode
Miss, Smith, 29 Hobsons Way, Bristol, BS6 5ER
Mr, Ahmed, 10 The Croft, Plymouth, PL2 7TR
Mrs, Zwetsloot, 109 Green Lane, Oxford, OX3 9TU
Dr, O'Byrne, 1 East Street, Norwich, NW8 4HR
Ms, Jones, Bryn Mawr, Llanfairfechan, LL13 6AW

Basic practice tasks

1   Start the word processor and open the file **Language**.
2   Save the document as **your initials module 3**.

3 Change the font in the document to Arial 12 pt.
4 Italicise the heading **Sample extract**.
5 Centre the heading.
6 Increase the font size of the heading to 18 pt.
7 Embolden the last paragraph.
8 Organise the courses in the last paragraph into bullet format.
9 Insert a blank line between paragraphs.
10 Insert a page break after the third paragraph.
11 Add a header **Languages Course Details** and today's date.
12 Format the header to Times New Roman 8 pt.
13 Add page numbers bottom right, starting at 5.
14 Insert your name in the first line of the document (Times New Roman 10 pt, right align).
15 Embolden all occurrences of the word **Old**.
16 Copy the first paragraph so that it appears at the end of the document.
17 Change the line spacing of the first paragraph to 1.5.
18 Fully justify the second paragraph.
19 Insert the following text in the paragraph containing the bulleted list after **course content**.

We have many others and we are confident that you will find something interesting and worthwhile.

20 Save the document with the name **your initials module 3 test1**.
21 Print the document.
22 Create a new document.
23 Copy all of the text to the new document.
24 Change the font throughout to Arial 10 pt.
25 Delete the page break so that it fits on one page.
26 Set the line spacing to single throughout.
27 Set the top and bottom margins to 2 cm.
28 Save the document as **Merge**.

Advanced practice tasks 1

29 Working with the **Merge** document, insert the text **Ref 9054** under your name.
30 Set a left aligned tab to align the text on these first two lines at 12 cm.
31 On the line above the heading **Sample extract,** key in **Dear**.
32 At the end of the document enter the text **Yours sincerely** and **your name**.
33 Insert a suitable ClipArt picture at bottom of the document. Adjust the picture to an appropriate size so that it fits neatly on the page.
34 Delete page numbers.
35 Save the document as **Merge2**.

Advanced practice tasks 2

1 Working with the **Merge2** document, delete the second paragraph.
2 Insert the following table after the first paragraph ending **is much clearer in Old English**:

1	Early Old English	450 – 850
2	Later Old English	850 – 1100
3	Middle English	1100 – 1450
4	Early modern English	1450 – 1750

3 Centre the table entries. Format in Times New Roman 12 pt.
4 Use the indent function to indent the last paragraph by approx.1.5 cm.
5 Set all other paragraphs with a first line indent of 0.8 cm.
6 Save the document as **Merge3**.
7 Print the **Merge3** document.
8 Open the Address file. This contains names and addresses of people who are to receive the letter. Insert merge fields for title, Name, Address, Town, Postalcode. Merge the letter with the address list. Adjust the letter (if necessary) so that it fits on one page.
9 Save the file with the name **M followed by your initials**.
10 Print the merged file.

Advanced practice tasks 3

1 Select the **Contemporary Fax** template.
2 Delete the field above *Facsimile Transmittal*.
3 In the To field key in **Lycée la Rochelle**.
4 In the Fax field key in **00 33 23 44 76 98 11**.
5 In the From field key in your name.
6 In the Re field key in **Exchange Visits**.
7 In the Pages field key in **1**.
8 Mark the fax **Please Comment**.
9 Enter the message:

   Thank you for your interest. I will send details as soon as possible.

10 Save the fax as **Exchange** and print a copy.

Note: This is only a practice test. Successful completion does not imply certification of the module by the ECDL Foundation.

Module 4

Spreadsheets

Section 1 Basics – getting started

In this section you will practise and learn how to:

- load Excel
- understand the parts of the document window
- modify the toolbar display
- enter spreadsheet contents: insert text, numeric data, simple formulae
- understand common error messages
- use the undo command
- delete cell contents
- use spellcheck
- save the spreadsheet structure and data
- print preview and print the spreadsheet
- display and print formulae
- use the page view magnification/zoom tool
- fit one page
- modify margins
- close the spreadsheet
- exit Excel.

1.1 Loading Excel

 Exercise 1

Load Excel.

 Method

Load Excel in the same way as other Office 2000 applications, this time selecting:

[X] Microsoft Excel from the **Start**, **Programs** menu *or* double-click on: the [X] **Excel** shortcut icon (if you have one).

1.2 Understanding the parts of Excel

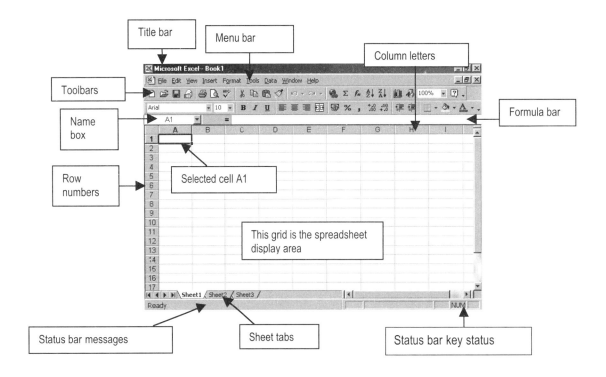

Figure 4.1 The application window

The **Title bar** and **Menu bar** are at the top of the application window.

The **Menu bar** has a set of *drop-down* menus that provide access to all Excel's features.

The **Toolbar** is a row of buttons and selection boxes that, in most cases, provide shortcuts to the menu options or quick ways of entering values. (In Figure 4.1 the Standard and Formatting toolbars are shown.)

To modify the toolbar display
From the **View** menu, select: **Toolbars**. Click on: the toolbars that you want displayed so that they have a tick next to them or select: **Customize** for further modifications options.

The **Formula bar** displays the data you enter into your worksheet.

The **Name box** displays the active cell reference.

The **Sheet tabs** allow you to move from one spreadsheet to the next.

The **Status bar**, located at the bottom of the window, displays messages about current events. **NUM** shows that the Num Lock on your keyboard is on, enabling you to use the number keys 0–9 to quickly enter numbers. Press the **Num Lock** key to turn Num Lock off so that you can use the keys for movement instead.

The document window is the area between the Formula bar and the Status bar where your document (spreadsheet) is displayed. It consists of cells, each with their own cell reference – e.g. A1, B7, F9. Rows go across and are labelled 1, 2, 3, 4... Columns go down and are labelled A, B, C, D... Figure 4.2 shows the position of cell C6.

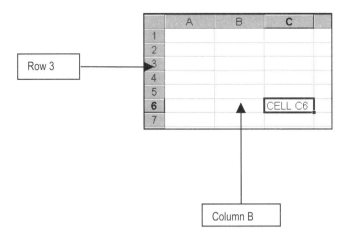

Figure 4.2 Cell references

Practice: Moving around the spreadsheet:

1 Moving around your document using the scroll bars (see Figure 4.3).

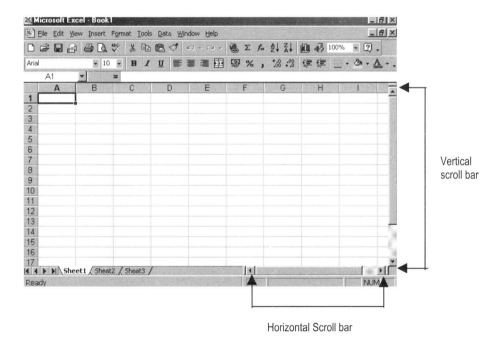

Figure 4.3 Scroll bars

2 Using navigation keys, **Page Up** and **Page Down**, to move up and down a page at a time.
3 Using the arrow keys.
4 Using the **Go To** command in the **Edit** menu. Enter the cell address e.g. C5 in the **Reference** text box and click on: **OK**.
5 Clicking in the **Name** box and key in the cell address.
6 Pointing to a cell with the mouse and clicking.

7 Pressing: **Ctrl + Home** (takes you to the top of your spreadsheet).

8 Pressing: **Ctrl + End** (takes you to the last entry on your spreadsheet where you have entered data).

1.3 Spreadsheet contents

You can enter:

- text
- numeric data
- formulae.

Text entries are used for titles, headings and any notes. They are entries that you do not want to manipulate arithmetically. Telephone numbers and stock numbers (although they contain numbers) are text entries.

Numeric data consists of numbers you want to add, subtract, multiply, divide and use in formulae.

Formulae are used to calculate the value of a cell from the contents of other cells. For instance, formulae may be used to calculate totals or averages. Formulae always start with an = sign. You must enter the formula for it to be activated by pressing: **Enter** or clicking on the ✓ **Enter** button on the Formula bar. A typical formula could look like:

=A1+A2 *or* **=SUM(A1:A6)**

The following operators (symbols) are used in formulae:

+ ADD   – SUBTRACT   * MULTIPLY   / DIVIDE

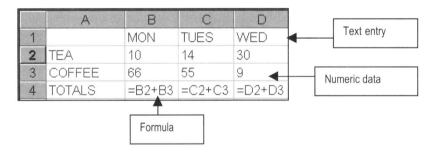

Figure 4.4 Types of spreadsheet entry

ℹ️ **Info**

Excel follows arithmetic protocol when carrying out calculations. It will perform multiplication and division first and then addition and subtraction. Sometimes you will need to force Excel to carry out the calculation in a different order. As in arithmetic, this can be achieved by adding brackets around the appropriate part – e.g. when cell A1, A2 and A3 contain the numbers 4, 3 and 2 respectively:

A1+A2*A3 in numbers is 4+3x2 which Excel would calculate to be (carrying out the multiplication first) 10.

Placing brackets around the addition section forces Excel to perform the calculation differently. (A1+A2)*A3 in numbers is (4+3)x2 and gives the result 14.

1.4 Inserting text and numeric data

Exercise 2

The spreadsheet below shows the sales figures for three different clothing companies over a four-month period. Enter the data into the spreadsheet.

Method

1 Move to cell A1 and key in: **Month**.
2 Move to cell B1 and key in: **Casualco**.
3 Move to cell C1 and key in: **Smartco**.
4 Complete the worksheet in this way until it looks like Figure 4.5:

	A	B	C	D
1	Month	Casualco	Smartco	Partyco
2	May	990	830	770
3	June	550	880	220
4	July	330	660	700
5	August	400	550	820

Figure 4.5 Spreadsheet data

1.5 Entering simple formulae

Exercise 3

Enter simple formulae to add up cell contents.

Method

Remember that formulae must always begin with the = sign

1 Move to cell A6 and key in **Total**.
2 We wish to add up the sales figures for Casualco. These are displayed in cells B2, B3, B4 and B5. Move to cell B6 (where you want the answer to appear).

Info

Notice as you key in that the formula appears on the Formula bar. It may be too long to fit the cell but you can ignore this. Cell references can be in upper or lower case. If you make a mistake use the **Undo** button or press: **Esc**.

Key in:

=B2+B3+B4+B5 and press: **Enter**

The answer 2270 appears in cell B6.

3 Add up the sales figures for Smartco in the same way by keying in:

=C2+C3+C4+C5 and press: **Enter**

The answer 2920 appears in cell C6.

Your spreadsheet will now look like Figure 4.6:

	A	B	C	D
1	Month	Casualco	Smartco	Partyco
2	May	990	830	770
3	June	550	880	220
4	July	330	660	700
5	August	400	550	820
6	Total	2270	2920	

Figure 4.6 Totalling column B and column C

Using the built-in sum function

On a large business spreadsheet you might need to add a huge number of cell contents and specifying each cell reference would not be practical. A quicker way to add up figures is by using one of Excel's built-in functions **SUM** to work out the formula as follows:

To produce a Total for Partyco this time:

1   Move to cell D6 (where you want the answer to appear).

2   Key in **=SUM(D2:D5)** and press: **Enter**.

> **ⓘ Info**
>
> The colon between the cell references in the formula above means 'to include all the cells in between D2 and D5'.

Your spreadsheet will now look like Figure 4.7:

	A	B	C	D
1	Month	Casualco	Smartco	Partyco
2	May	990	830	770
3	June	550	880	220
4	July	330	660	700
5	August	400	550	820
6	Total	2270	2920	2510

Figure 4.7 Totalling column D

Practise using the SUM function:

1   Delete the Totals of Casualco (cell B6) and Smartco (cell C6) by selecting them and pressing: **Delete**.

2   Add the Totals again this time using the SUM function, in cell B6 **=SUM(B2:B5)** and in cell C6 **=SUM(C2:C5)**.

Using the AutoSum button

There is an even quicker way to add cell values using the Σ **AutoSum** button.

To practise this, add up the totals for the three clothing companies for each month.

 Method

1   Move to cell E1 and key in **Sales**.

2   Move to cell E2, the cell where you want the total sales for May to appear.

3   Click on: the Σ **AutoSum** button. You will notice that a dotted line has appeared around cells B2 through to D2.

4   Press: **Enter**.
5   The answer 2590 appears in cell E2.
6   Use this method to calculate the sales total for June, July and August.

If you have done everything correctly the totals will be as in Figure 4.8.

	A	B	C	D	E
1	Month	Casualco	Smartco	Partyco	Sales
2	May	990	830	770	2590
3	June	550	880	220	1650
4	July	330	660	700	1690
5	August	400	550	820	1770
6	Total	2270	2920	2510	

Figure 4.8 Sales figures for June, July and August

1.6 Saving the spreadsheet structure and data

 Exercise 4

Save the spreadsheet structure and data.

 Method

1   Spellcheck the spreadsheet using the **Spelling** button and correct any errors.
2   From the **File** menu, select: **Save As**. The **Save As** dialogue box appears (see Figure 4.9).
3   Select the location where you want to save your file and key in **Sales** in the **File name** box.
4   Click on: **Save**.

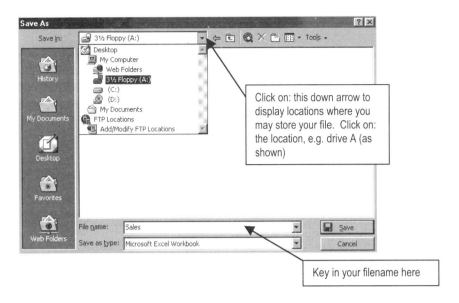

Figure 4.9 The Save As dialogue box

1.7 Printing spreadsheets

 Exercise 5

Print a copy of the spreadsheet onto A4 paper.

 Method

Previewing a spreadsheet before printing

It is always wise to preview your spreadsheet before printing so that you are sure that it will print exactly what you want. This will save paper as well as effort.

1   Click on: the ⬚ **Print Preview** button.
2   Click on: the **Zoom** option to see your spreadsheet contents. Click on: **Zoom** again to return to default view.
3   If you are happy with the Print Preview, click on: **Print**. (You can change default options here if necessary.)
4   Click on: **OK**.

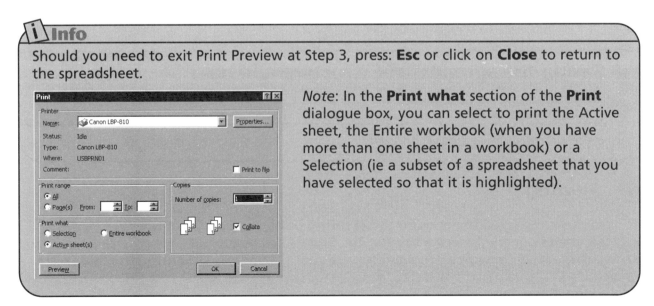

Info

Should you need to exit Print Preview at Step 3, press: **Esc** or click on **Close** to return to the spreadsheet.

Note: In the **Print what** section of the **Print** dialogue box, you can select to print the Active sheet, the Entire workbook (when you have more than one sheet in a workbook) or a Selection (ie a subset of a spreadsheet that you have selected so that it is highlighted).

Info

Printing on landscape

By default the spreadsheet will print a Portrait display (the narrow edge at the top of the page). If you prefer or if your spreadsheet does not fit across the page, you can change the display to Landscape.

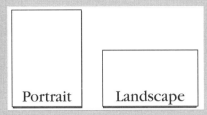

Portrait   Landscape

To do this from **Print Preview**, click on: **Setup**:

1   Click on: the **Page** tab, then on the **Landscape** option button.
2   Click on: **OK**.

If not using Print Preview:

1   From the **File** menu, select: **Page Setup**.
2   Click on: the **Page** tab, then on: the **Landscape** option button.
3   Click on: **Print**.

1.8 Printing formulae

Exercise 6

Print a copy of the spreadsheet showing the formulae used.

Info

It is useful to have a printout of the formulae used on your spreadsheet so that you can cross-reference for accuracy.

Method

Showing formulae on your spreadsheet

1   With your spreadsheet on screen, from the **Tools** menu, select: **Options**.
2   Click on: the **View** tab (if not already selected); the **Options** dialogue box appears (see Figure 4.10).
3   Click on: the **Formulas** check box so that a tick appears in this box.
4   Click on: **OK**.

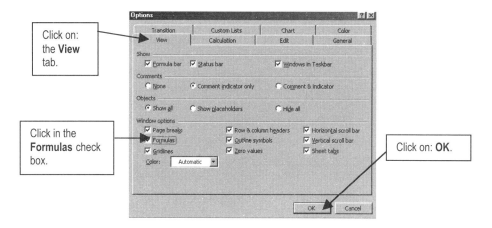

Click on: the **View** tab.

Click in the **Formulas** check box.

Click on: **OK**.

Figure 4.10 Showing formulae

Notice that the columns have widened to accommodate the formulae.

5   If you are unable to see all of the spreadsheet at once, use the ▢ `100%` ▾ **Zoom** button.

> **Info**
>
> Depending on your setup, you may notice a vertical dotted line has appeared. This denotes a page break. Do not adjust the column widths, as when you take the 'show formulas' off, the cell widths will need altering again.

> **Info**
>
> For a quicker way to show formulae, press **Ctrl +** (to the left of the number one key).

6   Check the spreadsheet using **Print Preview** (as above).
7   If it fits on one page, print as before.
8   If it does not fit, check that it is on landscape by following the instructions above.

> **Info**
>
> If you really want to print in portrait display, try the following:
>
> **Fitting to one page**
> 1   From the **File** menu, select: **Page Setup** *or* in **Print Preview**, click on: **Setup**.
> 2   With the **Page** tab selected, in the **Scaling** section, click in the option button next to **Fit to** 1 page.
>
> **Modifying margins**
> 1   From the **File** menu, select **Page Setup** or in **Print Preview**, click on: **Setup**.
> 2   With the **Margins** tab selected, decrease the left and right margin settings.

 Exercise 7

Change the spreadsheet so that numbers are displayed instead of formulae.

 Method

Removing showing formulae
1   From the **Tools** menu, select: **Options**.
2   Click on: the **View** tab (if not already selected).
3   Click in the **Formulas** check box so that the tick is removed.
4   Click on: **OK**.

Info

A quick way to change back to values display is to press: **Ctrl** + .

1.9 Closing a spreadsheet file

Exercise 8

Close the spreadsheet file.

Method

From the **File** menu, select: **Close**.

1.10 Exiting Excel

Exercise 9

Exit Excel.

Method

From the **File** menu, select: **Exit**.

Section 1 Spreadsheet practice

Practice 1

1 Load Excel.

2 On a new sheet enter the following data:

Leave the cells containing 'formula' blank

EXPENSES			
	AUG	OCT	NOV
RENT	350	350	350
ELEC	45	50	60
GAS	18	25	40
LOAN	55	55	55
PETROL	75	60	60
INS	20	20	20
TOTALS	formula	formula	formula

3 Enter a formula in the TOTALS row to calculate the total expenditure for AUG.

4 Save the spreadsheet as **p1 expenses**.

5 Print a copy of the spreadsheet showing values and another copy showing the formula used.

6 Close the spreadsheet file.

Practice 2

1 On a new sheet enter the following data:

Leave the cells containing 'formula' blank

Sales						
	Tue	Wed	Thu	Fri	Sat	Total
Food	550	660	500	900	1120	formula
Menswear	200	190	300	100	780	formula
Fashions	300	625	740	800	1500	formula
Baby	200	450	380	590	213	formula
Cosmetics	77	90	65	105	280	formula
Home	500	1800	1200	954	3080	formula

2 Enter a formula to calculate the Total for the Food row.

3 Save the spreadsheet as **p2 store sales**.

4 Print a copy of the spreadsheet showing values and one showing the formula used.

5 Close the spreadsheet.

Section 2 Basics – editing

In this section you will practise and learn how to:

- open an existing spreadsheet
- make alterations to cell contents
- select row/column
- delete/insert rows/columns
- copy or replicate formulae

- use find and replace
- understand relative and absolute cell references
- save an existing spreadsheet to disk
- save the document under another file format, including saving a document for posting on the web
- print part of a spreadsheet.

2.1 Opening an existing spreadsheet

 Exercise 1

Recall the spreadsheet **Sales** saved in section 1.

 Method

1 With Excel loaded, click on: the 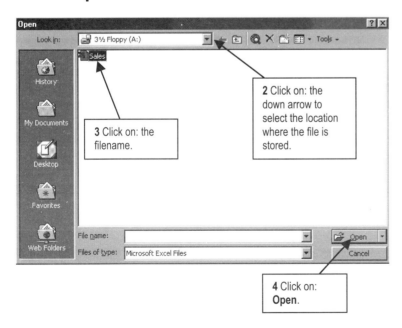 **Open** icon; the **Open** dialogue box appears (see Figure 4.11).
2 Select the location where your file is stored by clicking on the down arrow.
3 Click on: the filename **Sales**.
4 Click on: **Open**.

Figure 4.11 Opening a saved file

2.2 Making alterations to your spreadsheet

Exercise 2

The Sales figures for Casualco should be **850** (not **990**) in May and **470** (not **330**) in July.

We need to change these entries.

Method

1 Move to cell B2 and key in: **850** and press: **Enter**.
2 Move to cell B4 and key in: **470** and press: **Enter**.

Info

Notice that the original figures are overwritten. Look what has happened to the Total for Casualco. You will see that the formula has been recalculated to give a new Total. The Sales figures for May and July in column E have also updated to reflect the changes made. This will usually happen; when you change cell contents within a spreadsheet, all the formulae referring to that cell will be automatically recalculated.

Your spreadsheet will now look like Figure 4.12:

	A	B	C	D	E
1	Month	Casualco	Smartco	Partyco	Sales
2	May	850	830	770	2450
3	June	550	880	220	1650
4	July	470	660	700	1830
5	August	400	550	820	1770
6	Total	2270	2920	2510	

Figure 4.12 Updated spreadsheet

2.3 Deleting a row or column

Exercise 3

It has been decided that the figures for July are not required. Delete this row. Close up space, do not leave a blank row.

Method

1 Click in the box to the left of the row to be deleted, i.e. row 4. Row 4 is highlighted (Figure 4.13).

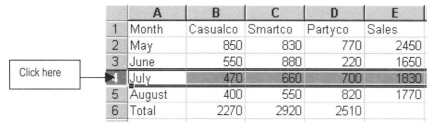

Figure 4.13 Selecting a row

2 Right-click on: the selected row. A pop-up menu appears (see Figure 4.14):

Figure 4.14 Right-clicking displays a pop-up menu

3 Click on: **Delete**. The spreadsheet contents move up to occupy the empty space and the figures are recalculated to reflect the change (see Figure 4.15).

	A	B	C	D	E
1	Month	Casualco	Smartco	Partyco	Sales
2	May	850	830	770	2450
3	June	550	880	220	1650
4	August	400	550	820	1770
5	Total	1800	2260	1810	

Figure 4.15 Spreadsheet after deletion of the July row

Info

When you have a large spreadsheet, use **Find/Replace** from the **Edit** menu to locate/replace entries.

Exercise 4

The figures for Smartco are no longer required; delete this column.

Method

1 Click in the box at the top of the column to be deleted – i.e. C. Column C is highlighted.
2 Right-click on: the selection; a pop-up menu appears.
3 Click on: **Delete**.

The spreadsheet now looks like Figure 4.16:

	A	B	C	D
1	Month	Casualco	Partyco	Sales
2	May	850	770	1620
3	June	550	220	770
4	August	400	820	1220
5	Total	1800	1810	

Figure 4.16 Spreadsheet after deletion of Smartco column

2.4 Copying or replicating formulae

Exercise 5

Replicate the formula used to calculate the Total for Partyco so that the Total for Sales is also calculated.

Method

1 Move to the cell in which the formula you want to copy is stored – in this case C5.
2 Point the mouse at the bottom right of this cell until a thin black cross + appears, then holding down the left mouse, drag across cell D5 (where you want the formula copied to).
3 Release the mouse.

The spreadsheet now looks like Figure 4.17:

	A	B	C	D
1	Month	Casualco	Partyco	Sales
2	May	850	770	1620
3	June	550	220	770
4	August	400	820	1220
5	Total	1800	1810	3610

Figure 4.17 Spreadsheet after replication of formula

Info

If you make an error performing this procedure, click on: the **Undo** button and try again.

Relative and absolute cell references
When replicating formulae, the cell references change to reflect their new position. (You can check this by looking at the formulae that you have just replicated.) A relative cell reference will change relatively to its position on the spreadsheet. By contrast, an absolute cell reference will not change even if it is replicated or moved to another part of the spreadsheet. If you need to make a cell reference absolute, add a $ sign in front of the column letter and another $ sign in front of the row number or press: **F4**.

Example: cell reference **C8** becomes **$C$8** when it is absolute

2.5 Adding a new column and a new row

Exercise 6

Adding a new column

Insert a new column, headed **Jeansco**, after **Casualco** and before **Partyco**. Enter the following information:

May, 600   **June, 700**   **August, 650**

 Method

1 Click in the box at the top of the column after where the new column is to appear – i.e. column C. Column C is highlighted (see Figure 4.18).

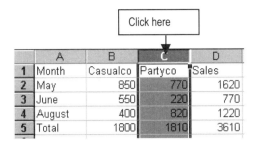

Click here

	A	B	C	D
1	Month	Casualco	Partyco	Sales
2	May	850	770	1620
3	June	550	220	770
4	August	400	820	1220
5	Total	1800	1810	3610

Figure 4.18 Selecting a column

2 Right-click on: the selection. A pop-up menu appears (see Figure 4.19).

3 Click on: **Insert**. An empty column appears.

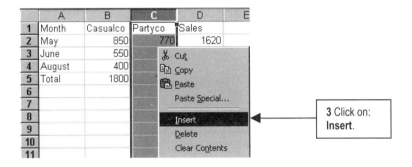

3 Click on: **Insert**.

Figure 4.19 Inserting a column

4 Enter the new text and data shown above.

The spreadsheet now looks like Figure 4.20:

	A	B	C	D	E
1	Month	Casualco	Jeansco	Partyco	Sales
2	May	850	600	770	2220
3	June	550	700	220	1470
4	August	400	650	820	1870
5	Total	1800		1810	5560

Figure 4.20 Spreadsheet after addition of Jeansco column and data

Calculate the Total for Jeansco, using one of the quicker methods you have learnt.

The Total is 1950.

 Exercise 7

It has been decided to reinsert the figures for July. Insert a new row for July with the following Information: **Casualco 470**, **Jeansco 850**, **Partyco 700**.

 Method

Adding a new row

1 Click in the box to the left of the row below where you want the new row to appear – i.e. row 4. Row 4 is highlighted (see Figure 4.21).

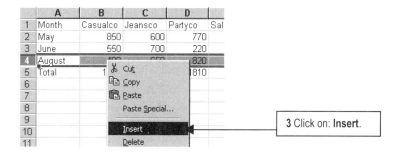

	A	B	C	D	E
1	Month	Casualco	Jeansco	Partyco	Sales
2	May	850	600	770	2220
3	June	550	700	220	1470
4	August	400	650	820	1870
5	Total	1800	1950	1810	5560

Click here.

Figure 4.21 Adding a new row

2 Right-click on: the highlighted row. A pop-up menu appears (see Figure 4.22).

3 Click on: **Insert**. An empty row appears.

3 Click on: **Insert**.

Figure 4.22 Inserting a row

4 Enter the new text and data shown above.

5 Replicate the formula from cell E3 to produce a Total in cell E4 for July Sales. The total is 2020.

2.6 Adding a new column or row to create new values

   Exercise 8

Insert a new column for Shoesco after Partyco and before the Sales column. (See above 2.5.)

Enter the following data:

May, 621   **June**, 890   **July**, 700   **August**, 440

Replicate the formula from D6 to give a Total value in cell E6 for Shoesco.

Info

Note: In Excel 2000, these figures (although at the end of the existing SUM cell range) are automatically included in the Sales column figures. This did not happen in earlier versions of Excel. Look out for this as you may not always want Excel to include new data in formulae.

   Method

Follow the Method in Section 2.5 (page 136).

The spreadsheet now looks like Figure 4.23:

	A	B	C	D	E	F
1	Month	Casualco	Jeansco	Partyco	Shoesco	Sales
2	May	850	600	770	621	2841
3	June	550	700	220	890	2360
4	July	470	850	700	700	2720
5	August	400	650	820	440	2310
6	Total	2270	2800	2510	2651	10231

Figure 4.23 Spreadsheet after adding the Shoesco column

2.7 Save your spreadsheet as **Sales1** and print one copy on A4 paper.

2.8 Saving documents under a different file format

 Exercise 9

Save the spreadsheet with the filename **Clothing** in a format suitable for posting on the web.

 Method

1 From the **File** menu, select: **Save As**.
2 Key in the filename.
3 In the **Save as type** section, click on: the down arrow to display type options (see Figure 4.24).
4 Select: **Web Page**.
5 Click on: **Save**.

> **i Info**
>
> By default Excel automatically saves files in a version of Excel format that you are using e.g. EXCEL 2000, and adds the extension .xls e.g. Sales.xls.
>
> In Excel the **Save as type** menu includes options specific to spreadsheets (see Figure 4.24). Compare this with Word in Module 3, Section 4.4 (page 88).

Figure 4.24 Excel's Save as type menu

> **i Info**
>
> **File formats available**
> Being able to save files in different formats is extremely useful. It means that you can share files with others who do not have the same software or version of software that you are using. You can save in a previous version of Excel, Lotus 1-2-3 or Quattro Pro format (Lotus 1-2-3 and Quattro Pro are other common spreadsheet applications.) You can also save in dBASE format (dBASE is a common database format). Other useful formats include:
>
> **Text Only** – This format saves spreadsheet contents but not formatting. The saved file can then be opened in programs that can handle text files. Note that only one sheet at a time can be saved in a text file so when saving ensure that you have the correct sheet displayed. Two commonly-used text formats include:
>
> - **Text (Tab-delimited)** - items separated by tabs.
> - **CSV (Comma delimited)** – items separated by commas.
>
> **Template** – This saves text labels and formulae and formatting so that you can reuse it to create similar spreadsheets with different content.

2.9 Printing part of a spreadsheet

 Exercise 10

Print only the figures for **Casualco** (include the month labels).

 Method

1 Select columns A and B (by dragging the mouse over the cells) to and including row 6.
2 From the **File** menu, select: **Print**.
3 In the **Print what** section, click in the option box next to **Selection** (see Figure 4.25).
4 Click on: **OK**.

Figure 4.25 Printing a selection

2.10 Close the file and exit Excel.

Section 2 Spreadsheet practice

Practice 3

1 Recall the spreadsheet **p1 expenses** saved in Section 1.
2 Change the following entries:

ELEC in **AUG** should be **35** not **45**.
GAS in **NOV** should be **54** not **40**.

3 Delete the row containing the PETROL data.
4 Replicate the formula for TOTALS for the other months.
5 In a new column after the NOV column, enter the heading TOTAL.
6 Enter a formula to calculate the total RENT for the months shown.
7 Replicate the formula for the other costs.
8 Save the spreadsheet with the name **p3 expenses**.
9 Insert a new column headed SEPT after the AUG column. Enter the data:

RENT	350
ELEC	50
GAS	20
LOAN	55
INS	20

10 Adjust the spreadsheet to show the TOTAL for SEPT.
11 Calculate an overall total in the TOTALS row/TOTAL column.
12 Save the spreadsheet as **p3 expenses1** and print one copy.
13 Print only the TOTAL column showing the formulae used.
14 Close the file.

Practice 4

1 Recall the spreadsheet **p2 store sales** saved in Section 1.
2 Change the following entries:

Menswear Thu should be **350** not **300**.
Baby Fri should be **610** not **590**.

3 Delete the Cosmetics row.
4 Replicate the formula calculating the Total for Food to all other departments.
5 Save the spreadsheet as **p4 store sales**.
6 Insert a column headed Profit after the Total column.
7 Calculate the profit for the Food department (20% of Total).
8 Replicate this formulae for the other departments.
9 Insert a new column headed Mon before the Tue column and enter the following data:

Food	25
Menswear	180
Fashions	270
Baby	52
Home	25

10 Adjust the spreadsheet formulae as necessary.
11 Save the spreadsheet as **p4 store sales1** and print one copy.
12 Close the spreadsheet file.

Section 3 Basics – formatting

In this section you will practise and learn how to:

- align cell contents

- modify column width and row height

- change text font, size and colour, italicise, embolden, change orientation

- use the Average function in formulae

- format number styles: decimal places, integers, with commas

- display numbers as percentages

- format currency symbols

- format different date styles

- use copy/cut and paste to duplicate/move cell contents in another part of the spreadsheet

- select non-adjacent rows or columns

- open several spreadsheets

- sort data into ascending/descending alphabetical/numerical order

- move cell contents between active spreadsheets

- use autofill to increment entries

- add borders

- add header/footer.

3.1 Aligning cell contents

Info

When data is first entered, text is placed on the left of the cell and numbers line up on the right. Three toolbar buttons can be used to apply a new alignment to a range that is selected.

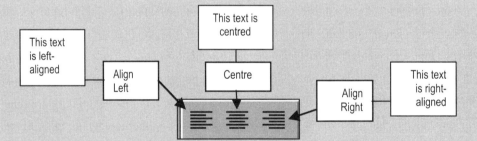

To align cell contents

Select the cells to be realigned.

Click on: the appropriate toolbar button.

Exercise 1

1 Reload the spreadsheet **Sales1** saved at the end of section 2.

2 Display the headings: **Month**, **Casualco**, **Jeansco**, **Partyco**, **Shoesco** and **Sales** so that **Month** is left-aligned and **Casualco**, **Jeansco**, **Partyco**, **Shoesco** and **Sales** are right-aligned.

Method

The heading Month is already left-justified. To right justify the other headings:

1 Select cells **B1** to **F1** (see Figure 4.26).

	A	B	C	D	E	F
1	Month	Casualco	Jeansco	Partyco	Shoesco	Sales
2	May	850	600	770	621	2841

Figure 4.26 Cells selected to right justify

2 Click on: the **Align Right** toolbar button.

 Exercise 2

Enter a main heading **CLOTHING COMPANY SALES** and centre it across the top of the spreadsheet.

 Method

1 Insert a row at the top of the spreadsheet.
2 Key in the text.
3 Select cells A1 to F1 – i.e. the full extent of spreadsheet columns.
4 Click on: the **Merge and Centre** button to centre the heading across the selected cells.

i Info

Text can also be given a different orientation – e.g. vertical instead of horizontal. To do this, from the **Format** menu, select: **Cells** (or whatever you have selected). Ensure that the **Alignment** tab is selected and alter settings in the **Orientation** section.

3.2 Modifying column width/row height

i Info

By default each column starts with a width of about nine numeric characters. You can adjust the column width so that it accommodates the entry within.

 Exercise 3

Change the heading **Sales** so that it becomes **Monthly Sales**.

 Method

1 Move to cell **F2**.
2 Click the cursor in front of the **S** of **Sales** (see Figure 4.27) on the formula bar and key in: **Monthly** and a space.
3 Press: **Enter**.

Figure 4.27 Positioning the cursor to alter a heading

4 The entry is now too long to fit the cell. There are several ways to widen the column:

Info

Click on: the **Undo** button after trying each method so that you can practise.

a) Position the cursor at the column border; a double arrow appears. Drag the right-hand edge of the column border (next to the column letter) to the right (see Figure 4.28):

Figure 4.28 Changing column width

b) Position the cursor as above and double-click the mouse (this action widens to exactly fit the longest entry).

c) With the cell selected, from the **Format** menu, select: **Column, AutoFit Selection** (see Figure 4.29).

d) Select the column, right-click and from the pop-up menu select: **Column Width**. Key in the new width. Click on: **OK**.

Figure 4.29 Widening a column using the menus

Info

Row height can be changed following these methods substituting Row for Column.

3.3 Changing text: size, colour, italicise and embolden

Exercise 4

In the Total row, change the font size to 16 pt and the text colour to blue. Italicise and embolden this row only.

 Method

1 Select the row.
2 Use the **Font Size** button to change to 16 pt.
3 Use the **Font Colour** button to change the text to blue.
4 Use the **Italic** and **Bold** buttons to italicise and embolden.

3.4 Using the Average function

 Exercise 5

Enter a column headed **Average Sales** after the **Monthly Sales** column. Right justify this heading and widen the cell to display this heading in full. Recentre the main heading to incorporate this additional column.

In cell **G3**, enter a formula to work out the **Average Sales** for **May**. Replicate this formula to cells **G4**, **G5**, **G6** and **G7**.

Info

Excel has a built in AVERAGE function to work out averages. The syntax is:

=AVERAGE(cell ref:cell ref)

Note: In some spreadsheet applications you can shorten the word AVERAGE. Excel does not allow this.

In this instance, in cell G2 the formula is =AVERAGE(B3:E3).

After replicating this formula, the spreadsheet will now look like Figure 4.30:

	A	B	C	D	E	F	G
1			CLOTHING COMPANY SALES				
2	Month	Casualco	Jeansco	Partyco	Shoesco	MonthlySales	Average Sales
3	May	850	600	770	621	2841	710.25
4	June	550	700	220	890	2360	590
5	July	470	850	700	700	2720	680
6	August	400	650	820	440	2310	577.5
7	*Total*	*2270*	*2800*	*2510*	*2651*	*10231*	*2557.8*

Figure 4.30 Spreadsheet with the Average Sales column added

Notice that there are integers (whole numbers) in cells G4 and G5. Cells G6 and G7 have 1 decimal place (1 numeric character after the decimal point) and cell G3 has 2 decimal places (2 numeric characters after the decimal point).

3.5 Using integer and decimal format to display numbers

 Exercise 6

Display the numeric data in the Average Sales column as integers (whole numbers).

 Method

1 Select the column entries i.e. cells G3 to G7.
2 Right-click the highlighted area. A pop-up menu appears (see Figure 4.31).

Figure 4.31 Formatting cells

3 From the menu, select: **Format Cells**; the Format Cells dialogue box is displayed (Figure 4.32).
4 Click on: the **Number** tab.
5 In the **Category** box, click on: **Number**.
6 In the **Decimal places** box, use the down arrow to set to zero (0).

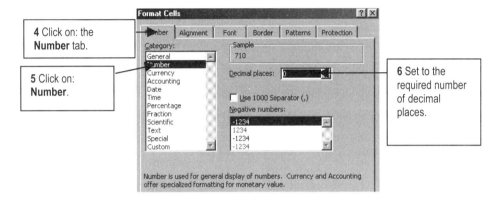

Figure 4.32 Format Cells dialogue box

7 Click on: **OK**.

The Average Sales column will now look like Figure 4.33:

G
Average Sales
710
590
680
578
2558

Figure 4.33 Average Sales figures displayed as integers

Exercise 7

Change the display of the numeric data in the **Average Sales** column to **2 decimal places** – i.e. two places after the decimal point.

 Info

General is the default number format in Excel and displays numbers with decimal places as in Figure 4.30. If a number has a zero positioned, as in 577.50 (the zero here is said to be 'trailing'), and Excel will only display 577.5 in the General format.

You can also use the ⊞ **Increase Decimal/Decrease Decimal** buttons to increase and decrease decimal places. Try this method in the following exercise.

The Average Sales column should now look like Figure 4.34:

G
Average Sales
710.25
590.00
680.00
577.50

2557.75

Figure 4.34 Average Sales figures displayed with 2 decimal places

---

3.6 Save the spreadsheet as **Sales2** and print one copy on A4 paper.

3.7 Adding currency symbols

 Exercise 8

In the **Total** row, **Average Sales** column, display the entry with the **UK** currency symbol (£).

Method

1   Select the relevant cell – i.e. **G7**.

2   Click on: the ⬚ **Currency** button.

> **i Info**
>
> Excel inserts the £ symbol, a comma to denote thousands and two decimal places so that pence can be displayed. Other currency options can be chosen by selecting: **Cells** from the **Format** menu.
>
> With the **Number** tab selected, in the **Category** section, select: **Currency** and then choose from the drop-down list in the **Symbol** section.
>
> Commas to denote thousands (so that 1234 becomes 1,234) can be inserted in numeric data using the ⬚ **, Comma Style** button.
>
> Other symbols can be inserted as follows:
>
> 1   From the **Start** menu, select: **Programs, Accessories, System Tools, Character Map**.
>
> 2   Select the symbol required by clicking on it.
>
> 3   Click on: **Select**.
>
> 4   Click on: **Copy**.
>
> 5   Click on: **Close**.
>
> 6   In Excel click on: the **Paste** button.

3.8 Copying and pasting

 Exercise 9

Copy the heading so that it appears in cell **A10**.

Method

Using drag and drop

1   Select the cell where the heading is displayed.

2 Hover the mouse over the selection border; the mouse pointer appears.
3 Hold down the **Ctrl** key. A **+** appears alongside the arrow.
4 Hold down the left mouse button and drag the selection to its new position – i.e. cell **A10**.
5 Release the mouse button.

 Exercise 10

Copy the **Month** and the **Shoesco** columns so that they appear adjacent underneath the main spreadsheet.

 Method

Copying using the Copy and Paste buttons

Selecting non-adjacent columns/rows

 Info

Adjacent means that the cells are next to one another. Non-adjacent means that they are not. The columns in this exercise are non-adjacent.

1 Select the **Month** column data, hold down the **Ctrl** key and select the **Shoesco** column data.
2 Click on: the **Copy** button. Flashing dotted lines appear around the selected columns.
3 Select the cells where you want to copy to – e.g. **A11** to **B16**.
4 Click on: the **Paste** button.
5 Press: **Esc** to remove flashing lines.
6 Reformat the copied cells if necessary.

 Info

Similarly you can cut and paste. This time do not hold down the **Ctrl** key.

3.9 Displaying numbers as percentages

 Exercise 11

In cell **C11**, enter the text **Commission Rates**. Enter the following commission rates for the months of **May**, **June**, **July** and **August** respectively:

0.05, **0.08**, **0.1** and **0.025**.

Display these commission rates as percentages.

 Method

1 Enter the text and data in the usual way.
2 Select the cells containing the commission rates.
3 Click on: the **%** **Percent Style** button. The commission column now looks like Figure 4.35.

Commission
5%
8%
10%
3%

Figure 4.35 Commission figures changed to percentages

3.10 Save the spreadsheet as **Sales3** and print one copy on A4 paper.

3.11 Opening several spreadsheets

Exercise 12

Keeping the current spreadsheet open, open a new workbook. Copy the main heading to the new spreadsheet. Save the new workbook with the filename: **Employees**.

Method

1 Click on: the **New** button.
2 Return to the **Sales3** spreadsheet display (from the **Window** menu, select: the filename *or* click on: the filename on the Taskbar).
3 Select the cell to copy, then click on: the **Copy** button.
4 Return to the new spreadsheet, select cell **A1** and click on: the **Paste** button.
5 Press: **Esc** to remove the selection from the **Sales3** spreadsheet.
6 Save the new spreadsheet.

Exercise 13

Enter the following employee information:

Surname	First Name	Start Date
Jones	Julia	14/02/96
Gill	Sanjit	10/10/99
Wright	Dominic	29/09/98
Jones	Bronwen	02/05/00

Note: You can also move the contents using the **Cut** button at Step 3.

3.12 Changing date format

Exercise 14

Change the date format so that the date is displayed in the format **14-Feb-1996**.

Method

1 Select the cells to format.
2 From the **Format** menu, select: **Cells**. The **Format Cells** dialogue box is displayed (see Figure 4.36).

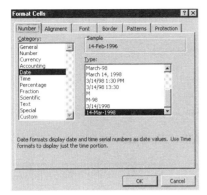

Figure 4.36 Formatting date styles

3 Ensure **Number** tab is selected.
4 In the **Category** section, click on: **Date**.
5 In the **Type** section, select the relevant format and click on: **OK**.

3.13 Sorting data into ascending/descending alphabetical/numerical order

 Exercise 15

Display the employee names in alphabetical order of surname.

 Method

Sorting using the toolbar Ascending/Descending buttons

1 Select the cell range containing the employee details – i.e. **A3** to **C6**.

Note: It is necessary to select the **First Name** and **Start Date** columns so that they will be kept together when sorted.

2 Click on: the **Ascending** button.

Info

The Ascending button will sort from A-Z or from the lowest number to the highest number in the selection. There is also a **Descending** button to use when necessary. This sorts from Z-A and from the highest number to the lowest number in a selection.

 Exercise 16

Sort the employee data, first by **Surname**, then by **First Name**.

 Method

1 Select the cell range containing the employee details as before – i.e. **A3** to **C6**.
2 From the **Data** menu, select: **Sort**.
3 The **Sort** dialogue box appears (see Figure 4.37).

4 In the **Sort by** section, select: **Surname**.
5 In the **Then by** section, select: **First Name**.
6 Ensure that **Ascending** is chosen in both cases.
7 Click on: **OK**.

Figure 4.37 Sorting on more than one criteria

You will notice that because Bronwen begins with a B and Julia begins with a J, Bronwen Jones is now placed above Julia Jones

 Exercise 17

Copy the whole of the **Employees** spreadsheet except the main heading to a second sheet within the same workbook. Name the new sheet: **Personnel data**.

 Method

1 Select the spreadsheet contents excluding the main heading.
2 Click on: the **Copy** button.
3 Open a new sheet by clicking on the **Sheet2** tab (see Figure 4.38).

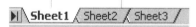

Figure 4.38 Selecting a new sheet

4 The new sheet appears.
5 Click on: the **Paste** button.
6 Reformat the cells as necessary.
7 Right-click on: the new sheet tab (**Sheet2**) and key in the new sheet name.

3.14 Formatting numbers as text

 Exercise 18

Key in **Tel** in cell D1 and key in the employee telephone numbers as follows:

Sanjit	01234 752999
Bronwen	01234 621900
Julia	01908 554211
Dominic	01908 338554

Method

1   Select the cells that are to contain the telephone numbers – i.e. cells **D2** to **D5**.
2   From the **Format** menu, select: **Cells**.
3   With the **Number** tab selected, in the **Category** section, select: **Text** from the list.
4   Click on: **OK**.

Note: It is essential that you format the cells *before* entering the telephone numbers.

3.15 Using AutoFill

 Exercise 19

Add the following column headings after **Tel**:

Week1, Week2, Week3, Week4

 Method

1   Enter **Week1** in cell **E1**.
2   Hover the mouse over the **Fill** handle (see below) at the bottom right of the cell. A cross appears.

3   Hold down the left mouse and drag across the cells you want to autofill – i.e. **F1**, **G1** and **H1**.
4   Release the mouse button.

3.16 Adding borders

 Exercise 20

Add a border around the entire spreadsheet and a double-line border under the heading row.

Method

1 Select the spreadsheet.

2 Click on: the down arrow of the 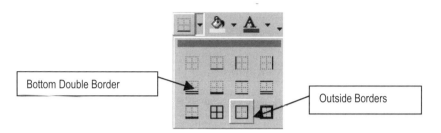 **Borders** button.

3 Select: **Outside Borders** as shown in Figure 4.39.

Bottom Double Border

Outside Borders

Figure 4.39 Adding borders

4 Select the heading row.

5 Using the **Borders** button, select: **Bottom Double Border** (see Figure 4.39).

3.17 Adding headers/footers

 Exercise 21

Add the header **Produced by (your name)** and the **date** to all of the open spreadsheets.

 Method

1 With the spreadsheet displayed, from the **File** menu, select: **Page Setup**. The **Page Setup** dialogue box appears.

2 Click on: the **Header/Footer** tab so that it is displayed (see Figure 4.40).

3 Click on: **Custom header**.

Note: Click on Custom Footer to add information to a footer.

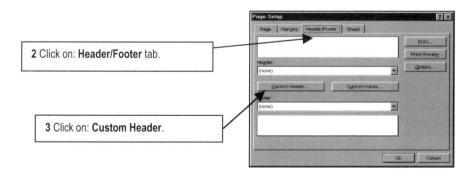

2 Click on: **Header/Footer** tab.

3 Click on: **Custom Header**.

Figure 4.40 Adding headers/footers

4 The Header dialogue box appears.

5 Click in the **Left** section and key in: **Produced by (your name)**.

6 Click in the **Center** section and key in the date (or click the **Date** button (see Figure 4.41) if you are certain that your computer's date is set correctly – the actual date will not be displayed here but you can practise and see what appears on your Print Preview).

7 Click on: **OK** and on **OK** again.

Figure 4.41 Inserting an automatic date into a header

8 Switch to the next open spreadsheet and repeat.

> **Info**
>
> Creating a footer. At Step 3 click on: **Custom Footer** and repeat as for Custom Header.

3.18 Save and print all of your work on A4 paper.

3.19 Close all files and exit Excel.

Section 3 Spreadsheet practice

Practice 5

1　Recall the spreadsheet **p3 expenses1** saved in Section 2.
2　Right align all the column headings.
3　Change the row headings to Times New Roman, 12 point, red, bold.
4　Display all the numeric data in the months columns to 1 decimal place.
5　Display the numeric data in the TOTAL column in UK pounds to 2 decimal places.
6　Add a new column after the TOTAL column headed AVERAGE.
7　Set the new column width to 10.
8　Enter a formula in the AVERAGE column to calculate the average expenditure over the four monthly period.
9　Display the numeric data in the AVERAGE column in integer format.
10　Open another sheet in the same workbook.
11　On the new sheet, enter the heading YEARLY EXPENSES. Format it to bold, 18 pt.
12　Copy the row headings from the first sheet to column A.
13　Enter column headings 1 Jan 99 and increment on a monthly basis to 1 Dec 99.
14　Copy the data for AUG to NOV to the appropriate columns on the second sheet.
15　Format the dates in the column headings to Jan-99, Feb-99 etc.
16　Add a border round the whole spreadsheet.
17　Add the header ECDL 2000 in the centre and today's date at the right.
18　Save the workbook as **p5 expenses2**.
19　Print a copy of both sheets in landscape display.
20　Close the file.

Practice 6

1　Recall the spreadsheet **p4 store sales1** saved in Section 2.
2　Embolden and centre the column headings.
3　Display all the numeric data to 2 decimal places.
4　Enter a new row headed Average Store Sales. Widen the column to display the new entry.
5　In this row, enter a formula to calculate the average daily sales for Mon.
6　Replicate the formula for the other days.
7　Change the row heading Fashions to Ladies Fashions.
8　Copy the Food and Home rows and column headings to a new workbook file.
9　Insert a row at the top of the new spreadsheet with the title HOUSEHOLD SALES.
10　Centre the heading across the cells.
11　Insert a column before the Profit column headed Predicted Increased Sales.
12　Enter 0.012 in the Food row and 0.035 in the Home row.
13　Format the figures in this column as %.
14　Add a border around the spreadsheet and between the cells.
15　Save the Household Sales spreadsheet file as **p6 house** and the original spreadsheet as **p6 store sales2**.
16　Print both spreadsheet files fitting them each to one page.
17　Close both files.

Section 4 Advanced – charting

In this section you will practise and learn how to:

- produce different types of charts/graphs from spreadsheet figures to analyse data: pie charts, column charts, bar charts, line graphs, comparative charts

- edit or modify a chart/graph: add a title or label, change the scale, change the colours
- change the chart type
- move and delete charts/graphs.

4.1 Different types of display

There are many different ways of graphically displaying data in Excel. The main ones that we will be looking at are pie charts, column/bar charts, line graphs and comparative charts.

Info

Excel uses the word chart and not graph for all of its graphical displays. In the UK we usually tend to differentiate between charts and graphs. For our purposes we can assume that they are the same thing.

4.2 Pie chart

A pie chart consists of a circle divided into a number of segments. In this example (Figure 4.42), there are three segments representing eye colours: blue, brown and green, in Tutor Group A. The largest segment is brown and it tells us that 44% of Tutor Group A have brown eyes, the next largest is green with 30%, and the smallest blue with 26%. There is a legend (key) to show us which colour or shade represents which eye colour.

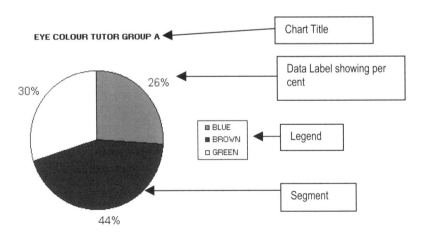

Figure 4.42 Pie chart

Chart components

Chart title. The chart title should be descriptive and clear.

Data labels. On a pie chart you can show percentage values or actual values. You can show the legend labels next to the segments instead of a legend.

Legend. A legend is a key showing the different colours/shades that correspond to the data represented in the pie chart.

Segment. The pie chart is made up of segments that represent different data types.

4.3 Column and bar charts

A column chart uses columns to represent values. The chart has two axes, the *x* (horizontal) axis and the *y* (vertical) axis. The *x* axis usually represents data that does not change, such as days of the week. The *y* axis usually represents values that fluctuate, such as monetary values or temperatures. This type of chart is useful for showing comparisons.

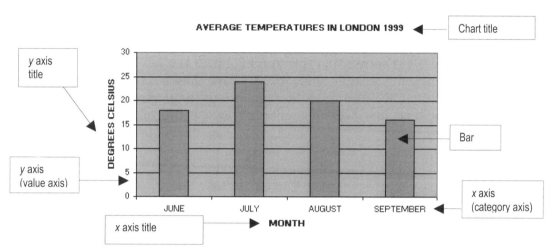

Figure 4.43 Column chart

The column chart (Figure 4.43) shows the comparison of average temperatures in London. The tallest column, July, shows the overall hottest average temperature. The shortest column, September, shows that it was the coolest month of those shown.

A bar chart has the same components as a column chart but shows the categories vertically and the values horizontally (see Figure 4.44).

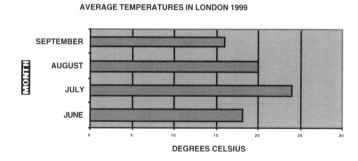

Figure 4.44 Bar chart

4.4 Line graph

A line graph (see Figure 4.45) shows trends in data at equal intervals. Points on the graph are joined together to form a continuous line. It has properties in common with a column/bar chart, such as *x* and *y* axes and axes titles.

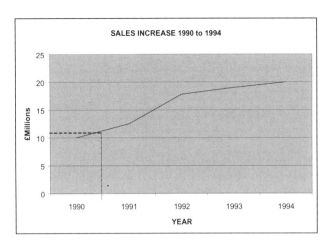

Figure 4.45 Line graph

The line graph (see Figure 4.45) shows that the trend is up, as the line is going up and not down. Sales have been increasing steadily since 1990. I have drawn a line from the *x* axis, at the end of 1990, to the plotted line and then drawn a line to the *y* axis. Where this line joins the *y* axis the value can be read, just over £11 million. This was the value of sales at the end of 1990.

4.5 Comparative charts

A comparative chart is used to compare sets of data. The display shows two or more columns (if a comparative column chart, Figure 4.46) or two or more lines (if a comparative line graph, Figure 4.47) of the same item.

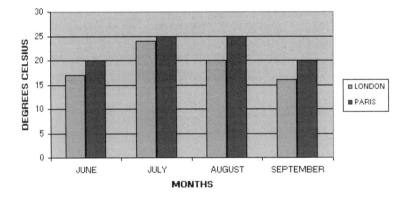

Figure 4.46 Comparative column chart

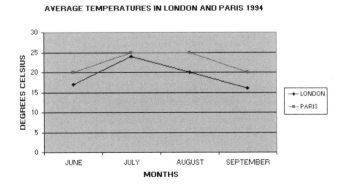

Figure 4.47 Comparative line graph

4.6 Creating a pie chart

Exercise 1

Produce a pie chart showing the branch sales percentages for Le Cafe for the months January to June 2000.

Method

1 Load Excel as shown in Section 1 (page 121).
2 Enter the data so that the spreadsheet looks like Figure 4.48.

	A	B
1	BOURNEMOUTH	22
2	LUTON	28
3	MANCHESTER	19
4	READING	31

Figure 4.48 Data entered into spreadsheet

3 Save the spreadsheet as **Le Cafe**.

Now create the pie chart including labels for each of the segments. Enter the following heading **BRANCH SALES PERCENTAGES – JANUARY TO JUNE 2000**.

Method

1 Select all of the data entered i.e. cells A1 to B4.

2 Click on: the 🔲 **Chart Wizard** button.

3 **Step 1 of 4 Chart Wizard** dialogue box appears: **Chart Type** (see Figure 4.49).

   a) The **Standard Types** tab is selected. In the **Chart type** box, click on: **Pie**.

   b) In the **Chart sub-type** box, click on: the top left pie type, as shown. This is usually already selected as the default setting.

   c) Click on: **Next**.

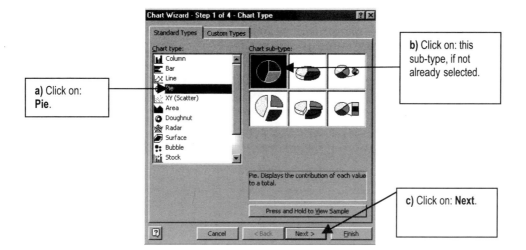

Figure 4.49 Step 1 of Chart Wizard

4   **Step 2 Chart Wizard** dialogue box appears: **Chart Source Data** (see Figure 4.50).

There is a preview of the pie chart together with a legend – a key to the different segments of the pie. With the **Data Range** tab selected, the data range selected is shown as:

=Sheet1$A$1:$B$4

Ignoring the $ signs, this represents Sheet1, cells A1 to B4.

5   Click on: **Next**.

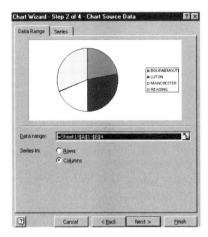

Figure 4.50 Step 2 of Chart Wizard

6 Step 3 Chart Wizard dialogue box appears: **Chart Options** (Figure 4.51).

    a) With the Titles tab selected, click in the Chart title box and key in: **BRANCH SALES PERCENTAGES – JANUARY TO JUNE 2000**.

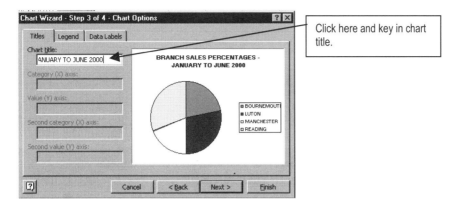

Figure 4.51 Step 3 of Chart Wizard

You will not be able to see all the title as it will scroll out of the visible section. Do not press **Enter** as this will result in moving to the next step of Chart Wizard. If you have pressed **Enter**, click on: **Back**.

    b) Click on: the **Legend** tab (see Figure 4.52).
    c) Click in the **Show legend** tick box to remove the tick.

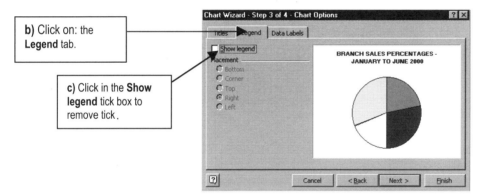

Figure 4.52 Removing a legend

Info

You have been asked to show labels for each of the segments, not a legend. Having segment data labels and a legend duplicates information and will make the chart appear cluttered.

    d) Click on: the **Data Labels** tab (see Figure 4.53).
    e) Click in the **Show label** option button.
    f) Click on: **Next**.

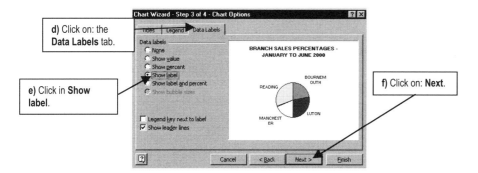

Figure 4.53 Showing labels

> **i Info**
>
> You will notice that labels and choices appear on the chart preview as you work. If you make an error, carry out the instruction again.

7 **Step 4 Chart Wizard** dialogue box appears: **Chart Location** (see Figure 4.54).

   a) Click in the **As new sheet** option button.
   b) In the box shown, key in the name **Le Cafe pie**.
   c) Click on: **Finish**.

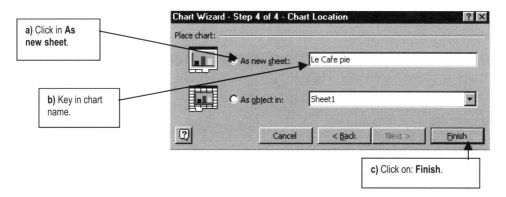

Figure 4.54 Step 4 of Chart Wizard

> **i Info**
>
> You can choose **As object in** if you want the chart to appear on the same sheet as the data. The chart will be located in the workbook (the same file) whichever option you choose.

The completed pie chart is displayed as shown in Figure 4.55:

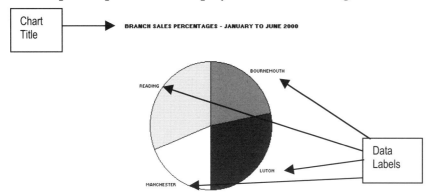

Figure 4.55 Completed pie chart

Should you need to make any changes – e.g. to the title, labels or you want to change to a different type of chart: with the chart displayed on screen, right-click in the chart area to bring up the menu shown. You will notice that the menu items in the second section – i.e. below **Format Chart Area**, correspond to the dialogue boxes of Chart Wizard. Choose from these options.

Note: Pie charts are generated from one data series only. You will need to bear this in mind if you are changing **Chart Type** (you may need to hide some of the original data for a correct result).To hide data Select the column(s)/row(s) to hide. Right-click on the selection and select: Hide. To unhide data Select the columns/rows on either side of the hidden data. Right-click on the selection, select: Unhide.

4.7 Saving the chart

 Method

Click on: the **Save** button.

You can use this quick saving method as you have already saved the chart as **Le cafe pie**. The chart and spreadsheet will be saved as one file.

You can swap between chart and spreadsheet display by clicking the relevant tab in the worksheet tab area at the bottom of the currently displayed spreadsheet.

Le Cafe pie \ **Sheet1** / Sheet2 / Sheet

4.8 Printing a chart

 Method

1   With the chart displayed on screen, from the **File** menu, select **Print**. The **Print** dialogue box appears (see Figure 4.56).

2 In the **Print what** section, ensure that the **Active sheet** option button is selected.
3 Click on: **OK**.

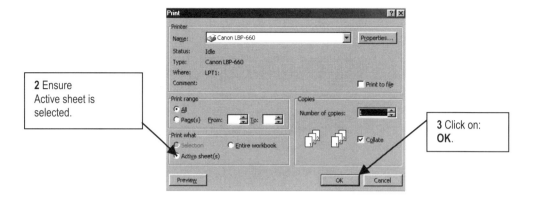

Figure 4.56 Print dialogue box

> **Info**
> By default the chart will print in landscape format. (See Module 4, Section 1 – page 129 – for how to change the orientation.)

4.9 Closing the chart

 Method

From the **File** menu, select: **Close**.

> **Info**
> You can close with the display on either the chart or the spreadsheet. They will be saved together with the same filename.

4.10 Creating a column chart

 Exercise 2

Produce a column chart showing the monthly sales from January to June for the Bournemouth branch.

 Method

1 Load Excel or click on: the **New** button if Excel is already loaded.
2 Enter the data so that your spreadsheet looks like Figure 4.57.

	A	B
1	MONTH	SALES - £
2	January	25000
3	February	23000
4	March	40000
5	April	11000
6	May	24000
7	June	19000

Figure 4.57 Spreadsheet with data entered

3 Save the spreadsheet as **BOURNEMOUTH SALES**.

Now create the column chart. Title the *x* (horizontal) axis **MONTHS** and the *y* (vertical) axis **£**. Give the bar chart the title **MONTHLY SALES, BOURNEMOUTH BRANCH**.

Method

1 From the data entered, select all except the headings i.e. cells A2 to B7.

2 Click on: the **Chart Wizard** button.

3 **Step 1** (of 4) **Chart Wizard** dialogue box appears: **Chart Type**.

   a) With the **Standard Types** tab selected, click on: **Column**.
   b) In the **Chart sub-type** box, click on: the top left chart. (This is the default so may already be selected.)
   c) Click on: **Next**.

Practice

Experiment with the different chart types.

---

4 **Step 2 Chart Wizard** dialogue box appears: **Chart Source Data**.
5 Click on: **Next**.
6 **Step 3 Chart Wizard** dialogue box appears: **Chart Options**.

   a) Select the **Titles** tab (if not already selected), click in the **Chart title** box and key in: **MONTHLY SALES, BOURNEMOUTH BRANCH**.
   b) Click in the **Category** (*x*) axis box and key in: **MONTHS**.
   c) Click in the **Value** (*y*) axis box and key in **£**.
   d) Click on: the **Legend** tab.
   e) Click in the **Show legend** tick box to remove the tick.
   f) Click on: **Next**.

7 **Step 4 Chart Wizard** dialogue box appears: **Chart Location**.

   a) Click on: **As new sheet** option button and key in the name **SALESBAR**.
   b) Click on: **Finish**.

The completed column chart is displayed as shown in Figure 4.58:

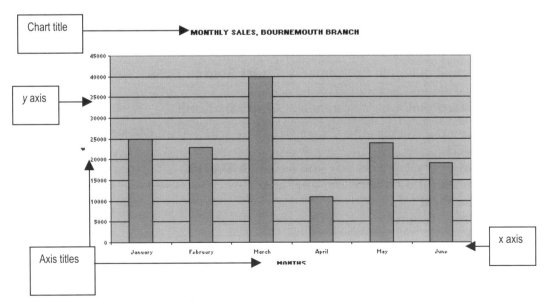

Figure 4.58 Completed column chart

8 Save the chart as in Section 4.7 (page 163).

9 Print the chart as in Section 4.8 (page 163).

10 Close the chart as in Section 4.9 (page 164).

4.11 Creating a line graph

 Exercise 3

Produce a line graph showing the monthly sales from January to June for the Luton branch.

 Method

1 Load Excel or click on: the **New** button.

2 Enter the data so that your spreadsheet looks like Figure 4.59.

	A	B
1	MONTH	SALES - £
2	January	17000
3	February	14000
4	March	26000
5	April	32000
6	May	22000
7	June	20000

Figure 4.59 Spreadsheet with data entered

3 Save the spreadsheet as **LUTON SALES**.

For the data create a line graph. Enter the x (horizontal) axis title **MONTHS** and the y (vertical) axis £. The title for the graph is **MONTHLY SALES – LUTON BRANCH**.

 Method

1 Select the data entered in the cells **A2** to **B7**.

2 Click on: the ▥ **Chart Wizard** button.

3 **Step 1** of 4 **Chart Wizard** dialogue box appears: **Chart type**.

    a) With the **Standard Types** tab selected, click on: **Line**.

    b) In the **Chart sub-type** box, click on: the top left chart.

    c) Click on: **Next**.

4 **Step 2 Chart Wizard** dialogue box appears: **Chart Source Data**.

5 Click on: **Next**.

6 **Step 3 Chart Wizard** dialogue box appears: **Chart Options**.

    a) Select the **Titles** tab, click in the **Chart title** box and key in: **MONTHLY SALES – LUTON BRANCH**.

    b) Click in the **Category (x) axis** box and key in: **MONTHS**.

    c) Click in the **Value (y) axis box** and key in: **£**.

    d) Click on: the **Legend** tab.

    e) Click in the **Show legend** tick box to remove the tick.

    f) Click on: **Next**.

7 **Step 4 Chart Wizard** dialogue box appears: **Chart Location**.

    a) Click on: **As new sheet** option button and key in the name **SALES LINE**.

    b) Click on: **Finish**.

The completed line graph is displayed as shown in Figure 4.60.

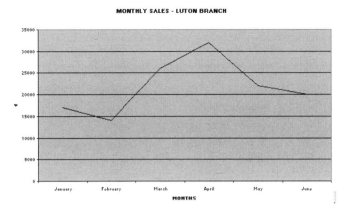

MONTHLY SALES - LUTON BRANCH

Figure 4.60 Completed line graph

8   Save the graph as in Section 4.7 (page 163).
9   Print the graph as in Section 4.8 (page 163).
10 Close the graph as in Section 4.9 (page 164).

4.12 Creating a comparative chart

Exercise 4

Produce a comparative column chart showing Le Cafe's daily sales of hot chocolate and cappuccino from Sunday to Saturday.

Method

1   Load Excel *or* click on: the **New** toolbar button.
2   Enter the data so that the spreadsheet looks like Figure 4.61.

	A	B	C
1		HOT CHOCOLATE	CAPPUCCINO
2	SUN	100	220
3	MON	40	98
4	TUE	70	106
5	WED	103	155
6	THU	207	198
7	FRI	264	189
8	SAT	298	68

Figure 4.61 Spreadsheet with data entered

3   Save the spreadsheet as **BEVERAGES**.

Create a comparative column chart using the data entered. Enter the *y* axis title **NUMBER OF BEVERAGES**. Enter the *x* axis title **DAY**. Create a legend to show Hot Chocolate and Cappuccino. The title for the graph is **BEVERAGE SALES**.

Method

1   Select all the data entered – i.e. cells **A1** to **C8**.
2   Click on: the **Chart Wizard** button.
3   **Step 1 Chart Wizard**

    a) With the **Standard Types** tab selected, click on: **Column**.

b) In the **Chart sub-type** box, click on: the first chart at the top left.

c) Click on: **Next**.

4 **Step 2 Chart Wizard**

a) Click on: **Next**.

5 **Step 3 Chart Wizard**

a) Select the **Titles** tab, click in the **Chart title** box and key in: **BEVERAGE SALES**.

b) Click in the **Category (x) axis** box and key in: **DAY**.

c) Click in the **Value (y) axis** box and key in: **NUMBER OF BEVERAGES**.

d) Click on: **Next**.

6 **Step 4 Chart Wizard**

a) Click on: the **As new sheet** option button and key in **BEVERAGE COMPARISON**.

b) Click on: **Finish**.

The completed comparative chart is displayed as shown in Figure 4.62.

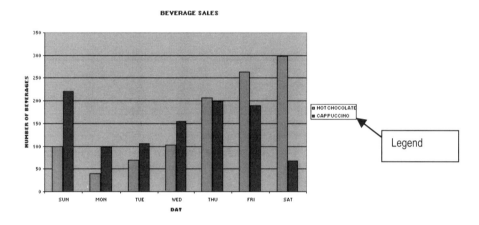

Figure 4.62 Completed comparative graph

ℹ️ **Info**

In this example, we need to show a legend to indicate which colour bars represent hot chocolate and which cappuccino. If you are printing in black and white, the bars and legend will display in differing patterns.

If you are printing a comparative line graph to a black and white printer, be careful to choose a chart type that displays different shapes on the lines to distinguish them.

---

7 Save the chart as in Section 4.7 (page 163).

8 Print the chart as in Section 4.8 (page 163).

4.13 Changing chart colours

A pop-up menu will be displayed when you double-click on: any part of the completed chart. There will be options to change colours, patterns, fonts etc. Practise this now.

4.14 Changing chart scales

To change the *y* axis value:

1 With the chart displayed on screen, double-click on: the **Value Axis** (see Figure 4.63).

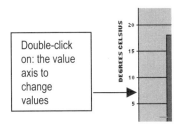

Figure 4.63 The Value Axis

2 The Format Axis dialogue box appears.
3 With the **Scale** tab selected, change the values in the **Minimum** and **Maximum** boxes.
4 Click on: **OK**.

Practise this now.

4.15 Moving a chart

Click on: it to select it.

Either

Use **Cut** and **Paste** to move it to another sheet or application.

or

Drag the chart using the mouse to another location on the same sheet.

4.16 Deleting a chart

1 Click on: the chart to select it.
2 Press: **Delete**.

4.17 Save and close the spreadsheets and exit Excel.

Section 4 Spreadsheet practice

Practice 7

1 Set up the following spreadsheet.
2 Enter the appropriate formulae in the relevant cells.

Note: To convert Degrees C to Degrees F, (°C x 1.8)+32

Temperature Chart						
	Degrees C					Degrees F
	May	**June**	**July**	**August**	**4-Month Average**	**May**
Amsterdam	18	21	22	22	formula	formula
Athens	25	30	33	33	formula	formula
Berlin	19	22	24	23	formula	formula
Budapest	22	26	28	27	formula	formula
Copenhagen	16	19	22	21	formula	formula
Dublin	15	18	20	19	formula	formula
Helsinki	14	19	22	20	formula	formula
London	17	20	22	22	formula	formula
Madrid	21	27	31	30	formula	formula
Oslo	16	20	22	21	formula	formula
Paris	20	23	25	24	formula	formula
Rome	23	28	30	30	formula	formula
Stockholm	14	19	22	20	formula	formula
Vienna	19	23	25	24	formula	formula
Zurich	19	23	25	24	formula	formula

3 Working with the degrees C columns, create a 3-D column chart comparing the temperatures in Helsinki and Rome.
4 Use the chart title Temperature Comparison (Helsinki, Rome).
5 Label the *x axis* Month and the *y axis* Degrees C.
6 Change the scale to display starting at 10.
7 Save the chart on a new sheet.
8 Print the chart in landscape.
9 Change the chart type to Line with markers displayed at each data value.
10 Print the Line graph.

Practice 8

1 Using the spreadsheet created in Practice 7, create a Clustered Bar chart with 3-D visual effect of the temperatures in May in degrees F for the cities Oslo through to Zurich.
2 Use the chart title May Temperatures.
3 Title the category axis Cities and the value axis Degrees F.
4 Save the chart on the same sheet as the spreadsheet data.
5 Reposition and resize the chart so that it does not obscure any of the spreadsheet data and shows all the city names.
6 Save the spreadsheet file and print a copy of the data and chart on one page.

Practice 9

1 Set up the following spreadsheet:

Football attendance figures
Adult Male	16,790
Adult Female	3,791
Male under 16	10,000
Female under 16	1,199

2 Create a pie chart on a new sheet in the same workbook to display the percentage attendance.

3 Add the title Attendance Figures.

4 Add a legend.

5 Save and print the chart in portrait display.

6 Copy the chart to a new sheet in the same workbook.

7 Change the chart on the sheet just created to an exploded pie.

8 Colour the segments as follows:

Adult Male = Black, Adult Female = Red, Male (under 16) = Yellow, Female (under 16) = Grey

9 Print the exploded pie chart in landscape display.

10 Save and close the file.

Section 5 Advanced – importing

In this section you will practise and learn how to:

- import objects into a spreadsheet: image files, charts/graphs, text files etc.

- move and resize imported objects within a spreadsheet.

5.1 Importing objects into a spreadsheet

 Exercise 1

Reload any of the spreadsheets created in Section 4. Import an image file, a chart/graph and a text file.

 Method

Inserting an image file

1 With the spreadsheet displayed on screen, select the place on the spreadsheet where you want the image to appear.
2 From the **Insert** menu, select: **Object** (see Figure 4.64).

Figure 4.64 Inserting an object

3 The Object dialogue box appears (see Figure 4.65). In this case select: **Microsoft Clip Gallery**.

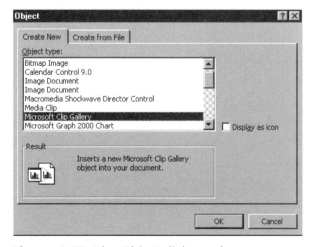

Figure 4.65 The Object dialogue box

4 The Microsoft Clip Gallery appears. Select a suitable clip and click on: **Insert**. The clip is inserted on the spreadsheet.

5.2 Resizing and moving imported objects

Resizing an imported object

You will notice that the import has handles. Resize it using the handles. Remember if you want to keep its proportions, then resize from a corner.

Moving an imported object

With the object selected, drag it to the required position using the mouse *or* use the cut and paste method.

5.3 Save and print the spreadsheet.

Note: There is no printout of this exercise as versions will differ considerably.

5.4 Close the file and exit Excel.

Section 5 Spreadsheet practice

Practice 10

1   Load any Excel spreadsheet that you have saved.
2   Practise importing different types of files.
3   Practise moving and resizing them.

Excel quick reference guide

Action	Keyboard	Mouse	Right-mouse menu	Menu
Absolute cell reference	Add $ sign in front of the cell reference column letter and in front of the cell reference row number or press: **F4**			
Align cell entries	Select cells to align			
		Click: the relevant button: ≡ ≡ ≡ ⊞	**Format Cells**	**F**or**mat**, **C**e**lls**
			Select the **Alignment** tab Select from the **Horizontal:** drop-down menu as appropriate	
Autofill	Select the first cell, drag the **Fill Handle** across the cells			
Bold text	Select cells to embolden			
	Ctrl + B	Click: the **B** **Bold** button	**Format Cells**	**F**or**mat**, **C**e**lls**
			Select the **Font** tab Select **Bold** from the **Font style:** menu	
Borders	Select the cells that you want to add a border to			
		Click on the down arrow of the ▢▾ **Borders** button. Select the border you require	**Format Cells**, **Border** tab	**F**or**mat**, **C**e**lls**
Capitals (blocked)	Caps Lock (Press again to remove)			
Close a file	**Ctrl + W**	Click: the ⊠ **Close window** icon		**F**i**le**, **C**lose
Columns, adding	Select the column following the one where you want the new column to appear – by clicking on the column ref box (at top of column)			
			Insert	**I**nsert, **C**olumns
Columns, changing width of		Drag the column border C ⟷ D to fit the widest entry	Select the column(s) by clicking (and dragging) on the column ref box (at top of column)	
			Column Width Key in the width you want	**F**or**mat**, **C**olumn, **W**idth Key in the width you want *or* Format, Column, AutoFit Selection
Columns, deleting	Select the column you want to delete by clicking on the column ref box (at top of column)			
	Delete		**D**elete	**E**dit, **D**elete

Action	Keyboard	Mouse	Right-mouse menu	Menu
Commas, inserting in numbers		Click: the **,** **Comma Style** button	**Format Cells**, **Number**, **Number**, **Use 1000 Separator**	**Format**, **Cells**, **Number**, **Number**, **Use 1000 Separator**
Copy/cut and paste	Select cell(s) to copy/cut			
	Using drag and drop Copy: Hold down Ctrl and drag to new position. Cut: Drag to new position			
	Using Cut/Copy and Paste Click: the **Cut/Paste** button. Select where you want to cut/copy to. Click: the **Paste** button			
Copy (replicate) formulae mouse	Select cell with formula to be copied Drag the mouse from bottom right corner of cell over cells to copy to, release			
Currency symbols		Click: the **Currency** button for UK currency		**Format**, **Cells**, **Number**, **Category**, **Currency**, select: symbol to use
Date, adding	From the **View** menu, select: **Header and Footer** Click: **Custom Header** Click: where you want the date to appear Click: the **Date** button			
Date, formatting			**Format cells**, **Category**, **Date**, **Type**	**Format**, **Cells**, **Category**, **Date**, **Type**
Decimal places		Click: the **Increase Decimal** button to increase the number of decimal places Click: the **Decrease Decimal** to decrease the number of decimal places	**Format Cells** Select the **Number** tab Click: **Number** in the **Category:** menu Select the number of decimal places you need	**Format**, **Cells**
Enter text	Click: in the cell where you want text to appear Key in: the text Press: **Enter**			
Enter numeric data	Click: in the cell where you want text to appear Key in: the data Press: **Enter**			
Enter formulae	Click: in the cell where you want text to appear Key in: = followed by the formula Press: **Enter**			
Exit the program		Click: the **Close Window** icon		**File**, **Exit**
Find and Replace				**Edit**, **Replace**
Fit to page				**File**, **Page Setup**, **Fit to (1) Page**

Action	Keyboard	Mouse	Right-mouse menu	Menu
Formulae, functions	Click on: the cell where the result is required Use: **=SUM(cell ref:cell ref)** for adding a range of cells or Click: **Σ** **AutoSum** button Click and drag over the cell range Press: **Enter**			
	Use: **=AVERAGE(cell ref:cell ref)** to find the average value in a range of cells			
	Use: **=COUNT(cell ref:cell ref)** to count the number of cells in range			
	Use: **=LOOKUP(cell that holds the compare value, range)** to find the cell that contains the value specified			
	Use: **=IF(test,"value if true", "value if false")** to return a value for the given test			
Formulae, operators	+ add - subtract * multiply / divide			
Formulae, showing	**Ctrl + `**			**Tools**, **Options**, **View** Under **Window options**, select **Formulas** so that a tick appears
Formulae, printing	Ensure the formulae are showing			
				File, **Page Setup**, **Page** tab, **Landscape** or **File**, **Page Setup**, **Page** tab Under **Scaling**, select **Fit to 1 page wide** and **1 page tall**
Help	**F1**			**Help** **Microsoft Excel Help**
	Shift + F1			**Help, What's This?**
Hide columns	**Ctrl + 0**		**Hide**	**Format, Column, Hide**
Hide rows			**Hide**	**Format, Row, Hide**
Import/insert objects				**Insert, Object**
Integers (whole numbers)		Click: the ⁰⁰/₊₀ **Decrease Decimal** button until you have reduced the number of decimal places to zero	**Format Cells**	**Format, Cells** Select the **Number** tab Click: **Number** in the **Category** menu Change the number of decimal places to zero

Action	Keyboard	Mouse	Right-mouse menu	Menu
Moving around	Use the cursor keys	Click where you want to move to		
Move to top of document	**Ctrl + Home**			
Move to end of document	**Ctrl + End**			
Naming cells	From the **Insert** menu, select: **Name**, **Define** Key in: the name Click: **OK**			
New file	**Ctrl + N**	Click: the 🗋 **New** button		**File**, **New**
Open an existing file	**Ctrl + O**	Click: the 📂 **Open** button		**File**, **Open**
	Select: the drive required Select: the filename Click: **Open**			
Page number, adding	From the **View** menu, select: **Header and Footer** Click: **Custom Header** Click: where you want the page number to appear Click: the 🔢 **Page** button			
Page Setup	From the **File** menu, select: **Page Setup** Choose from **Margins**, **Paper Size**, **Paper Source**, **Layout**			
Percentages, numbers as		Click: the **%** **Percent Style** button		
Print file	**Ctrl + P** Select the options you need Press: Enter	Click: the 🖨 **Print** button		**File**, **Print** Select the options you need and click **OK**
Printing in Landscape	From the **File** menu, select: **Page Setup** Click: the **Page** tab Select: **Landscape** Click: **OK**			
Printing selected cells only	Select the cells to print			
	Ctrl + P			**File**, **Print**
	Select: **Selection** Click: OK			
Print preview		Click: the 🔍 **Print Preview** button		**File**, **Print Preview**
Remove text emphasis	Select text to be changed			
	Ctrl + B (remove bold) **Ctrl + I** (remove italics) **Ctrl + U** (remove underline)	Click: the appropriate button: **B** *I* U	**Format Cells**	**Format**, **Cells** Select the **Font** tab Click: **Regular** in the **Font Style:** menu

Action	Keyboard	Mouse	Right-mouse menu	Menu
Replicate (copy) formulae	Select: the cell with the formula to be copied Drag the mouse from the bottom right corner of the cell over the cells to copy to Release mouse			
Restore deleted input	**Ctrl + Z**	Click: the ↶ **Undo** button		**Edit**, **Undo**
Rows, adding	Select the row by clicking in the row ref box (at side of row) below the one where you want the new row to appear			
			Insert	**Insert**, **Rows**
Rows, deleting	Select the row by clicking in the row ref box (at side of row) below the one that you want to delete			
			Delete	**Edit**, **Delete**
Save	**Ctrl + S**	Click: the 💾 **Save** button		**File**, **Save**
	If you have not already saved the file you will be prompted to specify the directory and to name the file. If you have already done this, then Excel will automatically save it.			
Save using a different name or to a different directory				**File**, **Save As**
	Select the appropriate drive and change the filename if relevant. Click: **Save**			
Save file in a different file format	Save as above, select from **Save as type**			
Selecting cells Selecting non-adjacent cells Remove selection	Click and drag across cells Select the first cell(s), hold down **Ctrl** and click the others Click in any white space			
Sheets, adding changing				**Insert**, **Worksheet**
	Click on: appropriate sheet tab			
copying		Use **Copy** and **Paste** buttons	Right-click on: sheet tab. Select: **Move or Copy**. In the **Before sheet** section, select appropriate sheet. Ensure **Create a copy** is ticked. Click: **OK**	
deleting			Right-click on: Sheet tab. Select: **Delete**	
renaming			Right-click on: sheet tab. Select: **Rename**	

Action	Keyboard	Mouse	Right-mouse menu	Menu
Sorting data	Select cells in the range to sort			
		Click: the ⬇️ **Ascending** or the ⬆️ **Descending** button		
Spell check	Move cursor to top of document			
	F7	Click: the ✓ **Spelling** button		**Tools**, **Spelling**
Text formatting: Font, size, colour, italicise, embolden, orientation	Select cell(s) to format			
	Ctrl + B Embolden **Ctrl + I** Italicise **Ctrl + U** Underline	Click: the relevant toolbar button on the formatting toolbar	**Format Cells**, **Font** tab For orientation: **Alignment** tab	**Format**, **Cells**, **Font** tab For orientation: **Alignment** tab
Toolbar, modify				**View**, **Toolbars**, **Customize**
Undo	**Ctrl + Z**	Click: the ↶ **Undo** button		**Edit**, **Undo**
Unhide columns	Select the columns on either side of the hidden ones			
	Ctrl + Shift + 0		**Unhide**	**Format**, **Column**, **Unhide**
Unhide rows	Select the rows on either side of the hidden ones			
			Unhide	**Format**, **Row**, **Unhide**
Zoom		Click: the 100% ▾ **Zoom** button		**View**, **Zoom**

Excel charts quick reference guide

Action	Keyboard	Mouse	Right-mouse menu	Menu
Change graphical display	*To change the scale ratios:* With the graph on screen Select: the **Plot Area** Drag the corner handles inwards (to reduce the scale) and outwards (to increase the scale) To set upper and lower limits for Y (vertical) axis: With the graph on screen Double-click: the **Value Axis** In the **Format Axis** dialogue box: Click: the **Scale** tab Key in: the new values in the **Maximum** and **Minimum** boxes Click: **OK** To set intermediate values: With the graph on screen Double-click: the **Value Axis** In the **Format Axis** dialogue box: Click: the **Scale** tab Change the **Major** unit to the required value Click: **Close**			
Create a chart	Select the data to chart			
		Click: the ▮▮ **Chart Wizard** button		**I**nsert, **C**hart
	STEP 1 Select: the chart type Click: **Next** **STEP 2** Check that the source data is correct, if not change it Click: **Next** **STEP 3** Select: the **Titles** tab Key in the title Select: the **Legend** tab Click: in the **Show legend** box to add/remove tick as appropriate (For pie charts only) Select: the **Data Labels** tab Click: **Show label** if appropriate Click: **Next** **STEP 4** Click: **As new <u>s</u>heet** or **As <u>o</u>bject in** Key in: the chart name Click: **<u>F</u>inish**			
Delete a chart	Select the chart. Press: **Delete**			
Edit a chart			Right-click on: the chart. Select from options	
Move a chart	Select the chart. Use **Cut** and **Paste** buttons or Drag and drop to new location.			

Action	Keyboard	Mouse	Right-mouse menu	Menu
Print a chart	With the chart displayed on screen			
	Ctrl + P Ensure **Active sheet** is selected. Click: **OK**	Click: the 🖨 **Print** button (This will automatically print the sheet)		**File**, **Print** Ensure **Active sheet** is selected. Click: **OK**
Save a chart	**Ctrl + S**	Click: the 💾 **Save** button		**File**, **Save**
Sheets, changing	Click on: appropriate sheet tab			

Module 4 practice tasks

Basic practice tasks 1

You work for a temporary employment agency. Create a spreadsheet to calculate weekly payments for staff on the temporary register.

1   Create the following spreadsheet. Leave the cells that contain formula blank.

Name	Hourly rate	Weekend rate	Weekly hours	Weekend hours	Hourly rate total	Weekend total	Total pay
Rachel Simms	6.80	formula	18	12	formula	formula	formula
Gareth Philips	10.50	formula	22.5	8	formula	formula	formula
Jeanna Larouse	6.80	formula	30	2	formula	formula	formula
Mark Anthony	7.80	formula	21	2	formula	formula	formula
Philip Smith	5.80	formula	10	7	formula	formula	formula
Greg Moore	6.80	formula	17	5	formula	formula	formula
Jayne Temple	7.80	formula	30	0	formula	formula	formula
Sara Janes	10.50	formula	30	0	formula	formula	formula
Tom Batco	10.50	formula	25	3	formula	formula	formula

2   Save the spreadsheet as **your initials wages**.
3   Enter your name in the upper left corner of the spreadsheet.
4   Add a header with the text centred **Spreadsheet produced by (your name)**.
5   Create a formula to calculate the Weekend rate for each employee:

Weekend rate is 20% more than hourly rate

*Formula = 120/100*Hourly rate*

6   Create a formula to calculate Hourly rate total *Hourly rate * Weekly hours*.
7   Create a formula to calculate Weekend total *Weekend rate * Weekend hours*.
8   Create a formula to calculate Total pay for each employee.

Hourly rate total + Weekend total

9   Format all columns with monetary amounts to £ currency 2 decimal places.
10 Add a title row with the text **Temporary register payments** centred across the columns.
11 Embolden the title and change the font size so that it is 4 pts larger than the rest of the spreadsheet.
12 Add a row at the bottom with the heading **Total temp pay**.
13 Enter a formula in the Total Pay column to calculate Total temp pay. Use *SUM*.
14 Change the Name column width to 16.
15 Embolden the column headings.
16 Put a border around the whole table and between each cell.
17 Save the spreadsheet as **your initials wages1**.
18 Print with landscape orientation.

Advanced practice tasks 1

19 Create a column chart on the same sheet to show the Total pay for each employee.

20 Use the title **Employee Total Pay**.

21 Insert a new sheet in the same workbook with the name **Total Pay Bar**.

22 Copy the chart to the **Total Pay Bar** sheet.

23 Print the **Total Pay Bar** sheet only.

24 Delete the chart from the original sheet.

25 Save the spreadsheets and close the spreadsheet program.

Basic practice tasks 2

Create a spreadsheet to calculate currency exchanges.

1 Set up the following spreadsheet:

Your £ Buys			
No of pounds for exchange	10,190		
Country	Currency	Exchange rate	Exchange result
France (Franc)	FRF	10.47	formula
Germany (Deutsche Mark)	DEM	3.11	formula
Spain (Peseta)	ESP	276	formula
Italy (Lira)	ITL	3086	formula

2 Save the spreadsheet as **your initials Currency**.

3 In the Exchange result column, enter a formula to convert the currency (use an absolute cell reference for the pounds for conversion).

4 Format all figures in the Exchange result column to the appropriate currency format with two decimal places.

5 Centre the title **Your £ buys** across the spreadsheet.

6 Embolden all row headings and increase the font size of the headings by 2 pts.

7 Set the width of the Currency column to 10.

8 Insert a new row below the France row with the following data:
   Belgium (Franc), BEF, 64.26

9 Add a thin line at the top of the spreadsheet and a thick line under the bottom cells.

10 Sort in ascending order of Country.

11 Save the spreadsheet as **your initials Currency1** and print.

Advanced practice tasks 2

12 Create a new workbook with the filename: **Conversions**.

13 Copy the original worksheet to the new workbook.

14 Delete the Italy row.

15 Insert a footer with the text **Conversions by (your initials)** on the right.

16 Create an exploded pie chart on a new sheet in the **Conversions** workbook showing the Countries and Results of exchange.

17 Include a legend for the countries.

18 Title the chart **Exchange result on 10,190GBP**.

19 On the first sheet of the conversions workbook, insert a suitable ClipArt.

20 Resize the ClipArt so that it fits on one page with the data.

21 Save all documents and print both sheets in the **Conversions** file.

Note: This is only a practice test. Successful completion does not imply certification of the module by the ECDL Foundation.

Database

Section 1 Getting started

In this section you will practise and learn how to:

- open access
- save a database
- close a database
- use Help functions
- modify toolbars
- change viewing modes

- design and plan a database
- create a table
- enter data
- define a primary key
- set up an index
- modify table layout attributes
- add records
- modify field attributes.

1.1 Understanding Access basics

Access is a very powerful database program with numerous features. We will be using only those features necessary to create simple databases and to edit, sort, search and print them. As Access is quite complicated for the new user, we will start by creating and manipulating a very small database in order to concentrate on understanding the processes involved, without the difficulties involved in keying in lots of data. Different aspects of Access will be explained as and when we meet them.

Common database terms, which are general to all types of database applications, include:

File. A file is a collection of related records.

Record. Each collection of information for each item in a file is called a record.

Field. A record is divided into separate categories, known as fields. There are different types of field. The common ones are:

- *Alphabetic* (in Access called **TEXT**) fields. These contain text that is manipulated alphabetically.

- *Numeric* (in Access called **NUMBER**) fields. These recognise numbers and sort in ascending or descending numerical order. In Access **CURRENCY** and **DATE/TIME** fields can also be used as number fields where appropriate.

- *Alphanumeric* (in Access called **TEXT**) fields. These contain numbers and text that do not need to be sorted in number order, such as telephone numbers.

- An Access database file contains database objects. We will be using four database objects – **Tables**, **Queries**, **Reports** and **Forms**. We will meet all the above terms as we progress through this module.

Exercise 1

You organise the college's fitness centre events and need to set up a database of classes.

Set up a database file using the following field titles:

CLASS	**the name of the class**
DAY	**the day the class takes place**
ROOM	**the location of the class**
INSTRUCTOR	**the instructor's name**
NUMBER OF WEEKS	**the number of weeks the class runs**

Info

There are five fields in each record of this database file: four text fields – **CLASS**, **DAY**, **ROOM** and **INSTRUCTOR** – and one numeric field – **NUMBER OF WEEKS**.

Enter the details shown below:

CLASS	DAY	ROOM	INSTRUCTOR	NUMBER OF WEEKS
AEROBICS	MONDAY	HALL	KENNY	10
AEROBIKING	WEDNESDAY	GYM	SALLY	10
FIT AND FUNKY	THURSDAY	DANCE STUDIO	LYNNE	15
SYNC AND SWIM	WEDNESDAY	POOL	DUNCAN	5
POWER HOUR	FRIDAY	HALL	LARRY	10
BODY BLITZ	TUESDAY	DANCE STUDIO	LYNNE	20

Each row of data (above), excluding field headings, makes up one record. Therefore there will be six records in this database file.

Info

When entering data, you can use codes instead of the full entry. For example, in the **DAY** field, the codes **M**, **TU**, **W**, **TH** and **F** would be suitable codes for days of the week. This can save time and storage space. For simplicity we will create this database without codes.

1.2 Loading Access

Exercise 2

Load Access.

  Method

Load Access in the same way as loading other Office applications, this time selecting:

 from the **Start**, **Programs** menu *or* using the **Access**

shortcut icon if you have one.

The **Access** window appears.

Info

You will notice that there are many similarities with other Office application windows, for example: Title Bar, Menu Bar and Standard toolbar. Other toolbar buttons will be displayed automatically to reflect the current task as you work through different components of the database. It is worth examining the toolbar buttons as you work through the exercises so that you become acquainted with them. As in other Office applications, you can customise the toolbars to your own preferences by selecting **Toolbars** from the **View** menu. Similarly, help is accessed from the **Help** menu or by pressing **F1**.

1.3 Creating a new database

Method

On loading Access, a dialogue box also appears (see Figure 5.1).

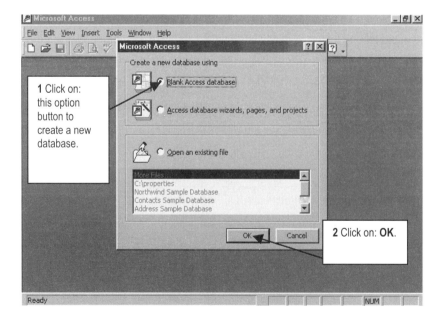

Figure 5.1 The Access window and opening dialogue box

1   Click on: the option button next to **Blank Access Database** in order to create a new one.

2   Click on: **OK**. The **File New Database** dialogue box is shown (see Figure 5.2).

Figure 5.2   The File New Database dialogue box

3   Choose where your file will be located and then key in the filename **SPORTS** (if saving to a floppy disk, remember to have the disk inserted in the drive).

4   Click on: **Create**. The **SPORTS: Database** window is shown (see Figure 5.3).

Figure 5.3   SPORTS Database window

1.4 Designing a table

 Method

1 The **Tables** button is selected by default (it looks as if it has been pressed in), if not, click it to select it.

2 Double-click on: **Create table in Design view** (see Figure 5.4).

Figure 5.4 Creating a table in Design view

The **Table** window in Design view is shown (see Figure 5.5).

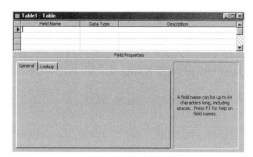

Figure 5.5 The Table window in Design view

 Exercise 3

Define the fields in the table.

 Method

1 In the **Field Name** column, with the **Caps Lock** on, key in the name of the first field, **CLASS** and press: **Enter** to move to the next column.

2 In the **Data Type** column, keep the default **Text** as this column will contain text entries – i.e. names of classes. Press: **Enter** to move to the next column.

3 In the **Description** column, you can type a description of the information this field will contain. This is optional, so leave it blank in this case and press: **Enter**.

Repeat steps 1 to 3 for the other fields except:

Choose Text as the Data Type for **DAY**, **ROOM** and **INSTRUCTOR**, but **NUMBER OF WEEKS** is a numeric field – i.e. it contains numbers – therefore choose **Number** as the Data Type. To do this:

In the Data Type column, next to the Field Name **NUMBER OF WEEKS**, click in the **Data Type** box, a down arrow appears. Click on: the down arrow and click on: **Number** (see Figure 5.6):

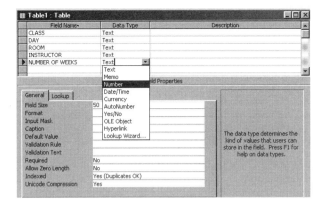

Figure 5.6 Changing the Data Type

Info

See the quick reference guide on page 229 for different data types.

The Field Properties can then be altered to choose the field size of the number that is required (see Figure 5.7).

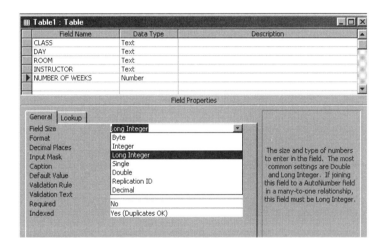

Figure 5.7 Setting Field Properties

1 Click in the box where **Long Integer** (the default) is displayed, a down arrow appears.

2 Click on: the down arrow to see the options available. The options we will use in this chapter are:

Long Integer (integer means a whole number – i.e. no decimal places).

Double (this allows decimal places).

In this case (as we do not require decimal places) we will leave the Field Size as **Long Integer**.

3 Click on: **Long Integer**.

The Table design should look like Figure 5.8.

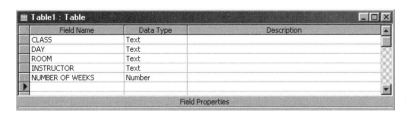

Figure 5.8 The Table design should look like this

Info

In the **Field Properties** section, the field size for text entries is set at 50 characters. This will accommodate most entries and can be left as it is. Should you be very short of storage space (this is unlikely in this instance), then you could save some space by reducing the field sizes as appropriate.

If you make a mistake when keying in, you can always go back and make corrections or use the **Undo** button.

Info

If you missed out a field, see Section 2 (page 197) or the quick reference guide (page 229) at the end of this module for the method to insert it.

1.5 Saving the table design

 Method

1 From the **File** menu, select: **Save As** (see Figure 5.9).

Figure 5.9 Saving a table

2 The **Save As** dialogue box appears (see Figure 5.10).
3 Key in the Table name: **CLASSES**.
4 Click on: **OK**.

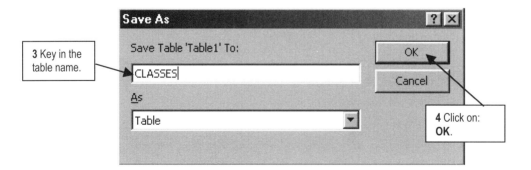

Figure 5.10 The Save As dialogue box

A message is displayed as shown in Figure 5.11:

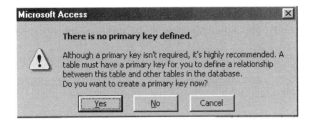

Figure 5.11 Primary Key message

5 Click on: **No.**

 Info

Primary keys and indexes

A Primary Key is not essential. It is a field that uniquely identifies each record in a table. Examples of this type of field would be car registration numbers or unique part numbers. In some databases, there is no field that can be guaranteed not to duplicate an entry. In such cases, at the Save stage, Access can create a Primary Key by setting up a field called ID and allocating a number to each record.

Setting a primary key on a specific field

In Table Design view, select the field you want for the primary key and then click on: the
⧉ **Primary Key** button. The primary key icon appears to the left of the chosen field as shown:

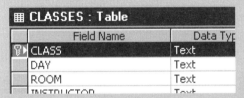

To change the Primary Key, follow the instructions above again, selecting the new field. Primary Keys speed up data retrieval and are useful when working with large databases or multiple databases.

Fields that have a primary key allocated are automatically indexed. With large databases, indexing fields that you often sort and search is another way of speeding up data retrieval. To set up an index:

1 With the table in Design View, position the cursor in the field that you want to index.

2 In the **Field Properties** section (below), and in the **Indexed** section, select: **Yes(Duplicates OK)** or **Yes(No Duplicates)**, depending on whether the indexed field entries are unique – e.g. car registration numbers set to **Yes(No Duplicates)**, surnames set to **Yes(Duplicates OK)**. Repeat with any other fields that you want to index.

3 Save the changes to the table design when prompted.

To delete an index:

In table Design view set the Indexed field property to **No**.

To view a list of indexed fields on an existing database:

With the table in Design View, click on: the ⧉ **Indexes** button.

To remove a Primary Key and not set a new one:

1 Click on: the ⧉ **Indexes** button. The **Indexes** dialogue box appears.

2 Select: **No** from the **Primary** menu.

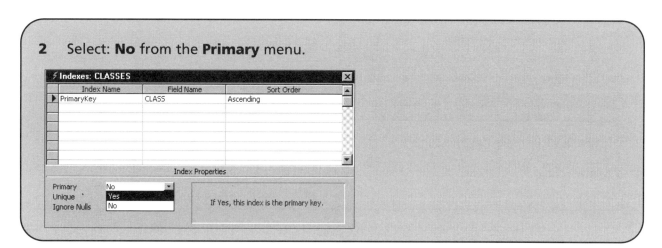

6 Close the database design window by clicking on the **Close** button (see Figure 5.12).

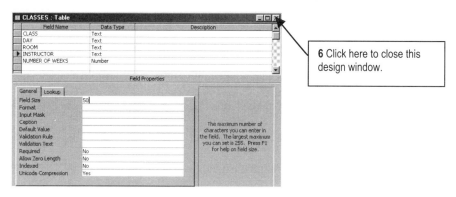

6 Click here to close this design window.

Figure 5.12 Closing the Design Window

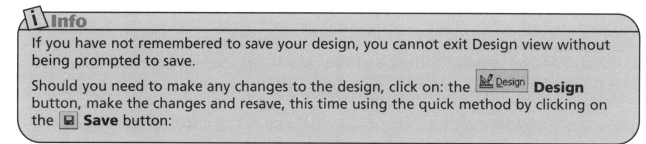

Info

If you have not remembered to save your design, you cannot exit Design view without being prompted to save.

Should you need to make any changes to the design, click on: the ☑ Design **Design** button, make the changes and resave, this time using the quick method by clicking on the 🔲 **Save** button:

7 You are returned to the **SPORTS: Database** window.

1.6 Entering data

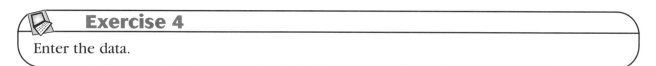

Exercise 4

Enter the data.

Method

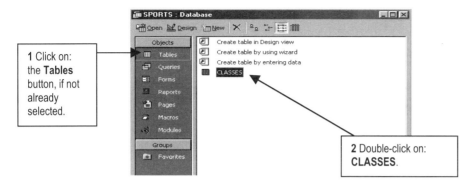

Figure 5.13 Opening a Table

3 The Table window appears (see Figure 5.14). The table is now displayed in Datasheet view so that you can enter and manipulate data.

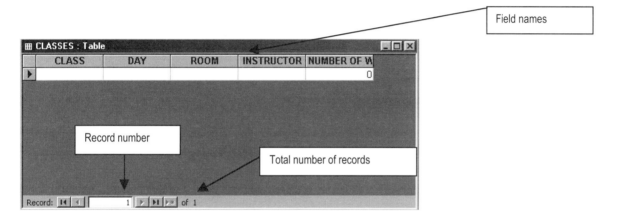

Figure 5.14 CLASSES table ready for data entry

4 As you can see, the **NUMBER OF WEEKS** field heading does not display in full. Widen this column by dragging the mouse, as shown in Figure 5.15:

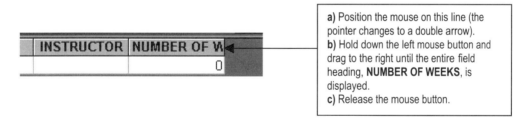

a) Position the mouse on this line (the pointer changes to a double arrow).
b) Hold down the left mouse button and drag to the right until the entire field heading, **NUMBER OF WEEKS**, is displayed.
c) Release the mouse button.

Figure 5.15 Widening columns

Note: To widen the column, you can also double-click where shown in Figure 5.15.

5 Key in the data in the appropriate fields as shown in Figure 5.16, pressing **Enter**, **Tab** or arrow keys to move from field to field.

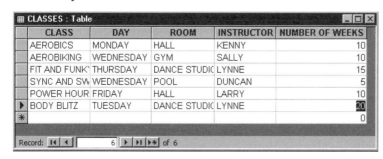

CLASS	DAY	ROOM	INSTRUCTOR	NUMBER OF WEEKS
AEROBICS	MONDAY	HALL	KENNY	10
AEROBIKING	WEDNESDAY	GYM	SALLY	10
FIT AND FUNK	THURSDAY	DANCE STUDIC	LYNNE	15
SYNC AND SW	WEDNESDAY	POOL	DUNCAN	5
POWER HOUR	FRIDAY	HALL	LARRY	10
BODY BLITZ	TUESDAY	DANCE STUDIC	LYNNE	20
				0

Figure 5.16 Data has been keyed in

6 You can see that **FIT AND FUNKY**, **SYNC AND SWIM** and **DANCE STUDIO** are too long to fit in the **CLASS** and **ROOM** field columns. Widen these columns as shown in Figure 5.15.

7 Proofread on screen against copy.

8 Correct any errors by clicking to position the cursor on the error, then correcting as necessary.

1.7 Saving data and closing the table

 Exercise 5

Save the data and close the table.

 Method

1 Click on: the **Close** button at the top right of the Table window.

2 The data is saved automatically.

3 If you have made any layout changes, you will be asked if you want to save these, click on: **Yes**.

1.8 Saving the database file

 Exercise 6

Save the database file **SPORTS**.

 Method

From the **File** menu, select: **Close**.

 Info

The database file and its components are automatically saved together. Each individual part, such as the Table **CLASSES**, has been saved as we have progressed through the exercises. If any parts are not saved, you will be prompted to save before closing.

1.9 Exiting Access

 Exercise 7

Exit Access.

 Method

From the **File** menu, select: **Exit**.

Section 1 Database practice

Practice 1

1 Start up Access.

2 Set up the following database with the filename: **Solicitor**.

3 Save the table as: **Clients**.

Note: The **TIME** and **PREVIOUS VISITS** should be numeric fields. Use **Date/Time** for the **TIME** field data type and **Field Properties** format: **Short Time**. For more information on **Data Types**, see the quick reference guide (page 229) at the end of the module.

ℹ️ Info

To repeat data as in the **SOLICITOR** field:

1 Key in the solicitor's name.
2 Select the name by double-clicking on it.
3 Click on: the **Copy** button.
4 Move to the cell you want to copy.
5 Click on: the **Paste** button.
6 Move to the next cell to copy to.
7 Click on: the **Paste** button.
8 Repeat as appropriate.

SOLICITOR	CLIENT NAME	REF NO	DAY	TIME	PREVIOUS VISITS
PATEL	JONES L	J120	WED	09:30	6
PATEL	SMITH C	J561	TUE	12:00	10
PATEL	CLARKSON J	M124	SAT	16:00	4
PATEL	GRIGGS S	N6570	FRI	13:45	10
COLLINS	DENT J	C780	SAT	09:00	12
COLLINS	JENKINS Z	E120	WED	10:30	0
COLLINS	DENNIS M	L833	SAT	10:00	8
COLLINS	MOWHILL S	H777	FRI	17:45	12
McBRIDE	HARMAN D	G652	THU	11:00	12
McBRIDE	PETERS H	Y444	FRI	18:30	6
McBRIDE	CLARKE F	R567	SAT	09:30	0
McBRIDE	PAUL G	H800	SAT	11:00	6
McBRIDE	MULERO M	D437	WED	15:00	2
SIMPSON	ANDREWS C	G123	WED	10:00	6
SIMPSON	GOODYEAR K	H321	WED	11:00	6
SIMPSON	STEWART J	L909	SAT	12:00	10
SIMPSON	GREGORY A	F549	THU	16:00	10

4 Close the database file.

Practice 2

1 Start up Access.
2 Set up the following database file with the filename: **Bikes**.
3 Save the table as: **Stock**.

Note: The **PRICE** and **NO IN STOCK** should be numeric fields. Use **Currency** for the **PRICE** field data type: Field Properties Format: **Fixed**.

STORE	TYPE	MODEL	COLOUR	PRICE	NO IN STOCK
MILTON KEYNES	RACER	SPIRIT20	BLUE	359.99	10
MILTON KEYNES	RACER	SPEEDY18	GREEN	359.99	2
MILTON KEYNES	TRICYCLE	PIXIE5	YELLOW	60.50	6
MILTON KEYNES	RACER	SPIRIT18	RED	279.99	10
OLNEY	TANDEM	TWIN20	RED	399.00	1
OLNEY	MOUNTAIN	ROUGHTRACK1	BLUE	89.99	5
OLNEY	MOUNTAIN	ROUGHTRACK6	SILVER	129.99	6
OLNEY	TRICYCLE	PIXIE5	YELLOW	60.50	8
OLNEY	TRICYCLE	PIXIE10	RED	65.99	6
NEWPORT PAGNELL	RACER	SPEEDY18	SILVER	339.99	4
NEWPORT PAGNELL	TRICYCLE	PIXIE5	YELLOW	60.50	2
NEWPORT PAGNELL	MOUNTAIN	ROUGHTRACK1	BLUE	89.99	14
NEWPORT PAGNELL	RACER	SPIRIT18	BRONZE	279.99	2
CRANFIELD	RACER	SPIRIT20	BLACK	359.99	5
CRANFIELD	MOUNTAIN	ROUGHTRACK6	GREEN	129.99	6

4 Close the database file.

Section 2 Editing

In this section you will practise and learn how to:

- open an existing database
- print data in table format
- navigate through a table
- modify data
- delete data
- delete/insert records
- add/delete a field
- change field order.

2.1 Opening an existing database

 Exercise 1

Load Access and the database file **SPORTS** created in the previous section.

 Method

Load Access (see Section 1.2 – page 186). Follow the instructions in Figure 5.17.

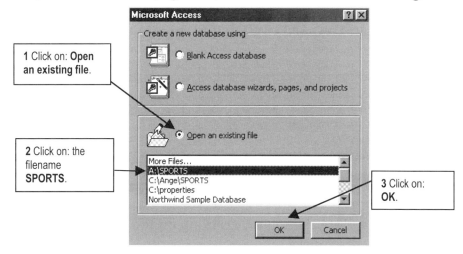

Figure 5.17 Opening an existing database file

Info

The most recently used files will appear in the box. If your file is not there, click on: **More Files** to locate your file.

2.2 Printing data in table format

 Exercise 2

Print the table **CLASSES**.

Method

1   Open the table **CLASSES**:

   In the Database window, ensure that the **Tables** tab is selected, if not select it.
   Double-click on: **Classes**.

2   From the **File** menu, select: **Print**.
3   The Print dialogue box appears; we do not need to change any settings.
4   Check that the printer is ready and loaded with paper.
5   Click on: **OK**.

 Info

The printout will automatically print the name of the database object (in this case the table name) and the date at the top of the page.

2.3 Editing data

 Exercise 3

Some errors have been found with the data entered:

AEROBICS, **MONDAY** should be in the **GYM** not the **HALL**.

The **NUMBER OF WEEKS** for **SYNC AND SWIM**, **WEDNESDAY** should be 6 not 5.

Make the necessary changes.

 Method

1   Open the table **CLASSES** if it is not already open.
2   Alter the data by positioning the cursor in the place where you want to alter data, delete the incorrect data using the **Delete** key or the ← Del (backspace) key and key in the correct data.
3   When all editing is complete, close the table by clicking on the **Close** button.

The changes will be saved automatically.

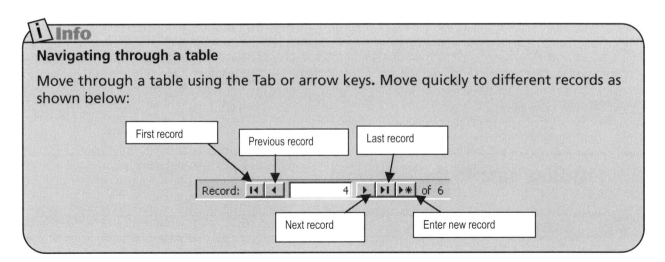

2.4 Deleting a record

Exercise 4

POWER HOUR on FRIDAY has been postponed. Delete all the details of this class from the database.

Method

1 Open the table **CLASSES** if it is not already open.
2 Click the row selection box to the far left of the record (see Figure 5.18).

Click in this box to select the record **POWER HOUR**.

	AEROBICS	MONDAY	GYM	KENNY	10
	AEROBIKING	WEDNESDAY	GYM	SALLY	10
▶	POWER HOUR	FRIDAY	HALL	LARRY	10
	FIT AND FUNKY	THURSDAY	DANCE STUDIO	LYNNE	15
	BODY BLITZ	TUESDAY	DANCE STUDIO	LYNNE	20
*					0

Figure 5.18 Selecting a record

3 An arrow appears in the box; the entire record is highlighted.
4 Right-click anywhere on the selection.
5 A pop-up menu appears (see Figure 5.19).

▶* New Record
✗ Delete Record

✂ Cut
▣ Copy
▣ Paste

↕▯ Row Height...

Figure 5.19 Pop-up menu

6 Select: **Delete Record**.
7 You will be asked to confirm that you want to delete this record, click on: **Yes**.

2.5 Adding a record

Exercise 5

A new class is to be started. The class name is **TONE AND TRIM**, it is to be on **FRIDAY** in the **GYM**, the instructor is **LYNNE** and it will run for **20** weeks. Add this record to the file.

Method

1 Open the table if it is not already open.
2 Move the cursor to the last (empty) row (see Figure 5.20).

Move the cursor here.

	FIT AND FUNKY	THURSDAY	DANC
	BODY BLITZ	TUESDAY	DANC
▶*			

Figure 5.20 Adding a record

3 Key in the data in the appropriate fields, pressing **Enter** or **Tab** after each entry.
4 Proofread on screen.
5 Close the table by clicking on the **Close** button of the Table window. Data is saved automatically.

2.6 Adding a field

 Exercise 6

Add the field **MEMBER** to the database between the **ROOM** and **INSTRUCTOR** fields. Use the Yes/No data type with Yes = must be a member of the fitness centre and No = does not need to be a member, as follows:

AEROBICS	No
AEROBIKING	Yes
FIT AND FUNKY	No
SYNC AND SWIM	No
BODY BLITZ	No
TONE AND TRIM	Yes

 Method

1 Open the table.
2 Change to Design view by clicking on the **View** button.
3 Position the cursor in the field below where you want to insert the new field – i.e. in the **INSTRUCTOR** field.
4 Click on: the ⭲ **Insert Rows** button.
5 Key in the new field name: **MEMBER**.
6 Set the Data Type to **Yes/No**.
7 Set the Field Properties format to **Yes/No**.
8 Save changes to the table design.
9 Enter the data in Datasheet view; clicking in the box for Yes, leaving the box empty for No.

i Info

To delete a field

1 In Design view, position the cursor in the field to delete.
2 Click on: the ⭲ **Delete Rows** button.
3 You will be asked to confirm the delete.
4 Click on: **Yes**.

2.7 Changing field order

 Exercise 7

Rearrange the fields so that the **DAY** field is positioned after the **ROOM** field.

Method

1 With the table in Design view, click in the selection box of the title of the field to move – i.e. DAY.
2 Click in the selection box again (an arrow and dotted box appears). Using the mouse drag the field to the new location.
3 Save the changes to the table.

2.8 Print the table on A4 paper.

 Info

You will need to change to landscape to display all the fields on one page. Use **Print Preview** and **Page Setup**, **Page tab**.

2.9 Close the database file and exit Access.

Section 2 Database practice

Practice 3

1 Start up Access and reload the database file **Solicitor**, saved in section 1.
2 Print out the complete file in table format.
3 Change the following records:

The appointment for Miss S Griggs to see Mr Patel should be on Saturday not Friday. The appointment time of Miss McBride's client Dr M Mulero should be at 16.00 not 15.00.

4 Mr M Dennis who was to see Mrs Collins has cancelled. Delete his details.
5 Add the following new client for Mr Patel. His name is Mr S Samuel and he has booked an appointment for Saturday at 10 am. His reference number is D321.
6 Save the file.
7 Add a new field to the database TITLE. Enter the clients' titles as follows:

CLIENT NAME	TITLE
JONES L	MISS
SMITH C	MRS
CLARKSON J	MS
GRIGGS S	MISS
DENT J	MR
JENKINS Z	MR
MOWHILL S	DR
HARMAN D	MISS
PETERS H	MS
CLARKE F	MR
PAUL G	MR
MULERO M	DR
ANDREWS C	MR
GOODYEAR K	MS
STEWART J	MR
GREGORY A	MISS
SAMUEL S	MR

8 Change the order of the fields so that the REF NO field is before the CLIENT NAME.
9 Save and print the table.
10 Close the database file.

Practice 4

1 Reload the database file **Bikes**, saved in section 1.
2 Print out the complete file in table format.
3 Change the following records:

The racer, Speedy18 bike at the Newport Pagnell store should be blue not silver.
The number of mountain, Roughtrack1s in the Newport Pagnell store should be 10 not 14.

4 Delete the red tandem, Twin20 at the Olney store.
5 Add two mountain bikes, Roughtrack3, bronze to the Cranfield store. The price is 99.99 each.
6 Save the file.
7 Add a new field to the database SALE PRICE. Enter all prices over £300 down by £30 – i.e. 359.99 becomes 329.99, all prices over £200 but less than £300 down by £20 and all other prices down by £10.
8 Change the field order so that the COLOUR field comes before the TYPE field.
9 Save and print the table.
10 Close the file.

Section 3 Sorting and searching

In this section you will practise and learn how to:

- find a record on given criteria
- create a simple query
- create a query with multiple criteria
- save a query
- add/remove filters
- add fields to a query/remove fields from a query
- select and sort data based on given criteria
- select and sort data based on common logical operators.

3.1 Sorting data

Exercise 1

Sort the database file **SPORTS**, saved in section 2, into alphabetical order of **CLASS**.

Info

There are three main methods to sort the database. Use the toolbar button method when you do not need to save the sort. Use the filter or the query method when you want to save the sort and not overwrite any other sort.

What is filtering?

Once you have stored information in your database, you will want to sort and question the database to obtain information in different forms. When you want to see a subset of the records in a table or you want to sort the table and save it (or do all of these) you can use filtering.

What is a query?

A query is a more sophisticated method of sorting and searching a database. It has advantages over a filter as it can:

enable you to select only certain fields to be displayed

be used when a table is closed

calculate sums, averages and other types of totals.

3.2 Sorting using the Sort buttons

 Method

1 Reload the saved file **SPORTS** so that the **SPORTS: Database** window is displayed.
2 Open the table **CLASSES** in Datasheet view.
3 Click on: the Field Name **CLASS** at the top of the field column so that the column is selected.
4 Click on: the [↓] **Sort Ascending** button.

Info

Use the **Sort Descending** button to sort in descending alphabetical/numerical order.

3.3 Sorting using a filter

Exercise 2

Sort the database file into descending numerical order of **NUMBER OF WEEKS** and ascending order of **INSRUCTOR**.

Info

Using the filtering method allows you to sort more than one field. This is called a multiple criteria sort as opposed to sorting on a single criterion, as in Exercise 1.

 Method

1 With the table **CLASSES** displayed in Datasheet view, position the cursor in the **NUMBER OF WEEKS** field.
2 From the **Records** menu, select: **Filter**, **Advanced Filter/Sort** (see Figure 5.21).

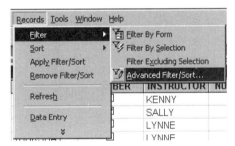

Figure 5.21 Applying a filter

3 The **Filter** dialogue box appears (see Figure 5.22). Click in the first Field column box, click on: the down arrow, and click on: **NUMBER OF WEEKS**.
4 Click the **Sort** box, click on: the down arrow and click on: **Descending**.
5 Click the second field column box, click on: the down arrow and click on: **INSTRUCTOR**.
6 In the **Sort** box, click on: the down arrow and click on: **Ascending**.
7 From the **File** menu, select **Save As Query** and key in the query name **Weeks des and Instructor asc**.
8 Click on: **OK**.

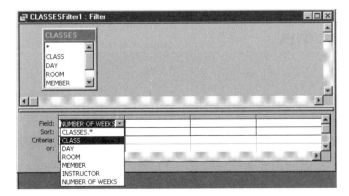

Figure 5.22 The Filter dialogue box

The table is unchanged by the filtering. The filtering result saves as a query. See the next section for more information on queries.

9 To view the result of the filtering, click on: the **Queries** button in the **SPORTS: Database** window.

10 Double-click on: the query name.

3.4 Printing a query

 Exercise 3

Print the query saved as **Weeks des and Instructor asc**.

 Method

1 In the **SPORTS: Database** window, click on: the **Queries** button.

2 Right-click on: **Weeks des and Instructor asc**.

3 From the pop-up menu, select: **Print** or **Print Preview**, then **Page Setup** from the **File** menu to change to landscape if necessary. Check that the printer is ready and loaded with paper.

4 Click on: **OK**.

3.5 Sorting in a query

 Exercise 4

Sort the database file into alphabetical order of **DAY** and print the file.

 Method

1 Reload the saved file **SPORTS** so that the **SPORTS: Database** window is displayed.

2 Click on: the **Queries** button (see Figure 5.23).

3 Double-click on: **Create query in Design view**.

Figure 5.23 Creating a Query

4 The **Show Table** dialogue box appears (see Figure 5.24).

5 Click on: **Add**, then on **Close**.

Figure 5.24 Show Table dialogue box

6 The Query – Design view window is displayed (see Figure 5.25).

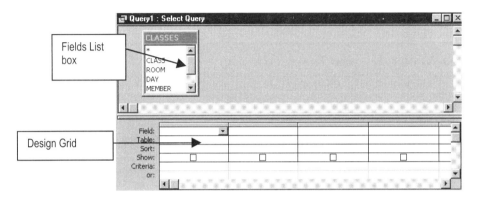

Figure 5.25 Query Design

7 The fields of the **CLASSES** table are displayed in a Fields List box. Place the fields in the Design Grid as follows:

a) in the Design Grid, click in the first field column
b) click on: the down arrow
c) click on: the name of the field that you want to appear – i.e. **CLASS**
d) click in the next field column, click on: the down arrow – i.e. **ROOM**
f) repeat steps (d) to (e) until all of the fields are on the grid.

Info

There are other ways to place the fields in the Design grid:

a) Double-click on: the field name that you want in the Design Grid.
b) Drag the field name onto the Design Grid.

8 In the field **DAY** column, click in the **Sort** row, then click on: the down arrow, then on **Ascending** (see Figure 5.26).

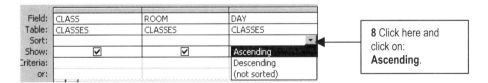

Figure 5.26 Sorting into Ascending order

9 To save the query, from the **File** menu, select **Save As**. Replace the default name **Query1** by deleting it and keying in the query name **Day ascending**. Click on: **OK**.
10 Return to the **Sports: Database** window.

11 View the results of the query as in Section 3.3 (page 204).

12 Print the query.

13 Click on: the **Close** button in the top right-hand corner of this window to return to the **SPORTS: Database** window.

 Exercise 5

Search the file for all classes taking place in the **GYM**.

3.6 Finding records specified by a single criterion

3.7 Finding data using Find

1 With the table displayed in Datasheet view, position the cursor in the field that you want to search on – i.e. **ROOM**.

2 Click on: the 🔍 **Find** button. The **Find and Replace** dialogue box appears (see Figure 5.27).

3 In the **Find What** box key in the data you want to find – i.e. **GYM**.

4 In the **Look In** box, select: **ROOM** (ROOM will already be selected if you positioned the cursor in this field at step 1).

5 Click on: **Find Next**.

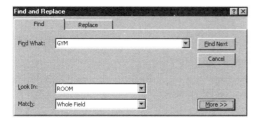

Figure 5.27 Find and Replace dialogue box

6 Access will find each record in turn.

7 When you have finished searching, close the dialogue box by clicking on the **Close** button or on **Cancel**.

ⓘ Info

Refining finds

*Using **Match***

Any Part of Field: This finds any data with **GYM** in it – e.g. **GYM**NASIUM, SPORTS **GYM**.

Whole Field: This finds only **GYM** not **GYMNASIUM** or **SPORTS GYM**.

Start of Field: This finds data with **GYM** at the beginning – e.g. **GYMNASIUM** but not **SPORTS GYM**.

Clicking on **More** in the **Find and Replace** dialogue box allows further refinements as shown:

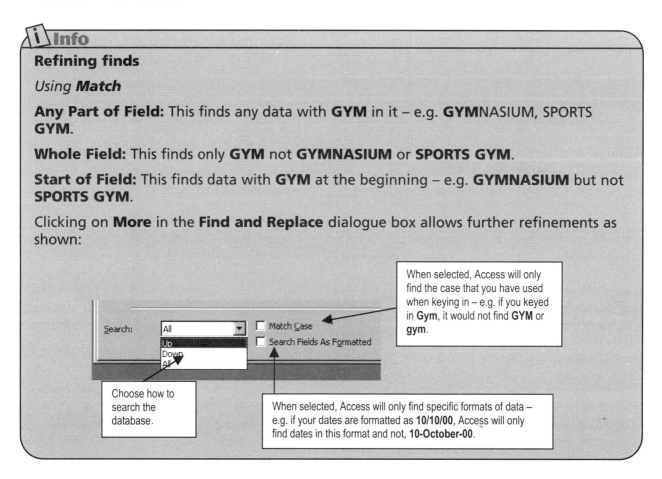

3.8 Finding data using a filter

 Method 1

1 With the table displayed in Datasheet view, position the cursor in a cell containing the data you want to find – i.e. **GYM**.

2 Click on: the 🔽 **Filter** button.

3 All the records with **GYM** are displayed.

Info

You can refine your search further by selecting another data entry – e.g. all classes in the GYM lasting 10 weeks. With the filtered **GYM** records displayed, repeat steps 1 and 2, this time positioning the cursor in a cell containing 10.

You can also select any part of a data entry – e.g. if you wanted to find all records beginning with the letter G, select only the G and run the filter.

Note: If you are filtering a Yes/No field, you will change the data when you click in the cell containing it. To overcome this, click it twice so that it keeps its original setting before filtering.

4 To remove the filter, click on: the ⧩ **Remove Filter** button.

Note: You cannot save the filter as a query using this method.

Method 2

1 With the table displayed in Datasheet view, from the **Records** menu select: **Filter**, **Advanced Filter/Sort** (see Figure 5.28).

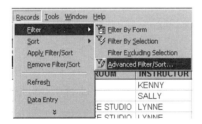

Figure 5.28 Adding a filter

2 The Filter box dialogue appears (see Figure 5.29):

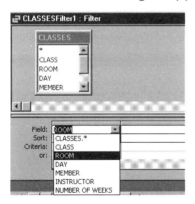

Figure 5.29 The Filter dialogue box

3 Select the field that contains the data you want to find – i.e. **ROOM** by clicking on the arrow in the **Field** row.
4 In the **Criteria** row, key in **GYM**.
5 Click on: the 💾 **Save As Query** button to save the filter as a query, named **GYM**.
6 Close the filter and table.
7 View the results of the filter by clicking on the **Queries** button and double-clicking on the query name.

3.9 Finding data using a query

 Method

Follow steps 1 – 7 in 3.5.

8 In the field **ROOM** column and the **Criteria** row, key in **GYM** and press: **Enter** (see Figure 5.30).

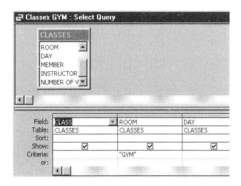

Figure 5.30 Selecting criteria

9 View the results of the query.
10 Save the query with the filename **Classes GYM**.
11 Print as in Section 3.4 (page 205).

3.10 Selecting records specified by more than one criterion

 Exercise 6

Using the query method, find all the records for classes taking place in the **GYM** lasting **less than 15 weeks**. Print details of the selected records and show all fields.

Method

1 In the **SPORTS: Database** window, click on: the **Queries** tab, double-click on: the query **Classes GYM**, then on the **View** button to switch from Datasheet view to Design view.
2 In the field **NUMBER OF WEEKS** column and the **Criteria** row, key in **<15** and press: **Enter** (see Figure 5.31).

ROOM	DAY	MEMBER	INSTRUCTOR	NUMBER OF W
CLASSES	CLASSES	CLASSES	CLASSES	CLASSES
☑	☑	☑	☑	☑
"GYM"				<15

Figure 5.31 Selecting more than one criteria

3 Save the query as **Gym less than 15 weeks** and print.

3.11 Printing specified fields from selected sorted records

 Exercise 7

Find all the records with the instructor **LYNNE** lasting **more than 15 weeks**. Sort the records into alphabetical order of class. Print the details of only these records. Show only the information for **CLASS**, **DAY** and **NUMBER OF WEEKS** fields.

 Method

Follow Steps 1–7 in Section 3.5 (page 205).

8 In the field **INSTRUCTOR** column and **Criteria** row, key in **LYNNE** and press: **Enter**.

9 In the field **NUMBER OF WEEKS** column and **Criteria** row, key in **>15** and press: **Enter**.

10 In the **CLASS** field, **Sort** row, select **Ascending** (see Figure 5.32).

Field:	CLASS	ROOM	DAY	MEMBER	INSTRUCTOR	NUMBER OF WEEKS ▾
Table:	CLASSES	CLASSES	CLASSES	CLASSES	CLASSES	CLASSES
Sort:	Ascending					
Show:	☑	☑	☑	☑	☑	☑
Criteria:					"LYNNE"	>15
or:						

Figure 5.32 Selecting more than one criteria and sorting in the same query

11 To show only the **CLASS**, **DAY** and **NUMBER OF WEEKS** fields, in the **Show** row and **ROOM** field column, click the tick in the box. The tick will disappear. Repeat for the **MEMBER** and **INSTRUCTOR** fields. This leaves ticks in the **CLASS**, **DAY** and **NUMBER OF WEEKS** fields only (see Figure 5.33).

CLASS	ROOM	DAY	MEMBER	INSTRUCTOR	NUMBER OF WEEKS
CLASSES	CLASSES	CLASSES	CLASSES	CLASSES	CLASSES
Ascending					
☑	☐	☑	☐	☐	☑
				"LYNNE"	>15

Figure 5.33 Showing only certain fields

12 Save the query as **Lynne more than 15 weeks**.

13 Check the result in Datasheet view.

14 Print the query.

ⓘ Info

You will notice that only the fields with ticks will appear on the printout.

Remember – it is always a good idea to check that your query is showing the correct result, so always view it in Datasheet view before printing. If it is not showing what you think you have asked for, return to Design view by clicking the **View** button and checking the details you have entered.

You can sort and search within the same query.

Common errors

Misspelling the criteria so that the query does not find an exact match (this can also be due to a spelling error in the data in the database).

Making the criteria plural – i.e. **GYMS** instead of **GYM**. The query will not find **GYMS** as this is not what was entered in the database and therefore is not an exact match.

Leaving spaces where they should not be.

3.12 Close the database file and exit Access.

Section 3 Database practice

Practice 5

1 Reload the database file **Solicitor** saved in Section 2.
2 Sort the file into alphabetical order of client name and print all the details.
3 Sort the file into ascending numerical order of previous visits and print all details.
4 Search for all the clients whose appointment day is **Wednesday**. Print details of the selected records showing all fields.
5 Find all the records of clients whose appointments are **before 12.00** and have previously **visited fewer than 8 times**. Print only the information in the **Client Name** and **Time** fields.
6 Save and close the file.

Practice 6

1 Reload the database file **Bikes**, saved in Section 2.
2 Sort the file into alphabetical order of model and print.
3 Sort the file into descending numerical order of price and print all details.
4 Search for all the yellow bikes. Print details of the yellow bikes only.
5 Find all records of mountain bikes costing **more than £100.00** (at original prices). Print only the **Store**, **Colour Type** and **Model** fields.
6 Save and close the file.

Section 4 Reporting

In this section you will practise and learn how to:

- create reports
- present selected data in a particular sequence on screen and in reports
- modify a report
- create and customise headers and footers
- group data in a report-totals, sub-totals, etc.

4.1 Creating a report

Exercise 1

Open the database file **SPORTS** and create a report in table format based on the table **CLASSES** displaying all the records.

  Method 1

Using AutoReport

1 With the **SPORTS: Database** window displayed, click on: the **Reports** button.
2 Click on: the 🔲 **New** button.
3 In the **New Report** dialogue box, select **AutoReport: Tabular** and choose the table **CLASSES** from the drop-down list (see Figure 5.34).
4 Click on: **OK**.

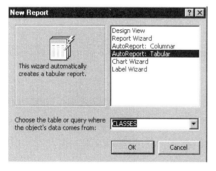

Figure 5.34 Creating an AutoReport

5 The report appears in Print Preview mode.
6 Save and print the report.

In this instance the report looks very good. Sometimes this is not the case and you will need to use the Report Wizard to create your report. Creating reports without the aid of the wizard is very advanced and time consuming.

  Method 2

Using the Report Wizard

1 With the **SPORTS: Database** window displayed, click on: the **Reports** button.

2 Double-click on: **Create report by using wizard** (see Figure 5.35).

Figure 5.35 Creating a report

3 The **Report Wizard** box appears (see Figure 5.36).

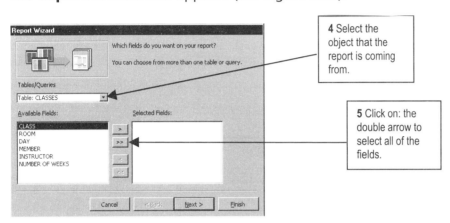

Figure 5.36 Report Wizard box

4 Choose the name of the object that the report's data is to come from, by clicking on the down arrow and then on the table **CLASSES**.

5 Choose all the fields by clicking on: the **>>** button, so the **Available Fields** move to the **Selected Fields** box (see Figure 5.36).

> **ℹ️ Info**
>
> It is not always necessary to show all fields on a report. If this is the case, select the field you want to include and click on the **>** button to move it to the **Selected Fields** box. Repeat as required. If you make a mistake and select the wrong fields, reverse the procedure by selecting and clicking on the **<** or **<<** button as appropriate. If you want to print the fields in a different order, select them individually and move them across using the **>** button in the order you want.

6 Click on **Next**.

7 The next **Report Wizard** box appears. If you need to group a report, select the groupings here. Let's select grouping by **INSTRUCTOR**, so select **INSTRUCTOR** in the left box and click on: the **>** button. Click on: **Next** (see Figure 5.37).

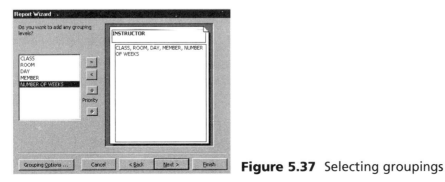

Figure 5.37 Selecting groupings

8 The next **Report Wizard** box appears. Let's sort in ascending order of **CLASS**. In box 1 click on: the down arrow, then click on: **CLASS** (see Figure 5.38). Ensure that the **A-Z** button is on A-Z. If not click on it to reverse it.

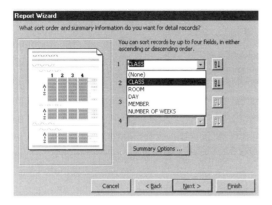

Figure 5.38 Selecting sort order

---

i Info

Sometimes it is better to ensure that the data has already been sorted in the object it has come from (e.g. a query), because if the sort order is chosen within Report Wizard, the wizard will automatically place the sorted field in the first column of your report. This will mean moving it to the position requested. In this case it does not apply since **CLASS** is the first database field.

---

9 Let's show a sum of the total number of weeks for each Instructor. To do this click on: **Summary Options** (see Figure 5.38).

10 In the **Summary Options** dialogue box (see Figure 5.39), click in the **NUMBER OF WEEKS** row and **Sum** column so that a tick appears. (This will show a sum total for each instructor and not just the overall sum total). In the **Show** section, select **Detail and Summary**.

11 Click on: **OK**, then on: **Next**.

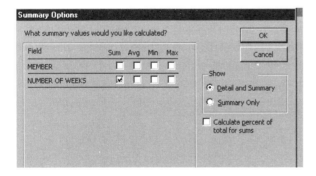

Figure 5.39 Summary Options dialogue box

12 The next **Report Wizard** box appears (see Figure 5.40). Use your discretion for the best **Layout** and **Orientation**. This report, because it is going to show all the fields, will be wide, therefore it is best suited to a landscape display. Click on: the **Landscape** option button. Ensure the **Adjust the Field widths** box is ticked.

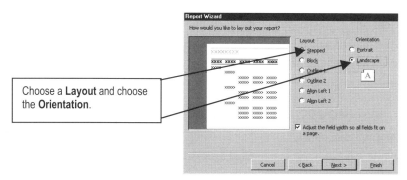

Choose a **Layout** and choose the **Orientation**.

Figure 5.40 Choosing Layout and Orientation

13 Click on: **Next**.

14 The next **Report Wizard** box appears (see Figure 5.41). Experiment with the styles. Each time you choose a style, example reports are displayed in the left box. **Corporate** is a good style because the layout is compact and the data will usually fit on one page.

15 Click on: **Next**.

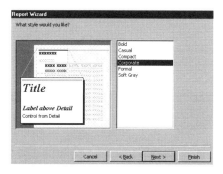

Figure 5.41 Choosing a style

16 The next **Report Wizard** appears (see Figure 5.42). Key in a report title.

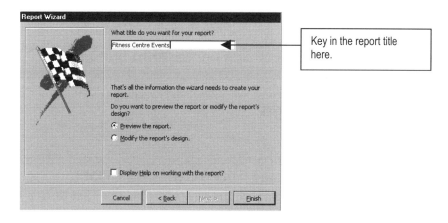

Key in the report title here.

Figure 5.42 Adding a title

Info

This may scroll out of view as you type. Do not worry. Always choose a descriptive title for your report. This will become the report name when it saves automatically.

17 Ensure that the **Preview the report** button is selected.

18 Click on: **Finish**.

19 Check the report (zoom in and out by clicking the mouse over it) to make sure that all details are displayed in full as requested. Access has a habit of cutting off the edges of some of the longer entries! This will not always happen. In this case, using the **Corporate** style, my report has displayed all of the entries.

20 You will notice that details of the calculations appear on the report (see Figure 5.43). Since these are distracting, we can delete them.

DUNCAN

SYNCHRONISED SWIMMING   POOL

Summary for 'INSTRUCTOR' = DUNCAN (1 detail record)

Sum

Figure 5.43 Details of calculations can be deleted

21 Click on: the **View** button to switch to Design view.
22 Delete the details of calculations by clicking on the box shown below (see Figure 5.44) so that it has handles. Press: **Delete**. Similarly delete **Sum** below.

♦ INSTRUCTOR Footer											
="Summary for " & "'INSTRUCTOR' =" & " " & [INSTRUCTOR] & " (" & Count(*) & " " & IIf(Count(*)=1,"de
Sum											

Figure 5.44 Select the detail to delete it

23 Review (using the View button) and save the report.

4.2 Printing a report

Exercise 2

Print the report including the field headings.

Method

From the **File** menu, select: **Print**, then click on: **OK** *or* click on: the **Print** button.

4.3 Further adjusting a report design

Exercise 3

In the Table **CLASSES**, in the **CLASS** field, change the entry **SYNC AND SWIM** to **SYNCHRONISED SWIMMING (BEGINNERS)**. Review the report created in Section 4.1 (page 214) and adjust as necessary.

Info

Making this entry longer has resulted in the report not displaying the entry in its entirety – i.e. it is not displaying **(BEGINNERS)**.

Method

1 Change the entry in Datasheet view. Then change to **Report Preview** of the report created in Section 4.1 (page 214). Click on: the **View** button.

2 **Report Design View** is now displayed (see Figure 5.45). The report is divided into panes:

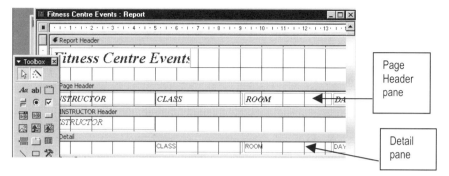

Figure 5.45 Report Design View

3 Using the scroll bars, ensure that the item that you want to alter is in view. In this case the item should already be visible – i.e. **CLASS** in the **Detail** pane.

4 Click on: the **CLASS** box to select it. Drag the handle to the right to widen the box so that it is wide enough to display all of the detail (see Figure 5.46). (You will have to make a guess as to how wide to make the box since the detail does not appear in Report Design view.)

Figure 5.46 Widening the CLASS field

5 Unfortunately the last action has obscured some of the **ROOM** Detail. Therefore we need to resize both the **ROOM** Detail and the **ROOM** Header (so that they line up). To do this, select the **ROOM** Header by clicking on it: drag the handle to the right (see Figure 5.47).

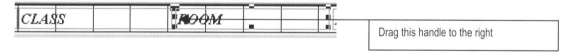

Figure 5.47 Resizing the ROOM field

6 Similarly resize the **ROOM** Detail.

7 Click on the **View** button (this has now changed to a Print Preview icon) to return to Report Preview.

8 From the **File** menu, select: **Save**, to save the report design. (This is necessary, even if your report is still not perfect, as failure to save at this point will result in losing the changes that you have already made.)

9 Check the Report Preview and continue to fine tune and save the design as above until you are happy with it.

10 Print the report.

4.4 Adding a header/footer

 Exercise 4

Add the header: **Report produced by (your name).**

Add the footer: **Report designed to show total hours for each instructor.**

 **Method**

1 From the **Toolbox**, select **Label** (see Figure 5.48).

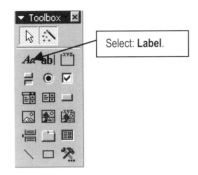

Select: **Label**.

Figure 5.48 The Toolbox

2 In the **Report Header** pane, click and drag out a text box.
3 With the text box selected, select the font, size etc and key in the header text.
4 Repeat for the footer text.
5 Save, preview and print the report.

Info

You can format any of the report text by clicking on it to select it and then formatting. To select more than one text box, hold down the **Shift** key. Resize the boxes as necessary or move them by pointing to a box border until a hand appears and then drag to the new position.

4.5 Close the database file and exit Access.

Section 4 Database practice

Practice 7

1 Reload the database file **Solicitor** saved in Section 3.
2 Produce a report as follows:

Display all of the records.
Group by Solicitor.
Sort in descending order of Client Name.
Title the report **Clients grouped by solicitor**.
Add a header with your name and current time of day in Arial, bold, 14 pt.

3 Print the report.
4 Change the report title to **Client appointments this week, grouped by solicitor**.
5 Save and print the report.
6 Close the database file.

Practice 8

1   Reload the database file **Bikes** saved in section 3
2   Produce a report as follows:

Include all fields except Colour.
Group the report by Store.
Add totals and sub-totals for the fields Price and Sale Price and No in Stock.
Sort the report into ascending order of Price.
Add a title **Store Stock (today's date)**
Add a footer containing the text: **Report produced by (your name)**

3   Save and print the report.

Section 5 Forms

In this section you will practise and learn how to:

- create a simple form
- enter data
- format text
- change background
- import an image or graphics file
- change arrangement of objects within a form layout.

5.1 What is a form?

 Info

Once you have created an Access database table you are able to view the data in Datasheet view. There are limitations in layout design in this view and so Access provides another way to view the same data so that you can see one complete record at a time, arranged to your liking, and this is called a Form. There are three ways to create a form:

Using Autoform

Using a Form Wizard

Manually

We will be using the first two methods as we work through this section.

5.2 Creating forms using AutoForm

 Exercise 1

Open the **SPORTS** database and create a form from the table **CLASSES**.

 Method

1 With the **SPORTS: Database** window open, click on: the **Forms** button in the **Objects** section.
2 Click on: the 　　 **New** button.
3 The **New Form** dialogue box appears (see Figure 5.49). Select: **AutoForm: Columnar** and choose the table **CLASSES**.
4 Click on: **OK**.

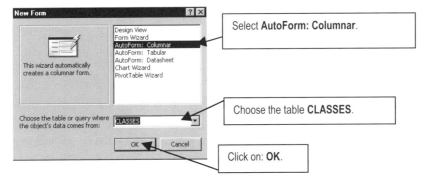

Figure 5.49 Creating a Form using AutoForm

The Autoform will appear as below (see Figure 5.50).

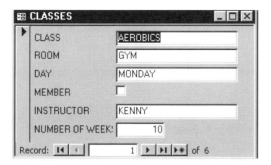

Figure 5.50 The table CLASSES in Form layout

Info

The first record of the database is displayed. To see the others, use the arrow buttons at the bottom as described in Section 2 (page 197). You can carry out all the procedures in a form that you can do in a table – i.e. edit, add, delete records, etc. When you make alterations in Form view, the contents of the table **CLASSES** will also be changed.

5.3 Creating forms using the Form Wizard

Exercise 2

Create a form based on the table **CLASSES** using the Form Wizard. Set out the form so that it is easy to read and attractive to look at.

 Method

1 With the **SPORTS**: **Database** window open, click on: the **Forms** button in the **Objects** section.
2 Double-click on: **Create form by using wizard**. A **Form Wizard** box appears (see Figure 5.51). Ensure that the table **CLASSES** is chosen. Move all the fields across to the Selected Fields section using the **>>** double arrow. Click on: **Next**.

Info

You can choose to show only some of the fields on a form.

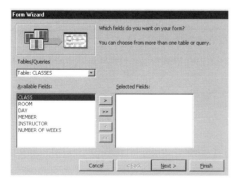

Figure 5.51 Form Wizard

3 The next **Form Wizard** box appears (see Figure 5.52). Select the layout you require (you are given a preview in the box to the left). In this instance select: **Columnar**. Click on: **Next**.

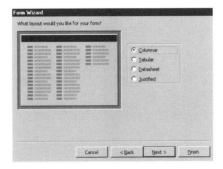

Figure 5.52 Choosing a layout

4 The next **Form Wizard** box appears (see Figure 5.53). Here you can choose a suitable style for your form. Examine the different styles. I will choose **Blends**. Click on: **Next**.

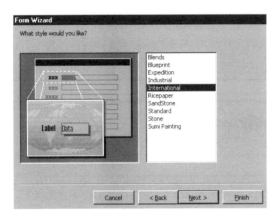

Figure 5.53 Choosing a style

5 The next **Form Wizard** box appears (see Figure 5.54). Give the form a suitable name – e.g. **FITNESS CLASSES** and click on: **Finish**.

Figure 5.54 Giving the form a title

6 The completed form appears on screen showing the first record.
7 Save the form using **Save As** from the **File** menu.

5.4 Entering and editing data in a form

 Exercise 3

Enter the following new record:

CLASS	ROOM	DAY	MEMBER	INSTRUCTOR	NO OF WEEKS
BADMINTON	SPORTS HALL	WEDNESDAY	YES	JANE	20

 Method

Click on: the **New Record** button and enter the data into the blank form, pressing: **Enter** after each field entry.

 Exercise 4

Delete the record for **BODY BLITZ**.

 Method

1 Find the **BODY BLITZ** record using the **Find** button.
2 Click on: the **Delete Record** button.
3 Click on: **Yes** to confirm the delete.

 Exercise 5

Sort the database into descending alphabetical order of **CLASS**.

 Method

This is done the same way as in Datasheet view. Use the **Sort descending** button.

 Info

You can also perform a multiple criteria sort as in datasheet view – i.e. from the **Records** menu, select: **Filter, Advanced Filter/Sort** and save it as a query.

Info

You can Filter by selection as in Datasheet view. The number of records found by the filtering is shown beside the navigation buttons. You can also use **Filter by Form** from the **Records** menu or by clicking in the **Filter by Form** button. In this case a blank form is displayed. Key in what you want to find, then click on: the **Apply Filter** button. Click on: the button again to remove the filter.

You can also perform an Advanced Filter and save it as a query as in Datasheet view.

5.5 Modifying a form

Info

You can change the appearance of a form in a similar way to changing a report's appearance. The exercises below will allow you to practise this.

 Exercise 6

Change the text in the form to a different font and enlarge it.

 Method

1 In the **SPORTS: Database** window, click on: the **Forms** button.
2 Click on: the form **FITNESS CLASSES** and click on: the 📐 Design **Design** button.
3 The form appears in Design view (see Figure 5.55).

Figure 5.55 Form in Design view and Toolbox

4 As with Report designing, select the boxes containing the text to alter, holding down **Shift**.
5 Format the text using the toolbar buttons.

 Exercise 7

Change the layout of the form so that the data is displayed in full – e.g. **SYNCHRONISED SWIMMING (BEGINNERS)** is not cropped. Enlarge and rearrange the form in any order you like.

 Method

Use the methods described for reports in Section 4 (page 214).

 Exercise 8

Change the background colours in the text boxes.

Method

With the form in Design view, select the objects to change. Right-click the mouse to view and select from a pop-up menu.

Practise changing other options. Save the form design when you are happy with it.

5.6 Import an image or graphics file

 Exercise 9

Import a suitable image or graphics file.

 Method

1 With the form in Design view, select: **Object** or **Picture** from the **Insert** menu.
2 Select what you want to insert.
3 When the graphic appears on the form, resize and reposition it as necessary, using the same methods as in report designing.

5.7 Change arrangement of objects within form layout

 Info

As with reports you can reposition objects within the form in Design view (see Section 4.3, page 218). Practise this now.

5.8 Print the file in form layout

 Method

1 Display the database form that you have just created.
2 Print in the normal way.

5.9 Close the file and exit Access.

Section 5 Database practice

Practice 9

1 Reload the database file **Solicitor** saved in section 4.
2 Create a simple form using the table **Clients**.
3 Change the text of the Field headings to Times New Roman, italic 18 pt.
4 Change the colour of the background in the Field headings boxes to green.
5 Import a suitable graphic image and position and resize it so that it fits in with the form design.
6 Enter the following new records:

SOLICITOR	CLIENT NAME	REF NO	DAY	TIME	PREVIOUS VISITS	TITLE
COLLINS	MUSGROVE D	B421	FRI	16.00	2	MR
PATEL	DANIELS Z	H555	TUE	10.00	0	MISS

7 Save the database and print the new records only in Form format.

8 Close the database file.

Practice 10

1 Reload the database file **Bikes** saved in section 4.

2 Create a simple form using the table **Stock**.

3 Change the text of the data to Arial, bold, 16pt.

4 Change the colour of the background in the data boxes to purple.

5 Import a suitable graphic image and position and resize it so that it fits in with the form design.

6 Enter the following new record:

STORE	COLOUR	TYPE	MODEL	PRICE	NO IN STOCK	SALE PRICE
CRANFIELD	APACHE	RACER	SPIRIT28	489.99	1	459.99

7 Save the database and print the new record only in Form format.

8 Close the database file.

Note: No answers are given for these exercises as the form designs will vary and the answers are obvious.

Access quick reference guide

Action	Keyboard	Mouse	Right-mouse menu	Menu
Close a database	**Ctrl + W**	Click: the ☒ **Close** icon on the database window		**F**ile, **C**lose
Close the Table window		Click: the ☒ **Close Window** icon		**F**ile, Save **A**s
Count records in a query	In the query Design grid, select the field to count			
		Click: the Σ **Totals** button	**T**otals	
	A Totals row appears. Click: the down arrow, select: **Count**			
Create a database	Load Access Click: **Blank Access Database**, **OK** Select: the location Enter: the filename Click: **Create** Click: **Tables** button. Double-click: **Create table in Design view** Enter the field names. These will all appear (by default) as text entries under Data Type			
Data Type, change	*(see separate table for Data Types)* Click: in the **Data Type** box next to the field name you wish to change Click: the arrow Click: the Data Type you require – e.g. Number Select the Field properties (see separate table for Field Properties) from the box below			
Primary key	If required, create a primary. Select the field for the primary key and click: the ⚷ **Primary Key** button			
	Close the Table window by clicking: the ☒ **Close** button of that window Save the table design			
Enter data	In the Database window, double-click: the table name Enter the data required in the correct fields. Widen the field columns as necessary. Close the Table window as before. The data is saved automatically.			
Edit data	Open the table (if it is not already open)			
	Click: in the entry you want to edit Delete/overwrite the old data Key in the new data			
Field, add	In Design View: Click in the field below where you want to insert a new field			
		Click: the ⌐ᴱ **Insert Rows** button	**Insert Rows**	**Insert**, **Rows**
	Add the field details. Resave the table design			
Field, delete	In Table Design View Select the field to be deleted by clicking to the left of it			

Action	Keyboard	Mouse	Right-mouse menu	Menu
	Delete	Click: the ⧉⧽ **Delete Rows** button	<u>D</u>elete Rows	<u>E</u>dit, Delete <u>R</u>ows
	Click: Yes			
Field order, change	With the table in Design view, click: the selection box of the field to move Click: the selection box again (an arrow and dotted box appears) Drag field to new location			
Filters, add/ remove	With the object displayed in Datasheet view			
	Select what you want to filter: Click: the ⧗⧸ **Filter** button *To remove filter:* Click the **Filter** button again		**Records**, **Filter**, **Advanced Filter/Sort**	
Find a record	With the Table displayed, position the cursor in the field you want to search.			
	Ctrl + F	Click: the 🔍 **Find** button		<u>E</u>dit, <u>F</u>ind
	In the **Fin<u>d</u> What** box, key in what you want to find Click: **Find <u>N</u>ext** Continue until all records have been found *Note:* You may need to choose a field that has a unique entry to ensure you find the correct record.			
Forms, create	With the database window open, click: the Forms button			
	Using Autoform Click: the ⧉New **New** button Select: **AutoForm: Columnar** Select object that the form is based on. Click: **OK** *Using the Wizard* Double-click: **Create form by using wizard** Follow the wizard's instructions			
Headers and footers in reports	From the **Toolbox**, select: **Label** In the Report header/footer section, click and drag out a box. Key in your text			
Index, set up	With the table in Design view, position the cursor in the field you want to index. In the **Field Properties**, **Indexed** section, make selection			
deleting	Set the **Indexed** field property to **No**			
Load Access	In the Windows 98 desktop			
		Double-click: the **Microsoft Access** shortcut icon		**Start**, **Programs**, **Microsoft Access**
Open a table In Datasheet view	In the Database window, make sure the **Tables** button is selected			
		Double-click: the table name Change to Design view by clicking: the 🔲 ⧸ **View** button		

Action	Keyboard	Mouse	Right-mouse menu	Menu
In Design view		Click: the table name Click: the ⊾ Design **Design** button		
Output a report *to Word*	Ensure you are in the **Report Preview** view			
		Click: the 🥈 **Publish It with MS Word** *OR* Click the ▾ next to the 🔀 **Analyze It with MS Excel** button and select **Publish It with MS Word**		<u>T</u>ools, Office Links, <u>P</u>ublish it with MS Word
to Excel		Click: the 🔀 **Analyze It with MS Excel button** *OR* Click the ▾ next to the 🥈 **Publish It with MS Word** button and select **Analyze It with Excel**		<u>T</u>ools, Office Links, <u>A</u>nalyze it with MS Excel
Print	Select the object you want to print.			
	Ctrl + P			<u>F</u>ile, <u>P</u>rint
	Make the necessary selections Choose Setup if you want to print Landscape Make the necessary selections from the <u>S</u>etup dialogue box Click: **OK, OK**			
Quick print		Click: the 🖨 button Access will automatically print the whole object.		
Record, add		Click: the ▶* **New Record** button *OR* Click: in the blank cell immediately after the last record	(Right-click to the left of any record) **Ne<u>w</u> Record**	**Insert, Ne<u>w</u> Record**
Record, delete	Select the record by clicking to the left of the first field of that record			
		Click: the 🗙 **Delete Record** button	**Delete Record**	**<u>E</u>dit, Delete <u>R</u>ecord**
	Click: **<u>Y</u>es** to save the change			
Replace field entries	**Ctrl + H**			**<u>E</u>dit, R<u>e</u>place**
Report, create	Ensure the Database window is displayed and that the Reports button is selected Double-click: **Create report by using wizard** In the Tables/Queries box, select: the name of the object – – e.g. query, table – that the report is to be generated from Click: **Next** Select the fields to include in the report using the >> or > buttons Click: **Next** (If you want to group the report – select the field(s) you want to group by here)			

Action	Keyboard	Mouse	Right-mouse menu	Menu
	Click: **Next** *Sorting (Preferably ensure that the original object is sorted. However, if you want to change the sort order here select the field you want to sort by. Note: this could rearrange field positions in the final report)* Click: **Summary Options** to include calculation results on the report Click: **Next** Select Layout Select the orientation you want – **Landscape or Portrait** Click: **Next** Select a style Click: **Next**. Key in: the report title Click: **Finish**			
Sort records (quick sort)	Open the Table if it is not already open. Select the field that you want to sort by clicking on the Field Name at the top of the field column			
ascending order		Click: the ⬆ **Sort Ascending** button	**Sort Ascending**	
descending order		Click the ⬇ **Sort Descending** button	**Sort Descending**	
Query, create in Design view	In the Database window ensure the **Queries** button is selected Double-click: **Create query in Design view** Select object query is based on Click: **Add**, **Close** The fields of the table are now displayed in a list box in the Query window. Place the fields that you want to see in your query in the field row of the query grid by double-clicking or dragging them. *Note:* Place the fields in the order that you want them to appear.			
Query, create a simple query using the wizard	In the database window, ensure the **Queries** button is selected Click: **Create query by using Wizard** Follow the wizard's instructions			
Query, sort	Click: in the Sort box of the appropriate field Click: the ⬇ arrow Select: **Ascending** or **Descending**.			
Specify criteria	Use the **Criteria** row in the grid to specify the conditions in a specific field – e.g. **RED** in the **Colour** field. (See *Working with Queries* section)			
Print specific fields	Use the **Show** row in the grid to choose whether or not to display a particular field in the query. A tick in the **Show** box means that the field will show, no tick means that it will not show. Click to toggle between them.			
Save a query	**Ctrl + S**	Click: the 🖫 **Save** button		**File**, Save **As**
	To see the results of your query			
		Change to Datasheet view or Click: the ❗ **Run** button		**Query**, **Run**

Important: Always close the database file properly.

DATA TYPE	PROPERTIES
Text (the default)	No need to set, unless requested or short of storage space.
Number	Field Size Long Integer is the default – this is OK for whole numbers. Double - for numbers with decimal places Format Choose **Fixed** for 2 decimal places to show (even if the last is a zero) Choose **Decimal Places** and enter the number required (Leave the Format blank for other numbers.)
Date/Time	Choose the most appropriate format for the task. (You can key in the date in any format and it will convert to the format you have set.)
Currency	Choose **Format Fixed** to display 2 decimal places with no commas or £ symbol.
Yes/No	No need to set
Memo	No need to set

Working with queries

When setting up queries, use the following as a guide. In the **Criteria** row you can enter any of the following:

> An exact match – e.g. SMITHSON

> The wildcard *

The * is a wildcard that stands for any number and type of character – e.g. if you were unsure how to spell the name you could enter **SM*THSON** or **SM*SON**. You can place the * wildcard before, after, and between characters and you can use it more than once in a single field – e.g. **SM*TH***.

The wildcard ?

The ? wildcard acts as a placeholder for one character – e.g. **SM?THSON**.

LIKE

This tells Access not to look for an exact match – e.g. **LIKE SMYTHSON**.

NOT

If you want to find all the records except **SMITHSON** you could enter **NOT SMITHSON**.

NULL

If you have records with no value in the field, you can type **NULL** to find these records, – e.g. you may be looking for all events that do not require a cake and the database design has allowed no value in the cake field if the event does not have a cake but a **YES** value if it does.

Mathematical operators

>	more than	>=	more than or equal to
<	less than	<=	less than or equal to
=	equal to	<>	not equal to

AND

You can use **AND** when you need restricted results – e.g. all events with a fee per guest of over £5.00 to under £10.00 – use:

> >5.00 and <10.00

Fields containing YES/NO data. If Yes the data will show as a ticked box.

Use **Yes** if you want to find the ticked box data and **No** if not.

Making a copy of a table

Sometimes it is useful to save your original table intact, follow the steps below:

1 With the table name selected in the Database window, click on: the **Copy** button.

2 Click on: the **Paste** button.

3 In the **Paste Table As** dialogue box, key in the new table name, ensure **Structure and Data** is selected.

4 Click on: **OK**.

You will now have two exact copies of the same table. Make amendments to one of them, leaving the other one intact.

Module 5 practice tasks

For this module you will need to have the following database file set up. Ask your supervisor or tutor to prepare it for you.

Preparation

Create the following database table. Save the database as **Lettings** and the table as **Properties**. Set Postcode as the primary key field.

Location	Postcode	Type	Beds	Garage	Garden	Rent £	Available
Elstow	BD41 5RW	House	3	Y	N	400	July
Bedford	BD23 1AS	Flat	1	N	N	600	June
Brickhill	MK54 3LP	House	2	Y	Y	550	June
Devonlly	MK29 7TD	Flat	2	N	Y	420	May
Goldington	BG31 8QT	House	5	Y	Y	875	August
Oakley	OS2 6RW	House	4	Y	Y	850	May
Rushden	NN14 8PT	House	2	Y	Y	500	June
Bodington	NN12 5RP	Flat	1	N	N	300	May
Carlton	MK44 9AS	House	3	Y	Y	1100	June
Harrold	MK49 4HX	Flat	2	Y	N	600	July

Practice tasks 1

Using the **Lettings** database and the table **Properties**:

1 Extract all records that have **3 bedrooms**. Save the query as **3 bedrooms** and print.
2 Extract all records that have **Locations beginning with B**. Save the query as **Location (B)** and print.
3 Extract all records of **properties without a garage**. Save the query as **No Garage** and print only the **Location**, **Rent** and **Availability** fields.
4 Using a query, count the records in the database on the **Location** field.
5 Using a text editor, enter the answer to 4 and save the file as **Count**.
6 Sort the database into alphabetical order of **Type** and **Beds**.
7 Add an additional record to the database (make it up).
8 In design view, format the **Rent(£)** field to two decimal places.
9 Save and print the table.
10 Create a report titled **Types of Rental Property** showing the fields **Location**, **Type**, **Rent** and **Available**. Group by **Type**.
11 Add a header to the report with **Your name**.
12 Save and print the report.

Practice tasks 2

The task is to create a database of CDs.

1 Create a database table in design view with 6 fields. Use appropriate data types, distinguishing between text, date etc with the field sizes shown.

Title (40), Artist (25), Release date, Category (15), Cost, Top 40 (Y/N)

2 Save the database as **Compact Disks** and the table as **CD**.
3 Create six records for any CDs (real or not) of your choice.
4 Sort the database in descending order of **Artist**.
5 Set the **Release** date field to **Long** date format.
6 Save and print the table.
7 Add a field **Label (20)** in between **Release date** and **Category**. Enter suitable label data.
8 Sort in alphabetical order of **Title**.
9 Save and print.

Note: There is no worked example of this task as versions will vary considerably.

___

Note: This is only a practice test. Successful completion does not imply certification of the module by the ECDL Foundation.

Presentation

Section 1 Getting started

In this section you will practise and learn how to:

- open PowerPoint
- use application Help functions
- close PowerPoint
- create a new presentation
- choose an appropriate automatic slide layout
- modify slide layout
- add text
- close document
- save presentation
- modify toolbar display
- use page view/zoom
- change display modes
- add an image, resize and move an image

- resize and move an image in a slide
- format font: italics, bold, underline, case, apply shadow, sub/superscript, apply colours
- align text: centre, left, right, top, bottom
- adjust line spacing
- change type of bullets
- resize and move text within a slide
- set line weights, style and colours in a text box
- use spellcheck
- preview: slide, outline, slide sorter, notes view
- print slides in various views
- select appropriate output.

1.1 Understanding PowerPoint basics

PowerPoint enables you to create, organise and design effective presentations. These can be used as handouts, overhead transparencies, 35 mm slides and automated presentations on a computer.

1.2 Loading PowerPoint

 Exercise 1

Load PowerPoint.

 **Method**

From the **Start** menu, select: **Programs**, **Microsoft PowerPoint** or double-click on: the
PowerPoint shortcut icon if you have one. Either method results in the **PowerPoint**
window being displayed on screen (see Figure 6.1).

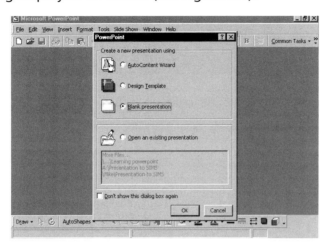

Figure 6.1 PowerPoint's opening window

1.3 Creating a new presentation

 Exercise 2

Create slide 1.

Note: PowerPoint uses the word slide for each page created, even for the production of
paper printouts or overhead transparencies.

 Method

1 Click on: **Blank presentation** and **OK**. The **New Slide** dialogue box appears (see Figure
6.2).

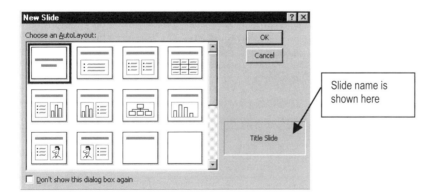

Figure 6.2 New Slide dialogue box

2 There are many different autolayouts to choose. In this case click the slide autolayout at
the top left – **Title Slide** (it may already be chosen). Click on: **OK**.
3 This first slide is displayed in **Normal View** (see Figure 6.3).

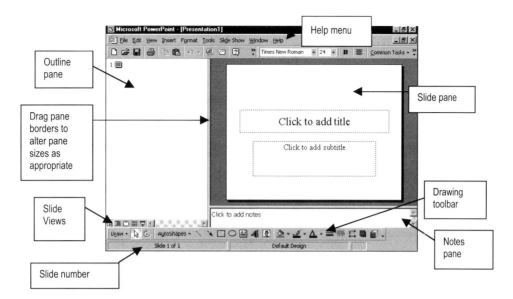

Figure 6.3 Slide in Normal View

Note: If you have selected the wrong layout, right-click in a white space on the slide (outside of the placeholders.

1 Select: **Slide Layout**.

2 Click on: a layout to select it.

3 Click on: **Reapply**.

Info

It is worth examining the PowerPoint window at this stage and noting the labels in Figure 6.3 and the following:

Modifying toolbars

The Standard and Formatting toolbars display (by default) on one row. It is quite useful to leave them like this so that you have more room to work on your slides. If you do want to modify the toolbar display, from the **View** menu, select: **Toolbars**, then **Customize**. Click on: the **Options** tab.

Slide views

The slide is displayed in **Normal View**. It contains three panes: outline, slide and notes. The pane sizes can be adjusted by dragging the pane borders. This view displays slides individually and can be used to work on/view all parts of your presentation. The notes pane allows you to input any notes that you want to make about the slide. This aids the speaker when making a presentation.

Other views include:

Outline. Displays an outline of your presentation. You can enter/review the text in your presentation in this view.

Slide. Displays one slide at a time. Use this view to create/edit slides.

Slide Sorter:

You can view all your slides in this view as miniatures (small versions or thumbnails).

Zoom in and out for more/less detail using **Zoom Control**.

Sort slides into a different presentation order by clicking on the slide you want to move and dragging it to a new location.

Add a new slide by placing the pointer between the slides where you want the new slide to appear and clicking on the **New Slide** button.

Delete a slide by selecting it and pressing the **Delete** key. Use the **Undo** button to reinstate the deleted slide.

Slide Show. Shows your slides on a full screen, as they will appear when you set a slide show in motion. Select the first slide. Click on: the **Slide Show** button. To view the next slide, press: **Page Down**. When all the slides have been viewed you will be returned to the previous view (this will be covered in more detail later).

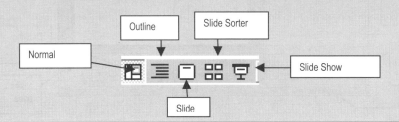

4   Change to **Slide View** by clicking on the **Slide View** button. The slide is shown as in Figure 6.4. It has pre-set placeholders (boxes with dotted-line borders to hold text, bulleted lists, etc.).

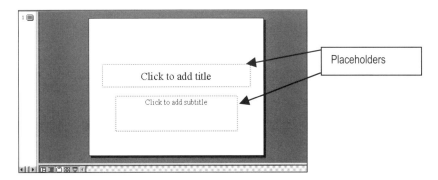

Figure 6.4 Slide View

5   In the slide window, click in the top placeholder (**Click to add title**) and key in **Learning PowerPoint**.
6   Click in the bottom placeholder (**Click to add subtitle**) and key in your name.

i Info

Title and sub-title can also be referred to as heading and sub-heading. Body text is usually the text that follows the sub-heading.

Exercise 3

Format the text on slide 1.

i Info

PowerPoint bases its default text formats on its default *master slide*. You will learn more about master slides in Section 2 (page 249).

Method

As in Word, select the text you want to format and then use the Formatting buttons (see Figure 6.5) and/or the **Format** menu, selecting **Font** to change the font type, point size, embolden, italicise or underline, apply text shadow, use sub and superscript.

Change case by selecting **Change Case** from the **Format** menu.

Figure 6.5 Formatting buttons

 Info

Serif and sans serif fonts

Serifs are small lines that stem from the upper and lower ends of characters. Serif fonts have such lines. Sans serif fonts do not have these lines. As a general rule, larger text in a sans serif font and body text in a serif font usually makes for easier reading.

Example: **Times New Roman** is a serif font.

Arial is a sans serif font.

1   Align the text within the placeholders using the buttons.

2   Align the text in relation to the slide:

   a) Select the placeholder box.
   b) On the **Drawing** toolbar, click on: **Draw** and then select: **Align or Distribute**.
   c) Click on: **Relative to Slide** so that a tick appears.
   d) Click on: **Draw** again, select: **Align or Distribute** and click on: the option you want – i.e. **Align Top**, **Bottom**, **Left**, **Right** (see Figure 6.6).

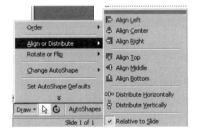

Figure 6.6 Aligning objects

3   Change the font colour by clicking the down arrow on the **A▾** **Font Colour** button on the **Drawing** toolbar. (By default this toolbar is at the bottom of the working area. If this is not visible, from the **View** menu, select: **Toolbars** and click on: **Drawing**.)

1.4 Saving the presentation

 Exercise 4

Save the presentation.

Method

1 From the **File** menu, select: **Save As**.
2 Choose where you want to save the file and key in a filename (if saving to a floppy disk, remember to have the disk inserted in the drive).
3 Click on **Save**.

1.5 Bulleted lists and adding graphics to a specified slide layout

 Exercise 5

Create a second slide in the presentation.

 Method

1 Click on: the ⬚ **New Slide** button.
2 Choose the autolayout **Text and Clip Art** as shown in Figure 6.7. Click on: **OK**.

Note: You now have two slides in the left hand pane.

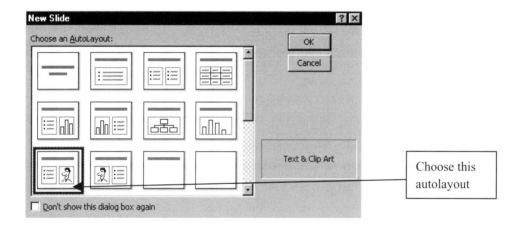

Figure 6.7 Creating Slide 2

3 In the **Click to add title** placeholder, key in **Bullets and Graphics**.
4 In the left-hand placeholder, key in the numbers 1 to 7, pressing **Enter** after each number except 7 (the last one). Notice that a bulleted list has been created.

Changing bullet type

5 Select the bulleted text. From the **Format** menu select: **Bullets and Numbering**.
6 Make your choices from the **Bullets and numbering** dialogue box. Click on: **OK**.
7 To insert a graphical image in the right hand placeholder, double-click in the placeholder.
8 Scroll through the Clip Art and decide which one to use.
9 Right-click on: the chosen one and then click on: the **Insert Clip** button (see Figure 6.8).

 Info

At step 6 you can select a numbered list by clicking on: the **Numbered** tab. You can also add bullets and numbered lists to slides using the appropriate toolbar buttons ie **Bullets** and **Numbering**. Click on the relevant toolbar button before keying in text or select the text to have bullets or numbering and then click on the relevant toolbar button.

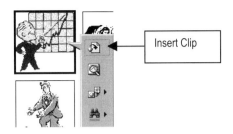

Figure 6.8 Inserting Clip Art

Slide 2 will now look something like Figure 6.9.

Figure 6.9 Slide 2

10 Resize the graphic image by dragging the handles.

> **Info**
>
> If you want to preserve the proportions (aspect ratio) of the image always resize from a corner.

1.6 Moving the elements of the slide

> **Exercise 6**
>
> Reduce the size of the image and reposition it at the right-hand corner of the slide.

Method

1 Click on: the image to select it.
2 Reduce the size as in step 10 above.
3 With the graphic still selected, hover the mouse over it. An arrowhead cross appears.
4 Holding down the left mouse button, drag the graphic to the required position.

> **Info**
>
> This repositioning can be carried out on any of the elements following the same method, but you will notice that you need to point the mouse at the border of some of the elements before the arrowhead cross appears. When this appears you can move the element.

Your slide will now look something like Figure 6.10:

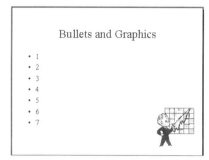

Figure 6.10 Graphic resized and repositioned

5 Save your work using the button method.

1.7 Adding text and images to a blank layout

 Exercise 7

Create slide 3 using the blank autolayout. Decide on your own text for this slide.

 Method

1 Click on: the **New Slide** button.
2 Choose the **Blank** autolayout.
3 Experiment with adding your own text and graphics.

Adding text

1 Click on: the **Text Box** button on the Drawing toolbar.
2 Click where you want the text to start. *Note:* You need not drag out a box, as the text will expand the box to fit.
3 Key in the text and format it as required.
4 Click in any white space on the slide when finished.
5 Adjust the text box size so that the text fits neatly on the slide.

Adjusting line spacing

When you have more than one line of text, you can adjust the line spacing.

Method

1 With the cursor positioned in the text box, from the **Format** menu, select: **Line Spacing**.
2 Make your choices from the **Line Spacing** dialogue box.

To add graphics

1 From the **Insert** menu, select: **Picture** and then **Clip Art** (see Figure 6.11).
2 Right-click on: the Clip Art you want to insert. Click on: the **Insert clip** button.

Figure 6.11 Adding a picture

Info

Notice that the menu shows other types of picture you can insert.

Note: The graphic is placed in the centre of the slide. Resize and reposition it as necessary following the method given above.

Use your imagination and practise adding and changing elements on this slide. When you are happy with the result, save your work.

You now have three slides in the presentation.

1.8 Viewing the slides

There are several ways to view your slides (see Section 1.3 – page 238). Practise using these views now.

1.9 Implementing a colour scheme

Exercise 8

For all three slides, change the background colour to light blue and the title text to red.

 Method

1   In **Slide View**, from the **Format** menu, select: **Slide Color Scheme**; the **Color Scheme** dialogue box appears. The default here is **Standard** and you can experiment with the colour schemes provided. However, to create your own scheme, ensure that **Custom** is selected, click on: **Background**, then **Change Color** (see Figure 6.12).

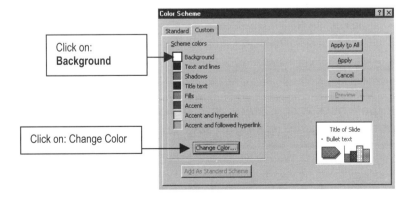

Figure 6.12 Color Scheme dialogue box

2 The **Background Color** dialogue box appears. With **Standard** selected, click on: a shade of light blue, then on **OK** (see Figure 6.13).

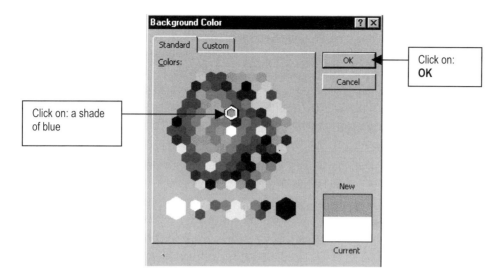

Figure 6.13 Adding a background color

3 You are returned to the **Color Scheme** dialogue box. This time select **Text and Lines** and follow the instructions above, choosing the colour red for the title text.

4 When you are returned to the **Color Scheme** dialogue box, click on: **Apply to All**. You are automatically returned to your slide.

Note: You could have chosen to apply to one slide only.

5 Change to **Slide Sorter View** and see how your slides look with this colour scheme.

Note: The text colour has not applied to the Title text. **Title Text** is not included in **Text and Lines** and must be chosen separately.

 Info

PowerPoint can do design work for you by selecting **Apply Design Template** from the **Format** Menu, and selecting something suitable.

6 Save your work.

1.10 Spellcheck the presentation

 Exercise 9

Spellcheck the presentation.

 Method

Click on: the **Spelling** button. The spellcheck is consistent with other Office 2000 applications. Always resave your work after spellchecking to save any corrections.

1.11 Printing your presentation

Exercise 10

Print the presentation of three slides, one slide per page.

Note: There is no worked example of this exercise as answers may vary.

Method

From the **File** menu, select: **Print**. The **Print** dialogue box appears (see Figure 6.14).

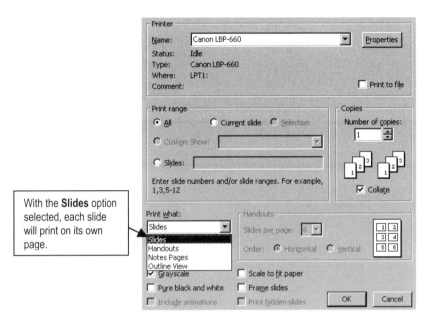

With the **Slides** option selected, each slide will print on its own page.

Figure 6.14 Print dialogue box

1.12 Closing and exiting PowerPoint

Info

You can print slides in various views including as individual **Slides** (one per page), as **Handouts** (several slides on one page, you can decide the number per page), as **Notes Pages** (slides and notes) or **Outline View**. You can also decide on **Greyscale** or **Black and White** output.

Method

1 From the **File** menu, select: **Close**.
2 From the **File** menu, select: **Exit**.

Section 1 Presentations practice

1 Create a three-slide presentation as follows and format it to good effect using the layout given as a guide.

Slide 1

Using Title slide autolayout, enter the text shown:

> # Multimedia on the web
> # Multimedia Workshop 2000
>
> The Grand Hotel Conference Centre
> Bristol BS8 2TS
> ## Tel 0117 2102102
> *E-mail: mow@multicon.ac.uk*

Slide 2

Using the Bulleted list autolayout, enter the following. Format the bullets as squares. Add a suitable piece of clip art in the bottom right corner.

> **The following topics will form the basis of the multimedia workshop:**
>
> ✓ Text
> ✓ Graphics
> ✓ Video
> ✓ Sound

Slide 3

Using the 2 Column Text autolayout, enter the following text. Adjust the line spacing in the body text to 1.25 lines. *Note:* Delete the bullets by selecting them and pressing: **Delete**.

> ### Video and Sound Workshops
>
> **Video**
>
> This will concentrate on accessing two websites with video content. The content will be compared and contrasted with a view to finding out what works and what falls flat. Website addresses will be specially selected for this workshop.
>
> **Sound**
>
> For this workshop there will be four websites to focus on. Some have streaming audio. The quality and accessibility of the sound will be judged and rated out of ten for each of the two categories.

2   Apply a light grey background to all the slides. Set all title text to dark red.
3   Save the presentation.
4   Print all slides, one per page.
5   Close the presentation file and exit PowerPoint.

Section 2 Editing and refining

In this section you will practise and learn how to:

- open an existing presentation
- create and use a master slide
- number the slides
- add different types of line, move lines, change line colour/modify line width
- add shapes: boxes, circles etc; rotate or flip an object; add free drawn lines
- change attributes: colour, line type, apply shadow
- set line weights, style and colours in a text box

- use copy/cut and paste to duplicate slides/text images within presentation(s)
- use cut and paste as above
- reorder slides
- open several presentations
- delete an image/selected text/slides
- add notes to slides
- change slide orientation: landscape or portrait
- save existing presentation
- save under different formats and for the web.

2.1 Opening an existing presentation

 Exercise 1

Open the presentation created in Section 1.

 Method

1 Open PowerPoint as in Section 1 (page 237).
2 Click in the option button **Open an existing presentation**.
3 Click on: the filename and then on **OK**.
4 If the filename is not visible, to locate it click on: **More files**.

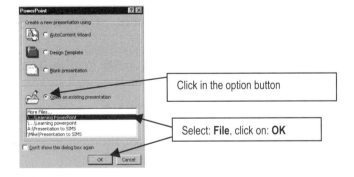

Figure 6.15 Opening an existing presentation

2.2 Creating and using a master slide

 Exercise 2

Create a master slide for the presentation, containing the date and the footer **Learning PowerPoint**.

Method

1 From the **View** menu, select: **Master, Slide Master**. The master slide appears (see Figure 6.16).

Figure 6.16 The Master slide

2 In this instance we will keep the default settings and enter the common information for this presentation in the **Date Area** and **Footer Area**.

Note: You may want to increase the zoom to be able to read the text you are working with. Change back to the default 33% when you have finished.

3 In the **Date Area**, click on: **Date/time** to select it and key in today's date.
4 In the **Footer Area**, key in: **Learning PowerPoint**.
5 Change to **Slide Sorter View** to view the effects of creating a master slide.

2.3 Adding lines and shapes

Exercise 3

Create a new slide and practise adding lines and shapes.

 Method

1 In **Slide View**, click on: the last slide in the presentation in the Outline pane. (This will ensure that the new slide is correctly positioned as slide 4 of the presentation.)
2 Click on: the **New Slide** button.
3 Select **Blank AutoLayout**.
4 Ensure that you are in **Slide View** with the Drawing toolbar visible. If not, from the **View** menu, select: **Toolbars**, **Drawing** so that a tick appears next to it. The Drawing toolbar is shown in Figure 6.17.

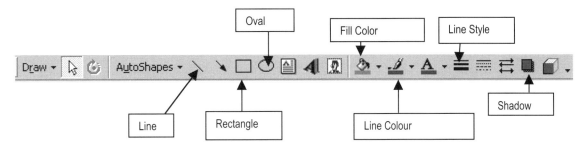

Figure 6.17 Drawing toolbar

Adding a line

1 Click on: the **Line** button.
2 Position the crosshair where you want the line to start.
3 Hold down the left mouse button and drag the mouse to where you want the line to end. Release the mouse.

Formatting the line

1 Select the line by clicking on it. When it is selected, handles appear at each end.
2 Click on: the **Line Style** button.
3 Click on: the line style that you want.
4 Click on: the **Line Color** button to choose the line colour.

Changing line length and moving a line

1 Click on: the line to select it.
2 Change the length by dragging the handles to the required length.
3 Move the line by holding down the mouse anywhere along its length until the arrowhead cross appears and then drag it to the new position.

Adding a circle or ellipse

1 Click on: the **Oval** button.
2 Hold down the left mouse button and drag out to the required shape.
3 Release the mouse button.

Adding a box

Follow the method for a circle/ellipse, shown above.

Filling a shape with colour

1 Select the shape to fill.
2 Click on: the **Fill Color** button.
3 Click on: the chosen colour.

Filling a shape with a pattern

Follow steps **1** and **2** above.

3 Click on: **Fill Effects**. The **Fill Effects** dialogue box appears.
4 Click on: the **Pattern** tab.
5 Click on: the chosen pattern. Click on: **OK**.

Applying a shadow

1 Select the required object.
2 Click on: the **Shadow** button.

Adding free drawn lines

1 Click on: the **Autoshapes** arrow button.
2 Select: **Lines**, **Freeform** or **Scribble** (see Figure 6.18).

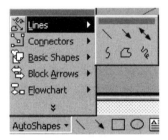

Figure 6.18 Free drawn lines

3 Hold down the left mouse and draw with the 'pencil'.

Note: Check the other options on this menu – they are very useful.

Rotating or flipping an object

1 Select the object.
2 Click on: the **Draw** arrow.
3 Select: **Rotate or Flip** and then select from the next menu (see Figure 6.19).

Figure 6.19 Rotating and flipping objects

> **ⓘ Info**
>
> Objects can be grouped so that they stay together. To do this: hold down Shift and click in turn on the objects to group. From the Drawing toolbar, **Draw**, **Menu**, select: **Group** (ungroup from the menu).
>
> Experiment with the other Drawing buttons to create some stunning effects.

2.4 Setting line weights, styles and colours in text boxes

Exercise 4

Create a text box at the top of the slide. Insert the text: **Adding shapes and lines**.
Format the text box.

Method

1 Add a text box in the normal way and key in the text.
2 With the text box selected, format it using the Drawing buttons.

2.5 Copying/cutting and pasting within a presentation

Exercise 5

Copy the text box created in Exercise 4 so that it appears centred on slide 2 under
Bullets and Graphics.

Method

1 In **Slide View**, select the text box.
2 Click on: the **Copy** button.
3 Select slide 2 from the left pane.
4 Click on: the **Paste** button.
5 Position the object as appropriate.

Exercise 6

Move the graphical image on slide 2 to a new blank slide.

Method

1 Create a new slide using the **Blank AutoLayout**.
2 Select slide 2 from the left pane, and then select the image.
3 Click on: the **Cut** button.
4 Select the new slide from the left pane.
5 Click on: the **Paste** button.

Exercise 7

Copy the image from slide 3 so that it appears in the box on slide 2 (in place of the
moved image).

Method

1 In **Slide View**, select the image on slide 3.
2 Click on: the **Copy** button.
3 Select slide 2 from the left pane.
4 Select the image placeholder and click on: **Paste**.

2.6 Duplicating whole slides

 Exercise 8

Duplicate slide 1.

 Method

1   In **Slide Sorter View**, select slide 1.
2   From the **Insert** menu, select: **Duplicate Slide**.
3   The duplicate of the slide appears next to slide 1.

Note: You can also duplicate slides by selecting the slide to copy and clicking on the **Copy** button. Click where you want the slide to appear and click on: the **Paste** button. You can cut and paste whole slides using the **Cut** instead of the **Copy** button.

2.7 Reordering slides

 Exercise 9

Reorder the slides so that the duplicate slide becomes the last slide.

 Method

In **Slide Sorter View**, hold down the left mouse on slide 2 and drag the slide to the required position.

2.8 Opening more than one presentation

 Exercise 10

Open a new presentation and copy slide 2 of the **Learning PowerPoint** presentation to the new presentation.

 Method

1   Click on: the ▯ **New** button.
2   Select **Blank AutoLayout**. Click on: **OK**.
3   On the **Taskbar**, click on: the **Learning PowerPoint** button (see Figure 6.20).

Figure 6.20 Switching presentations

4   In **Slide Sorter View** select slide 2.
5   Click on: the **Copy** button.
6   On the **Taskbar**, switch to the new presentation by clicking on the button **Presentation1**.
7   In **Slide View**, click on: the **Paste** button.
8   Resize to fit the slide if necessary.

Note: Although you have copied this slide, it will not implement the master slide for slides in this new presentation. You can use the methods in Section 2.5 (page 253) for copying/pasting between presentations, switching presentations using the taskbar buttons.

2.9 Deleting images/text

To delete images or text from slides, select the image/text and press: **Delete**.

Practise this now.

2.10 Deleting slides

 Exercise 11

Delete slide 3 from the presentation **Learning PowerPoint**.

 Method

1 In **Slide Sorter View**, select slide 3.
2 Press: **Delete**.

2.11 Adding notes to slides

Info

You can add notes to your slides. These are useful 'prompts' for key points when you are delivering a presentation. You can print notes for each slide together with a small version of each slide as handouts.

 Exercise 12

Add a note to slide 1 of the new presentation: **This slide has been copied from another presentation**. Print the slide together with the notes.

 Method

1 Ensure that the correct presentation is displayed.
2 Click on: the **Normal View** button.
3 Key in the text in the **Notes** pane.
4 From the **File** menu, select: **Print**.
5 In the **Print what** section, select: **Notes Pages** (see Figure 6.21).

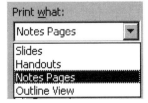

Figure 6.21 Printing notes

2.12 Changing slide orientation and sizing

Exercise 13

Print the slides in the **Learning PowerPoint** presentation in portrait display.

Note: There is no worked example of this exercise as answers may vary.

Method

1 From the **File** menu, select: **Page Setup**. The **Page Setup** dialogue box appears (see Figure 6.22).
2 In the **Orientation**, **Slides** section, click next to **Portrait**.
3 Click on: **OK**.

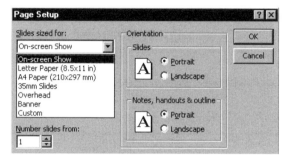

Figure 6.22 Page Setup

From the **Page Setup** dialogue box, you can resize the slides to suit different requirements – e.g. 35mm slides, overheads, etc. – using the **Slides sized for** drop-down list. You can also key in exact dimensions for your slides.

2.13 Saving an existing presentation and in different formats

Exercise 14

Save both presentations. Save the new presentation in a form suitable for the web.

Method

1 Save the existing presentation by clicking on: the **Save** button.
2 Save the new presentation by clicking on: the **Save** button. The **Save As** dialogue box is displayed. Select the location where you want to save it.
3 Key in a suitable filename.
4 Click on: the arrow in the **Save as type** box and select **Web Page** (see Figure 6.23).
5 Click on: **Save**.

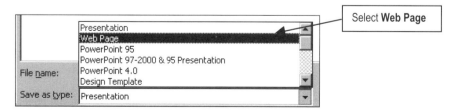

Figure 6.23 Saving as Web page

File formats available

Being able to save files in different formats is extremely useful. It means that you can share files with others who do not have the same software or version of software that you are using. Saving in web format will usually reproduce reliably. You can save in a previous version of PowerPoint but beware since some functions may not have been available in earlier versions so some elements may be lost or changed. Other useful formats include:

Outline/RTF – This saves the text of the presentation so that it can be opened in Word, for example.

Presentation Template – This saves the layout so that you can reuse it thus saving time. You need only add content to the slides.

Image formats – Use **JPEG** or **GIF** formats when you want to insert the slides on webpages or use them in other graphics programs.

2.14 Close both presentations and exit PowerPoint.

Section 2 Presentations practice

1 Reload the presentation saved in Practice Section 1.
2 Create a master slide containing the date and a footer: **Created by (your name)**.
3 Add a suitable graphic to this master slide at the top left. Resize it to approximately 2 cm square (keep the original aspect ratio).
4 Add a new slide at the end of the presentation.
5 Using the Drawing buttons, create the following diagram in the centre of the newly created slide:

6 Add a text box below the diagram with the text: **Using Multimedia**.
7 Format the text box with a background colour light green and text colour dark purple.
8 Create a new slide at the end of the presentation.
9 Copy the text box in step 7 to the new slide.
10 Open a new PowerPoint presentation and copy the last slide to become the first slide of the new presentation.
11 Add a text box to the slide in step 10 with the text **Multimedia is fun!**
12 Add a note to this slide: **Opening slide for uses of multimedia in web designs**.
13 Return to the original presentation. Reorder the slides so that slide 1 becomes the last slide.
14 Save the original presentation and print as **Handouts** (all slides on one page) in portrait display.
15 Save the new presentation in a format suitable for the web.
16 Print the new presentation as **Notes Pages**.
17 Close both files and exit PowerPoint.

Section 3 Working with objects

In this section you will practise and learn how to:

- create an organisational chart
- modify the structure of an organisational chart
- create different kinds of chart; bar, pies, etc.
- import images from other files
- copy an imported object to a master slide
- add borders to an object.

3.1 Creating an organisational chart

 Exercise 1

Load PowerPoint and a new presentation. On slide 1 enter the text: **Types of Chart**. Add a bulleted list containing **Organisational**, **Bar** and **Pie**. On the master slide for this presentation, insert a footer containing your name and slide number. Save the presentation with the filename **Cybercafe Company**. On slide 2 create an organisational chart.

 Method

1 Create slide 1 and edit the master slide.
2 Create slide 2 by clicking on the **New Slide** button and selecting: **Organization Chart AutoLayout** (see Figure 6.24). Click on: **OK**.

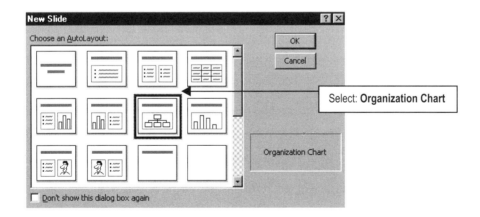

Figure 6.24 Creating an Organisational chart

3 Change to Slide View.
4 Key in the title: **Personnel** in the Title placeholder.
5 Double-click in the chart box to add the organisation chart. The **Organization Chart** window appears (see Figure 6.25).
6 Title the chart: **Cybercafe Company**. Key in the following details by clicking in the first relevant box and overwriting the original text. Click on: the second relevant box and so on.

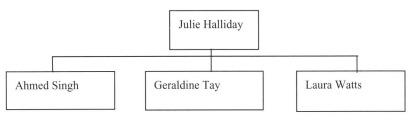

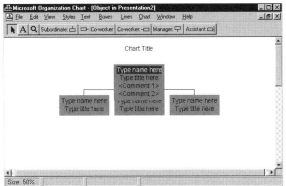

Figure 6.25 Organizational Chart window

Adding chart boxes

Exercise 2

Simeon Hardie works alongside Ahmed Singh and is also a Technical Manager. Add a Co-worker box and enter his name and his position.

Method

1　Click on: the **Left Co-worker** button.
2　Click on: Ahmed Singh's chart box and key in Simeon Hardie's details.

Exercise 3

Pat Hodge's line manager is Geraldine Tay. Her title is Administrator. Enter a chart box for Pat.

Method

1　Click on: the **Subordinate** button.
2　Click on: Geraldine Tay's chart box and key in Pat Hodge's details.

To return to the slide, from the **File** menu, select: **Exit and Return to Cybercafe Company** (see Figure 6.26). Click on: **Yes** to update the object.

Info

You can continue adding as many boxes as necessary to complete an organisational chart. Use the menus to format the chart.

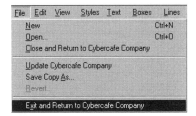

Figure 6.26 Returning to the slide

3.2 Creating a bar/pie chart

Exercise 4

Create slide 3 containing the title: **Weekly Sales – January to March 2000**. Include a column chart showing the sales set out below:

	Week 1	Week 2	Week 3	Week 4
Jan	106	98	270	106
Feb	49	50	98	200
Mar	208	41	111	119

 Method

1 Click on: the **New Slide** button.
2 Select **Chart AutoLayout** (see Figure 6.27).
3 Click on: **OK**.

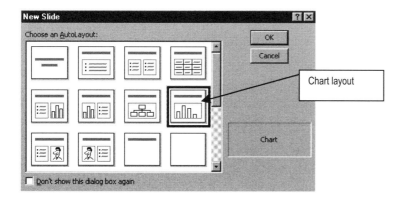

Figure 6.27 Chart layout

4 Key in the title in the Title placeholder.
5 Double-click to add the chart. A datasheet (see Figure 6.28), a column chart and charting menus and buttons appear (see Figure 6.29).
6 Key in the data above in the appropriate cells overwriting the sample data.

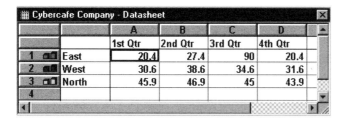

Figure 6.28 Datasheet

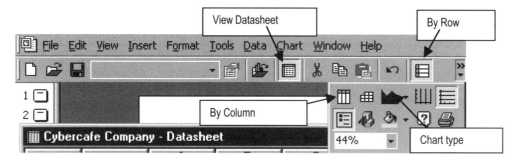

Figure 6.29 Charting menu and button options

7 Click on: the **View Datasheet** button (see Figure 6.29) to display the chart only.

 Exercise 5

Change the column chart to a 3-D bar chart.

 Method

1 With the chart selected, click on: the **Chart Type** button arrow and select: **3-D Bar Chart**.
2 The chart changes to the requested chart.

Info

Depending on how you lay out the data you can use the buttons to plot by row or by column. Add/delete rows or columns and format as in Excel. You can also create other types of chart – e.g. pie. Remember that pie charts use only one data series so you may need to hide data on the datasheet to get an accurate result. **To hide data**: Select the column(s)/row(s) to hide. Right-click on the selection and select: **Hide**. **To unhide data**: Select the columns/rows on either side of the hidden data. Right-click on the selection, and select: **Unhide**.

3.3 Importing objects and images from other files

Info

Sometimes you will want to import objects and images from other files – e.g. a company logo – and add it to the master slide so that it will be visible throughout the presentation. If you have an image to import practise with it now. If not, make a note of the methods used below.

You can use the copy and paste methods described in Section 2 (page 249). You can also use:

1 The **Insert** menu and select: **Object** (see Figure 6.30).

Figure 6.30 Inserting objects

2 The **Insert Object** dialogue box is displayed (see Figure 6.31).

3 Click in the **Create from file** button.

4 Click on: **Browse** to locate the file.

5 Click on: **OK**.

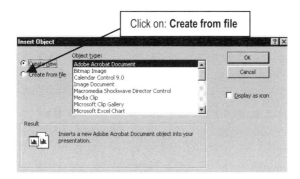

Figure 6.31 Insert Object box

6 The file is inserted into your presentation.

7 Resize and reposition it as appropriate.

 Info

If you want to add it to the master slide, first from the **View** menu, select: **Master**, **Slide Master**. Then follow the method above.

3.4 Adding borders to an object

 Exercise 6

Add a border to the imported object.

 Method

1 Select the object by clicking on it. On the Drawing toolbar, click on: the **Line Color** button arrow (see Figure 6.32).

2 Click on: the colour you want.

3 Use the **Line Style** button to alter the line's format.

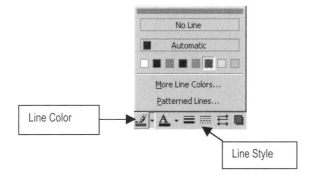

Figure 6.32 Adding a border

3.5 Save and print the presentation (as slides).

Note: There is no worked example of this exercise as versions may vary.

3.6 Close the presentation and exit PowerPoint.

Section 3 Presentation practice

1   Open a new PowerPoint presentation, choose a suitable template background to be used throughout and create the following 3 slides:

Slide 1

Using the Title slide layout enter the title **Arts Department, North Weston College** and the sub-title **Friarsmith Mansion, Heathcliff Road, Leeds LS6 9YQ e-mail arts@nwc.ac.uk**.

Slide 2

Using the Organisation chart layout, enter the title **Structure of Arts**. Enter the organisational chart with the title **Current Staff** as shown:

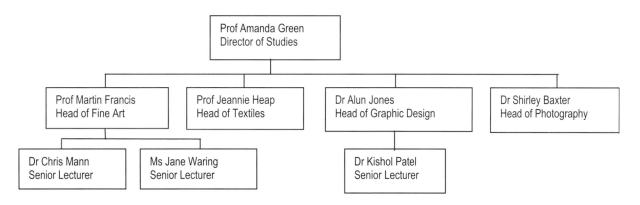

Slide 3

Using the Chart slide layout, add the title **Number of Students**. Use the following chart data to produce a 3-D column chart.

	Art	Text	Graphics	Photo
TERM 1	28	36	20	18
TERM 2	61	43	39	50
TERM 3	25	41	60	70

2   Insert a footer on all three slides: **Arts Department**, **your initials** and **the date**.
3   Insert a suitable piece of clip art on the first slide.
4   Change the text in the title of slide 2 to **March 2000 – Structure of the Arts Faculty**.
5   Save the presentation and print the slides as handouts (all on the same page).
6   Close the presentation.

Section 4 Automating a presentation

In this section you will practise and learn how to:

• add slide transitions

• start a slide show

• add preset animation effects

• change preset animation effects

• use on-screen navigation tools

• hide slides.

4.1 Creating transitional timings

 Info

In Slide Show View you can see how the slides look on a full screen moving to the next/previous slide using the **Page Up/Page Down** keys (other keys will also perform the same task. Pressing the **Home** key will take you to slide 1 and pressing the **End** key will take you to the last slide). The slides do not run automatically. In order for them to do this you need to set up transitional timings (slide durations) that automatically show the next slide after a set number of seconds.

Exercise 1

Load PowerPoint and load one of the presentations you have created in the last sections. Create an automated presentation with slide durations shown below:

SLIDE NO	SLIDE DURATION
Slide 1	5 secs
Slide 2	7 secs
Slide 3	15 secs
Slide 4	10 secs

 Method

1 In **Slide Sorter View,** click on: slide 1 to select it.
2 Click on: the **Slide Transition** button.
3 The **Slide Transition** dialogue box appears (see Figure 6.33).

Figure 6.33 Slide Transition box

4 In the **Advance** section, click in the box: **On mouse click** so that there is no tick in the box. Click in the box: **Automatically after** so that a tick is shown, and in the box beneath, key in the slide duration for slide 1 – i.e. 5 (see Figure 6.34).

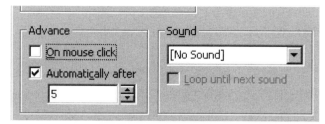

Figure 6.34

5 Click on: **Apply**. Slide 1 now has the duration (05) shown underneath at the left-hand side (see Figure 6.35).

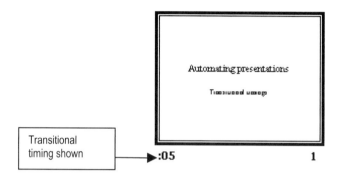

Figure 6.35 Transitional timing

6 Repeat steps 2 to 5 for each of the other slides ensuring that you have selected the timing requested.

7 Save the presentation.

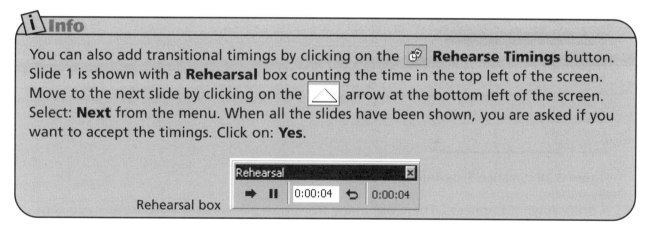

Info

You can also add transitional timings by clicking on the ⬚ **Rehearse Timings** button. Slide 1 is shown with a **Rehearsal** box counting the time in the top left of the screen. Move to the next slide by clicking on the ◺ arrow at the bottom left of the screen. Select: **Next** from the menu. When all the slides have been shown, you are asked if you want to accept the timings. Click on: **Yes**.

Rehearsal box

4.2 Starting a slide show

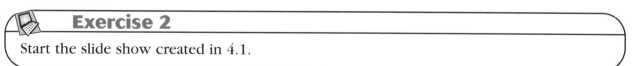

Exercise 2

Start the slide show created in 4.1.

Method

1 From the **Slide Show** menu, select: **View Show**.
2 The presentation will run automatically with the timings that have been set.

4.3 Changing transitional timings

Info

If you are not happy with the timings set, change them by selecting the slide with the time you want to change. Click on: the **Slide Transition** button, edit the time next to the **Automatically after** box. Click on: **Apply**. Repeat for any other slides you want to change.

4.4 Creating transitional effects

Info

Transitional effects control how slides appear on the screen during a presentation. They are used to enhance the display and to ensure that the audience of the presentation stays interested in it.

Exercise 3

Create different transition effects for each of the slides.

 Method

1 Click on: the **Slide Sorter View** button.
2 Click on: slide 1 to select it.
3 Click on: the down arrow on the **Slide Transition Effects** toolbar box (see Figure 6.36).

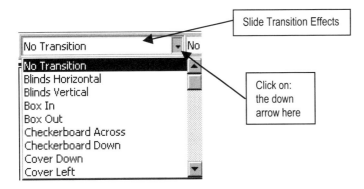

Figure 6.36 Creating Slide Transition Effects

4 A drop-down list appears. There are many transition effects to choose from – you can scroll down for more. Click on: a transition effect – you will see a preview of the effect on slide 1. Experiment with the different effects. When you find one you like, click on it so that it remains visible in the **Slide Transition Effects** box.

5 An icon appears beneath the slide to show that it has a transition effect applied to it (see Figure 6.37).

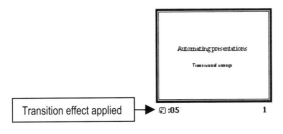

Figure 6.37 Applying a Transition Effect

6 Repeat for the other slides, choosing a different transitional effect for each one.

7 Save the presentation.

8 You can now run the presentation so that you can view how the transitional effects look.

4.5 Creating preset animation effects

 Exercise 4

Add different preset animation effects to all of the slides except slide 4.

 Method

1 Click on: the **Slide Sorter View** button.

2 Click on: slide 1 to select it.

3 Click on: the down arrow on the **Preset Animation** toolbar box (see Figure 6.38).

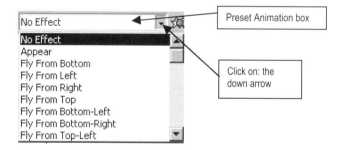

Figure 6.38 Setting a Build Effect

4 A drop-down list appears. There are many effects to choose from – you can scroll down for more. Click on: an effect. You will not see a preview, as with transition effects.

5 An icon appears beneath the slide to show that an animation effect has been applied to it (see Figure 6.39).

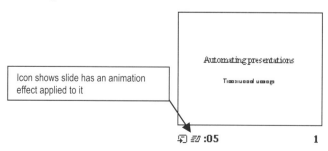

Figure 6.39 Preset animation effect applied

6 To view the animation effect, change to **Slide Show View**. The presentation will begin. To exit the slide show, press: **Esc**.

7 Add preset animation effects to the other slides as appropriate.

8 Save the presentation.

9 View the automated presentation.

Note: to change animation effect, repeat the method above selecting a different effect.

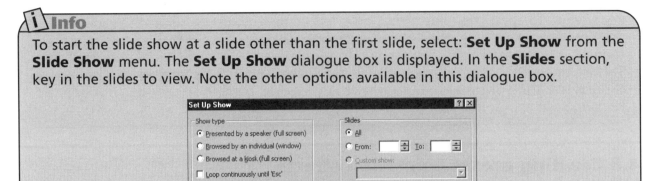

To start the slide show at a slide other than the first slide, select: **Set Up Show** from the **Slide Show** menu. The **Set Up Show** dialogue box is displayed. In the **Slides** section, key in the slides to view. Note the other options available in this dialogue box.

Info

When presenting a show, you can navigate through as follows:

1 With the slide show running, right-click.

2 From the pop-up menu, select: **Go**, then: **Slide Navigator**.

3 Click on the slide to show next, then on: **Go To**.

4.6 Hiding slides

Exercise 5

Hide one of the slides in your show.

Method

1 In **Slide Sorter View**, select the slide to hide.

2 Click on: the **Hide Slide** button.

Hidden slides have a cross through their number – e.g.

4.7 Save and close the presentation and exit PowerPoint.

Section 4 Presentations practice

1 Reload the presentation saved in Practice Section 3.

2 Add transitional timings to the presentation.

3 Add preset animation effects to the presentation.

4 Hide slide 3.

5 Review the slide show and reset timings and effects as necessary.

6 Save the presentation.

PowerPoint quick reference guide

Action	Keyboard	Mouse	Right-mouse menu	Menu
Alignment, in relation to slide		Select object **Drawing** toolbar, **Draw**, **Align or Distribute**, **Relative to Slide** then **Draw**, **Align or Distribute**, select option you want		
Bold text	Ctrl + B	Click: the **B** **Bold** button	**Font**	**Format**, **Font**
			Select: **Bold** from the **Font style:** menu	
Borders		Select object Drawing toolbar, Click: ✐ **Line Color** button Click: ≡ **Line Style** button		
Bullets, changing type			**Bullets and Numbering**	**Format**, **Bullets and Numbering**
Capitals (blocked)	**Caps Lock** Key in the text **Caps Lock** again to remove			Select text to be changed to capitals: **Format**, **Change Case**, **UPPERCASE**
Centre text	Select the text			
	Ctrl + E	Click: the ≡ **Center** button		**Format**, **Alignment**, **Center**
Change case	Select the text to be changed			
	From the **Format** menu, select: **Change Case** Select the appropriate case			
Chart, inserting data organisation	Select appropriate slide AutoLayout, – i.e. chart or organisation chart Data chart – overwrite sample data, click: ▦ **View Datasheet** button Organisation – key in text. **File** menu, **Exit and Return to (presentation)**			
Close a file	Ctrl + W	Click: the ✕ **Close** icon		**File**, **Close**
Colours, slide				**Format**, **Slide Color Scheme**
Cut text	Select the text to be cut			
	Ctrl + X	Click: the ✂ **Cut** button	**Cut**	**Edit**, **Cut**
Delete a character	Press **Delete** to delete the character to the right of the cursor Press ← (Backspace) to delete the character to the left of the cursor			
Delete an image	Select the image, press: **Delete**			
Delete a word	Double-click: the word to select it Press: **Delete**			
Delete an slide	Select the slide in Slide Sorter View. Press: **Delete**			

Action	Keyboard	Mouse	Right-mouse menu	Menu
Delete/cut a block of text	Select the text you want to delete			
	Delete or **Ctrl + X**	Click: the ✄ **Cut** button	**Cut**	**E**dit, **Cu**t
Duplicate slide	**I**nsert menu, **Duplicate Slide**			
Effects, transitional timings	In **Slide Sorter** view			
		Click: the ⊡ **Slide Transition** button	**Slide Transition**	**Sli**de Show, **Slide Transition**
	In the **Advance** section Select: the timing you require			
Effects, transitional effects	In **Slide Sorter** view			
		Click: the ▾ down arrow next to the **Slide Transition Effects** box	**Slide Transition**	**Sli**de Show, **Slide Transition**
			In the **Effects** section	
	Select: the effect you want from the drop-down menu			
Effects, preset animation	In **Slide Sorter** view			
		Click: the ▾ down arrow next to the **Text Preset Animation** box	**Slide Transition**	**Sli**de Show, **Slide Transition**
			In the **Effects** section	
	Select: the effect you want from the drop-down menu			
Exit PowerPoint		Click: the ✕ **Close Window** icon		**F**ile, **E**xit
Font size	Select the text you want to change			
		Click: the ▾ down arrow next to the **Font Size** box Select: the font size you require	**Font**	F**o**rmat, **F**ont
			Select: the required size from the **Size:** menu	
Font	Select the text you want to change			
		Click: the ▾ down arrow next to the **Font** box Select: the font you require	**Font**	F**o**rmat, **F**ont
			Select: the required font from the **Font:** menu	
Serif	Serif fonts have small lines at upper and lower ends of characters – e.g. **Times New Roman**			
Sans serif	Sans serif fonts do not have lines – e.g. **Arial**			
Headers and footers				**View**, **Header and Footer**
Help	**F1**			**Help, Microsoft PowerPoint Help**
	Shift + F1			**What's This?**
Hide a slide		Click: the ⊡ **Hide Slide** button		**Slide Show, Hide Slide**

Action	Keyboard	Mouse	Right-mouse menu	Menu
Importing	From the **Insert** menu, select: **Picture** or **Object**			
graphic *extract text,* *Excel graph or* *other object*	Use copy (in the source application) and paste into PowerPoint			
Insert text	Position the cursor where you want the text to appear Key in the text			
Lines, adding formatting	Use the relevant Drawing buttons			
Load PowerPoint	In Windows 98 desktop			
		Double-click: the **PowerPoint** shortcut icon		**Start**, **Programs**, **Microsoft** **PowerPoint**
Master Slide setup				**View**, **Master**, **Slide** **Master**
New presentation, creating	**Ctrl + N**	Click: the ▢ **New** button		**File**, **New**
New Slide	**Ctrl + M**	Click: the ▣ **New Slide** button		**Insert**, **New Slide**
Notes, adding	In **Normal View,** add to the **Notes** pane			
Numbering slides				**Insert**, **Slide** **Number**
Open an existing file	**Ctrl + O**	Click: the 🖿 **Open** button		**File**, **Open**
	Select the appropriate directory and filename Click: **Open**			
Orientation of slides				**File**, **Page Setup**
Print	**Ctrl + P**			**File**, **Print**
– Slides, Handouts, Notes Pages, Outline View	Select from the **Print what**: drop-down menu			
Remove text emphasis	Select text to be changed			
	Ctrl + B (remove bold) **Ctrl + I** (remove italics) **Ctrl + U** (remove underline)	Click: the appropriate button: **B** *I* U̲	**Font**	**Format, Font**
				Select **Regular** from the **Font Style**: menu
Resize objects	Select the object. Resize using the handles. To preserve aspect ratio, resize from a corner.			

Action	Keyboard	Mouse	Right-mouse menu	Menu
Run automated presentation		Click: the ▣ **Slide Show** button at the bottom left of the screen		**View**, **Slide Show**
Save	**Ctrl + S**	Click: the ▣ **Save** button		**File**, **Save**
	If you have not already saved the file you will be prompted to specify the directory and to name the file.				
Save using a different name or to a different directory or in a different format				**File**, **Save As**
	Select the appropriate drive and change the filename and file type if relevant. Click: **Save**				
Shadow, adding	On the Drawing toolbar, click: the ▣ **Shadow** button				
Slide order	In **Slide Sorter** View Click and drag the slide to required position				
Spellcheck	**F7**	Click: the ▣ **Spelling** button		**Tools**, **Spelling**
Superscript and subscript text			**Font, Effects**	**Format**, **Font**, **Effects**
Templates, using		Formatting toolbar, **Common Tasks**, **Apply Design Template**		**Format**, **Apply Design Template**
Toolbars modifying	**View, Toolbars, Customize**				
Undo	**Ctrl + Z**	Click: the ↺ **Undo** button		**Edit**, **Undo**
View		Click: a **View** button ▣ ≣ ▢ ▦ ▣		**View**, make selection
Zoom		Click: the 100% ▾ **Zoom** button		**View, Zoom**

Module 6 practice tasks

Practice tasks 1

Make a 3-page presentation for Chellington Car Sales.

1 First slide is the Title slide. Key in the text: **Summer Madness 2000**.
2 Add your name and date in the bottom centre and ensure it appears on all three slides.
3 Insert a suitable piece of clip art on slide 1. Resize and centre it so it looks effective.
4 On slide 2 key in the text: **Many models on offer:**
5 Underneath key in the bulleted list:

> **Vauxhalls**
> **Fords**
> **Toyotas**
> **Volkswagens**

6 Format the bullets as ticks.
7 On slide 3 create an organisational chart entitled **Meet the Team** as follows:

Jean Moneypenny – Managing Director, Jack Quincy and Jill Bailey are Sales Managers immediately subordinate to Jean MoneyPenny. Paul Jones and Kiki Young are co-workers subordinate to Jill Bailey.

8 Create a slide show.
9 Save the presentation and print slides as **Handouts** (all 3 on one page).

Practice tasks 2

Make a 3-page presentation for Gardening World.

1 Select a template (background) that you think will be appropriate.
2 Key in the following on Slide 1 (the Title Slide): **Gardening World, Annual Report**.
3 At the bottom left corner, add your initials and a relevant piece of clip art (resize to fit in the corner) so that they appear on all three slides.
4 Slide 2 will contain text and a chart. Key in the text: **Performance**.
5 Create a column chart using the data below:

	Qtr 1	Qtr 2	Qtr 3	Qtr 4
Plants	1900	2380	1700	4000
Trees	2000	4000	6000	3000
Equipment	5500	3322	6622	1890

6 Enter the following text on slide 3:

We strive to provide the very best for all your gardening needs. We are always ready to provide Information and advice that will turn your fingers green.

7 Centre the text on the slide.
8 Italicise the words **fingers green** and change the text colour to green (if it is appropriate for the design).
9 Create the following graphic (use the Drawing toolbar). Centre it under the text.

10 Add a note to slide 2: **Figures do not include bedding plant sales**.

11 Create a slide show and save it with an appropriate name.

12 Set the slide orientation to **Portrait**.

13 Print the slides as **Notes Pages**.

14 Save the presentation.

Note: This is only a practice test. Successful completion does not imply certification of the module by the ECDL Foundation.

Information and Communication

Section 1 Getting started with the World Wide Web

In this section you will practise and learn how to:

- open a web browsing application
- understand the make-up and structure of a web address
- display a given web page
- change the web browser home page
- save a web page as a file

- use application Help functions
- close the web browsing application
- change view/display modes
- modify toolbar display
- display images on web page
- do not load image files onto web page.

1.1 What is a web browser?

A web browser is software that allows you to view, navigate and interact with the World Wide Web. Currently the two most commonly used browsers are Internet Explorer and Netscape Navigator. In this chapter the examples use Internet Explorer. You will need to check which browser your ECDL test centre uses. If it uses Netscape Navigator, this can be downloaded free from the Internet. There are some differences between them but check that you know how to transfer the skills practised in Internet Explorer.

1.2 Opening Internet Explorer

 Exercise 1

Open Internet Explorer.

 Method

From the **Start** menu, select **Programs, Internet Explorer** *or* click on: the 🎴 **Launch Internet Explorer Browser** icon on the Taskbar.

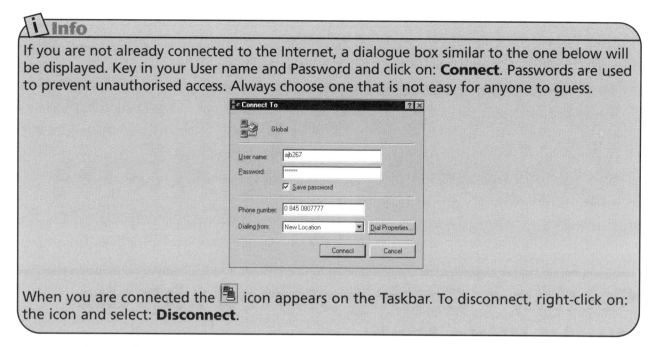

Info

If you are not already connected to the Internet, a dialogue box similar to the one below will be displayed. Key in your User name and Password and click on: **Connect**. Passwords are used to prevent unauthorised access. Always choose one that is not easy for anyone to guess.

When you are connected the 🖳 icon appears on the Taskbar. To disconnect, right-click on: the icon and select: **Disconnect**.

Either method will result in the Internet Explorer window being displayed (see Figure 7.1). Toolbar buttons are labelled in Figure 7.2

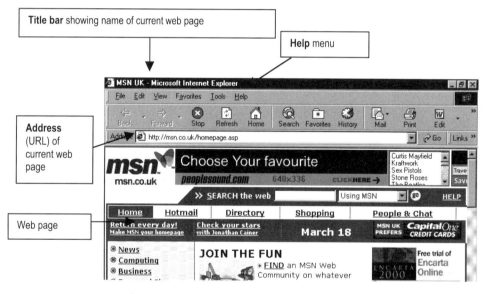

Figure 7.1 Internet Explorer window

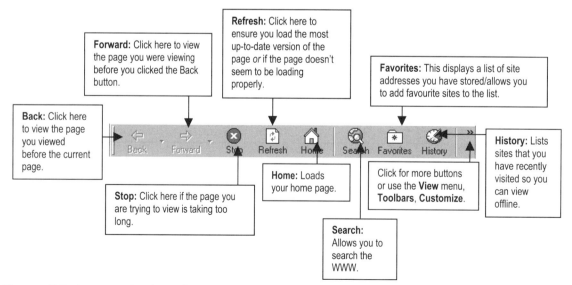

Figure 7.2 Internet Explorer buttons

1.3 What is a web address?

A *website* is a collection of pages on the Web owned by an individual or organisation. The first page of a website is the *home page*. Every web page has a unique address. This is known as a **URL** (**U**niform **R**esource **L**ocator). It usually begins with 'http://www.' (http stands for *HyperText Transfer Protocol* and tells the web browser that it is looking for a web page). Most modern browsers have 'http://' stored so you can start at 'www'. Some URLs include:

* http://www.bbc.co.uk

* http://www.bargainholidays.com

* http://www.nhm.ac.uk

The text after the www shows the *domain name*, the organisation's name – e.g. **BBC**, **bargainholidays** and **nhm** (Natural History Museum), the type of site, – e.g. **.co** and **.com** are commercial companies; **.ac** is an academic community, and the country, – e.g. **.uk** is United Kingdom. If there is no country name this often means that the website is American.

Note: The dots are important in a web address and the address must be spelt correctly.

Sometimes URLs are longer because they include the pathname to the web page e.g.:

www.bbc.co.uk/weather/worldweather/europe/index.shtml

| Folders where the Information is stored | Name of the page document |

1.4 Displaying a given web page

Exercise 2

Display the following web page:

http://www.britannica.com

Method

1   Key in the web address in the address box, press: **Enter** *or* click on: the [⟲Go] **Go to** button.
2   The first page of the **Encyclopaedia Britannica** website is displayed.

1.5 Changing your web browser's home page

Exercise 3

Change your web browser's home page so that it is the home page of **This is London**. The address is **http://www.thisislondon.co.uk**.

Info

Notice that I have used the words Home page twice in the question above. A home page can mean the page that your browser displays when it first starts up or it can mean the first page of a website. The home page of the **This is London** website is the first page you see when you enter its address.

Method

1   Go to the **This is London** home page by keying in the web address.
2   The **This is London** home page appears.

3 From the **Tools** menu, select **Internet Options**. The **Internet Options** dialogue box is displayed (see Figure 7.3).

4 With the **General** tab selected, in the **Home Page** section, click on: **Use Current**.

5 Click on: **Apply** and then on: **OK**.

Figure 7.3 Setting a browser's home page

1.6 Displaying/not displaying images

Info

It is quicker to load a web page when you do not load the images contained in it since image files are quite large. You are able to set up your browser so that it does not display images.

 Exercise 4

Load the Natural History Museum home page without images. The address is:
http://www.nhm.ac.uk

Then change the settings back to load the page with images.

 Method

1 From the **Tools** menu, select: **Internet Options**.

2 Click on: the **Advanced** tab.

3 In the **Multimedia** section, click in the boxes next to **Show pictures**, **Play videos**, **Play Animations** so that there are no ticks.

4 Click on: **Apply** and then on: **OK**.

5 Key in the **Natural History Museum** address.

6 The **Natural History Museum** home page is displayed without images.

Re-loading with images

1 Follow steps 1 to 5 again, this time placing ticks where they were removed.

2 Click on: the **Refresh** button to redisplay the page with images.

1.7 Changing view/display

Info

You may find that you want to change the look of web pages to suit your needs – i.e. colours, fonts, etc which you find easier to read. To change settings:

1 From the **Tools** menu select: **Internet Options**.

2 With the **General** tab selected, click on: **Colors** and make your choices. Similarly, click on: **Fonts** to set your preferences.

3 Click on: **Apply** and then on: **OK**.

Changing text size

From the **View** menu, select: **Text Size**. Select the size you prefer.

1.8 Saving a web page as a file

Exercise 5

Save one of the web pages you have visited as a file.

 Method

1 Load the web page by keying in the address in the **Address** box.
2 From the **File** menu, select: **Save As**.
3 The **Save As** dialogue box is displayed.
4 Select the location where you want to save the web page and key in a file name.
5 In the **Save as type** section, select from the list (see Figure 7.4).
6 Click on: **Save**.

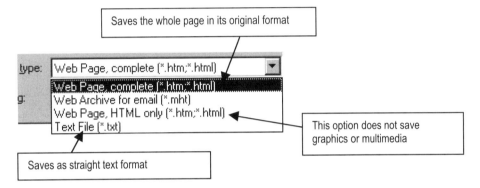

Figure 7.4 Saving a web page

1.9 Closing Internet Explorer

 Method

From the **File** menu, select: **Close**.

Section 1 Information and Communication practice

Practice 1

1 Open a web browser.
2 Display one of the following website home pages:

http://www.bbc.co.uk

http://www.channel4.co.uk

3 Set one of the site home pages as your web browser home page.
4 Save the web page as a file.
5 Change the browser's settings so that images are not loaded.
6 Display the following website home page

http://www.thisisbritain.co.uk

7 Change the browser's settings so that images are displayed.

Section 2 Browsing and favorites

In this section you will practise and learn how to:

- browse a specific site and collect data
- open a hyperlink or an image link and return to the original page
- add a web page to favorites
- add web pages to a favorites folder
- open a favorites web page.

2.1 Using hyperlinks

Web pages have links (called *hyperlinks*) that you can click on to take you to other places within the current site or to other websites. Links can take the form of underlined text, text in a different colour or they can be image links. When you hover over a link, a hand (usually) appears. The home page of the **Natural History Museum** site has text and image links (see Figure 7.5).

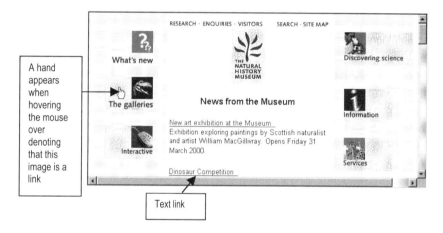

Figure 7.5 Text and image links

 Exercise 1

Follow one of the links on the **Natural History Museum** home page to find out specific information – e.g. What galleries are there? What is new?

 Method

1 Click on the link. Another page of the site is displayed. Notice that the address and Title bar have changed to reflect that you are viewing another page.

2 Collect the information you are looking for.

   a) Select the data so that it is highlighted.

   b) Click on: the **Copy** button.

   c) Open an application to copy it to e.g. Word.

   d) Click on: the **Paste** button.

3 Return to the original page by clicking on the **Back** button.

2.2 Saving a list of your favourite web sites

Info

When you find a site that you would like to visit again, or a site that you visit often, it is a good idea to save the address of the site to make it easier to re-visit in the future. These sites are then known as *Favorites* or *Bookmarks*.

Exercise 2

Save the **Natural History Museum** site in your **Favorites** list.

Method

1 With the home page of the site displayed, from the **Favorites** menu, select: **Add to Favorites**.
2 The **Add Favorite** dialogue box is displayed.
3 A default name already appears in the **Name** box. Change the name if you want to.
4 Click on: **OK**.

Accessing Favorites

Method

From the **Favorites** menu, select: the website name.

2.3 Organizing favorites

So that your list of favorites does not become unmanageable, you can organise it by creating folders to store similar content pages.

Method

1 From the **Favorites** menu, select: **Organize Favorites**.
2 The **Organize Favorites** dialogue box is displayed (see Figure 7.6).
3 Click on: the **Create Folder** button.
4 Key in a name for the new folder and press: **Enter**.
5 Drag the relevant favorites into the folder.
6 Click on: **Close**.

Note: Use the **Move to Folder** button when moving multiple favorites.

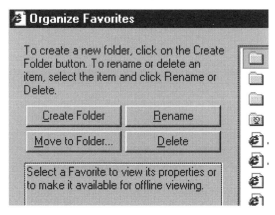

Figure 7.6 Organizing favorites

Section 2 Information and Communication practice

Practice 2

1 Access one of the sites listed below:

The Louvre	**http://www.louvre.fr**
Good Book Guide	**http://www.good-book-guide.com**
British Space Centre	**http://www.bnsc.gov.uk**
The Guardian	**http://www.newsunlimited.co.uk**
ITN Online	**http://www.itn.co.uk**

2 Using hyperlinks find out some information that is not available on the home page.

3 Add the home page of your chosen website to your favorites in a folder with the name **ECDL practice**

Section 3 Searching

In this section you will practise and learn how to:

- define search requirements
- use a key word in a search
- use common logical operators in a search

- modify page setup options
- print a web page
- present a search report as a printed document.

3.1 Searching the web

There are many ways that you can find information on the web:

- If you know the web address of the site where you can find the information, go straight to the site by keying in the address and using hyperlinks to navigate through the site (or use the site's search box if it has one).

- Using Internet Explorer's **Search** button enables you to key in a word(s) (known as a **key word**) or phrase. It then uses a search engine that will look for the key word(s) on a database of web sites. A search engine looks like a normal web page with a form to enter key words that you are looking for. It runs a program that searches its own database, an up-to-date list of websites, and provides you with a list of 'hits' – i.e. sites that contain the keyword(s).

- Using a chosen search engine: you may find that a particular search engine usually finds what you are looking for and/or you find it easy to use. Common search engines include:

  http://www.altavista.com
  http://www.hotbot.com
  http://www.excite.co.uk
  http://www.Infoseek.com
  http://www.ask.co.uk

- Using a search directory. A search directory sets out information in subject categories. This is useful if you are conducting a broad search. Currently, the most common search directory is Yahoo: **http://www.yahoo.com**. Other common search directories include:

Magellan	**http://www.mckinley.com**
Lycos	**http://www.lycos.com**
LookSmart	**http://www.looksmart.com**
What's New	**http://www.whatsnew.com**
UK Online	**http://www.ukonline.com**

 Exercise 1

Find the addresses of ECDL test centres using the different search methods. Compare the different methods as you progress – i.e. time taken, usefulness of results, ease of use.

3.2 Using the Search button

 Method

1 Click on: the **Search** button.
2 Key **ECDL** into the **Search** box and enter it by clicking on: **Search**.
3 My search revealed four possible links (see Figure 7.7).
4 Follow the links for Information.

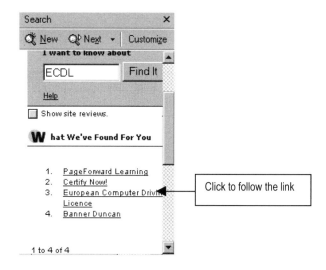

Figure 7.7 Finding Information using Search

3.3 Using a search engine

 Method

1 Access the Altavista web site.
2 In the **Search** box, key in: **ECDL** and enter it by clicking on **Search**.
3 My search resulted in the following (see Figure 7.8).
4 Follow up the links.

Figure 7.8 Using a search engine

I clicked on **ECDL test** and found 90 pages (see Figure 7.9).

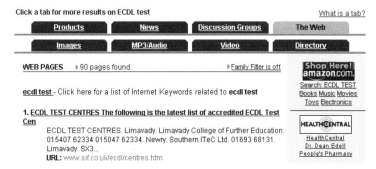

Figure 7.9 Following a link in Alta Vista

3.4 Using a search directory

 Method

1 Log on to the **Yahoo** site. Figure 7.10 shows some of the site's categories.

Reproduced with permission of Yahoo! Inc
© 2000 by Yahoo! Inc. Yahoo! and the
Yahoo! logo are trademarks of Yahoo! Inc.

Figure 7.10 Using Yahoo

2 Click on: links in the directory that you think are appropriate.

3.5 Using logical operators

You can refine your searches by keying in more than one word and using logical operators: **AND**, **NOT** (or their equivalents **AND**, **+**, **&**; **NOT**, **-**) and **OR**. Different search engines have slightly different rules about how you enter searches with logical operators.

Using AND

Use **AND** or one of the symbols when searching for more than one word. Results will list sites that contain all the search words.

Examples:

• You are interested in finding information on football and in particular Everton. In the **Search** box, key in **Football + Everton**.

• You are interested in finding information about Oscars and Disney. In the **Search** box, key in **Oscars + Disney**.

Using OR

You are interested in finding information about cameras. You could key in **Camera OR Photography**, since both of these might find useful information.

 Info

For some search engines, quotation marks can be used to group words together – e.g. **"motor racing"** may find more confined results than **motor racing**.

Try out some other searches with logical operators. Note the different search format requirements and which methods give the most relevant results.

3.6 Modifying page setup ready for printing

 Method

1   From the **File** menu, select: **Page Setup** (see Figure 7.11).
2   Change the paper size, orientation and margins.
3   Use **Internet Explorer Help** if you want to set headers and footers.
4   Click on: **OK**.

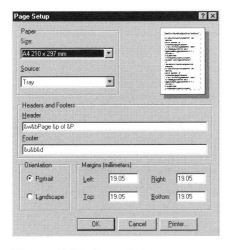

Figure 7.11 Page Setup

3.7 Printing a web page

 Method

1   From the **File** menu, select: **Print**.
2   The Print dialogue box is displayed (see Figure 7.12).

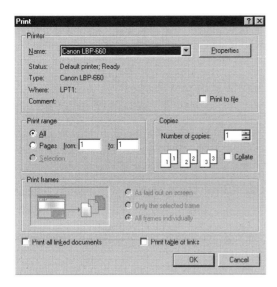

Figure 7.12 Printing

3 Make selections as appropriate.
4 If the web page is divided into frames, enter your choices in the **Print Frames** section.
5 Click on: **OK**.

---

i Info

You can also choose to print a table of links. This is useful for reference.

WARNING: Remember anyone can set up a website and Information may not always be correct or may be misleading. Always check that information is from a reliable source.

3.8 Exit Internet Explorer.

Section 3 Information and communication practice

Practice 3

1 Using a search engine or a search directory, find answers to some of the following questions:

What is the current line-up of the Leicester City football team?
What is on BBC1 and ITN at 8 pm this evening?
What is the population of the UK?
What time do trains depart from Bristol tomorrow morning (leaving at approx 9.30 am), destination Leeds? Are there any changes en route?

2 Print out the results of your searches detailing the information requested.

Section 4 Getting started with e-mail

In this section you will practice and learn how to:

- open an electronic mail application
- use application Help functions
- change display modes
- modify toolbar display
- create a new message
- insert a mail address in the mail to box

- insert a title in the subject field
- use a spell checking tool (if available)
- send a message with low/high priority
- copy a message to another address
- use blind copy tool
- receive messages
- add an auto-signature to a message
- close the electronic mail application.

Introduction

The following sections focus on sending and receiving e-mail using Microsoft Outlook Express 5. By demonstrating the methods used by Outlook Express you will gain an insight into the procedures involved even though you may be using a different e-mail system. It should be relatively easy to apply what you learn here to your own e-mail system.

Note: Since Outlook Express can be configured to suit your needs, the Outlook Express settings used in the examples may differ slightly from your settings. This could result in some of the methods given not conforming exactly to those that you may see on your computer.

4.1 Opening Outlook Express

 Exercise 1

Open Outlook Express.

 Method

From the **Start** menu, select: **Programs, Outlook Express** *or* click on: the 🔄 **Launch Outlook Express** icon on the **Taskbar**.

Either method will result in the Outlook Express window being displayed on screen (see Figure 7.13):

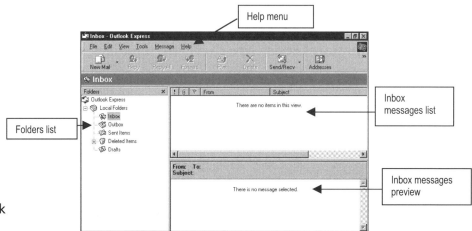

Figure 7.13 Outlook Express 5 window

The Folders list contains:

- **Inbox** folder – where incoming messages are stored
- **Outbox** folder – where outgoing messages are stored
- **Sent Items** folder – where sent messages are stored
- **Deleted Items** folder – where deleted items are stored
- **Drafts** folder – where draft messages are stored.

Info

You can change the layout and modify the toolbar to suit your needs by selecting: **Layout** from the **View** menu. The **Window Layout Properties** dialogue box is displayed as shown below:

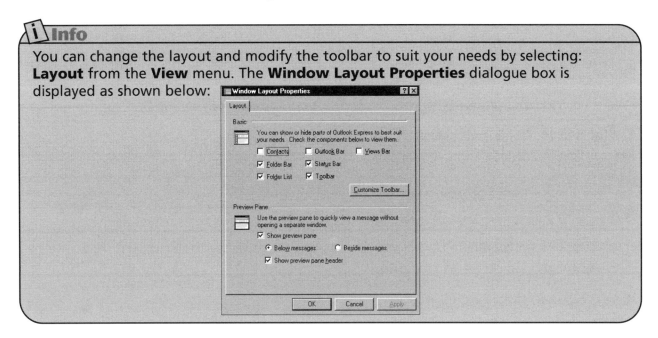

4.2 Creating messages

Exercise 2

Create the message (shown below) and send it to someone you know who has an e-mail address.

Note: If you do not have anyone to send it to, then send it to your own e-mail address.

Hi there [insert person's name]

I am learning how to use e-mail. Please let me know if you have received this message.

Thanks.

[Insert your name]

 Method

1 Click on: the [New Mail] **New Mail** button.
2 The **New Message** window appears (see Figure 7.14).
3 Click in the **To:** box and key in the e-mail address of the person you are sending the message to. Check that you have keyed in the address correctly.

Header section:
Click in the boxes and key in the e-mail address(es) of recipient(s) and subject here.

Message section:
Click in this area and key in your message here.

Figure 7.14 Creating a message

Info

It is very important that the address is keyed in correctly, otherwise it will not reach its destination. Each dot (full stop) is important. If you have made an error, you can delete it and key it in again.

E-mail addresses are made up of: the user's name, followed by the **@** symbol, followed by the address of the user's service provider. This includes the domain category; in this example **co**, meaning a company or commercial organisation in the UK, followed by the country, **uk** (United Kingdom).

Example   A.Smith@somewhere.co.uk

Common domain categories include the following:

ac = academic community (in the UK)
co = company or commercial organisation (in the UK)
com = company or commercial organisation
edu = educational institution
org = non-profit organisation

Each country has its own unique code, – e.g. **fr** =France, **ca** = Canada, **se** =Sweden.

4   Click in the header section, subject line and key in: **Just testing**.
5   Click in the message section underneath and key in the message.

Note: The subject of your message 'Just testing' has replaced 'New Document' on the Title bar.

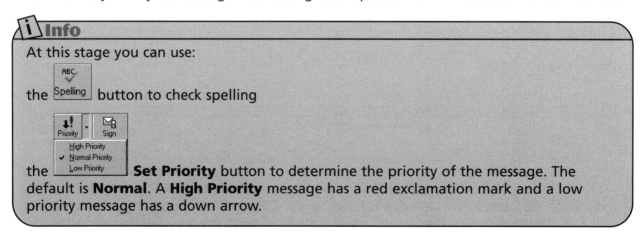

Info

At this stage you can use:

the Spelling button to check spelling

the Set Priority button to determine the priority of the message. The default is **Normal**. A **High Priority** message has a red exclamation mark and a low priority message has a down arrow.

6   Click on: the Send button.

Note: This will not send the message at this stage but will transfer it to your **Outbox** folder.

7 You are returned to the original **Outlook Express** window with the **Outbox** contents displayed (see Figure 7.15).

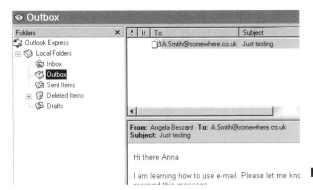

Figure 7.15 Outbox contents are displayed

4.3 Transmitting and receiving messages

Exercise 3

Transmit the message that you have prepared.

Method

1 Click on: the Send/Recv **Send and Receive All** button.
2 Outlook Express will send the message automatically and will display that it is sending the message.
3 When it has been transmitted, it is placed in the **Sent Items** folder. Click on: the folder to check.

4.4 Copying messages

The same message can be sent to more than one address at a time.

Sending the message on equal terms to more than one address

In the **To:** box, key in the e-mail addresses and separate them with semicolons.

Example   A.Smith@somewhere.co.uk;J.Jones@somewhereelse.ac.uk

Note: You don't need a space after the semi-colon.

Sending 'carbon copies'

1 In the **To:** box, key in the first person's e-mail address.
2 In the **Cc:** box, key in the second person's e-mail address.

The main recipient(s) is the person in the **To:** box, with a 'carbon copy' sent to the second addressee(s).

Sending blind copies

Sometimes you may want to send a copy of the e-mail to an addressee(s) without other recipients' knowledge.

1 From the **View** menu, select: **All Headers**.
2 A **Bcc** box appears where you can enter the recipient's address(es).

Note: With all of the above, the message is again placed in your **Sent Items** folder and is still treated as one message, even though it has been transmitted to more than one e-mail address.

4.5 Setting up an auto-signature

An auto-signature consists of text that you want to include at the end of your message (and saves keying it in each time). You can set up more than one signature for different types of recipient.

Setting a signature

1 In the main **Outlook Express** window, from the **Tools** menu, select: **Options**.
2 In the **Options** dialogue box, click on: the **Signatures** tab (see Figure 7.16).
3 In the **Signatures** section, click on: **New**.
4 Select **Text** and key in your text in the **Edit Signature** box.
5 Click on: **Apply**, then on: **OK**.

Inserting a signature in a message

You can select **Add signatures to all outgoing messages** by clicking in the box next to this option (see Figure 7.16).

OR

In the **New Message** window, after you have keyed in your message, from the **Insert** menu, select: **Signature**.

Figure 7.16 Setting up a signature

4.6 Close Outlook Express

 Method

From the **File** menu, select: **Exit** *or* click on: the **Close** button.

Section 4 Information and Communication practice

Practice 4

1   Open an electronic mail application.
2   Send the following message with high priority to someone you know and a copy to someone else. Give the message the title **Seminar**.

Hello

Thank you for letting me know about the seminar. I will certainly be there. Perhaps we could meet in the cafeteria afterwards?

Regards

[Add an auto-signature]

Auto-signature should include your name, job title and ext no.

Section 5 Organising messages

In this section you will practice and learn how to:

- open a mail message
- open a mail inbox for a specified user
- attach a file to a message
- delete text in a message
- delete a file attachment from a message
- open and save an attachment
- use reply to sender/reply to all
- reply with/without original message insertion
- forward a message
- use copy and paste to duplicate text within a message or to another active message
- use cut and paste to insert text from another source into a message
- use cut and paste to move text within a message or to another active message
- create a new mail folder
- delete a message
- sort messages by name, subject, date etc
- move messages to a new mail folder
- mark/highlight a message in a mail folder
- search for a message.

5.1 Opening received mail messages

 Exercise 1

Open messages received.

Note: If you have not yet received replies to your e-mails then you will need to send an e-mail to your own e-mail address so that there is a message received.

 Method

1 Load Outlook Express as in Section 4.1 (page 288) – if not already loaded.
2 You will notice that there is a number (in this example, 2) next to your **Inbox** folder, indicating that two messages have been received (see Figure 7.17).

Figure 7.17 Messages have been received

3 The message(s) are displayed in the right-hand window.
4 Click once on the message to see it in the **Preview** window (bottom right), or double-click it to see it in a separate window (see Figure 7.18).

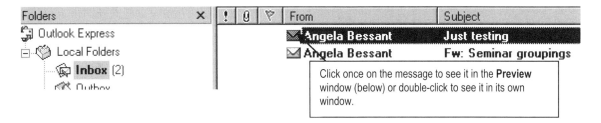

Figure 7.18 Viewing a received message

5.2 Opening another user's Inbox messages

Creating folders for other users

There may be several people accessing mail on the same account. If this is the case, you can add new identities for the other users as follows:

1 From the **File** menu, select **Identities** then **Add New Identity**.
2 Key in the name of the new user.
3 Enter a password if you want to use one for this user.
4 Repeat these steps until all users have been entered.

Opening user's inboxes

If another user wants you to check their mail, look to see if they have a number next to their folder. If so, click on: the folder so that their messages appear in the right hand window. Access as in Section 5.1 (page 294).

5.3 Attaching files to messages

Sometimes you may want to enclose something with your message – e.g. a picture or a different type of file. In such cases you can add a file to your message. This is called an attachment. You can add more than one file. These then are called attachments.

 Exercise 2

Create a simple Excel or a Word file. Save the file with the filename **TEST**. Send a message, together with the file **TEST** (the attachment) to an e-mail address. Ask the recipient to send you an attachment.

 Method

1 Create a simple file and save it with the name **TEST** in a place you will know where to find it (e.g. on a floppy disk in drive A).
2 Load Outlook Express and key in the following new message:

Hi [name of recipient]

I am practising sending and receiving attachments to e-mail messages. Please find the attached file TEST.

Please could you let me know that you have received this and also please could you send me an example attachment?

Thanks.

[Your name]

Note: **DO NOT CLICK SEND YET**

3 Click on: the **Attach File** button.

4 The **Insert Attachment** dialogue box appears (see Figure 7.19).

Figure 7.19 Insert Attachment dialogue box

5 Select the drive where the file is located, – e.g. Drive A. Click on: the file so that it appears in the **File name** box (or key in the file name).

6 Click on: **Attach**.

7 You will notice that your attachment is now shown in the header section (see Figure 7.20).

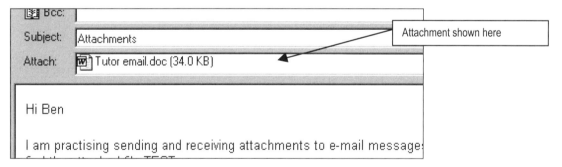

Figure 7.20 E-mail with an attachment

You can now send the file in the normal way.

ⓘ Info

You can attach more than one file to a message by repeating steps 3 to 6 for each extra file.

5.4 Viewing attachments

Exercise 3

View an attachment you have received.

 Method

When you receive a message with an attachment, the message has a paperclip icon next to it (see Figure 7.21).

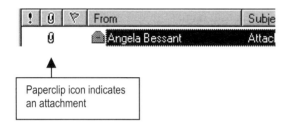

Figure 7.21 Receiving attachments

1 Double-click on: the message to view it in a separate window.
2 In the **Attach** box, double-click on: the attached file (see Figure 7.22). The file will appear in its own program window.

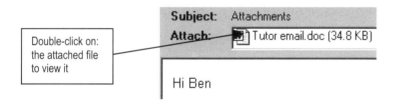

Figure 7.22 Viewing an attachment

3 When you have finished viewing the file, close its window in the normal way. You are returned to Outlook Express.

5.5 Saving a file attachment

1 Double-click on: the message with the attachment so that it appears in its own window.
2 From the **File** menu, select: **Save Attachments**.
3 The **Save Attachments** dialogue box is displayed (see Figure 7.23).

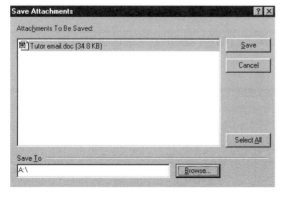

Figure 7.23 Saving attachments

4 Click on: **Browse** to choose where to save it.

5 Click on: **Save**.

or

Right-click on: the attachment and select: **Save As** (see Figure 7.24).

Figure 7.24 Saving the attachments by right-clicking

5.6 Deleting a file attachment from a message

When sending attachments, if you have chosen the wrong one or need to delete one for any other reason, select the attachment by clicking on it. Press: **Delete**.

5.7 Replying to a message

 Method

1 Click on: the [Reply] **Reply to Sender** button. The address and subject are already entered.

2 Key in your reply.

3 If you want to delete the original message, select it and press: **Delete**.

4 Send the message in the usual way.

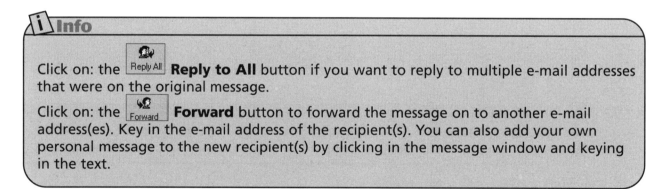

5.8 Using cut/copy and paste

You can use the **Cut/Copy** and **Paste** from the **Edit** menu, as in other Office applications, to move and duplicate text within a message or to another active message.

You can also **Cut/Copy** and **Paste** to insert text from another source – e.g. a Word document or web page.

5.9 Deleting a message

In the main window, select the message to delete. Press: **Delete**.

To select adjacent messages, hold down **Shift** when selecting.

To select non-adjacent messages, hold down **Ctrl** when selecting.

Info

Deleted messages are sent to the **Deleted Items** folder. You can recover deleted messages from here. It is a good idea to empty this folder from time to time. To do this right-click on: the folder and select: **Empty 'Deleted Items' Folder**. You can also delete messages by selecting them and pressing: **Delete**

5.10 Sorting messages

When you have numerous messages, you may want to sort them so that they are easier to locate. To sort by name, subject or date, click on: the relevant heading at the top of the messages window (see Figure 7.25). In Figure 7.25 there is a down arrow next to **Sent** indicating that the messages are sorted in descending date order.

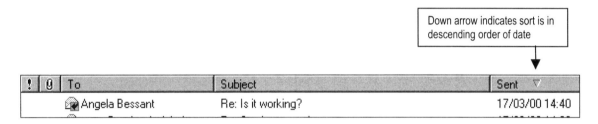

Figure 7.25 Sorting messages

For a more comprehensive sort, from the **View** menu, select: **Sort By**. Options available are shown in Figure 7.26:

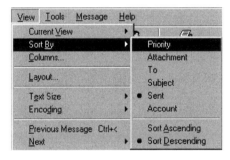

Figure 7.26 Sorting messages using the View menu

5.11 Moving/copying messages to a new mail folder

To move messages

 Method

1 Select the message(s) to move.
2 From the **Edit** menu, select: **Move to Folder** or **Copy to Folder**.
3 The **Move** or **Copy** dialogue box is displayed (see Figure 7.27).

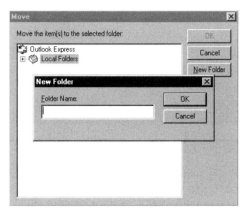

Figure 7.27 Moving messages to a new folder

4 Click on: **New Folder** and key in a name for the folder.
5 Click on: **OK**.
6 The message(s) is moved or copied to the new folder.

5.12 Marking/highlighting a message in a mail folder

In order to help you process mail effectively and efficiently, you can set rules so that messages are automatically categorised. For instance you can highlight messages in colour or let Outlook automatically put them into specified folders.

 Exercise 4

Mark all messages containing the words **Cybercafe Company** in red.

 Method

1 From the **Tools** menu, select **Message Rules, Mail**.
2 The **New Mail Rule** dialogue box is displayed (see Figure 7.28).
3 In section **1 – Select the condition for your rule**. Place a tick by the line: **Where the subject line contains specific words**.
4 In section **2 – Select the Actions for your rule**, place a tick in by the line: **Highlight it with color**.
5 In section **3 – Rule Description**, click on: **contains specific words**.

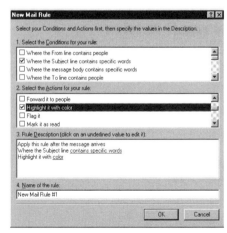

Figure 7.28 New Mail Rule dialogue box

The **Type Specific Words** dialogue box is displayed.

6 Key in the words **Cybercafe Company** and click on: **Add** then on: **OK**.

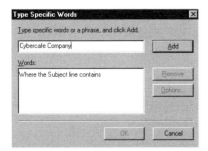

Figure 7.29 Type Specific Words dialogue box

7 Still in section 3, click on: **Color**.

8 Select **Red** from the colour list, click on: **OK**.

9 Click on: **Apply Now** and then click on: **OK** again.

Test this by sending a message to your e-mail address containing the words **Cybercafe Company**.

5.13 Searching for a message

 Method

1 Select the folder where you think the message is saved.

2 From the **Edit** menu, select: **Find**, **Message** or click on: the [Find] **Find** button.

3 The **Find Message** dialogue box appears (see Figure 7.30).

> **i Info**
>
> In this example, I have selected the **Inbox** folder at step 1. This method searches the **Inbox** folder and its subfolders when the **Include subfolders** box is ticked. If you do not find your message in a particular folder, click on: **Browse** to select other possible locations.

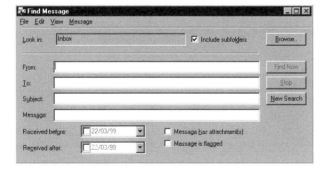

Figure 7.30 Finding messages

4 Key in details of your message in the appropriate boxes and then click on: **Find Now**.

5.14 Close Outlook Express as shown in Section 4.6 (page 292).

Section 5 Information and Communication practice

Practice 5

1 Access any received message and forward it to someone.
2 Copy one sentence from a received message to a new e-mail message.
3 Title the new message: **Attachments**.
4 Send it to someone and send a blind copy to someone else.
5 Create a short Word file and send it as an attachment with the e-mail.
6 Save any received e-mail to a folder named: **ECDL**.
7 Set a rule so that all messages relating to **ECDL** are highlighted.
8 Save a received attachment onto a floppy disk.
9 Look for all messages from a particular person using **Find**, **Message**.
10 Sort your emails into date order.
11 Delete an old message that you don't need to keep.

Section 6 The Address Book

In this section you will practise and learn how to:

- add a mail address to an address list
- update an Address Book for incoming mail
- delete a mail address from an address list
- create a new address list/distribution list
- reply to a message using a distribution list.

6.1 About the Address Book

The Outlook Address Book enables you to store addresses you often use. Using the Address book means that you do not have to remember all those cumbersome e-mail addresses and saves you having to key in addresses each time you send messages.

6.2 Adding an address to the Address Book

 Method

1 Click on the **Address Book** button.
2 The Address Book – Main Identity dialogue box is displayed (Figure 7.31).

Figure 7.31 Displaying the Address Book

3 Click on the **New** button and then **New Contact**.
4 The Properties dialogue box is displayed (Figure 7.32).

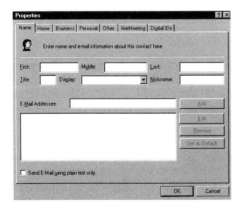

Figure 7.32 Properties dialogue box awaiting new contact details

5 With the **Name** tab selected, key in the details of your contact.

Note: By selecting other tabs you can enter further details of your contact as appropriate.

6 Click on **OK**. The new contact is added to your Address Book list.

Outlook Express can automatically add addresses to your Address Book when you send e-mail. To set this option:

1 From the **Tools** menu, select: **Options**.
2 Click on the **Send** tab.
3 Click next to **Automatically put people I reply to in my address book**.

Output Express can add addresses to your Address Book by the following method:

1 Open the mail message from the contact.
2 From the **Tools** menu, select **Add to Address Book** and click on the contact name.
3 Click on **OK**.

6.3 Deleting an address

 Method

1 Open the Address Book as in 6.2.
2 Select the address to delete.
3 Press: **Delete**.
4 You will be asked to confirm the delete. Click on **Yes**.

6.4 Creating an address list

If you want to send a message to people who belong to a certain group, you can create a group address list. When you have set up the group list you will need to key in the name of the group only to send the message to all members.

 Method

1 Click on the **Address Book** button.
2 Click on the **New** button, then on **New Group**. The properties dialogue box is displayed (Figure 7.33).

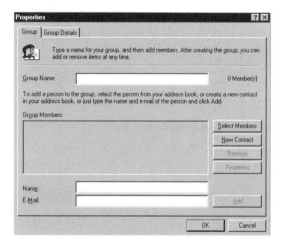

Figure 7.33 Adding a group

3 In the **Group Name** box, key in the name of the new group.
4 Click on **Select Members** to add addresses already in your address book.
5 Click on **New Contact** to add new addresses to both the list and your address book.

Note: If you want to add an address to the group list only, enter the name and e-mail address in the boxes at the bottom of the Properties dialogue box.

6 When you have completed the group entries, click on **OK**.

6.5 Sending messages using the Address Book

 Method

1 Click on the **New Message** button.

2 In the header section, click on the **To**: section.
3 The Select Recipients dialgoue box is displayed.
4 Click on the recipient's name or the group name and click on the ⬜ To: -> button.
5 Click on **OK**.

> **ℹ️ Info**
> You can select as many recipients as you want and add them to the To, Cc or Bcc boxes.

6.6 Close Outlook Express

Section 6 Information and Communication practice

Practice 6

1   Add the following contact to the Address Book: Jackie Louise Watson, Ms: <u>J.L.Watson@</u>
<u>anywhere.com</u>

2   Delete one of the names in your address book.
3   Set up a new group called **Sports**. Include the following in the group:

Jackie Watson and two other contacts in your address book.

4   Send a message to the Sports mailing list with the title **Newsflash** as follows:

NEWS JUST IN
Carl De Vere has just been announced team captain for the under 18s Rugby Club.
I think you will agree that it is justly deserved.

Your name

5   Close the electronic mail application.

Using the Web quick reference guide

Action	Keyboard	Mouse	Right-mouse menu	Menu
Access a website	Key in the web address (URL) in the address box			
Change View/ display				**Tools**, **Internet** **Options**, **General** and Make selections from **View**
Exit Internet Explorer		Click: the ☒ Close button		**File**, **Close**
Favorites, add to open		Click: the [Favorites] **Favorites** button, click: the [Add..] **Add** button	**Add to Favorites**	**Favorites**, **Add** **to Favorites**
Folder, create favorites folder		Click: the [Favorites] **Favorites** button, Click: the [Organize...] **Organize** button		**Favorites**, **Organize Favorites**
Help	**F1**			**Help**, **Contents** **and Index**
Hyperlink, following		Click: the hyperlink		
Images Display Do not display				**Tools**, **Internet** **Options**, **Multimedia**, **Show** **Pictures**
Open Internet Explorer	In Windows 98 desktop			
		Click: the 🅔 **Launch** **Internet Explorer** **Browser** icon on the Taskbar		**Start**, **Programs**, **Internet Explorer**
Page setup				**File**, **Page Setup**
Print	**Ctrl + P**	Click: the 🖨 **Print** button	**Print**	**File**, **Print**
Return to original page		Click: the [Back] **Back** button		
Searching, using common logical operators	Use **Search** button *or* a Search Engine Use **AND**, **+**, **&**, or **NOT**, **-**, or use **OR**			

Electronic mail quick reference guide

Action	Keyboard	Mouse	Right-mouse menu	Menu
Access received messages		Click: **Inbox** in left-hand window Click: the message (to view in Preview) or Double-click: the message (to view in own window		
Address Book, *Open*		Click: the [Addresses] **Address Book** button		**Tools, Address Book**
Add address	Open Address Book.			
		Click: the [New] **New** button		**File, New Contact**
	Click: the **Name** tab. Enter details. Click: **OK**			
Delete address	Open Address Book			
	Delete	Click: the [Delete] **Delete** button	**Delete**	**File, Delete**
Create address/ distribution list	Open Address Book	Click: the [New] **New** button		**File, New Group**
		Click: the **Group** tab. Enter **Group Name** Select Members to add addresses already in the address book New Contact to add new addresses. Click: **OK**		
Attach files to messages		Click: the [📎] **Attach File** button		**Insert, File**
Attachment, delete	Double-click the message with the attachment so that it appears in its own window. Select attachment			
	Delete	Click: the [Delete] **Delete** button		
Attachments, save	Select the attachment			
			Save **As**	**File, Save Attachments**
Auto-signature, add				**Tools, Options, Signatures**
Copy/paste	**Ctrl + C** **Ctrl + V**			**Edit, Copy** **Edit, Paste**
Copy/Move messages to folders			**Copy to Folder** **Move to Folder**	**Edit, Move to Folder** **Copy to Folder**
Create messages		Click: the **Compose Message** button		

Action	Keyboard	Mouse	Right-mouse menu	Menu
Delete, message,	Select message			
	Delete	Click: the X **Delete** button	**Delete**	**Edit**, **Delete**
Delete, text	Select text			
	Delete			
Exit Outlook Express		Click: the ⊠ **Close** button		**File**, E**x**it
Folders, create new				**File**, **New**, **Folder**
Forward a message	**Ctrl + F**	Click: the Forward **Forward** button	**Forward**	**Message**, **Forward**
Help	**F1**			**Help**, **Contents and Index**
Highlight message				**Tools**, **Message Rules**, **Mail**
Load Outlook Express	In Windows 98 desktop			
		Click: the 🖫 **Launch Outlook Express** icon on the Taskbar		**Start**, **Programs**, **Outlook Express**
Print messages	(With transaction details and message visible in its own window)			
	Ctrl + P	Click: the 🖨 **Print** button		**File**, **Print**
Prioritise messages		With the message displayed, click: the Priority **Set Priority** button arrow		
Reply to all	**Ctrl + Shift + R**	Click: the Reply All **Reply All** button	**Reply to All**	
Reply to sender	**Ctrl + R**	Click: the Reply **Reply** button	**Reply to Sender**	
Route/address messages Multiple recipients	Key in the address in the **To:** box Separate addresses with semicolons (;) Use **Cc** box to send a 'carbon copy'. Use **Bcc** box to send a 'blind copy			
Search for a message		Click: the Find **Find** button		**Edit**, **Find**, **Message**
Sort messages	Click on: the relevant heading at the top of the messages window			
Spellcheck	**F7**			**Tools**, **Spelling**
Transmit messages		Click: the Send/Recv **Send and Receive** button		**Tools**, **Send and Receive**
View attachments	(With message in its own window – attachment visible)			
		Double-click: the attachment		

Module 7 practice tasks

Answers to the following questions can be found in Module 7 or Module 1 text.

1   What is a web browser?
2   Explain what a hyperlink is.
3   Give an example of a web address (real or made up). Explain how each part is derived.
4   What is another name for a web address?
5   Home page can have two different meanings. Explain.
6   When carrying out a search, what is a key word?
7   Explain how a search engine would help you find something on the web.
8   Why are passwords used when accessing the Internet?
9   What is an e-mail attachment?
10 How do you send e-mail messages to more than one person at the same time?
11 What is an e-mail signature? Why would you use one?
12 In e-mail, what is an address book and why is it useful?
13 How do you save a copy of an e-mail for yourself?
14 What is a group address list?

Practical tasks

1   Find out what is on at the London theatres. Send two sentences about two events via e-mail to your supervisor/tutor.
2   Find two different airline sites. What are the differences between them and which one do you prefer? Send an e-mail to your supervisor/tutor containing the names of the sites and three points in favour of your preferred site.
3   Find two organisations specialising in distance learning. Do either of them offer qualifications in languages? Send a short e-mail to your supervisor/tutor reporting what you have found.

Note: This is only a practice test. Successful completion does not imply certification of the module by the ECDL Foundation.

Answers to Exercises

Module 3, Section 1.8, Exercise 5

LANDMARKS IN LONDON

St Paul's Cathedral

St Paul's Cathedral is one of London's landmarks and is renowned throughout the world. It is the largest church in the city and was built on the same site and to replace a Norman church that was destroyed by the Great Fire of 1666.

The Whispering Gallery

This famous Renaissance building was designed by Sir Christopher Wren and has many interesting features. One of its most intriguing is the Whispering Gallery which runs round the inside of the great dome. If you speak in this gallery the sound waves of your voice are carried round the entire circumference of the gallery because the waves are prevented from going outwards by the stones lining the circular wall. These acoustic properties enable someone sitting far away on the opposite side of the gallery to hear your voice, even if you are whispering.

Famous people

Many famous people are buried at St Paul's and their tombs can be found either in the church or in the crypt beneath. They include Nelson, Wellington, Turner and Sir Christopher Wren.

Module 3, Section 2.13, Exercise 12

LANDMARKS IN LONDON

St Paul's Cathedral

St Paul's Cathedral is one of London's landmarks and is renowned throughout the world. It is the largest cathedral in the city and was built to replace a Norman cathedral that was destroyed by the Great Fire of 1666.

Sir Christopher Wren

Over the north door, Wren's epitaph is inscribed in Latin. It is - Si monumentum requiris, circumspice. This translated into English means - If you seek his memorial, look around you.

The Whispering Gallery

This famous Renaissance building was designed by Sir Christopher Wren and has many interesting features. One of its most intriguing is the Whispering Gallery which runs round the inside of the great dome. If you speak in this gallery the sound waves of your voice are carried round the entire circumference of the gallery because the waves are prevented from going outwards by the stones lining the circular wall. These acoustic properties enable someone sitting far away on the opposite side of the gallery to hear your voice, even if you are whispering.

Famous people

Many famous people are buried at St Paul's and their tombs can be found either in the cathedral or in the crypt beneath. They include Roberts, Jellicoe, Beatty, Nelson, Wellington, Turner and Sir Christopher Wren.

LANDMARKS IN LONDON

Module 3, Section 2.14, Exercise 15(a)

Picnics can be enjoyed in the summer when the weather is usually warm and dry.

St Paul's Cathedral is one of London's landmarks and is renowned throughout the world. It is the largest cathedral in the city and was built to replace a Norman cathedral that was destroyed by the Great Fire of 1666.

Module 3, Section 2.14, Exercise 15(b)

St Paul's Cathedral is one of London's landmarks and is renowned throughout the world. It is the largest cathedral in the city and was built to replace a Norman cathedral that was destroyed by the Great Fire of 1666.

Famous people

Many famous people are buried at St Paul's and their tombs can be found either in the cathedral or in the crypt beneath. They include Roberts, Jellicoe, Beatty, Nelson, Wellington, Turner and Sir Christopher Wren.

LANDMARKS IN LONDON Walkabouts Company ©

Module 3, Section 2, Practice 3, Step 4

THE WORLD WIDE WEB

Many commercial services are now offered on the WWW. You can order books, arrange a car rental anywhere in the world, and even purchase and download new software direct to your computer. If you live in the right area, you can even order a pizza via the WWW!

It was developed to help scientists share information and has rapidly become a general service for everyone. Using a suitably configured computer, users can access information on the WWW (known as web pages) from anywhere in the world. These pages can be created by anyone, from schoolchildren right up to the world's largest companies.

The ability to combine text, pictures, videos and sound makes the WWW ideal for entertainment pages. Most bands, films and computer games have their own official pages, and there are often many more set up by fans.

Be wary of what you find on the WWW. Always check the source of any information given. Remember that anyone can set up a website and the content authenticity will not always have been scrutinized.

THE WORLD WIDE WEB

Many commercial services are now offered on the web. If you live in the right area, you can even order a pizza via the web! You can order books, arrange a car rental anywhere in the world, and even purchase and download new software direct to your computer.

The possibilities are endless. User groups are growing daily. Who would have thought that people would be doing their weekly grocery shopping using the web?

It was developed to help scientists share information and has rapidly become a general service for everyone. Using a suitably configured computer, users can access information on the web (known as web pages) from anywhere in the world.

The ability to combine text, pictures, videos and sound makes the web ideal for entertainment pages. Most bands, films and computer games have their own official pages, and there are often many more set up by fans.

Be wary of what you find on the web. Always check the source of any information given. Remember that anyone can set up a website and the content authenticity will not always have been scrutinized.

The ability to combine text, pictures, videos and sound makes the web ideal for entertainment pages. Most bands, films and computer games have their own official pages, and there are often many more set up by fans.

Be wary of what you find on the web. Always check the source of any information given. Remember that anyone can set up a website and the content authenticity will not always have been scrutinized.

Module 3, Section 2, Practice 4, Step 4

Thank you for filling in our recent Holiday questionnaire.

We are constantly striving to improve our services for you and to offer the kind of holidays that you will enjoy. Your comments have been noted and we will do our best to exceed your expectations.

Our new brochure features more than 1,100 idyllic cottages, 160 luxury villas with pools (usually available in the summer months only), more than 2,000 hotels and over 40 apartments at holiday villages, with superb on-site facilities. We also offer deluxe camping and mobile homes at 20 wonderful 4-star sites and theme parks including Disneyland, Paris, Parc Asterix and Futuroscope.

We would like to reward you for helping us with our survey. We are delighted to offer you a 10% saving on your next holiday. If you would like to benefit from this offer, please quote code Q2000 when you call.

We look forward to hearing from you soon.

Module 3, Section 2, Practice 4, Step 11

Thank you for filling in our recent Holiday questionnaire.

We are continually striving to improve our services for you and to offer the kind of holidays that you will enjoy.

We would like to reward you for helping us with our survey. We are delighted to offer you a 10% saving on your next holiday. However, you must act within 28 days. If you would like to benefit from this offer, please quote code Q2000 when you call.

Our new brochure features more than 1,100 idyllic cottages, 160 luxury villas with pools (usually available in the summer months only), more than 2,000 hotels and over 40 apartments at holiday villages, with superb on-site facilities. We also offer deluxe camping and mobile homes at 20 wonderful 4-star sites and theme parks including Disneyland, Paris, Parc Astérix and Futuroscope.

We look forward to hearing from you soon.

Module 3, Section 3.9, Exercise 7

LANDMARKS IN LONDON

St Paul's Cathedral

St Paul's Cathedral is one of London's landmarks and is renowned throughout the world. It is the largest cathedral in the city and was built to replace a Norman cathedral that was destroyed by the Great Fire of 1666.

Sir Christopher Wren

Over the north door, Wren's epitaph is inscribed in Latin. It is - *Si monumentum requiris, circumspice.* This translated into English means - If you seek his memorial, look around you.

The Whispering Gallery

This famous Renaissance building was designed by Sir Christopher Wren and has many interesting features. One of its most intriguing is the Whispering Gallery which runs round the inside of the great dome. If you speak in this gallery the sound waves of your voice are carried round the entire circumference of the gallery because the waves are prevented from going outwards by the stones lining the circular wall.

These acoustic properties enable someone sitting far away on the opposite side of the gallery to hear your voice, even if you are whispering.

Famous people

Many famous people are buried at St Paul's and their tombs can be found either in the cathedral or in the crypt beneath. They include Roberts, Jellicoe, Beatty, Nelson, Wellington, Turner and Sir Christopher Wren.

LANDMARKS IN LONDON Walkabouts Company ©

LANDMARKS IN LONDON

St Paul's Cathedral

St Paul's Cathedral is one of London's landmarks and is renowned throughout the world. It is the largest cathedral in the city and was built to replace a Norman cathedral that was destroyed by the Great Fire of 1666.

Sir Christopher Wren

Over the north door, Wren's epitaph is inscribed in Latin. It is

- *Si monumentum requiris, circumspice.* This translated into English means - If you seek his memorial, look around you.

London Information   24/03/00   Angela Bessant

2

The Whispering Gallery

This famous Renaissance building was designed by Sir Christopher Wren and has many interesting features. One of its most intriguing is the Whispering Gallery which runs round the inside of the great dome. If you speak in this gallery the sound waves of your voice are carried round the entire circumference of the gallery because the waves are prevented from going outwards by the stones lining the circular wall. These acoustic properties enable someone sitting far away on the opposite side of the gallery to hear your voice, even if you are whispering.

Famous people

Many famous people are buried at St Paul's and their tombs can be found either in the cathedral or in the crypt beneath. They include Roberts, Jellicoe, Beatty, Nelson, Wellington, Turner and Sir Christopher Wren.

LANDMARKS IN LONDON Walkabouts Company ©

London Information   24/03/00   Angela Bessant

Angela Bessant

3

World Wide Web

THE WORLD WIDE WEB

Many commercial services are now offered on the web. If you live in the right area, you can even order a pizza via the web! You can order books, arrange a car rental anywhere in the world, and even purchase and download new software direct to your computer.

The possibilities are endless. User groups are growing daily. Who would have thought that people would be doing their weekly grocery shopping using the web?

Angela Bessant

World Wide Web

It was developed to help scientists share information and has rapidly become a general

service for everyone. Using a suitably configured computer, users can access information

on the web (known as web pages) from anywhere in the world.

The ability to combine text, pictures, videos and sound makes the web ideal for

entertainment pages. Most bands, films and computer games have their own official pages,

and there are often many more set up by fans.

Be wary of what you find on the web. Always check the

source of any information given. Remember that anyone can

set up a website and the content authenticity will not always

have been scrutinized.

4

Module 3, Section 3, Practice 6, Step 7

Details of your reward

Thank you for filling in our recent Holiday questionnaire.

We are continually striving to improve our services for you and to offer the kind of holidays that you will enjoy.

We would like to reward you for helping us with our survey. We are delighted to offer you a 10% saving on your next holiday. However, you must act within 28 days. If you would like to benefit from this offer, please quote code Q2000 when you call.

Our new brochure features more than 1,100 idyllic cottages, 160 luxury villas with pools (usually available in the summer months only), more than 2,000 hotels and over 40 apartments at holiday villages, with superb on-site facilities. We also offer deluxe camping and mobile homes at 20 wonderful 4-star sites and theme parks including Disneyland, Paris, Parc Astérix and Futuroscope.

We look forward to hearing from you soon.

Module 3, Section 4.4, Exercise 7

VOLUNTEERS REQUIRED

Do you meet the following criteria?

$\Rightarrow$ Age range 16 to 40
$\Rightarrow$ Computer literate
$\Rightarrow$ Available during the hours of 16.00 and 18.00

We are looking for volunteers to take part in a survey on computer usage. We are able to offer you a small payment and a cup of tea or coffee! If you think that you may be able to help us, we would like to hear from YOU.

Please contact one of the following:

Mike	ext 4448
Chris	ext 4462
Jane	ext 4463
Felicity	ext 6884

We look forward to your call.

Park House, London SW6 3JT Tel: 020 8223 3555 Fax: 020 8223 3566

Really Advertising

To:	Paul Young	From:	Angela Bessant
Fax:	01234 734999	**Pages:**	2
Phone:	01234 734820	**Date:**	09/05/00
Re:	Posters	**CC:**	Jane Harris

☐ **Urgent**   ☐ **For Review**   ☐ **Please Comment**   ✓ **Please Reply**   ✓ **Please Recycle**

● **Comments:**

Just to let you know that your posters, ordered last week, are now ready for collection. As it is your first order, please notice that we have added a few extra at no cost to yourself.

Thank you for choosing to order from us. We look forward to receiving your custom in the future.

GRAND OPENING
THE COMPUTER SHOP
SATURDAY 25 MARCH 2000

Many opening bargains including

→ **Computers**

→ **Printers**

→ **Scanners**

→ **Modems**

→ **Software**

Come and see for yourself

Our prices are keen:
Internal Zip drives from £102.95
Hard drives 20Gb from £129.99
Scanners from £79.99

The first 10 customers will each receive boxed software of their choice up to the value of £50

We look forward to welcoming you!

THE COMPUTER SHOP

Memo

To: Andrea Whitely

From: Paul Hunter

CC: Gita Meehan

Date: 19/04/00

Re: Delivery of laptops

Thank you for the delivery that I received this morning. As you know we are opening next Saturday and you would be most welcome to come and join us then. Please let me know if you can make it.

Best Regards

1

Module 3, Section 5.5

Largest Continents	Largest Countries	Largest Oceans and Seas	Largest Islands
Asia	Russian Federation	Pacific	Greenland
North America	China	Indian	Borneo
South America	USA	Arctic	Madagascar
Antarctica	Brazil	South China	Baffin

Module 3, Section 5, Practice 9, Step 9

Mercalli	Richter	Characteristics
1	Less than 3.5	Only detected by seismograph
2	3.5	Only detected by people at rest
3	4.2	Similar to vibrations from HGV
4	4.5	Felt indoors; rocks parked cars
5	4.8	Generally felt; awakens sleepers
7	6.1	Causes general alarm; building walls crack
12	Greater than 8.1	Total destruction of area

Earthquake Measurements

The magnitude of earthquakes is measured in units on the Richter Scale and their intensity on the Mercalli Scale.

Richter	Characteristics
Less than 3.5	Only detected by seismograph
3.5	Only detected by people at rest
4.2	Similar to vibrations from HGV
4.5	Felt indoors; rocks parked cars
4.8	Generally felt; awakens sleepers
6.1	Causes general alarm; building walls crack
Greater than 8.1	Total destruction of area

10 February 2000

Mr Murray Dixon
63 Harpur Street
Luton
LU6 1AS

Dear Murray

Box Office Film Club

I am pleased to enclose details of our forthcoming film season.

All films will be shown in the Lecture Room on the Hemsley Hall Campus. Ample free parking spaces are available at both sides of the hall. If you are travelling by public transport, the nearest bus stop is in Regent Avenue. May I remind you that guest tickets will be on sale in the Hemsley Bar 20 minutes before each performance.

I look forward to welcoming you this season.

Yours sincerely

Club Secretary

Enc

Letters also to: Miss Lynne Carter;
Mr Jack Hobson; Mrs Susi Malucci

Module 3, Section 6, Practice 11, Step 5

19 April 2000

Miss King
8 Wendover Place
Kempston
Bedford
MK32 9TG

Dear Miss King

Town and Country Enterprise AGM

Please note that the AGM will take place on Tuesday 20 June at 7.30 pm in the Coleridge Meeting Room. I am enclosing the agenda. Please let me know if you have any further items to add.

Coffee and light snacks will be provided. I look forward to seeing as many of our members as possible.

Yours sincerely

Jenny Jinx
Secretary

Enc

> Letters also to: Mr Gregory; Dr Walpole

Miss King
8 Wendover Place
Kempston
Bedford
MK32 9TG

Mr Gregory
10 George Gardens
Silsoe
Bedford
BD27 9JU

Dr Walpole
118 Exeter Way
Harrold
Bedford
MK55 2AS

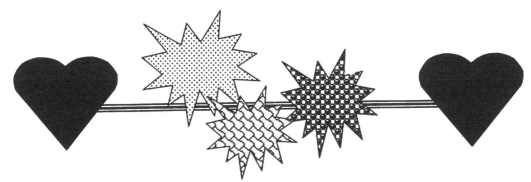

Shakespeare Season

ROMEO AND JULIET

All this week at 7 pm in the Drama Studio

Tickets available at the door

Module 3, Practice Task, Step 21

Angela Bessant

Sample extract

The people of Europe speak many different languages. English is termed a 'Germanic' language. This is because it is related to languages such as Dutch as well as German. The links are not as easily noticed in modern day English but the relationship is much clearer in **Old** English.

Old English is the name given to the English language up to *c.*1150. It was spoken from the fifth century. It has different vocabulary, word meanings and spellings to modern English. It even has letters, such as þ that are not found in modern English. Its pronunciation and grammar and the ways it was used are also different. So much so in fact that it would be most unlikely that **Old** English would be understood by the average English speaker today. Although anyone speaking or writing English at the beginning of the 21st century is using a language that dates back to Anglo Saxon times.

There is also the subject of accents and dialects to consider. Accents can be defined as the same language but differing in terms of pronunciation. Dialects differ in terms of grammar and vocabulary as well.

5

Module 3, Practice Task, Step 21 continued

Languages Course Details   19 April 2000

Nearly one billion people speak different varieties of modern-day English. There are mother tongue speakers, second language speakers and those for whom it is a foreign language. The spread of English to different parts of the world and it being used as an 'international' language has caused much debate.

This is just a taster of course content. We have many others and we are confident that you will find something interesting and worthwhile. Please ring for details of courses in:

- **French**
- **German**
- **Spanish**
- **Welsh**
- **Italian**

The people of Europe speak many different languages. English is termed a 'Germanic' language. This is because it is related to languages such as Dutch as well as German. The links are not as easily noticed in modern day English but the relationship is much clearer in **Old** English.

6

Module 3, Advanced Practice Tasks 2, Step 7

Languages Course Details   19 April 2000

Angela Bessant
Ref 9054

Dear

Sample extract

The people of Europe speak many different languages. English is termed a 'Germanic' language. This is because it is related to languages such as Dutch as well as German. The links are not as easily noticed in modern day English but the relationship is much clearer in **Old** English.

1	Early Old English	450 – 850
2	Later Old English	850 – 1100
3	Middle English	1100 – 1450
4	Early modern English	1450 – 1750

There is also the subject of accents and dialects to consider. Accents can be defined as the same language but differing in terms of pronunciation. Dialects differ in terms of grammar and vocabulary as well.

Nearly one billion people speak different varieties of modern-day English. There are mother tongue speakers, second language speakers and those for whom it is a foreign language. The spread of English to different parts of the world and it being used as an 'international' language has caused much debate.

This is just a taster of course content. We have many others and we are confident that you will find something interesting and worthwhile. Please ring for details of courses in:

- **French**
- **German**
- **Spanish**
- **Welsh**
- **Italian**

The people of Europe speak many different languages. English is termed a 'Germanic' language. This is because it is related to languages such as Dutch as well as German. The links are not as easily noticed in modern day English but the relationship is much clearer in **Old** English.

Yours sincerely

Angela Bessant

Languages Course Details

19 April 2000

Angela Bessant
Ref 9054

Miss Smith
29 Hobsons Way
Bristol
BS6 5ER

Dear Miss Smith

Sample extract

The people of Europe speak many different languages. English is termed a 'Germanic' language. This is because it is related to languages such as Dutch as well as German. The links are not as easily noticed in modern day English but the relationship is much clearer in **Old** English.

1	Early Old English	450 – 850
2	Later Old English	850 – 1100
3	Middle English	1100 – 1450
4	Early modern English	1450 – 1750

There is also the subject of accents and dialects to consider. Accents can be defined as the same language but differing in terms of pronunciation. Dialects differ in terms of grammar and vocabulary as well.

Nearly one billion people speak different varieties of modern-day English. There are mother tongue speakers, second language speakers and those for whom it is a foreign language. The spread of English to different parts of the world and it being used as an 'international' language has caused much debate.

This is just a taster of course content. We have many others and we are confident that you will find something interesting and worthwhile. Please ring for details of courses in:

- **French**
- **German**
- **Spanish**
- **Welsh**
- **Italian**

The people of Europe speak many different languages. English is termed a 'Germanic' language. This is because it is related to languages such as Dutch as well as German. The links are not as easily noticed in modern day English but the relationship is much clearer in **Old** English.

Yours sincerely

Angela Bessant

Letters also to: Mr Ahmed; Mrs Zwetsloot; Dr O'Byrne; Ms Jones

facsimile transmittal

To:	Lycée La Rochelle	**Fax:**	00 33 23 44 76 98 11
From:	Angela Bessant	**Date:**	19/04/00
Re:	Exchange Visits	**Pages:**	1
CC:	[Click here and type name]		

☐ Urgent   ☐ For Review   ✓ Please Comment   ☐ Please Reply   ☐ Please Recycle

Thank you for your interest. I will send details as soon as possible.

Module 4, Section 1.7, Exercise 5

Month	Casualco	Smartco	Partyco	Sales
May	990	830	770	2590
June	550	880	220	1650
July	330	660	700	1690
August	400	550	820	1770
Total	2270	2920	2510	

Module 4, Section 1.8, Exercise 6

Month	Casualco	Smartco	Partyco	Sales
May	990	830	770	=SUM(B2:D2)
June	550	880	220	=SUM(B3:D3)
July	330	660	700	=SUM(B4:D4)
August	400	550	820	=SUM(B5:D5)
Total	=SUM(B2:B5)	=SUM(C2:C5)	=SUM(D2:D5)	

Module 4, Section 1, Practice 1, Step 5(a)

EXPENSES

	AUG	OCT	NOV
RENT	350	350	350
ELEC	45	50	60
GAS	18	25	40
LOAN	55	55	55
PETROL	75	60	60
INS	20	20	20
TOTALS	563		

Module 4, Section 1, Practice 1, Step 5(b)

EXPENSES

	AUG	OCT	NOV
RENT	350	350	350
ELEC	45	50	60
GAS	18	25	40
LOAN	55	55	55
PETROL	75	60	60
INS	20	20	20
TOTALS	=SUM(B3:B8)		

Module 4, Section 1, Practice 2, Step 4(a)

Sales

	Tue	Wed	Thu	Fri	Sat	Total
Food	550	660	500	900	1120	3730
Menswear	200	190	300	100	780	
Fashions	300	625	740	800	1500	
Baby	200	450	380	590	213	
Cosmetics	77	90	65	105	280	
Home	500	1800	1200	954	3080	

Sales	Tue	Wed	Thu	Fri	Sat	Total
Food	550	660	500	900	1120	=SUM(B3:F3)
Menswear	200	190	300	100	780	
Fashions	300	625	740	800	1500	
Baby	200	450	380	590	213	
Cosmetics	77	90	65	105	280	
Home	500	1800	1200	954	3080	

Module 4, Section 2.7

Month	Casualco	Jeansco	Partyco	Shoesco	Sales
May	850	600	770	621	2841
June	550	700	220	890	2360
July	470	850	700	700	2720
August	400	650	820	440	2310
Total	2270	2800	2510	2651	10231

Module 4, Section 2.9, Exercise 10

Month	Casualco
May	850
June	550
July	470
August	400
Total	2270

Module 4, Section 2, Practice 3, Step 12

EXPENSES

	AUG	SEP	OCT	NOV	TOTAL
RENT	350	350	350	350	1400
ELEC	35	50	50	60	195
GAS	18	20	25	54	117
LOAN	55	55	55	55	220
INS	20	20	20	20	80
TOTALS	478	495	500	539	2012

Module 4, Section 2, Practice 3, Step 13

TOTAL
=SUM(B3:E3)
=SUM(B4:E4)
=SUM(B5:E5)
=SUM(B6:E6)
=SUM(B7:E7)
=SUM(F3:F7)

Module 4, Section 2, Practice 4, Step 11

Sales	Mon	Tue	Wed	Thu	Fri	Sat	Total	Profit
Food	25	550	660	500	900	1120	3755	751
Menswear	180	200	190	350	100	780	1800	360
Fashions	270	300	625	740	800	1500	4235	847
Baby	52	200	450	380	610	213	1905	381
Home	25	500	1800	1200	954	3080	7559	1511.8

Module 4, Section 3.6

CLOTHING COMPANY SALES

Month	Casualco	Jeansco	Partyco	Shoesco	Monthly Sales	Average Sales
May	850	600	770	621	2841	710.25
June	550	700	220	890	2360	590.00
July	470	850	700	700	2720	680.00
August	400	650	820	440	2310	577.50
Total	**2270**	**2800**	**2510**	**2651**	**10231**	**2557.75**

Module 4, Section 3.10

CLOTHING COMPANY SALES

Month	Casualco	Jeansco	Partyco	Shoesco	Monthly Sales	Average Sales
May	850	600	770	621	2841	710.25
June	550	700	220	890	2360	590.00
July	470	850	700	700	2720	680.00
August	400	650	820	440	2310	577.50
Total	**2270**	**2800**	**2510**	**2651**	**10231**	**£ 2,557.75**

CLOTHING COMPANY SALES

Month	Shoesco	Commission rates
May	621	5%
June	890	8%
July	700	10%
August	440	3%
Total	**2651**	

Module 4, Section 3.18

Produced by Angela Bessant   27 March 2000

CLOTHING COMPANY SALES

Surname	First Name	Start Date
Gill	Sanjit	10-Oct-99
Jones	Bronwen	2-May-00
Jones	Julia	14-Feb-96
Wright	Dominic	29-Sep-98

Module 4, Section 3.18

Produced by Angela Bessant   15/09/00

CLOTHING COMPANY SALES

Month	Casualco	Jeansco	Partyco	Shoesco	Monthly Sales		Average Sales
May	850	600	770	621	2841		710.25
June	550	700	220	890	2360		590.00
July	470	850	700	700	2720		680.00
August	400	650	820	440	2310		577.50
Total	*2270*	*2800*	*2510*	*2651*	*10231*	*£*	*2,557.75*

CLOTHING COMPANY SALES

Month	Shoesco	Commission rates
May	621	5%
June	890	8%
July	700	10%
August	440	3%
Total	*2651*	

Module 4, Section 3.18

Produced by Angela Bessant   27 March 2000

Surname	First Name	Start Date	Tel	Week1	Week2	Week3	Week4
Gill	Sanjit	10-Oct-99	01234 752999				
Jones	Bronwen	2-May-00	01234 621900				
Jones	Julia	14-Feb-96	01908 554211				
Wright	Dominic	29-Sep-98	01908 338554				

EXPENSES	AUG	SEP	OCT	NOV	TOTAL	AVERAGE
RENT	350.0	350.0	350.0	350.0	£ 1,400.00	350
ELEC	35.0	50.0	50.0	60.0	£ 195.00	49
GAS	18.0	20.0	25.0	54.0	£ 117.00	29
LOAN	55.0	55.0	55.0	55.0	£ 220.00	55
INS	20.0	20.0	20.0	20.0	£ 80.00	20
TOTALS	478.0	495.0	500.0	539.0	£ 2,012.00	503

20/4/00

ECDL 2000

YEARLY EXPENSES

	Jan-99	Feb-99	Mar-99	Apr-99	May-99	Jun-99	Jul-99	Aug-99	Sep-99	Oct-99	Nov-99	Dec-99
RENT								350.0	350.0	350.0	350.0	
ELEC								35.0	50.0	50.0	60.0	
GAS								18.0	20.0	25.0	54.0	
LOAN								55.0	55.0	55.0	55.0	
INS								20.0	20.0	20.0	20.0	
TOTALS								478.0	495.0	500.0	539.0	

Sales

	Mon	Tue	Wed	Thu	Fri	Sat	Total	Profit
Food	25.00	550.00	660.00	500.00	900.00	1120.00	3755.00	751.00
Menswear	180.00	200.00	190.00	350.00	100.00	780.00	1800.00	360.00
Ladies Fashions	270.00	300.00	625.00	740.00	800.00	1500.00	4235.00	847.00
Baby	52.00	200.00	450.00	380.00	610.00	213.00	1905.00	381.00
Home	25.00	500.00	1800.00	1200.00	954.00	3080.00	7559.00	1511.80
Average Store Sales	110.40	350.00	745.00	634.00	672.80	1338.60		

Module 4, Section 3, Practice 6, Step 15(b)

HOUSEHOLD SALES

	Mon	Tue	Wed	Thu	Fri	Sat	Total	Predicted Increased Sales		Profit
Food	25.00	550.00	660.00	500.00	900.00	1120.00	3755.00		1%	751.00
Home	25.00	500.00	1800.00	1200.00	954.00	3080.00	7559.00		4%	1511.80

Module 4, Section 4, Practice 7, Step 8

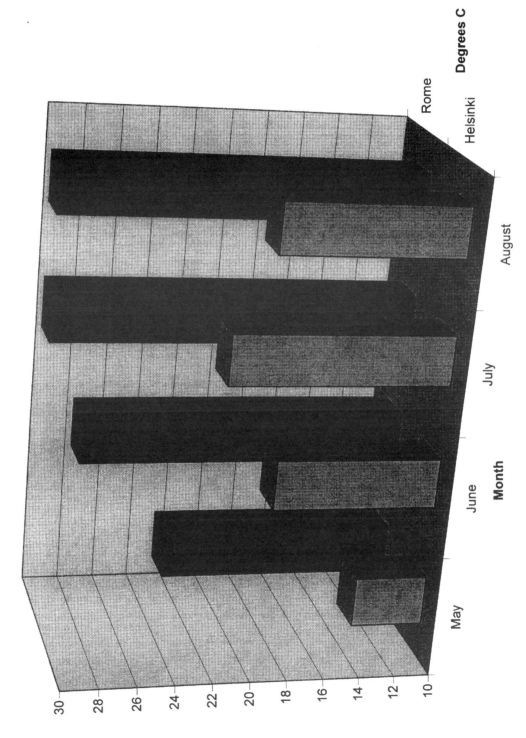

Temperature Comparison (Helsinki, Rome)

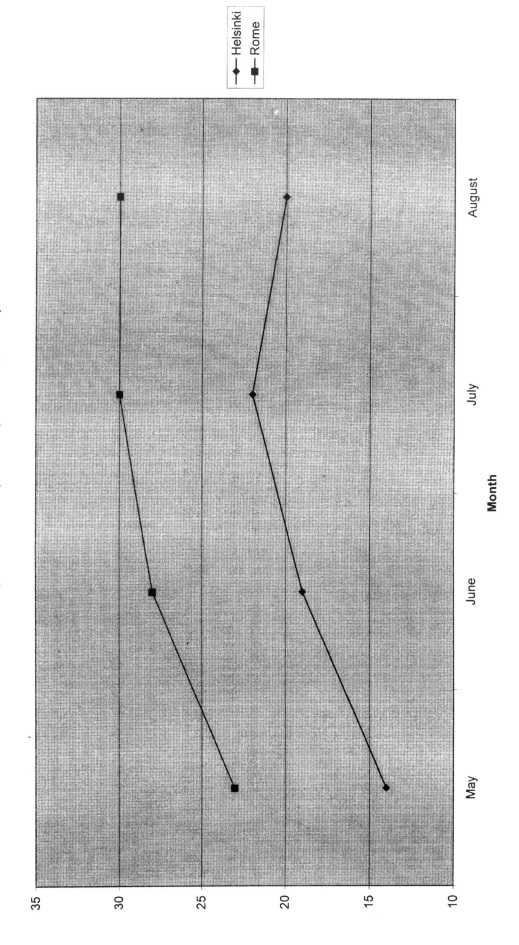

Temperature Comparison (Helsinki, Rome)

Module 4, Section 4, Practice 8, Step 6

Temperature Chart						
	Degrees C					Degrees F
	May	June	July	August	4-Month Average	May
Amsterdam	18	21	22	22	20.75	64.4
Athens	25	30	33	33	30.25	77
Berlin	19	22	24	23	22	66.2
Budapest	22	26	28	27	25.75	71.6
Copenhagen	16	19	22	21	19.5	60.8
Dublin	15	18	20	19	18	59
Helsinki	14	19	22	20	18.75	57.2
London	17	20	22	22	20.25	62.6
Madrid	21	27	31	30	27.25	69.8
Oslo	16	20	22	21	19.75	60.8
Paris	20	23	25	24	23	68
Rome	23	28	30	30	27.75	73.4
Stockholm	14	19	22	20	18.75	57.2
Vienna	19	23	25	24	22.75	66.2
Zurich	19	23	25	24	22.75	66.2

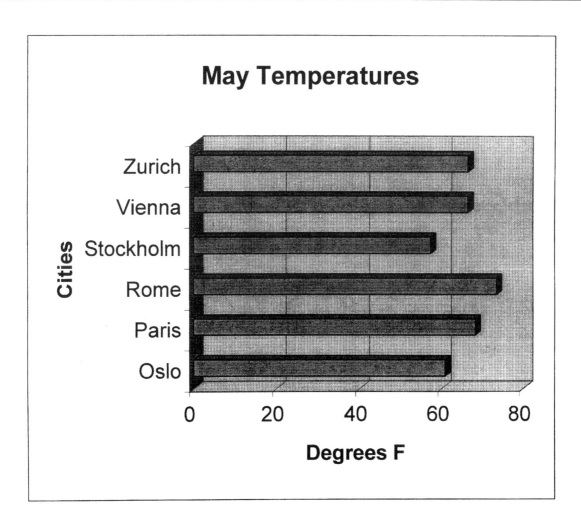

Attendance Figures

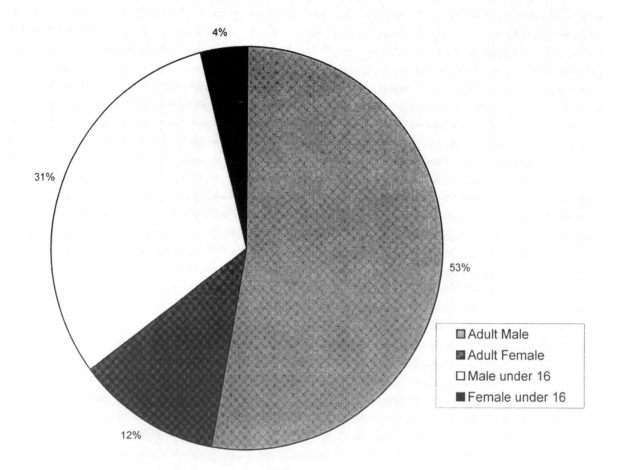

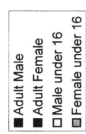

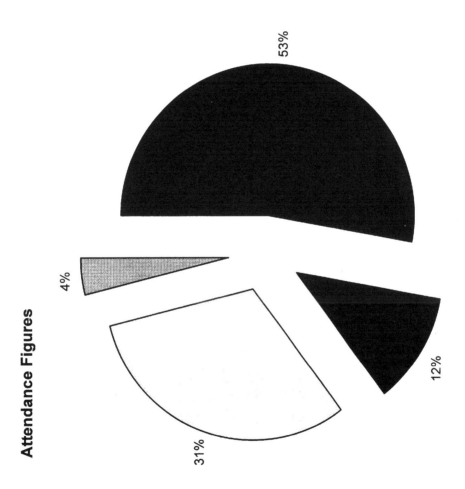

Attendance Figures

Angela Bessant

Spreadsheet produced by Angela Bessant

Temporary register payments

Name	Hourly rate		Weekend rate		Weekly hours	Weekend hours	Hourly rate total		Weekend total		Total pay	
Rachel Simms	£	6.80	£	8.16	18	12	£	122.40	£	97.92	£	220.32
Gareth Philips	£	10.50	£	12.60	22.5	8	£	236.25	£	100.80	£	337.05
Jeanna Larouse	£	6.80	£	8.16	30	2	£	204.00	£	16.32	£	220.32
Mark Anthony	£	7.80	£	9.36	21	2	£	163.80	£	18.72	£	182.52
Philip Smith	£	5.80	£	6.96	10	7	£	58.00	£	48.72	£	106.72
Greg Moore	£	6.80	£	8.16	17	5	£	115.60	£	40.80	£	156.40
Jayne Temple	£	7.80	£	9.36	30	0	£	234.00	£	-	£	234.00
Sara Janes	£	10.50	£	12.60	30	0	£	315.00	£	-	£	315.00
Tom Batco	£	10.50	£	12.60	25	3	£	262.50	£	37.80	£	300.30
Total Temp pay											£	2,072.63

Module 4, Advanced Practice Tasks 1, Step 23

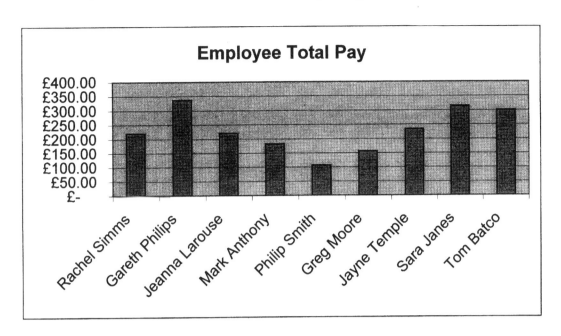

Module 4, Basic Practice Tasks 2, Step 11

	Your £ buys		
No of pounds for exchange	10,190		
Country	Currency	Exchange rate	Exchange result
Belgium (Franc)	BEF	64.26	BEF 654,809.40
France (Franc)	FRF	10.47	FRF 106,689.30
Germany (Deutsche Mark)	DEM	3.11	DEM 31,690.90
Italy (Lira)	ITL	3086	ITL 31,446,340.00
Spain (Peseta)	ESP	276	ESP 2,812,440.00

	Your £ buys		
No of pounds for exchange	10,190		
Country	Currency	Exchange rate	Exchange result
Belgium (Franc)	BEF	64.26	BEF 654,809.40
France (Franc)	FRF	10.47	FRF 106,689.30
Germany (Deutsche Mark)	DEM	3.11	DEM 31,690.90
Spain (Peseta)	ESP	276	ESP 2,812,440.00

Conversions by AJB

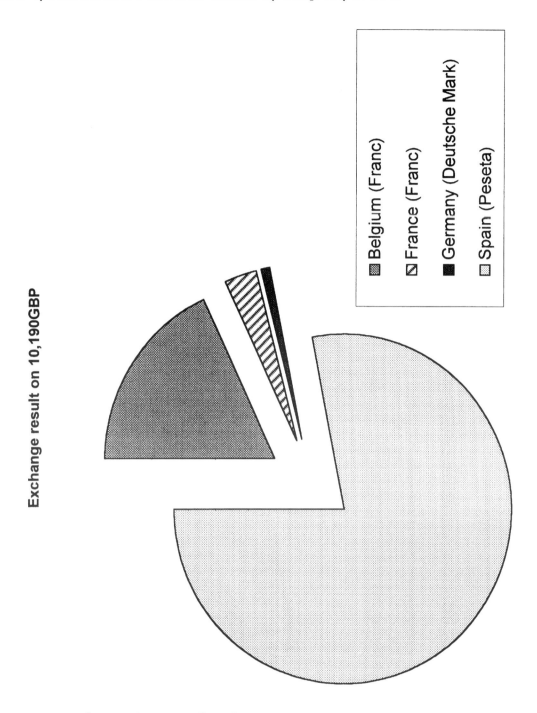

Exchange result on 10,190GBP

- Belgium (Franc)
- France (Franc)
- Germany (Deutsche Mark)
- Spain (Peseta)

Module 5, Section 2.2, Exercise 2

CLASSES   24/02/00

CLASS	DAY	ROOM	INSTRUCTOR	NUMBER OF WEEKS
AEROBICS	MONDAY	HALL	KENNY	10
AEROBIKING	WEDNESDAY	GYM	SALLY	10
FIT AND FUNKY	THURSDAY	DANCE STUDIO	LYNNE	15
SYNC AND SWIM	WEDNESDAY	POOL	DUNCAN	5
POWER HOUR	FRIDAY	HALL	LARRY	10
BODY BLITZ	TUESDAY	DANCE STUDIO	LYNNE	20

24/02/00

CLASSES

CLASS	ROOM	DAY	MEMBER	INSTRUCTOR	NUMBER OF WEEKS
AEROBICS	GYM	MONDAY	☐	KENNY	10
AEROBIKING	GYM	WEDNESDAY	☑	SALLY	10
FIT AND FUNKY	DANCE STUDIO	THURSDAY	☐	LYNNE	15
SYNC AND SWIM	POOL	WEDNESDAY	☐	DUNCAN	6
BODY BLITZ	DANCE STUDIO	TUESDAY	☐	LYNNE	20
TONE AND TRIM	GYM	FRIDAY	☑	LYNNE	20

Page 1

Module 5, Section 2, Practice 3, Step 2

Clients

29/03/00

SOLICITOR	CLIENT NAME	REF NO	DAY	TIME	PREVIOUS VISITS
PATEL	JONES L	J120	WED	09:30	6
PATEL	SMITH C	J561	TUE	12:00	10
PATEL	CLARKSON J	M124	SAT	16:00	4
PATEL	GRIGGS S	N6570	FRI	13:45	10
COLLINS	DENT J	C780	SAT	09:00	12
COLLINS	JENKINS Z	E120	WED	10:30	0
COLLINS	DENNIS M	L833	SAT	10:00	8
COLLINS	MOWHILL S	H777	FRI	17:45	12
McBRIDE	HARMAN D	G652	THU	11:00	12
McBRIDE	PETERS H	Y444	FRI	18:30	6
McBRIDE	CLARKE F	R567	SAT	09:30	0
McBRIDE	PAUL G	H800	SAT	11:00	6
McBRIDE	MULERO M	D437	WED	15:00	2
SIMPSON	ANDREWS C	G123	WED	10:00	6
SIMPSON	GOODYEAR K	H321	WED	11:00	6
SIMPSON	STEWART J	L909	SAT	12:00	10
SIMPSON	GREGORY A	F549	THU	16:00	10

Module 5, Section 2, Practice 3, Step 9

Clients

29/03/00

SOLICITOR	REF NO	CLIENT NAME	DAY	TIME	PREVIOUS VISITS	TITLE
PATEL	J120	JONES L	WED	09:30	6	MISS
PATEL	J561	SMITH C	TUE	12:00	10	MRS
PATEL	M124	CLARKSON J	SAT	16:00	4	MS
PATEL	N6570	GRIGGS S	SAT	13:45	10	MISS
COLLINS	C780	DENT J	SAT	09:00	12	MR
COLLINS	E120	JENKINS Z	WED	10:30	0	MR
COLLINS	H777	MOWHILL S	FRI	17:45	12	DR
McBRIDE	G652	HARMAN D	THU	11:00	12	MISS
McBRIDE	Y444	PETERS H	FRI	18:30	6	MS
McBRIDE	R567	CLARKE F	SAT	09:30	0	MR
McBRIDE	H800	PAUL G	SAT	11:00	6	MR
McBRIDE	D437	MULERO M	WED	16:00	2	DR
SIMPSON	G123	ANDREWS C	WED	10:00	6	MR
SIMPSON	H321	GOODYEAR K	WED	11:00	6	MS
SIMPSON	L909	STEWART J	SAT	12:00	10	MR
SIMPSON	F549	GREGORY A	THU	16:00	10	MISS
PATEL	D321	SAMUEL S	SAT	10:00	0	MR

Module 5, Section 2, Practice 4, Step 2

Stock   29/03/00

STORE	TYPE	MODEL	COLOUR	PRICE	NO IN STOCK
MILTON KEYNES	RACER	SPIRIT20	BLUE	359.99	10
MILTON KEYNES	RACER	SPEEDY18	GREEN	359.99	2
MILTON KEYNES	TRICYCLE	PIXIE5	YELLOW	60.50	6
MILTON KEYNES	RACER	SPIRIT18	RED	279.99	10
OLNEY	TANDEM	TWIN20	RED	399.00	1
OLNEY	MOUNTAIN	ROUGHTRACK1	BLUE	89.99	5
OLNEY	MOUNTAIN	ROUGHTRACK6	SILVER	129.99	6
OLNEY	TRICYCLE	PIXIE5	YELLOW	60.50	8
OLNEY	TRICYCLE	PIXIE10	RED	65.99	6
NEWPORT PAGNELL	RACER	SPEEDY18	SILVER	339.99	4
NEWPORT PAGNELL	TRICYCLE	PIXIE5	YELLOW	60.50	2
NEWPORT PAGNELL	MOUNTAIN	ROUGHTRACK1	BLUE	89.99	14
NEWPORT PAGNELL	RACER	SPIRIT18	BRONZE	279.99	2
CRANFIELD	RACER	SPIRIT20	BLACK	359.99	5
CRANFIELD	MOUNTAIN	ROUGHTRACK6	GREEN	129.99	6

Module 5, Section 2, Practice 4, Step 9

29/03/00

Stock

STORE	COLOUR	TYPE	MODEL	PRICE	NO IN STOCK	SALE PRICE
MILTON KEYNES	BLUE	RACER	SPIRIT20	359.99	10	329.99
MILTON KEYNES	GREEN	RACER	SPEEDY18	359.99	2	329.99
MILTON KEYNES	YELLOW	TRICYCLE	PIXIE5	60.50	6	50.50
MILTON KEYNES	RED	RACER	SPIRIT18	279.99	10	259.99
OLNEY	BLUE	MOUNTAIN	ROUGHTRACK1	89.99	5	79.99
OLNEY	SILVER	MOUNTAIN	ROUGHTRACK6	129.99	6	119.99
OLNEY	YELLOW	TRICYCLE	PIXIE5	60.50	8	50.50
OLNEY	RED	TRICYCLE	PIXIE10	65.99	6	55.99
NEWPORT PAGNELL	BLUE	RACER	SPEEDY18	339.99	4	300.99
NEWPORT PAGNELL	YELLOW	TRICYCLE	PIXIE5	60.50	2	50.50
NEWPORT PAGNELL	BLUE	MOUNTAIN	ROUGHTRACK1	89.99	10	79.99
NEWPORT PAGNELL	BRONZE	RACER	SPIRIT18	279.99	2	259.99
CRANFIELD	BLACK	RACER	SPIRIT20	359.99	5	329.99
CRANFIELD	GREEN	MOUNTAIN	ROUGHTRACK6	129.99	6	119.99
CRANFIELD	BRONZE	MOUNTAIN	ROUGHTRACK3	99.99	2	89.99

Page 1

Module 4, Section 3.4, Exercise 3

Weeks des and Instructor asc

CLASS	ROOM	DAY	MEMBER	INSTRUCTOR	NUMBER OF WEEKS
TONE AND TRIM	GYM	FRIDAY	✓	LYNNE	20
BODY BLITZ	DANCE STUDIO	TUESDAY	☐	LYNNE	20
FIT AND FUNKY	DANCE STUDIO	THURSDAY	☐	LYNNE	15
AEROBICS	GYM	MONDAY	☐	KENNY	10
AEROBIKING	GYM	WEDNESDAY	✓	SALLY	10
SYNC AND SWIM	POOL	WEDNESDAY	☐	DUNCAN	6

Page 1

24/02/00

Day ascending

CLASS	ROOM	DAY	MEMBER	INSTRUCTOR	NUMBER OF WEEKS
TONE AND TRIM	GYM	FRIDAY	☑	LYNNE	20
AEROBICS	GYM	MONDAY	☐	KENNY	10
FIT AND FUNKY	DANCE STUDIO	THURSDAY	☐	LYNNE	15
BODY BLITZ	DANCE STUDIO	TUESDAY	☐	LYNNE	20
SYNC AND SWIM	POOL	WEDNESDAY	☐	DUNCAN	6
AEROBIKING	GYM	WEDNESDAY	☑	SALLY	10

Page 1

24/02/00

Classes GYM

CLASS	ROOM	DAY	MEMBER	INSTRUCTOR	NUMBER OF WEEKS
AEROBICS	GYM	MONDAY	☐	KENNY	10
AEROBIKING	GYM	WEDNESDAY	✓	SALLY	10
TONE AND TRIM	GYM	FRIDAY	✓	LYNNE	20

Page 1

Module 4, Section 3.10, Exercise 6

24/02/00

Gym less than 15 weeks

CLASS	ROOM	DAY	MEMBER	INSTRUCTOR	NUMBER OF WEEKS
AEROBICS	GYM	MONDAY	☐	KENNY	10
AEROBIKING	GYM	WEDNESDAY	☑	SALLY	10

Page 1

Module 4, Section 3.11, Exercise 7

Lynne more than 15 weeks   24/02/00

CLASS	DAY	NUMBER OF WEEKS
BODY BLITZ	TUESDAY	20
TONE AND TRIM	FRIDAY	20

Module 4, Section 3, Practice 5, Step 2

Clients   30/03/00

SOLICITOR	REF NO	CLIENT NAME	DAY	TIME	PREVIOUS VISITS	TITLE
SIMPSON	G123	ANDREWS C	WED	10:00	6	MR
McBRIDE	R567	CLARKE F	SAT	09:30	0	MR
PATEL	M124	CLARKSON J	SAT	16:00	4	MS
COLLINS	C780	DENT J	SAT	09:00	12	MR
SIMPSON	H321	GOODYEAR K	WED	11:00	6	MS
SIMPSON	F549	GREGORY A	THU	16:00	10	MISS
PATEL	N6570	GRIGGS S	SAT	13:45	10	MISS
McBRIDE	G652	HARMAN D	THU	11:00	12	MISS
COLLINS	E120	JENKINS Z	WED	10:30	0	MR
PATEL	J120	JONES L	WED	09:30	6	MISS
COLLINS	H777	MOWHILL S	FRI	17:45	12	DR
McBRIDE	D437	MULERO M	WED	16:00	2	DR
McBRIDE	H800	PAUL G	SAT	11:00	6	MR
McBRIDE	Y444	PETERS H	FRI	18:30	6	MS
PATEL	D321	SAMUEL S	SAT	10:00	0	MR
PATEL	J561	SMITH C	TUE	12:00	10	MRS
SIMPSON	L909	STEWART J	SAT	12:00	10	MR

Module 5, Section 3, Practice 5, Step 3

Clients   30/03/00

SOLICITOR	REF NO	CLIENT NAME	DAY	TIME	PREVIOUS VISITS	TITLE
McBRIDE	R567	CLARKE F	SAT	09:30	0	MR
COLLINS	E120	JENKINS Z	WED	10:30	0	MR
PATEL	D321	SAMUEL S	SAT	10:00	0	MR
McBRIDE	D437	MULERO M	WED	16:00	2	DR
PATEL	M124	CLARKSON J	SAT	16:00	4	MS
PATEL	J120	JONES L	WED	09:30	6	MISS
McBRIDE	Y444	PETERS H	FRI	18:30	6	MS
McBRIDE	H800	PAUL G	SAT	11:00	6	MR
SIMPSON	G123	ANDREWS C	WED	10:00	6	MR
SIMPSON	H321	GOODYEAR K	WED	11:00	6	MS
SIMPSON	L909	STEWART J	SAT	12:00	10	MR
PATEL	N6570	GRIGGS S	SAT	13:45	10	MISS
SIMPSON	F549	GREGORY A	THU	16:00	10	MISS
PATEL	J561	SMITH C	TUE	12:00	10	MRS
COLLINS	H777	MOWHILL S	FRI	17:45	12	DR
COLLINS	C780	DENT J	SAT	09:00	12	MR
McBRIDE	G652	HARMAN D	THU	11:00	12	MISS

Module 5, Section 3, Practice 5, Step 4

Clients   30/03/00

SOLICITOR	REF NO	CLIENT NAME	DAY	TIME	PREVIOUS VISITS	TITLE
COLLINS	E120	JENKINS Z	WED	10:30	0	MR
McBRIDE	D437	MULERO M	WED	16:00	2	DR
SIMPSON	H321	GOODYEAR K	WED	11:00	6	MS
SIMPSON	G123	ANDREWS C	WED	10:00	6	MR
PATEL	J120	JONES L	WED	09:30	6	MISS

Module 5, Section 3, Practice 5, Step 5

step 5   30/03/00

CLIENT NAME	TIME
JONES L	09:30
JENKINS Z	10:30
CLARKE F	09:30
PAUL G	11:00
ANDREWS C	10:00
GOODYEAR K	11:00
SAMUEL S	10:00

Module 5, Section 3, Practice 6, Step 2

Stock

STORE	COLOUR	TYPE	MODEL	PRICE	NO IN STOCK	SALE PRICE
OLNEY	RED	TRICYCLE	PIXIE10	65.99	6	55.99
NEWPORT PAGNELL	YELLOW	TRICYCLE	PIXIE5	60.50	2	50.50
OLNEY	YELLOW	TRICYCLE	PIXIE5	60.50	8	50.50
MILTON KEYNES	YELLOW	TRICYCLE	PIXIE5	60.50	6	50.50
NEWPORT PAGNELL	BLUE	MOUNTAIN	ROUGHTRACK1	89.99	10	79.99
OLNEY	BLUE	MOUNTAIN	ROUGHTRACK1	89.99	5	79.99
CRANFIELD	BRONZE	MOUNTAIN	ROUGHTRACK3	99.99	2	89.99
CRANFIELD	GREEN	MOUNTAIN	ROUGHTRACK6	129.99	6	119.99
OLNEY	SILVER	MOUNTAIN	ROUGHTRACK6	129.99	6	119.99
NEWPORT PAGNELL	BLUE	RACER	SPEEDY18	339.99	4	300.99
MILTON KEYNES	GREEN	RACER	SPEEDY18	359.99	2	329.99
NEWPORT PAGNELL	BRONZE	RACER	SPIRIT18	279.99	2	259.99
MILTON KEYNES	RED	RACER	SPIRIT18	279.99	10	259.99
CRANFIELD	BLACK	RACER	SPIRIT20	359.99	5	329.99
MILTON KEYNES	BLUE	RACER	SPIRIT20	359.99	10	329.99

Page 1

30/03/00

Stock

STORE	COLOUR	TYPE	MODEL	PRICE	NO IN STOCK	SALE PRICE
CRANFIELD	BLACK	RACER	SPIRIT20	359.99	5	329.99
MILTON KEYNES	GREEN	RACER	SPEEDY18	359.99	2	329.99
MILTON KEYNES	BLUE	RACER	SPIRIT20	359.99	10	329.99
NEWPORT PAGNELL	BLUE	RACER	SPEEDY18	339.99	4	300.99
NEWPORT PAGNELL	BRONZE	RACER	SPIRIT18	279.99	2	259.99
MILTON KEYNES	RED	RACER	SPIRIT18	279.99	10	259.99
CRANFIELD	GREEN	MOUNTAIN	ROUGHTRACK6	129.99	6	119.99
OLNEY	SILVER	MOUNTAIN	ROUGHTRACK6	129.99	6	119.99
CRANFIELD	BRONZE	MOUNTAIN	ROUGHTRACK3	99.99	2	89.99
NEWPORT PAGNELL	BLUE	MOUNTAIN	ROUGHTRACK1	89.99	10	79.99
OLNEY	BLUE	MOUNTAIN	ROUGHTRACK1	89.99	5	79.99
OLNEY	RED	TRICYCLE	PIXIE10	65.99	6	55.99
NEWPORT PAGNELL	YELLOW	TRICYCLE	PIXIE5	60.50	2	50.50
OLNEY	YELLOW	TRICYCLE	PIXIE5	60.50	8	50.50
MILTON KEYNES	YELLOW	TRICYCLE	PIXIE5	60.50	6	50.50

Page 1

Module 5, Section 3, Practice 6, Step 4

Stock

STORE	COLOUR	TYPE	MODEL	PRICE	NO IN STOCK	SALE PRICE
NEWPORT PAGNELL	YELLOW	TRICYCLE	PIXIE5	60.50	2	50.50
OLNEY	YELLOW	TRICYCLE	PIXIE5	60.50	8	50.50
MILTON KEYNES	YELLOW	TRICYCLE	PIXIE5	60.50	6	50.50

Page 1

Module 5, Section 3, Practice 6, Step 5

Query1   30/03/00

STORE	COLOUR	TYPE	MODEL
OLNEY	SILVER	MOUNTAIN	ROUGHTRACK6
CRANFIELD	GREEN	MOUNTAIN	ROUGHTRACK6

CLASSES

CLASS	ROOM	DAY	MEMBER	INSTRUCTOR	NUMBER OF WEEKS
AEROBICS	GYM	MONDAY	☐	KENNY	10
AEROBIKING	GYM	WEDNESDAY	☑	SALLY	10
BODY BLITZ	DANCE STUDIO	TUESDAY	☐	LYNNE	20
FIT AND FUNKY	DANCE STUDIO	THURSDAY	☐	LYNNE	15
SYNC AND SWIM	POOL	WEDNESDAY	☐	DUNCAN	6
TONE AND TRIM	GYM	FRIDAY	☑	LYNNE	20

Fitness Centre Events

INSTRUCTOR	CLASS	ROOM	DAY	MEMBER	NUMBER OF WEEKS
DUNCAN					
	SYNC AND SWIM	POOL	WEDNESDAY	☐	6
					6
KENNY					
	AEROBICS	GYM	MONDAY	☐	10
					10
LYNNE					
	BODY BLITZ	DANCE STUDIO	TUESDAY	☐	20
	FIT AND FUNKY	DANCE STUDIO	THURSDAY	☐	15
	TONE AND TRIM	GYM	FRIDAY	☑	20
					55
SALLY					
	AEROBIKING	GYM	WEDNESDAY	☑	10
					10
Grand Total					81

24 April 2001

Fitness Centre Events

INSTRUCTOR	CLASS	ROOM	DAY	MEMBER	NUMBER OF WEEKS
DUNCAN					
	SYNCHRONISED SWIMMING (BEGINNERS)	POOL	WEDNESDAY	☐	6
					6
KENNY					
	AEROBICS	GYM	MONDAY	☐	10
					10
LYNNE					
	BODY BLITZ	DANCE STUDIO	TUESDAY	☐	20
	FIT AND FUNKY	DANCE STUDIO	THURSDAY	☐	15
	TONE AND TRIM	GYM	FRIDAY	✓	20
					55
SALLY					
	AEROBIKING	GYM	WEDNESDAY	✓	10
					10
Grand Total					81

24 April 2001

Module 5, Section 4.4, Exercise 4

Fitness Centre Events

Report produced by Angela Bessant

INSTRUCTOR	CLASS	ROOM	DAY	MEMBER	NUMBER OF WEEKS
DUNCAN	SYNCHRONISED SWIMMING (BEGINNERS)	POOL	WEDNESDAY	☐	6
					6
KENNY	AEROBICS	GYM	MONDAY	☐	10
					10
LYNNE	BODY BLITZ	DANCE STUDIO	TUESDAY	☐	20
	FIT AND FUNKY	DANCE STUDIO	THURSDAY	☐	15
	TONE AND TRIM	GYM	FRIDAY	☑	20
					55
SALLY	AEROBIKING	GYM	WEDNESDAY	☑	10
					10
Grand Total					81

Report designed to show total hours for each instructor

24 April 2001

Page 1 of 1

Clients grouped by solicitor   Angela Bessant 10.00 am

SOLICITOR	CLIENT NAME	REF NO	DAY	TIME	PREVIOUS VISITS	TITLE
COLLINS						
	MOWHILL S	H777	FRI	17:45	12	DR
	JENKINS Z	E120	WED	10:30	0	MR
	DENT J	C780	SAT	09:00	12	MR
McBRIDE						
	PETERS H	Y444	FRI	18:30	6	MS
	PAUL G	H800	SAT	11:00	6	MR
	MULERO M	D437	WED	16:00	2	DR
	HARMAN D	G652	THU	11:00	12	MISS
	CLARKE F	R567	SAT	09:30	0	MR
PATEL						
	SMITH C	J561	TUE	12:00	10	MRS
	SAMUEL S	D321	SAT	10:00	0	MR
	JONES L	J120	WED	09:30	6	MISS
	GRIGGS S	N6570	SAT	13:45	10	MISS
	CLARKSON J	M124	SAT	16:00	4	MS
SIMPSON						
	STEWART J	L909	SAT	12:00	10	MR
	GREGORY A	F549	THU	16:00	10	MISS
	GOODYEAR K	H321	WED	11:00	6	MS
	ANDREWS C	G123	WED	10:00	6	MR

31 March 2000

Client appointments this week, grouped by solicitor   Angela Bessant 10.00 am

SOLICITOR	CLIENT NAME	REF NO	DAY	TIME	PREVIOUS VISITS	TITLE
COLLINS						
	MOWHILL S	H777	FRI	17:45	12	DR
	JENKINS Z	E120	WED	10:30	0	MR
	DENT J	C780	SAT	09:00	12	MR
McBRIDE						
	PETERS H	Y444	FRI	18:30	6	MS
	PAUL G	H800	SAT	11:00	6	MR
	MULERO M	D437	WED	16:00	2	DR
	HARMAN D	G652	THU	11:00	12	MISS
	CLARKE F	R567	SAT	09:30	0	MR
PATEL						
	SMITH C	J561	TUE	12:00	10	MRS
	SAMUEL S	D321	SAT	10:00	0	MR
	JONES L	J120	WED	09:30	6	MISS
	GRIGGS S	N6570	SAT	13:45	10	MISS
	CLARKSON J	M124	SAT	16:00	4	MS
SIMPSON						
	STEWART J	L909	SAT	12:00	10	MR
	GREGORY A	F549	THU	16:00	10	MISS
	GOODYEAR K	H321	WED	11:00	6	MS
	ANDREWS C	G123	WED	10:00	6	MR

31 March 2000

Store Stock 31 March 2000

STORE	TYPE	MODEL	PRICE	NO IN STOCK	SALE PRICE
CRANFIELD					
	MOUNTAIN	ROUGHTRACK3	99.99	2	89.99
	MOUNTAIN	ROUGHTRACK6	129.99	6	119.99
	RACER	SPIRIT20	359.99	5	329.99
			589.97	13	539.97
MILTON KEYNES					
	TRICYCLE	PIXIE5	60.50	6	50.50
	RACER	SPIRIT18	279.99	10	259.99
	RACER	SPEEDY18	359.99	2	329.99
	RACER	SPIRIT20	359.99	10	329.99
			1060.47	28	970.47
NEWPORT PAGNELL					
	TRICYCLE	PIXIE5	60.50	2	50.50
	MOUNTAIN	ROUGHTRACK1	89.99	10	79.99
	RACER	SPIRIT18	279.99	2	259.99
	RACER	SPEEDY18	339.99	4	300.99
			770.47	18	691.47

31 March 2000

Report produced by Angela Bessant

STORE	TYPE	MODEL	PRICE	NO IN STOCK	SALE PRICE
OLNEY					
	TRICYCLE	PIXIE5	60.50	8	50.50
	TRICYCLE	PIXIE10	65.99	6	55.99
	MOUNTAIN	ROUGHTRACK1	89.99	5	79.99
	MOUNTAIN	ROUGHTRACK6	129.99	6	119.99
			346.47	25	306.47
Grand Total			2767.38	84	2508.38

31 March 2000

Report produced by Angela Bessant

Page 2 of 2

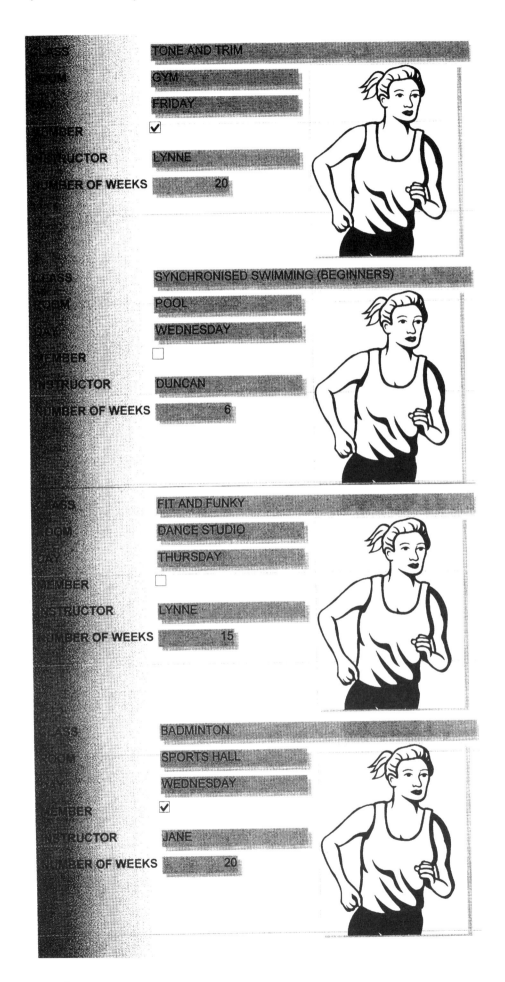

CLASS	TONE AND TRIM
ROOM	GYM
DAY	FRIDAY
MEMBER	✔
INSTRUCTOR	LYNNE
NUMBER OF WEEKS	20

CLASS	SYNCHRONISED SWIMMING (BEGINNERS)
ROOM	POOL
DAY	WEDNESDAY
MEMBER	☐
INSTRUCTOR	DUNCAN
NUMBER OF WEEKS	6

CLASS	FIT AND FUNKY
ROOM	DANCE STUDIO
DAY	THURSDAY
MEMBER	☐
INSTRUCTOR	LYNNE
NUMBER OF WEEKS	15

CLASS	BADMINTON
ROOM	SPORTS HALL
DAY	WEDNESDAY
MEMBER	✔
INSTRUCTOR	JANE
NUMBER OF WEEKS	20

CLASS   AEROBIKING
ROOM   GYM
DAY   WEDNESDAY
MEMBER   ☑
INSTRUCTOR   SALLY
NUMBER OF WEEKS   10

CLASS   AEROBICS
ROOM   GYM
DAY   MONDAY
MEMBER   ☐
INSTRUCTOR   KENNY
NUMBER OF WEEKS   10

Module 5, Practice Tasks 1, Step 1

3 beds   20/04/00

Location	Postcode	Type	Beds	Garage	Garden	Rent £	Available
Elstow	BD41 5RW	House	3	✔	☐	400	July
Carlton	MK44 9AS	House	3	✔	✔	1100	June

Module 5, Practice Tasks 1, Step 2

Properties   20/04/00

Location	Postcode	Type	Beds	Garage	Garden	Rent £	Available
Bedford	BD23 1AS	Flat	1	☐	☐	600	June
Brickhill	MK54 3LP	House	2	✔	✔	550	June
Bodington	NN12 5RP	Flat	1	☐	☐	300	May

Module 5, Practice Tasks 1, Step 3

Query1   20/04/00

Location	Rent £	Available
Bedford	600	June
Devonlly	420	May
Bodington	300	May

Module 5, Practice Tasks 1, Step 9

sorted   20/04/00

Location	Postcode	Type	Beds	Garage	Garden	Rent £	Available
Glasgow	GL4 6RP	Flat	1	☐	☐	400.00	June
Bodington	NN12 5RP	Flat	1	☐	☐	300.00	May
Bedford	BD23 1AS	Flat	1	☐	☐	600.00	June
Harrold	MK49 4HX	Flat	2	✔	☐	600.00	July
Devonlly	MK29 7TD	Flat	2	☐	✔	420.00	May
Rushden	NN14 8PT	House	2	✔	✔	500.00	June
Brickhill	MK54 3LP	House	2	✔	✔	550.00	June
Carlton	MK44 9AS	House	3	✔	✔	1100.00	June
Elstow	BD41 5RW	House	3	✔	☐	400.00	July
Oakley	OS2 6RW	House	4	✔	✔	850.00	May
Goldington	BG31 8QT	House	5	✔	✔	875.00	August

Types of Rental Properties

Angela Bessant

Type	Location	Rent £	Available
Flat	Glasgow	400.00	June
	Harrold	600.00	July
	Bodington	300.00	May
	Devonlly	420.00	May
	Bedford	600.00	June
House	Carlton	1100.00	June
	Rushden	500.00	June
	Oakley	850.00	May
	Goldington	875.00	August
	Brickhill	550.00	June
	Elstow	400.00	July

Multimedia on the web
Multimedia Workshop 2000

The Grand Hotel Conference Centre

Bristol BS8 2TS

Tel 0117 21021102

E-mail: mow@multicon.ac.uk

The following topics will form the basis of the multimedia workshop:

☐ Text

☐ Graphics

☐ Video

☐ Sound

Video and Sound Workshops

Video

This will concentrate on accessing two websites with video content. The content will be compared and contrasted with a view to finding out what works and what falls flat. Website addresses will be specifically selected for this workshop.

Sound

For this workshop there will be four websites to focus on. Some have streaming audio. The quality and accessibility of the sound will be judged and rated out of ten for each of the two categories.

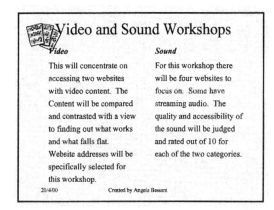

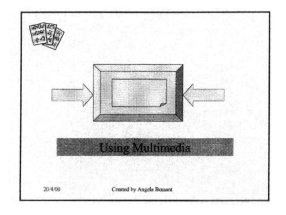

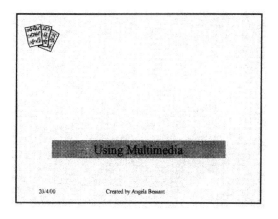

Multimedia is fun!

Using Multimedia

Opening slide for uses of multimedia in web designs.

1

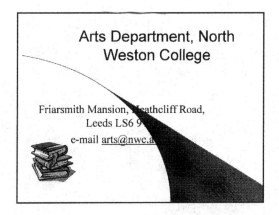

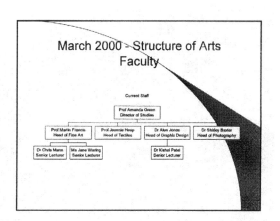

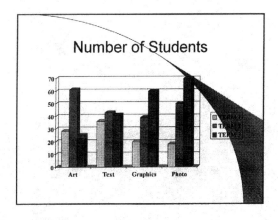

Module 6, Practice Tasks 1, Step 9

Summer Madness 2000

Angela Bessant 20/4/00

Many models on offer

✓ Vauxhalls
✓ Fords
✓ Toyotas
✓ Volkswagens

Angela Bessant 20/4/00

Meet the Team

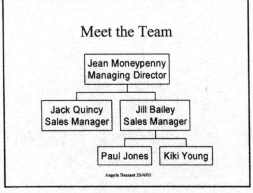

Angela Bessant 20/4/00

1

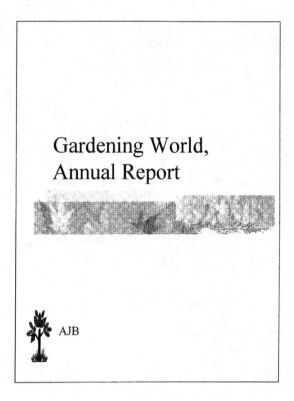

Gardening World,
Annual Report

AJB

1

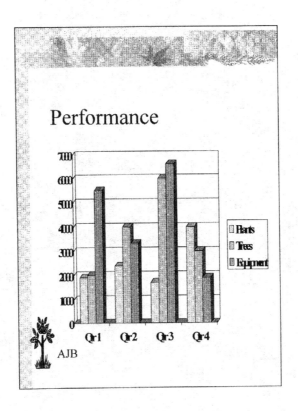

Figures do not include bedding plant sales.

We strive to provide
the very best for all
your gardening needs.
We are always ready
to provide information
and advice that will
turn your *fingers*
green.

AJB

Glossary

This glossary gives a short description of commonly used computing terms used throughout the book.

Alignment	Positioning of text or graphics on a page in relation to other elements.
Application	Another word for 'program' or 'application program'. An application enables you to do something specific e.g. word processing, payroll.
Aspect ratio	The ratio of width to height of an object. Maintaining the aspect ratio means not making the object taller or wider.
Backup	A second, safe copy of data on a different storage media made for security reasons.
Browser	A program that enables you to view web pages on the Internet.
Bullets	A small graphic – e.g. ● or ■ – used to emphasise and separate items in a list.
Buttons	Using the mouse you click on buttons to select actions. There are toolbar buttons, dialogue box buttons and so on.
Character formatting	Changing a character's look by altering font, size, style and so on.
Chart	Graphical display of information e.g. bar chart, organisational chart.
Clicking	Pressing and releasing the left mouse button.
Clip Art	Artwork that is available for you to insert into documents.
Clipboard	The Clipboard is where the computer stores items that you have copied or cut, ready to paste somewhere else.
Cursor	A symbol (which changes shape depending on what you are doing) displayed on the screen showing where the next character will be displayed.
Dialogue box	A window that is displayed asking you for information.
Document	A file containing text or pictures.
Double-clicking	Quickly pressing and releasing the left mouse button twice.
Dragging	Moving things around using the mouse.
Drive	The device that reads and writes onto disks.
E-mail	Short for 'Electronic Mail'. Mail sent via a network or the Internet.
File	A unit of information stored on the computer e.g. a Word file, an Excel file.
File name + extensions	The name given to a file. The extension is the letters after the filename that allow the computer to identify its type.
Floppy disk	A portable storage medium that is floppy but protected by having a plastic case.
Folder	A storage location to keep related files together. Sometimes known as a 'directory'.
Font	A character set with predefined styles and sizes e.g. Times New Roman, Courier.
Form letter	The main document used in a mail merge.
Header and footer	Special areas at the top and bottom of pages for information that can appear on all pages of a document.
Help	Press F1 to access information on topics you are unsure of.
Hover	Place the mouse pointer over an object for a few seconds.
Icon	Small pictures that represent objects in a Graphical User Interface (GUI).

Margin	The distance of text and graphics from the edges of printed pages.
Menu	A menu is a list of commands grouped into related tasks from which you can choose.
drop-down and pop-up	A drop-down (or pull-down) menu is displayed from the top of the screen downward when it is selected.
	A pop-up menu (usually activated using the right mouse button) pops up on screen.
Menu bar	A row of menu options.
Multitasking	The ability of a computer to run two or more programs at the same time.
Non-printing characters	Symbols that can be displayed on screen using the Show/Hide facility but which are not printed out.
Panes	When a window is split into several parts, each part is called a pane.
Pointer	The symbol on the screen that moves when you move the mouse or another pointing device.
Print queue	When more than one document has been sent to the printer, a print queue forms so that documents are stored and printed in turn. Print queues are common on networks.
Recycle Bin	Deleted files are sent to the Recycle Bin. They can be recovered from here if necessary depending on the setup. Files deleted from floppy disks are not sent to the Recycle Bin.
Right-click	Click the right mouse button. Usually this reveals a context-sensitive menu.
Scrollbar	A horizontal or vertical strip that appears on the right or bottom of the window and lets you move through a document using the mouse to reveal previously hidden parts that couldn't fit in the window.
Select	To highlight a portion of text or an object on the screen so that you can manipulate it.
Spellcheck	A command that compares the spelling in a document with that in the program's dictionary.
Style	A collection of formatting choices applied to text that can be saved and used again.
Subfolder	A folder within a folder.
Tab (in text)	A pre-set position for aligning text.
Taskbar	A strip (usually) along the bottom of the Windows desktop containing the Start button, icons for all active tasks, quick launch icons and the system tray.
Template	Templates have styles and page layout settings pre-set that you can use to create a document.
Text editor	A very basic word processing program for editing plain text.
Toolbar	A line of buttons containing clickable short-cut icons.
Undo	A command that reverses your most recent action(s).
Wildcard	A character – e.g. *, ? – used to represent unknown characters when searching for information/files.
Window	A rectangular screen area in which applications and documents are displayed.
Word wrap	A word processing feature that automatically starts a new line when the text reaches the end of the current line.
World Wide Web	The visible part of the Internet containing linked HTML documents accessed through browsers. Often abbreviated to 'the Web'.

Appendix

Changing defaults in Word

Office Assistant

To hide the Office Assistant:
Right-click: over the Office assistant, select: **Options** and set them to your preferences, click on: **OK**.

To turn the Office Assistant on:
From the **Help** menu, select: **Show the Office Assistant**.

Checking spelling and grammar

There are many options available. Throughout the book, I have chosen not to check on an ongoing basis but after keying in entire documents. Should you wish to choose other options:

From the **Tools** menu, select: **Options**. Click on the **Spelling & Grammar** tab. Select your preferences and click on: **OK**.

Changing the unit of measure

To change the unit of measure from inches to cms or vice versa:

1   From the **Tools** menu, select: **Options**, and then click on: the **General** tab.

2   In the **Measurement units** box, click on: the down arrow and then on the option you want.

3   Click on: **OK**.

File maintenance within programs

In addition to using Windows Explorer and My Computer, you can carry out file maintenance within programs. When opening or saving a file, you are able to gain access to your files within the window (shown below). This is common to most Office programs. This window was opened in Word and displays only Word documents (by default).

If you want to see other documents, click on: the down arrow next to **Files of Type** and make your selection. Click on: the **History** button to see recently opened files.

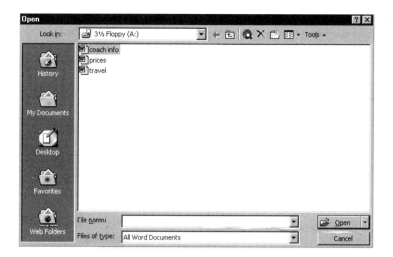

The main shortcut buttons that you will find useful are shown below. Using these will enable you to create folders, find out details of your files.

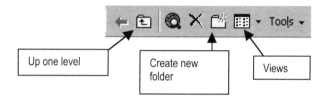

Up one level   Create new folder   Views

Clicking on the down arrow next to the **Views** button produces a menu where you can select what detail you want to see in the **Open** window. The choices are: **List** (the default), **Details**, **Properties** and **Preview**.

Right-clicking on a file/folder will bring up the pop-up menu shown. This allows you to carry out any of the tasks on the menu.

A quicker way to delete a file or folder is by selecting it and pressing: **Delete**.

Note: You cannot carry out file maintenance when a file is open.

A guide to document layout

When you have edited text or moved text within an exercise, remember that adjustment of line spacing is often necessary. When proofreading pay particular attention to line spacing between paragraphs.

When inserting a sentence within a paragraph, make sure the spacing after any punctuation marks remains consistent. Make the necessary adjustments if required.

Use the Spellchecker but do realise its limitations.

Line spacing between paragraphs

Press: **Enter/Return** twice to leave one clear line space between paragraphs.

Underlining/Underscoring

Underlining should not extend beyond the word.
Example   word is correct   word is incorrect

Punctuation

Be consistent with your spacing after punctuation marks. Use the following as a guide:

Punctuation	Mark	Number of spaces before/after
Comma	,	No space before – 1 space after
Semicolon	;	No space before – 1 space after
Colon	:	No space before – 1 or 2 spaces after
Full Stop	.	No space before – 1 or 2 spaces after
Exclamation Mark	!	No space before – 1 or 2 spaces after
Question Mark	?	No space before – 1 or 2 spaces after

Hyphen

No space is left before or after a hyphen – e.g. dry-clean.

Dash

One space precedes and follows a dash – never place a dash at the left-hand margin when it is in the middle of a word or a sentence, always place it at the end of the previous line.

Brackets

No spaces are left between brackets and the word enclosed within them – e.g. (solely for the purposes of assignments).

Keyboard shortcuts that work (almost) everywhere

Keyboard	Menu
F1	Help
F7	Tools, Spelling and Grammar
Ctrl + N	File, New
Ctrl + O	File, Open
Ctrl + S	File, Save
F12	File, Save As
Ctrl + W	File, Close
Ctrl + P	File, Print
Alt + F4	File, Exit
Ctrl + X	Edit, Cut
Ctrl + C	Edit, Copy
Ctrl + V	Edit, Paste
Ctrl + Z	Edit, Undo
Ctrl + A	Edit, Select All
Esc	Cancels items

Don't forget

Right-clicking over objects displays pop-up menus in Office 2000.

Forward

This exam guide and example assessments follows on from the Introduction to Bookkeeping study guide and is designed to prepare students specifically for the exam. This exam guide and assessments have been prepared as:

a) The mocks available tend to be quite similar to the released AAT draft assessments following the same path as in those assessments. However, the exam questions typically look at a similar scenario but from a different perspective confusing/reversing the entries;

b) Certain terminology used in the exam is counterintuitive/not consistent with real life bookkeeping and requires explanation just for the exam setting;

c) The practice questions do not link different parts of the five stage accounting system together to sufficiently embed knowledge;

d) There is often little relationship between marks allocated and time taken. An upfront question that uses considerable time for few marks often disturbs anxious students whereas overall time will not be a factor.

This guide and assessment will help students recognise and react to these points.

This exam assessment guide includes:

1) An exam guide breaking down:
   a. Question types;
   b. Different directions the examiner may approach questions;
   c. Potential new questions following the introduction of digital accounting systems into the syllabus;

2) Five practice exam assessments. Within the assessments there are no easy questions whereas the exam will contain a few high scoring questions requiring limited knowledge. The questions will also mirror the often confusing terminology.

Combined this is designed to provide an experience for students that better prepares them for the exam and will be slightly (but not too much) tougher than the real assessment.

Contents

1 Exam Guide

This exam guide is a brief review of the requirements for the exam. It follows on from the Introduction to Bookkeeping study guide. This guide is specifically about approaches to be used in the exam situation for questions that are counterintuitive and/or questions with confusing terminology – i.e. it is purely about passing the exam. Some of this guide will be useful as preparation for other units but not about accountancy knowledge itself. Often it will explain where the examiner is attempting to test in a particular manner that would not be used in the workplace.

It covers the main factors to be aware of in the exam including:

- T account/balance questions;
- The different perspectives of the five stage accountancy system to determine how to correctly complete documents/daybooks etc;
- Recurring entry journals
- The bank statement;
- VAT
- Discounts

1.1 T Accounts/What are the Balances Questions?

Many questions will ask for the different balances in a T account, including the cashbook balances (the cashbook really just being a T account for the bank and cash accounts with more detail provided in analysis columns to allow the posting of journals to the general ledger). In the workplace the balance on an account is the total of the debits less the credits (being either a positive or negative money amount to the company). However, confusingly the examiner refers to the following balances:

Examiners terminology	What is this really
Balance at the start of the month Balance bfwd Balance on 1 (and then month) Balance at the opening of the period	This is the opening balance on the account. The debit or credit at the start of the accounting period. Create a T account and put this in it
Balance at the end of the month Balance carried forward Balance on 30/31 of the month	This is the carried forward balance. However, it is important to understand that the carried forward balance is only a figure that makes the totals of both sides of the T account balance. It exists in a manual system because improves an ability to add up numbers without errors. Being: Step 1 total both sides add in the carried forward balance Step 2 re-total both sides

	If the total of both sides are the same you know the balancing figure is correct (this will be more accurate than simply adding both sides again because it approaches the task from a different perspective and is an approach known as triangulation).
	The reason such effort is put into adding correctly in a manual system is because if a miscasting error appears the whole set of books for that period has to redone. Throughout the five stage accounting system for manual accounting there will be numerous approaches that are wholly designed to add correctly.
	The carried forward balance is then brought down to the other side of the T account and it is that balance which is used for the trial balance.
Balance brought forward at the start of the following month	This is the final balance on the account which will be used in the trial balance. In a digital system this would be the balance on the account at the end of the month (not needed in the exam but highlights that the carried forward balance is not a balance but a balancing figure).

A high number of marks in the exam are going to be gained or lost by understanding what the examiner is referring to in a T account. It is important to enter into the exam with a good knowledge of:

1) Using T accounts for your workings;
2) Knowing which "balance" the examiner is referring to and looking for it in the question.

But again in real life the brought forward balance (at either the start of the month of the beginning of the next month) is the balance on the account and the figure to be used for the trial balance. The carried forward figure is only a balancing figure used to ensure arithmetical accuracy but for the purposes of the exam you will have to refer to it as a balance.

1.2 Whose Perspective?

The documents, daybooks and ledger accounts are from the perspective of either the buyer, the seller or the company's bank. When reading the scenario you should:

1) Set out who is the buyer and who is the seller. This will determine which parts of the five stage system is being used and the correct entries;
2) Determine the documents being used so you know what is the correct entries to the daybooks etc. For example, if the company is the seller and there is an invoice for credit sales this will be entered into the sales daybook, there will be a sales ledger control account and the journals will be dr trade receivables cr sales and VAT. The same invoice for the buying company is now in the purchases day book etc.

3) Determine if the sale is on credit or for cash. This will determine whether the sale/purchase is in the sales/purchase ledger or the cashbook.

The detail of each part of the five stage accounting system is set out in detail the study guide. The perspectives of each part is set out below:

Buyer	Seller
Negotiation undertaken between both	
Prepares purchase order States order number	Receives purchase order Uses purchase order number to allow tracking
Receives goods, prepares goods inwards note	Sends goods with delivery note
Purchase invoice Receives the invoice from the seller and for them is the purchase invoice Uses invoice number to allow tracking	Sales invoice The seller prepares the invoice and for them it is the sales invoice. They state the invoice number
Purchase ledger daybook	Sales ledger daybook
Discounts received daybook	Discounts allowed daybook
Purchase returns daybook	Sales return daybook
Credit note given to buyer	Credit note prepared by seller Seller creates the credit note number
Remittance advice	Supplier statement
Purchase ledger and purchase ledger control account	Sales ledger and sales ledger control account
Cashbook cash purchases on the credit side	Cashbook cash sales on the debit side·
Cashbook payments for credit supplies on credit side	Cashbook receipts for credit sales on debit side
VAT paid to the seller for onward payment to HMRC is then recoverable by the purchaser from HMRC	VAT charged on sales. Taken from customer and paid to HMRC

1.3 Bank Statement

Bank statements are typically considered in the Principles of Bookkeeping Controls unit however with the introduction of digital accounting into this unit it is possible that bank statements may be introduced in greater detail. The reason is that:

1) The syllabus sets some of the major advantages of digital accounting systems. One of the few that is provided is the ability to download bank statements and upload them into the digital accounting system;
2) The SAGE accounting software unit has been removed. The coding of a bank statement to be uploaded into a digital accounting system could be a good substitute question;
   3) The low potential quality of recurring journal questions (see below) that might force alternative sources of digital accounting questions.

It is important to remember that the bank statement is from the bank's perspective. A debit for the bank is a credit for the company and vice versa. The bank statement shows the amount the bank owes the company (credit) which would be a debit in the company's general ledger. A debit for the bank in the bank statement shows the amount the company owes the bank (overdraft) and is a credit in the company's general ledger.

Bank Statement from Bank of Norton				Company Bank Account in General Ledger			
			Balance	Debits	£	Credits	£
Starting balance	credit		1,020	Balance b/d	1,020		
Payment out 1	debit	46	974			Payment out 1	46
Payment in 1	credit	51	1,025	Payment in 1	51		
Payment out 2	debit	70	955			Payment out 2	70
Payment in 2	credit	94	1,049	Payment in 2	94		
Payment in 3	credit	56	1,105	Payment in 3	56		
Payment out 3	debit	67	1,038			Payment out 3	67
Payment in 4	credit	73	1,111	Payment in 4	73		
Payment out 4	debit	47	1,064			Payment out 4	47
Payment out 5	debit	65	999			Payment out 5	65
Payment in 5	credit	70	1,069	Payment in 5	70		
Payment out 6	debit	33	1,036			Payment out 6	33
Closing balance	credit		1,036			Balance c/d	1,036
				Total	1,364	Total	1,364
				Balance b/d	1,036		

Whilst it is possible that the bank statement will not appear in the exam, this is needed in full in the Principles of Bookkeeping Controls exam (it will appear at least once) so is not wasted effort at this stage.

1.4 Recurring Entries (Journals) for Income and Payments

The syllabus includes the following section regarding recurring entries (journals):

4.4	Process recurring receipts and payments	
	Learners need to understand:	Learners need to be able to:
	4.4.1 the information required to set up a recurring entry. 4.4.2 the effect of recurring entries in the digital bookkeeping system.	4.4.3 set up a recurring entry. 4.4.4 process a recurring entry.

This is stated as an important advantage of digital accounting systems. However in the workplace such journals would never be used as:

1) The transactions undertaken at level 2 are not appropriate for recurring journals. Recurring receipts and payments are not set up as recurring journals because of the high probability of:

a. Overpaying if circumstances change;
b. Not chasing debts if they are not paid – it has been assumed they have been paid;
c. The threat of not receiving necessary invoices/authorisation checks if the journals have been set up many months in advance and managers do not have to chase or sign off invoices.

2) Recurring journals are only potentially useful for areas considered at level 3 such as depreciation rather than payments to the bank account (as set out in the questions). Even here there are risks that errors are introduced into the system that go unchecked.

Recurring journals is only a theoretical advantage pushed by software developers rather than something a Finance Director would implement. However:

1) It should be a relatively easy question if it comes up (fill in the boxes) ;
2) This question could only become difficult if say the facts were to change and the question was asking for a particular length of time the journal should be set up for. If the price is subject to a variable change this would limit the length of the journal (such that the assessments test this).

1.5 VAT

There will be a very high number of marks in the exam for the correct calculation of VAT. This could appear in the following questions:

1) invoice/credit note preparation
2) cashbook - VAT is on cash sales or purchases but not on credit sales or purchases (credit sales or purchases going in the trade receivables or trade payables analysis columns)
3) Petty cashbook
4) Error journals

You must know how to calculate VAT for the exam and this is set out in detail in the study guide. The assessments highlight how this can appear in the questions.

1.6 Discounts

It is likely there will be at least one question on the calculation of discounts. The trick that will appear for this question is:

1) Trade and bulk discount are deducted before net amounts payable (and the VAT calculation;
2) Prompt payment discounts are not included in the net amounts payable and only deducted later.

The wording can often be confusing (providing a single prompt payment discount and asking for the amounts due before and after discounts) or in the credit note question providing the prompt payment discount that would not be applicable.

Care is required with discount questions to ensure you understand what the question is asking and also where a trap has been placed.

1.7 The Danger of DEAD CLIC

Throughout the study guide and associated playlist I highlight where I believe the use of DEAD CLIC to answer questions (in comparison to the positive money, negative money method) is a dangerous approach. The reasons is that DEAD CLIC (or PEARLS) only states what a general ledger account is (debit or credit) not why it is. It is similar to the money in money out description but without then considering the direction of travel of the money movement that makes the account a debit or a credit.

In the Introduction to Bookkeeping exam about 80% of the answers will follow the DEAD CLIC approach, however there will be a number of places where DEAD CLIC will fail such as:

1) Trial balance questions where the:
    a. Bank is stated as an overdraft (negative money);
    b. VAT is stated as from HMRC (positive money).
2) Error or credit note questions where items can be in reverse;
3) Irrecoverable debts where the VAT payable is now reversed.

Whilst DEAD CLIC can be used with little effort to get a low pass (sufficient marks can be achieved using it to pass) nothing has actually been learned, which will mean that the student has an insufficient knowledge of double entry bookkeeping to do well in the Principles of Bookkeeping Controls unit (where they will now struggle) and will most likely fail at the level 3 Advanced Bookkeeping unit later.

In addition, longer term the use of DEAD CLIC turns a simple matter of understanding positive and negative money to the company (that can be applied in all situations) to a grueling and very unpleasant memory test at level 3 and beyond for worse results.

If you are struggling with double entry bookkeeping at this stage and tempted to use the DEAD CLIC method (or are already using it) you should review the paper and cups exercise for learning double entry bookkeeping in this unit's playlist on the Michael Norton channel:

Double Entry Bookkeeping for AAT Level 2 and AAT Level 3: Paper and cups method - YouTube

You cannot fail to understanding double entry bookkeeping by the end of 40 minutes.

1.8 The Assessment Instructions

At the start of the assessment there will be a series of instructions that will apply unless stated otherwise. You must read them carefully as a few marks in the assessment will be associated with the correct interpretation of the instructions for the given scenario.

They will typically be:

All businesses use a manual bookkeeping system	This requires the use of Daybooks. There should now be a reference to digital systems somewhere in the assessment
Double entry takes place in the general ledger. Individual accounts of trade receivables and trade	This sets up the use of control accounts in the general ledger for trade receivables and trade payables

payables are kept in the sales and purchase ledgers as subsidiary accounts	
The cashbook and petty cashbook should be treated as part of the double entry system unless the task instructions state otherwise	The cashbook and petty cashbook are therefore the ledger accounts as well as the daybooks. This means the bank and cash amounts are already posted as journals and just the analysis columns require further posting to the general ledger (if this is asked)
The VAT rate is 20%	Be mindful that VAT can always change (unlikely but possible).

These instructions are to be use throughout the following assessments.

1.9 Workings and Exam Technique

The playlist that accompanies this unit provides walkthroughs of each type of question for the exam. The answers to these assessments also provides workings or notes rather than just the answer. When marking your work you should be mindful of the quality of your workings.

Even where you get an answer right you should consider whether your approach would result in you getting it right every time rather than just this time. Where possible your workings should:

1) Produce full T accounts with balances and totals as a cross check;
2) You net, VAT and gross figures should be determined independently then added together to see if they give a consistent answer;
3) The totals and analysis columns for your daybooks should be added and checked to see if the sum of the analysis columns is the same as the total columns.

This is what is meant by checking your work. If you do not take this approach checking your work becomes doing the exam twice and worrying about the times when you arrived at different answers.

1.10 Time and Anxiety

Time is unlikely to be a factor in this exam. You should remain calm throughout as the marks often have little relationship to the time taken. You may see an upfront question for few marks that takes up a lot of time. Learn to recognise this and complete that question at the end (you will still have lots of time then but be less anxious).

1.11 The Assessment Question Matrix

For tutors looking to use this assessment book for formative assessment question setting or for students looking to practice particular questions, the question types throughout the assessments are as follows:

Type of Question	Assessment				
	1	2	3	4	5
Five Stage Accounting System	1a		1a 1e		1a
Codes	1 b-c		1 b-c		1 b-c
Digital accounting systems	1d 5a	3a	1d		1d
Errors	1e				1e
Accounting Equation	2 4b 8	2 6	7 9d	3 4b 6 8d	2 7
Processing Sales inc discounts	3 6	1 4	2 5 6	1 7a	3 10a
Credit notes				2	
Discounts		5		4a	6
Processing purchases	4 7		3		4
Bank account and cashbook	5a-b 9	3a-b 7	4a-b 8 9a-c	5a 8a-c	5a-b 8 10b
Two column cashbook		9			9
Daybooks	5c	3c 10	3c 4c	7b	5c
Financial statements	10a				
Petty Cashbook	10b-c	8		5b	
Recurring Entries				9	

Note that in the above questions many will follow the same template. This is deliberate because the wording will be slightly different such that the answer is from a different perspective and often reversed. The same template is used to ensure the question is read fully and students understand that the examiner's wording has a large impact upon which daybooks etc are being used. They are not simply copies of each other with the numbers changed.

YOU HAVE 1 HOUR AND 30 MINUTES FOR EACH OF THE FOLLOWING ASSESSMENTS

aat

Practice Assessment

Introduction to Bookkeeping

Practice Assessment 1

Task 1 (10 marks)

This task is about manual and digital bookkeeping systems

(a) Identify which document would be used for each of the purposes below:

Document from the supplier of the amounts delivered signed by the person accepting the delivery	
Document prepared by the buyer of the amounts delivered and the person checking the quality of delivery	
Reminder from the supplier of amounts due	
Detailing the goods supplied to credit customers and the amount to be paid	

4 marks

(b) Supplier accounts are made up of the first three letters of their name and a sequential number separated by a -. The next available number is 63. Assign the supplier codes to the following two new suppliers:

Supplier	Code to be assigned
Dastardy Ltd	
Mutley plc	

2 Marks

c) A code is made up of a combination of letters and numbers separated by a -. This type of code is:

	Which code?
Alphabetic	
Alphanumeric	
Numeric	

(d) Identify whether the following statements about digital bookkeeping systems are true or false:

	True/False
Digital systems prevent duplicate entries into the general ledger	
Digital systems allow journals to be automated	

2 Marks

(e) A purchase invoice has been omitted from the purchases day book. Identify one possible consequence of this error:

	Pick correct option
The supplier may be overpaid	
VAT may be overpaid in the short-term	
The supplier may allow the goods to not be paid for	
A prompt payment discount can be obtained	

1 Mark

Task 2 (10 Marks)

This task is about principles of double-entry bookkeeping

(a) At the end of July a business had the following assets and liabilities

Assets and liabilities	£
Property	4,411.56
Fixtures and Fittings	6,272.37
Cash at bank	8,585.63
Trade receivables	8,645.97
Trade payables	8,361.62
Bank loan	6,897.15

What is the total of the following:

Assets	Liabilities	Capital
£	£	£

3 Marks

(b) The first transaction recorded in August related to the payment by a customer of a debt due. The effect of this transaction:

Effect	Pick option
Increase assets and reduce liabilities	
Both increase and reduce liabilities	
Both increase and reduce assets	

1 Mark

(c) Identify the opposite effect of each bank trasaction.

Bank transaction	Opposite effect	Options
Payment of sales tax due to HMRC		Repairs
Received money for cash sales		Trade receivables
Paid for employees wages		VAT control
Money received from customer for goods purchased on credit		Loan
Repaid a loan		Wages
Paid to repair the warehouse roof		Sales

6 Marks

Task 3 (10 marks)

A sales invoice is being prepared for goods supplied, as shown in the customer order below:

ABAC Plc	
Order number 3425	
Please supply	30 July 20XX
5 Pulleys	
@ 4.20 each less 10% trade discount	

a) Calculate the amounts to be included on the invoice

	Amount £
Net amount before discount	
Net amount after discount	
VAT	
Gross amount	

4 Marks

b) what will be the amount entered into the sales daybook when the invoice in a) has been processed?

Date	Details	Invoice number	Total	VAT	Net
30 July 20XX	ABAC Plc	1559242			

3 Marks

c) a cheque has been received from ABAC Plc for £7478.71 which they incorrectly state as being in full payment of any amounts due. The customer's account from the sales ledger is shown below. Which three items are outstanding?

Customer account

Date	Details	Amount	Date	Details	Amount
	Balance bfwd	3393.70			
1 July 20XX	Invoice 425	3410.20	6 July 20XX	Credit note 85497	192.42
3 July 20XX	Invoice 470	2042.90	4 July 20XX	Payment	3201.28
13 July 20XX	Invoice 499	3995.20	15 July 20XX	Credit note 52334	757.79
14 July 20XX	Invoice 565	4826.30	18 July 20XX	Credit note 51475	778.95

Circle three omitted	
Balance bfwd	
Invoice 425	Credit note 85497
Invoice 470	Payment
Invoice 499	Credit note 52334
Invoice 565	Credit note 51475

3 Marks

Task 4 (10 Marks)

The following order and invoice have been created

Invoice	
XYZ LLP	
VAT Reg no 3597881	
invoice number 3409	
To ABC Ltd Date 27/02/2022	
	£
FF06 @	
217 each	11.00
Less trade discounts @	0.00
VAT 20%	2.20
Total	13.20
Terms 3% discount for payment received by the end of the month	

Purchase Order		
ABC Ltd		
Purchase order 6250		
To XYZ LLP Date 19/02/2022		
Please supply		
	FF06 @	
	Product each	
217 code: £		10.00
Less 5% trade discount		
As agreed, terms 3% discount for payment by the end of the month		

(a) identify any discrepancies on the invoice by selecting the correct option in the table below

	Not shown on invoice	Correctly shown on invoice	Incorrectly shown on invoice
Terms of payment			
Quantity			
Price			
Discounts			

4 Marks

(b) The balances on GHER's sales and purchase ledger are as follows

Sales ledger (owed from customers)   98,313
Purchase ledger (owed to suppliers)   14,575

Complete the partially completed trial balance extracted below.

	Debit	Credit
Amount	369,052	122,454
Trade receivables control account		
Trade payables control account		
Shareholders funds		
Total		

5 marks

(c) Invoices for goods bought on credit are posted to which daybook:

Daybook	Choice
Cashbook	
Sales	
Purchases	
Petty cashbook	
Discounts received	
The Journal	

1 mark

Task 5 (10 Marks)

(a) At 30 July the balance on the cashbook is £2821 debit

Code the following transactions have been downloaded from the bank account on 31 July.	Amount £	Code
Payment to suppliers for purchases on credit	173	
Bank interest paid	399	
Bank interest received	477	
Wages paid	930	

2 Marks

General ledger codes	Code
Van at cost	1001
Computers at cost	1010
Trade receivables	1101
Trade payables	1201
Cash	1301
Sales	2101
Interest received	2302
Wages expense	3101
Repairs expense	3151
Purchases	3201
Interest paid	3305

(b) What are the cashbook balances on the following dates	Debit £	Credit £
Balance on 31 July		
Balance on 1 August		

4 Marks

(c) How are the following daybooks posted to the additional (not general) ledgers.

Daybook	Choice	Options
Sales		Debit to the trade receivables ledger
Sales returns		Credit to the trade receivables ledger
Discounts allowed		Debit to the trade payables ledger
Discounts received		Credit to the trade payables ledger

4 Marks

Task 6 (10 Marks)

ABC Ltd has received two remittance advices and cheques from XYZ Ltd totalling £ 13501.91

XYZ Ltd	
Remittance Advice 158422	
	Amount £
Invoice 472254	2,257.87
Invoice 472261	2,293.24
Invoice 472269	2,144.60
Invoice 472274	1,589.66
Amount paid	7,033.07

XYZ Ltd	
Remittance Advice 158434	
	Amount £
Invoice 472278	3,331.76
Invoice 472288	2,193.81
Amount paid	5,525.57

There are no prompt payment discounts

ABC has a policy of allocating all payments received against individual invoices/credit notes

The balances on the sales ledger before the payments are below. Allocate the payments

	Amount £	Select Option
Invoice 472254	2,427.82	
Invoice 472261	2,294.24	
Invoice 472269	2,145.60	
Invoice 472274	1,588.66	
Credit note re 472254	-169.95	
Invoice 472278	3,330.76	
Invoice 472288	2,193.81	

	Paid in full
	Underpaid - follow up
Options	Overpaid - Query

6 Marks

(a) The amounts owed to ABC Ltd are set out below. Determine any amounts remaining due (overpayments to be shown as negative figures)

	Invoice date	Amounts invoiced	Prompt payment terms	Date Paid	Amount paid	Discount due	Amount due
XYZ Ltd	05/04/2022	54,941.00	5% by end of month	09/04/2022	49,446.90		
UTD Plc	10/04/2022	35,827.00	5% Net monthly	09/06/2022	35,827.00		
OBO LLP	14/04/2022	99,277.00	10% within 7 days	19/04/2022	84,385.45		
PERDY Ltd	19/04/2022	22,952.00	5% Net monthly	15/06/2022	22,952.00		

4 Marks

Task 7 (10 Marks)

ABC Ltd has received the following supplier invoice on credit

Jones Plumbers	
Date	17/12/2021
Invoice number	9041479
	£
Services rendered	200
VAT	40
Total due	240
Prompt payment discount of 2% if paid within 7 days	

ABC Ltd would post this invoice to which daybook

Sales	
Sales returns	
Purchases	
Discounts received	

1 Mark

Complete the relevant daybook

Detail	Date	Invoice number	Total	VAT	Net
Fred Ltd	06/09/2021	A-7977102	270	45	225
Scoob Plc	09/09/2021	B/1676521	216	36	180
Velma LLP	12/09/2021	ZO-3684708	162	27	135
Daphnie	15/09/2021	A/8081440	186	31	155
Jones Plumbers	18/09/2021	9041479			
Total					

6 Marks

The journal to the general ledger will be	Debit	Credit
Options		
Options		
Options		

3 Marks

Options	
Trade Payables	Purchases
Trade Receivables	Purchases Returns
VAT	Discount Received
Sales	Discount Allowed
Sales Returns	

Task 8 (10 Marks)

The following accounts have been extracted from the sales ledger

b/d	4,236	b/d	3,284

b/d	3,897	b/d	3,193

The following balances have been extracted from the general ledger. Determine the debit and credit values

	Amount £	Debit	Credit
Van at cost	3,390		
Fixtures and fittings	3,663		
Trade receivables	extracted above		
Trade payables	3,537		
Bank	5,796		
Purchases expense	5,523		
Wages	5,958		
Sales	4,170		
Sales returns	4,212		
Discounts allowed	5,271		
Shareholders funds			

7 Marks

The totals of assets, liability and capital are:		
Assets	Liability	Capital

3 Marks

Task 9 (10 Marks)

(a) The following is to be posted into the cashbook for the month of July:

Cash sale to Fred Jones (subject to VAT) amount excluding VAT is £2042

Amount received from John Smith to pay for sale on credit (that included VAT) £8245

Date	Detail	Trade receivables	Sales	VAT	Total
30-Jul-22	Balances to date	8,338.00	3,530.50	706.10	12,574.60
31-Jul-22	Fred Jones				
31-Jul-22	John Smith				
	Total				

4 Marks

(b) The above entries will be posted to which side of the cashbook	

1 Mark

The amounts to be posted to the general ledger are:			
	Amount	Debit	Credit
Options			
Options			
Options			

3 Marks

Options		
Bank	VAT	Sales
Trade receivables	Trade payables	

(c)The total on the opposite side of the cashbook is £26229			
	Amount	Debit	Credit
Carried down balance on 31 July is			

2 Marks

Task 10 (10 Marks)

(a) Classify the following transactions

Transaction	Answer	Option
Purchase a computer		Capital expenditure
Fill the van with fuel		Revenue expenditure
Sell a van		Capital income
Purchase goods for resale		Capital expenditure

4 Marks

(b) Check the following petty cash voucher to attached receipt. It is company policy to not pay for expenses which do not have a valid till receipt or to pay for alcohol or cigarettes. Meals are capped at £12.00 per person.

Petty Cash Voucher		
	Amount	Checked by Finance
Coffee for meeting	2.40	
Refreshments for meeting	12.00	
Lunch 2 staff members	24.00	
Total	38.40	
I confirm that the following expense is validly incur and in line with the company's petty cash policy		
Michael Norton		06/11/2021

Till receipt	
Coffee	2.40
Alcohol	12.00
Total	14.40
Inc VAT	2.40

Options		
Valid expense	Not valid expense	No receipt

3 Marks

(c) Post this petty cash voucher to the petty cash book and return the petty cash holding to the imprest amount

Petty Cash Voucher		
	Amount	Checked by Finance
Coffee for meeting	2.40	Valid expense
Refreshments for meeting	12.00	Valid expense
Lunch	24.00	Valid expense
Total	38.40	
I confirm that the following expense is validly incur and in line with the company's petty cash policy		
Michael Norton	04/08/2022	

Till receipt	Amount
Coffee	2.40
Soft drinks	12.00
Lunch	24.00
Total	38.40
Inc VAT	6.40

Petty Cashbook								
Detail	Total £	Total £	VAT	Meeting expenses	Purchases	Fuel	Detail	Date
Bfwd	150.00	30.00	5.00			25.00	James Jim	02/08/2022
		72.00	12.00		60.00		Geoff Jay	02/08/2022
							Michael Norton	04/08/2022
From Bank							To Bank	31/08/2022
cfwd							cfwd	31/08/2022
Total							Total	

3 Marks

Answers

Task 1 (10 marks)

(a)

Document from the supplier of the amounts delivered signed by the person accepting the delivery	Delivery note
Document prepared by the buyer of the amounts delivered and the person checking the quality of delivery	Goods inwards note
Reminder from the supplier of amounts due	Supplier statement
Detailing the goods supplied to credit customers and the amount to be paid	Invoice

b)

Supplier	Code to be assigned
Dastardy Ltd	Das-63
Mutley plc	Mut-64

c)

	Which code?
Alphabetic	
Alphanumeric	Alphanumeric
Numeric	

(d)

	True/False
Digital systems prevent duplicate entries into the general ledger	False
Digital systems allow journals to be automated	True

(e)

	Pick correct option
The supplier may be overpaid	
VAT may be overpaid in the short-term	Possible because the VAT on the expense is not deducted from the VAT control account
The supplier may allow the goods to not be paid for	
A prompt payment discount can be obtained	

Task 2 (10 Marks)

(a)

Assets	Liabilities	Capital
£	£	£
27,915.53	15,258.77	12,656.76

(b)

Effect	Both increase and reduce assets

(c) Identify the opposite effect of each bank trasaction. You should ignore VAT

Bank transaction	Opposite effect
Payment of sales tax due to HMRC	VAT control
Received money for cash sales	Sales
Paid for employees wages	Wages
Money received from customer for goods purchased on credit	Trade receivables
Repaid a loan	Loan
Paid to repair the warehouse roof	Repairs

Task 3 (10 marks)

a)

	Amount £
Net amount before discount	21.00
Net amount after discount	18.90
VAT	3.78
Gross amount	22.68

b)

Date	Details	Invoice number	Total	VAT	Net
30 July 20XX	ABAC Plc	1559242	22.68	3.78	18.90

c)

Omitted	
Balance bfwd	
Invoice 425	Credit note 85497
Invoice 470	Payment
Invoice 499	Credit note 52334
Invoice 565	**Credit note 51475**

Task 4 (10 marks)

(a) identify any discrepancies on the invoice by selecting the correct option in the table below

	Not shown on invoice	Correctly shown on invoice	Incorrectly shown on invoice
Terms of payment		answer	
Quantity		answer	
Price			answer
Discounts			answer

(b)	Debit	Credit
Amount	369,052	122,454
Trade receivables control account	98,313	
Trade payables control account		14,575
Shareholders funds		330,336
Total	467,365	467,365

(c) Invoices for goods bought on credit are posted to which daybook:

Daybook	Purchases daybook

1 mark

Task 5 (10 Marks)

Code the following transactions have been downloaded from the bank account.	Amount £	Code
Payment to suppliers for purchases on credit	173	1201
Bank interest paid	399	3305
Bank interest received	477	2302
Wages paid	930	3101

2 Marks

(b) What are the cashbook balances on the following dates	Debit £	Credit £
Balance on 31 July – note that this is really only a balancing figure		1,796
Balance on 1 August - this would be used in the trial balance	1,796	

Date	Detail	Amount	Date	Detail	Amount
			30 Jul	bfwd	7462
			31 Jul	Trade payables	537
			31 Jul	Interest paid	563
31 Jul	Interest received	435			
			31 Jul	Wages expense	521
31 Jul	cfwd	8648			
	Total	9083			9083
			1 Aug	bfwd	8648

Page 25

Daybook	Choice
Sales	Debit to the trade receivables ledger
Sales returns	Credit to the trade receivables ledger
Discounts allowed	Credit to the trade receivables ledger
Discounts received	Debit to the trade payables ledger

4 Marks

Task 6 (10 Marks)

	Amount £
Invoice 472254	2,427.82
Invoice 472261	2,294.24
Invoice 472269	2,145.60
Invoice 472274	1,588.66
Credit note re 472254	-169.95
Invoice 472278	3,330.76
Invoice 472288	2,193.81

Paid in full
Underpaid - follow up
Underpaid - follow up
Overpaid - Query
Paid in full
Overpaid - Query
Paid in full

6 Marks

(b) The amounts owed to ABC Ltd are set out below. Determine any amounts remaining due
(overpayments to be shown as negative figures)

	Invoice date	Amounts invoiced	Prompt payment terms	Date Paid	Amount paid	Discount due	Amount due
XYZ Ltd	05/04/2022	54,941.00	5% by end of month	09/04/2022	49,446.90	5%	2,747.05
UTD Plc	10/04/2022	35,827.00	5% Net monthly	09/06/2022	35,827.00	0%	0.00
OBO LLP	14/04/2022	99,277.00	10% within 7 days	19/04/2022	84,385.45	10%	4,963.85
PERDY Ltd	19/04/2022	22,952.00	5% Net monthly	15/06/2022	22,952.00	0%	0.00

4 Marks

Task 7 (10 Marks)

ABC Ltd would post this invoice to which daybook

Purchases

Complete the relevant daybook

Detail	Date	Invoice number	Total	VAT	Net
Fred Ltd	06/09/2021	A-7977102	270	45	225
Scoob Plc	09/09/2021	B/1676521	216	36	180
Velma LLP	12/09/2021	ZO-3684708	162	27	135
Daphnie	15/09/2021	A/8081440	186	31	155
Jones Plumbers	18/09/2021	9041479	240	40	200
Total			1074	179	895

6 Marks

The journal to the general ledger will be	Debit	Credit
Purchases	895	
VAT	179	
Trade payables		1074

3 Marks

Task 8

The following balances have been extracted from the general ledger. Determine the debit and credit values

	Amount £	Asset	Liability	Capital	Debit	Credit
Van at cost	3,390	3,390			3,390	
Fixtures and fittings	3,663	3,663			3,663	
Trade receivables Bfwd used which is the balance on accounts	extracted above	8,224			8,224	
Trade payables	3,537		3,537			3,537
Bank	5,796	5,796			5,796	
Purchases expense	5,523			-5,523	5,523	
Wages	5,958			-5,958	5,958	
Sales	4,170			4,170		4,170
Sales returns	4,212			-4,212	4,212	
Discounts allowed	5,271			-5,271	5,271	
Shareholders funds				34,330		34,330
		21,073	3,537	17,536	42,037	42,037

Assets		Liability		Capital	
	21,073		3,537		17,536

Task 9

(a) Date	Detail	Trade receivables	Sales	VAT	Total
30-Jul-22	Balances to date	8,338.00	3,530.50	706.10	12,574.60
31-Jul-22	Fred Jones		2,042.00	408.40	2,450.40
31-Jul-22	John Smith	8,245.00			8,245.00
	Total	16,583.00	5,572.50	1,114.50	23,270.00

4 Marks

(b)The above entries will be posted to which side of the cashbook	Debit

1 Mark

(c) The amounts to be posted to the general ledger are:			
	Amount	Debit	Credit
Trade receivables	16,583.00		16,583.00
Sales	5,572.50		5,572.50
VAT	1,114.50		1,114.50

3 Marks

Note that because the cashbook is the daybook **and ledger** the totals column for Bank have already been posted to the bank account etc

The total on the opposite side of the cashbook is £26,229			
	Amount	Debit	Credit
Carried down balance on 31 July is	2,959.00	2,959.00	

2 Marks

Note this is 31 July so is the carried down balance to make the T account balance. The balance on the account is the brought down balance in the following month. This is simply an examiners quirk. The balance for the trial balance (if this were requested) would be credit £2,959

Task 10 (10 Marks)

Purchase a computer	Capital expenditure
Fill the van with fuel	Revenue expenditure
Sell a van	Capital income
Purchase goods for resale	Revenue expenditure

4 Marks

Petty Cash Voucher		
	Amount	Checked by Finance
Coffee for meeting	2.40	Valid expense
Refreshments for meeting	12.00	Not valid expense
Lunch 2 staff members	24.00	No receipt
Total	38.40	
I confirm that the following expense is validly incur and in line with the company's petty cash policy		
Michael Norton		06/11/2021

Till receipt	
Coffee	2.40
Alcohol	12.00
Total	14.40
Inc VAT	2.40

3 Marks

Petty Cashbook								
Detail	Total £	Total £	VAT	Meeting expenses	Purchases	Fuel	Detail	Date
Bfwd	150.00	30.00	5.00			25.00	James Jim	02/08/2022
		72.00	12.00		60.00		Geoff Jay	02/08/2022
		38.40	6.40	32.00			Michael Norton	04/08/2022
From Bank	140.40							31/08/2022
		150.00					cfwd	31/08/2022
Total	290.40	290.40	23.40	32.00	60.00	25.00	Total	

3 Marks

aat

Practice Assessment

Introduction to Bookkeeping

Practice Assessment 2

Task 1 (10 marks)

A sales invoice is being prepared for goods supplied, as shown in the customer order below:

ABAC Plc	
order 906521	
Please supply	30 July 20XX
100 Stakes	
@ 5.65 each less 5% bulk discount	

a) Calculate the amounts to be included on the invoice

	Amount £
Net amount before discount	
Net amount after discount	
VAT	
Gross amount	

4 Marks

b) what will be the amount entered into the sales daybook when the invoice in a) has been processed?

Date	Details	Invoice number	Total	VAT	Net
30 July 20XX	ABAC Plc	1670548			

3 Marks

c) a cheque has been received from ABAC Plc for £13675.20 which they incorrectly state as being in full payment of any amounts due. The customer's account from the sales ledger is shown below. Which three items are outstanding?

Customer account

Date	Details	Amount	Date	Details	Amount
	Balance bfwd	6098.20			
1 July 20XX	Invoice 425	9189.90	6 July 20XX	Credit note 41161	141.42
3 July 20XX	Invoice 470	2233.70	4 July 20XX	Payment	5509.25
13 July 20XX	Invoice 499	5367.80	15 July 20XX	Credit note 28015	588.95
14 July 20XX	Invoice 565	2251.60	18 July 20XX	Credit note 54987	330.77

Circle omitted	
Balance bfwd	
Invoice 425	Credit note 41161
Invoice 470	Payment
Invoice 499	Credit note 28015
Invoice 565	Credit note 54987

3 Marks

Task 2 (10 Marks)

This task is about principles of double-entry bookkeeping

(a) At the end of July a business had the following assets and liabilities

Assets and liabilities	£
Cash at bank	4,639.86
Fixtures and Fittings	5,362.60
Trade payables	3,104.37
Trade receivables	732.52
Property	8,163.65
Bank loan	9,551.98

What is the total of the following:

Assets	Liabilities	Capital
£	£	£

3 Marks

(b) The first transaction recorded in August related to the receipt of a loan from the bank. The effect of this transaction:

Effect	Pick option
Increase assets and increase liabilities	
Both increase and reduce liabilities	
Both increase and reduce assets	
Reduce assets and reduce liabilities	

1 Mark

(c) Identify the opposite effect of each bank trasaction. You should ignore VAT

Bank transaction	Opposite effect	Options
Fill van with petrol		Office expenses
Make a loan repayment		Van asset at cost
Payment from customer who purchased goods on credit		Wages
Purchase van		Loan
Purchase office stationery		Trade receivables
Pay employee		Motor vehicle expenses

6 Marks

Task 3 (10 Marks)

At 30 July the balance on the cashbook is £7193 debit

a) Code the following transactions have been downloaded from the bank account.	Amount £	Code
Bank interest paid	772	
Bank interest received	857	
Wages paid	433	
Cash sales	696	

4 Marks

General ledger codes	Code
Van at cost	1001
Computers at cost	1010
Trade receivables	1101
Trade payables	1201
Cash	1301
Sales	2101
Interest received	2302
Wages expense	3101
Repairs expense	3151
Purchases	3201
Interest paid	3305

(b) What are the cashbook balances on the following dates	Debit £	Credit £
Balance on 31 July		
Balance on 1 August		

2 Marks

(c) The following daybooks have been totalled. What is a correct entry to the ledgers

Daybook	Choice	Options
Sales returns		Debit to the trade receivables ledger
Discounts received		Credit to the trade receivables ledger
Purchases		Debit to the trade payables ledger
Purchases returns		Credit to the trade payables ledger

4 Marks

Task 4 (10 Marks)

ABC Ltd has received two remittance advices and cheques from XYZ Ltd totalling £ 13501.91

XYZ Ltd	
Remittance Advice 473917	
	Amount £
Invoice 389539	2,076.98
Invoice 389547	4,897.49
Invoice 389557	4,805.67
Invoice 389565	3,365.24
Amount paid	7,033.07

XYZ Ltd	
Remittance Advice 473945	
	Amount £
Invoice 389570	1,220.33
Invoice 389580	4,380.18
Amount paid	5,600.51

There are no prompt payment discounts

ABC has a policy of allocating all payments received against individual invoices/credit notes
The balances on the sales ledger before the payments are below. Allocate the payments

	Amount £
Invoice 389539	2,076.98
Invoice 389547	4,896.49
Invoice 389557	4,903.74
Invoice 389565	3,365.24
Credit note re 389557	-98.07
Invoice 389570	1,220.33
Invoice 389580	4,380.18

Select Option

6 Marks

	Paid in full
	Underpaid - follow up
Options	Overpaid - Query

(b) The amounts owed to ABC Ltd are set out below. Determine any amounts remaining due

	Invoice date	Amounts invoiced	Prompt payment terms	Date Paid	Amount paid	Discount due	Amount due
XYZ Ltd	05/04/2022	46,082.00	5% Net monthly	25/05/2022	42,856.26		
UTD Plc	09/04/2022	82,296.00	5% Net monthly	20/05/2022	78,181.20		
OBO LLP	10/04/2022	95,773.00	5% by end of month	10/05/2022	90,984.35		
PERDY Ltd	13/04/2022	96,763.00	5% by end of month	12/05/2022	96,763.00		

4 Marks

Task 5 (10 Marks)

ABC Ltd takes advantage of the prompt payment discount on the following invoice

Jones Plumbers	
Date	31/08/2021
Invoice number	9581927
	£
Services rendered	240
VAT	48
Total due	288
Prompt payment discount of 2% if paid within 7 days	

ABC Ltd would post the discount to which daybook   1 Mark

Sales	
Discounts allowed	
Purchases	
Discounts received	

(a) Complete the relevant daybook for this entry

Detail	Date	Invoice number	Total	VAT	Net
Fred Ltd	19/08/2021	A-1203698	20.40	3.40	17.00
Scoob Plc	22/08/2021	B/9224276	16.80	2.80	14.00
Velma LLP	25/08/2021	ZO-3179791	17.40	2.90	14.50
Daphnie	28/08/2021	A/5501501	12.00	2.00	10.00
Jones Plumbers	31/08/2021	9581927			
Total					

6 Marks

(b) The journal to the general ledger from this daybook will be	Debit	Credit
Options		
Options		
Options		

3 Marks

Options		
Trade Payables	Purchases	Sales
Trade Receivables	Purchases Returns	Discount Allowed
VAT Control	Discount Received	Sales Returns

Task 6 (10 Marks)

The following accounts have been extracted from the sales ledger

b/d	4,125		b/d	4,584	

b/d	3,783			b/d	5,908

(a) The following balances have been extracted from the general ledger. Determine the debit and credit values

	Amount £	Debit	Credit
Van at cost	5,839		
Fixtures and fittings	4,185		
Trade receivables	extracted above		
Trade payables	3,810		
Bank (overdraft)	5,758		
Purchases expense	4,417		
Wages	3,780		
Sales	4,723		
VAT to HMRC	5,443		
Discounts allowed	3,760		
Shareholders funds			

7 Marks

(b)The totals of assets, liability and capital are:		
Assets	Liability	Capital

3 Marks

Task 7 (10 Marks)

(a)The following is to be posted into the cashbook for the month of July:
Cash purchase from Frankie Chico (subject to VAT) amount including VAT is £3920.40
Amount paid to Tony Batts to pay for purchase on credit (that included VAT) £3367.00

Date	Detail	Trade payables	Purchases	VAT	Total
30-Jul-22	Balances to date	9,525.00	4,082.00	816.40	14,423.40
31-Jul-22	Frankie Chico				
31-Jul-22	Tony Batts				
	Total				

4 Marks

(b)The above entries will be posted to which side of the cashbook	Debit/Credit

1 Mark

(c) The amounts to be posted to the general ledger are:			
	Amount	Debit	Credit
Options			
Options			
Options			

3 Marks

Options		
Bank	VAT	Sales
Trade receivables	Trade payables	Purchases

(d) The total on the opposite side of the cashbook is £52,044			
	Amount	Debit	Credit
The balance on 1 August 2022 is			

2 Marks

Task 8 (10 Marks)

(a) Post the following petty cash vouchers to the cashbook and return the cashbook to the imprest amount

Petty cash voucher		
Detail	Amount Claimed	VAT
Fuel	16.00	3.20
Total	16.00	
Dated	03/04/2022	

Petty cash voucher		
Detail	Amount Claimed	VAT
Meeting expense	20.50	4.10
Total	20.50	
Dated	13/04/2022	

Petty Cashbook									
Date	Detail	Other	VAT	Amount	Amount	VAT	Fuel	Office stationery	Meeting expense
01/04/2022	bfwd			150.00					
03/04/2022	Fuel								
06/04/2022	Xmas Party	15.00		15.00					
11/04/2022	Xmas Party	15.00		15.00					
13/04/2022	Meeting expense								
18/04/2022	Xmas Party	15.00		15.00					
30/04/2022	From/To bank								
	cfwd								
	Totals								

7 Marks

(b)This petty cashbook is used as a daybook and general ledger account. The journal of the credit side of the petty cashbook to the general ledger is:

	Debit	Credit
Options		
Options		
Options		

3 Marks

Options		
Xmas Party	VAT	Amount
Fuel	Office stationery	Meeting expense
Petty cash	Bank	

Task 9 (10 Marks)

ALL Ltd posts its cashbook by downloading its bank statement first and posting the bank statement. All items except wages are subject to VAT @20%		
The bank statement for April is as follows:		
Bank of Norton	Debit	Credit
Balance bfwd		465.00
Purchase of goods for cash	1725.60	
Sale of goods for cash		742.20
Wages	1180.00	
Amounts received from customers for sales on credit		2222.00

(a) A cashbook has been prepared from the above bank statement. Post the remaining highlighted item in the bank statement to the debit side of the cashbook as well as a sale for cash of £240.00 including VAT and total the cashbook

		Debit Side					
Date	Detail	Sales	VAT	Trade receivables	Cash	Bank
01/04/2022	Balance bfwd				69.00	465.00
07/04/2022	Sale of goods for cash	618.50	123.70			742.20
13/04/2022	Amounts received from customers for sales on credit					
30/04/2022	Cash sale					
	Total					

5 Marks

(b)The credit side of the cashbook is set out below. Determine the balances on 30/04/2022 and total the cashbook.

		Credit side				
Date	Detail	Bank	Cash	VAT	Purchases	Wages
01/04/2022	Balance bfwd					
04/04/2022	Purchase of goods for cash	1725.60		287.60	1438.00	
10/04/2022	Wages	1180.00				1180.00
30/04/2022	Balance cfwd					
	Total					

3 Marks

(c)ALL Ltd has a policy of only holding £200 in cash on-site. What is the entry into the cashbook to reflect the necessary transfer of cash:

	Debit side		Credit side	
	Cash	Bank	Bank	Cash
from/to the bank				

2 Marks

Task 10 (10 Marks)

(a) What journals would be made to the general ledger accounts and other ledgers from the following daybooks? VAT is applicable.

Daybook	Debit	Debit	Credit	Credit
Purchases	Options	Options	Options	Options
Sales	Options	Options	Options	Options
Sales returns	Options	Options	Options	Options
Discounts Received	Options	Options	Options	Options
Purchase Returns	Options	Options	Options	Options

10 Marks

Options	
Dr Purchases	Cr Purchases
Dr Trade Receivables Control	Cr Trade Receivables Control
Dr Trade Payables Control	Cr Trade Payables Control
Dr VAT	Cr VAT
Dr Sales Ledger	Cr Sales Ledger
Dr Purchase Ledger	Cr Purchase Ledger
Dr Discounts Received	Cr Discounts Received
Dr Discounts Allowed	Cr Discounts Allowed

ANSWERS

Task 1 (10 marks)

(a)	Amount £
Net amount before discount	565.00
Net amount after discount	536.75
VAT	107.35
Gross amount	644.10

4 Marks

b) Date	Details	Invoice number	Total	VAT	Net
30 July 20XX	ABAC Plc	1670548	644.10	107.35	536.75

3 Marks

c) Omitted	
Balance bfwd	
Invoice 425	**Credit note 41161**
Invoice 470	Payment
Invoice 499	Credit note 28015
Invoice 565	**Credit note 54987**

3 Marks

Task 2 (10 Marks)

This task is about principles of double-entry bookkeeping

(a)

Assets	Liabilities	Capital
£	£	£
18,898.63	12,656.35	6,242.28

(b)

Effect	Pick option
Increase assets and increase liabilities	Increase assets and increase liabilities

1 Mark

(c) Bank transaction	Opposite effect
Fill van with petrol	Motor vehicle expenses
Make a loan repayment	Loan
Payment from customer who purchased goods on credit	Trade receivables
Purchase van	Van asset at cost
Purchase office stationery	Office expenses
Pay employee	Wages

6 Marks

Task 3 (10 Marks)

At 30 July the balance on the cashbook is £7193 debit

Code the following transactions have been downloaded from the bank account.	Amount £	Code
Bank interest paid	772	3305
Bank interest received	857	2302
Wages paid	433	3101
Cash sales	696	2101

(b) What are the cashbook balances on the following dates	Debit £	Credit £
Balance on 31 July		7,541
Balance on 1 August	7,541	

Date	Detail	Amount	Date	Detail	Amount
30 Jul	bfwd	7193			
			31 Jul	Interest paid	772
31 Jul	Interest received	857			
			31 Jul	Wages expense	433
31 Jul	Sales	696			
			31 Jul	cfwd	7541
	Total	8746			8746
1 Aug	bfwd	7541			

Daybook	Choice
Sales returns	Credit to the trade receivables ledger
Discounts received	Debit to the trade payables ledger
Purchases	Credit to the trade payables ledger
Purchases returns	Debit to the trade payables ledger

Task 4 (10 Marks)

	Amount £	Select Option
Invoice 389539	2,076.98	Paid in full
Invoice 389547	4,896.49	Overpaid - Query
Invoice 389557	4,903.74	Paid in full
Invoice 389565	3,365.24	Paid in full
Credit note re 389557	-98.07	Paid in full
Invoice 389570	1,220.33	Paid in full
Invoice 389580	4,380.18	Paid in full

6 Marks

(b) The amounts owed to ABC Ltd are set out below. Determine any amounts remaining due							
	Invoice date	Amounts invoiced	Prompt payment terms	Date Paid	Amount paid	Discount due	Amount due
XYZ Ltd	05/04/2022	46,082.00	5% Net monthly	25/05/2022	42,856.26	5%	921.64
UTD Plc	09/04/2022	82,296.00	5% Net monthly	20/05/2022	78,181.20	5%	0.00
OBO LLP	10/04/2022	95,773.00	5% by end of month	10/05/2022	90,984.35	0%	4788.65
PERDY Ltd	13/04/2022	96,763.00	5% by end of month	12/05/2022	96,763.00	0%	0.00

4 Marks

Task 5 (10 Marks)

(a) Discounts received

1 Mark

(b) Detail	Date	Invoice number	Total	VAT	Net
Fred Ltd	19/08/2021	A-1203698	20.40	3.40	17.00
Scoob Plc	22/08/2021	B/9224276	16.80	2.80	14.00
Velma LLP	25/08/2021	ZO-3179791	17.40	2.90	14.50
Daphnie	28/08/2021	A/5501501	12.00	2.00	10.00
Jones Plumbers	31/08/2021	9581927	5.76	0.96	4.80
Total			72.36	12.06	60.30

6 Marks

(c) The journal to the general ledger will be	Debit	Credit
Trade Payables	72.36	
VAT Control		12.06
Discount Received		60.30

3 Marks

Task 6

	Amount £	Asset	Liability	Capital	Debit	Credit
Van at cost	5,839	5,839			5,839	
Fixtures and fittings	4,185	4,185			4,185	
Trade receivables	extracted above	6,584			6,584	
Trade payables	3,810		3,810			3,810
Bank (overdraft)	5,758		5,758			5,758
Purchases expense	4,417			-4,417	4,417	
Wages	3,780			-3,780	3,780	
Sales	4,723			4,723		4,723
VAT to HMRC	5,443		5,443			5,443
Discounts allowed	3,760			-3,760	3,760	
Shareholders funds				8,831		8,831
		16,608	15,011	1,597	28,565	28,565
The totals of assets, liability and capital are:						

Assets	Liability	Capital
16,608	15,011	1,597

Note that income and expenditure is shareholders funds (capital) in year which gets transferred to shareholders funds at the end of the year. You will do this at level 3.

Task 7 (10 Marks)

Date	Detail	Trade payables	Purchases	VAT	Total
30-Jul-22	Balances to date	9,525.00	4,082.00	816.40	14,423.40
31-Jul-22	Frankie Chico		3,267.00	653.40	3,920.40
31-Jul-22	Tony Batts	3,367.00			3,367.00
	Total	12,892.00	7,349.00	1,469.80	21,710.80

The above entries will be posted to which side of the cashbook			Credit	

The amounts to be posted to the general ledger are:

	Amount	Debit	Credit
Trade payables	12,892.00	12,892.00	
Purchases	7,349.00	7,349.00	
VAT	1,469.80	1,469.80	

The total on the opposite side of the cashbook is £52,044

	Amount	Debit	Credit
The balance on 1 August 2022 is	30,333.20	30,333.2	

Task 8 (10 Marks)

								Office	Meeting
Date	Detail	Other	VAT	Amount	Amount	VAT	Fuel	stationery	expense
01/04/2022	bfwd			150.00					
03/04/2022	Fuel				16.00	3.20	12.80		
06/04/2022	Xmas Party	15.00		15.00					
11/04/2022	Xmas Party	15.00		15.00					
13/04/2022	Meeting expense				20.50	4.10			16.40
18/04/2022	Xmas Party	15.00		15.00					
30/04/2022	From/To bank				8.50				
	cfwd				150.00				
	Totals	45.00	0.00	195.00	195.00	7.30	12.80	0.00	16.40

Petty Cashbook

7 Marks

	Debit	Credit
VAT	7.30	
Fuel	12.80	
Meeting expense	16.40	

3 Marks

Task 9 (10 Marks)

				Trade		
Date	Detail	Sales	VAT	receivables	Cash	Bank
01/04/2022	Balance bfwd				69.00	465.00
07/04/2022	Sale of goods for cash	618.50	123.70			742.20
13/04/2022	Amounts received from customers for sales on credit			2222.00		2222.00
30/04/2022	Cash sale	200.00	40.00		240.00	
	Total	818.50	163.70	2222.00	309.00	3429.20

Debit Side

5 Marks

		Credit side				
Date	Detail	Bank	Cash	VAT	Purchases	Wages
01/04/2022	Balance bfwd					
04/04/2022	Purchase of goods for cash	1725.60		287.60	1438.00	
10/04/2022	Wages	1180.00				1180.00
	Balance cfwd	523.60	309.00			
		3429.20	309.00	287.60	1438.00	1180.00

3 Marks

	Debit side		Credit side	
	Cash	Bank	Bank	Cash
from/to the bank		109.00		109.00

2 Marks

Task 10 (10 Marks)

What journals would be made to the general ledger accounts and other ledgers from the following daybooks? VAT is applicable.

Daybook	Debit	Debit	Credit	Credit
Purchases	Dr Purchases	Dr VAT	Cr Trade Payables Control	Cr Purchase Ledger
Sales	Dr Trade Receivables Control	Dr Sales Ledger	Cr Sales	Cr VAT
Sales returns	Dr Sales	Dr VAT	Cr Trade Receivables Control	Cr Sales Ledger
Discounts Received	Dr Trade Payables Control	Dr Purchase Ledger	Cr Discounts received	Cr VAT
Purchase Returns	Dr Trade Payables Control	Dr Purchase Ledger	Cr Purchases	Cr VAT

aat

Practice Assessment

Introduction to Bookkeeping

Practice Assessment 3

Task 1 (10 marks)

This task is about manual and digital bookkeeping systems

(a) Identify which document would be used for each of the purposes below:

Detailing the goods supplied to credit customers and the amount to be paid	
Details an offer for goods and services including quantities, price and terms of payment	
Document prepared by the buyer of the amounts delivered and the person checking the quality of delivery	
Reminder from the supplier of amounts due	

4 marks

(b) Products held in the warehouse are provided a product code based upon their product type and next available number for that product type separated by a -. Assign the following two new product codes:

Product	Code
Copper wire 5mm	Wi-107
Copper wire 7mm	
Wooden pegs 10mm	Wo-42
Wooden pegs 12mm	

2 Marks

c) A company sets up its general ledger codes into sections with income being 100-199, wages being 200-299 and non staff expenses being 300-399. Such a coding system uses

	Which code?
Block	
Alphanumeric	
Hierarchical	

1 mark

(d) Identify whether the following statements about digital bookkeeping systems are true or false:

	True/False
Digital systems automatically balances	
Digital systems eliminate the possibility of error	

2 Marks

(e) A company does not use goods inwards notes. What possible outcome could occur from not using this control

	Pick correct option
Goods will be more easily found	
The delivery note will always be correct	
The quality of goods received may not be checked	
The purchase invoice will be correct	

1 Mark

Task 2 (10 marks)

A sales invoice is being prepared for goods supplied, as shown in the customer order below:

HABNY Ltd	
order 984913	
Please supply	30 May 20XX
40 Toy rifles	
@ 10.5 each less 5% Prompt payment	

a) Calculate the amounts to be included on the invoice

	Amount £
Net amount before discount	
Net amount after discount	
VAT	
Gross amount	

b) what will be the amount entered into the sales daybook when the invoice in a) has been processed?

Date	Details	Invoice number	Total	VAT	Net
30 May 20XX	HABNY Ltd	1536538			

c) a cheque has been received from HABNY Ltd for £8293.04 which they incorrectly state as being in full payment of any amounts due. The customer's account from the sales ledger is shown below. Which three items are outstanding?

Customer account

Date	Details	Amount	Date	Details	Amount
	Balance bfwd	2733.40			
1 July 20XX	Invoice 425	9514.10	6 July 20XX	Credit note 88806	783.56
3 July 20XX	Invoice 470	1996.50	4 July 20XX	Payment	3946.34
13 July 20XX	Invoice 499	8957.00	15 July 20XX	Credit note 81676	663.96
14 July 20XX	Invoice 565	8249.50	18 July 20XX	Credit note 65100	665.44

Circle omitted	
Balance bfwd	
Invoice 425	Credit note 88806
Invoice 470	Payment
Invoice 499	Credit note 81676
Invoice 565	Credit note 65100

Task 3 (10 Marks)

The invoice and purchase order below relate to goods from XYZ LLP

Invoice	
AOC Ltd	
VAT Reg no 3024481	
invoice number 5820	
To LOL Ltd Date 16/02/2022	
	£
WY-072 @ each	
103 £	11.00
Discounts	-0.22
VAT @ 20%	2.24
Total	13.24

Purchase Order	
LOL Ltd	
Purchase order 5405	
To XYZ LLP Date 12/02/2022	
Please supply	
103 Product code: WY-072 @ each £ 9.00	
Less 2% bulk discount	
As agreed Terms: Payment within 7 days	

(a) identify any discrepancies on the invoice by selecting the correct option in the table below

	Not shown on invoice	Correctly shown on invoice	Incorrectly shown on invoice
Terms of payment			
Quantity			
Price			
Discounts			

4 Marks

(b) The balances on GHER's cashbook and VAT control account are as follows:

Bank	16,612
VAT owed from HMRC	19,817

Complete the partially completed trial balance extracted below.

	Debit	Credit
Amount	371,939	137,651
Bank		
VAT owed from HMRC		
Shareholders funds		
Total		

5 marks

(c) Supplies to customers for cash are posted to which daybook:

Daybook	Choice
Cashbook	
Discounts allowed	
Sales	
Purchases	
Sales returns	
The Journal	

1 mark

Task 4 (10 Marks)

At 30 July the balance on the cashbook is £5869 credit

(a) Code the following transactions have been downloaded from the bank account.	Amount £	Code
Payment to suppliers for purchases on credit	945	
Income from customers for sales on credit	966	
Cash sales	290	
Repairs to office	925	

2 Marks

General ledger codes	Code
Van at cost	1001
Computers at cost	1010
Trade receivables	1101
Trade payables	1201
Cash	1301
Sales	2101
Interest received	2302
Wages expense	3101
Repairs expense	3151
Purchases	3201
Interest paid	3305

(b) What are the cashbook balances on the following dates	Debit £	Credit £
Balance on 31 July		
Balance on 1 August		

4 Marks

(c) The following daybooks have been totalled. What is a correct entry to the ledgers

Daybook	Choice	Options
Purchases		Debit to the trade receivables ledger
Purchases returns		Credit to the trade receivables ledger
Sales		Debit to the trade payables ledger
Discounts allowed		Credit to the trade payables ledger

2 Marks

Task 5 (10 Marks)

ABC Ltd has received two remittance advices and cheques from XYZ Ltd totalling £ 13,501.91

XYZ Ltd	
Remittance Advice 298639	
	Amount £
Invoice 165733	2,065.63
Invoice 165743	2,444.52
Invoice 165748	2,456.78
Invoice 165750	4,859.84
Amount paid	7,033.07

XYZ Ltd	
Remittance Advice 298663	
	Amount £
Invoice 165756	4,999.76
Invoice 165759	4,796.99
Amount paid	9,796.75

There are no prompt payment discounts

ABC has a policy of allocating all payments received against individual invoices/credit notes
The balances on the sales ledger before the payments are below. Allocate the payments

	Amount £
Invoice 165733	2,158.63
Invoice 165743	3,094.33
Invoice 165748	2,456.78
Invoice 165750	4,860.84
Credit note re 165743	-649.81
Invoice 165756	5,000.76
Invoice 165759	4,795.99

Select Option

6 Marks

(b) The amounts owed to ABC Ltd are set out below. Determine any amounts remaining due

	Invoice date	Amounts invoiced	Prompt payment terms	Date Paid	Amount paid	Discount due	Amount due
XYZ Ltd	05/04/2022	67,644.00	5% Net monthly	24/04/2022	62,908.92		
UTD Plc	10/04/2022	37,399.00	10% within 7 days	17/04/2022	31,789.15		
OBO LLP	15/04/2022	96,053.00	5% Net monthly	08/06/2022	96,053.00		
PERDY Ltd	17/04/2022	42,252.00	10% within 7 days	24/04/2022	35,914.20		

4 Marks

Task 6 (10 Marks)

Jones Plumbers has provided the following invoice to ABC Ltd on credit

Jones Plumbers	
Date	30/03/2022
Invoice number	1771421
	£
Services rendered	110
VAT	22
Total due	132
Prompt payment discount of 2% if paid within 7 days	

(a) Jones Plumbers would post this invoice to which daybook

Sales	
Sales returns	
Purchases	
Discounts received	

1 Mark

(b) Complete the relevant daybook

Detail	Date	Invoice number	Total	VAT	Net
Fred Ltd	18/03/2022	1771417	120	20	100
Scoob Plc	21/03/2022	1771418	174	29	145
Velma LLP	24/03/2022	1771419	216	36	180
Daphnie	27/03/2022	1771420	216	36	180
Jones Plumbers	30/03/2022	1771421			
Total					

6 Marks

(c) The journal to the general ledger will be	Debit	Credit
Options		
Options		
Options		

3 Marks

Options		
Trade Payables	Purchases	Sales
Trade Receivables	Purchases Returns	Discount Allowed
VAT	Discount Received	Sales Returns

Task 7 (10 Marks)

The following accounts have been extracted from the sales ledger

b/d	5,197			b/d	3,792		

b/d	5,418					b/d	5,491

The following balances have been extracted from the general ledger. Determine the debit and credit values

	Amount £	Debit	Credit
Van at cost	4,799		
Fixtures and fittings	5,350		
Trade receivables	extracted above		
Trade payables	5,682		
Bank	3,154		
Purchases expense	5,302		
Wages	3,422		
Sales	4,499		
Sales returns	5,668		
Discounts allowed	5,121		
Shareholders funds			

7 Marks

The totals of assets, liability and capital are:		
Assets	Liability	Capital

3 Marks

Task 8 (10 Marks)

The following is to be posted into the cashbook for the month of July:					
Cash sale to Harry Rico (subject to VAT) amount excluding VAT is £7747					
Amount received from Phillip Leon to pay for sale on credit (that included VAT) £5860					
Date	Detail	Trade receivables	Sales	VAT	Total
30-Jul-22	Balances to date	8,348.00	4,977.50	995.50	14,321.00
31-Jul-22	Harry Rico		7,747.00	1,549.40	9,296.40
31-Jul-22	Phillip Leon	5,860.00			5,860.00
	Total	14,208.00	12,724.50	2,544.90	29,477.40

4 Marks

The above entries will be posted to which side of the cashbook	Debit (receipts) side

1 Mark

The amounts to be posted to the general ledger are:			
	Amount	Debit	Credit
Trade receivables	5,860.00		5,860.00
Sales	7,747.00		7,747.00
VAT	1,549.40		1,549.40

3 Marks

Options		
Bank	VAT	Sales
Trade receivables	Trade payables	Purchases

The total on the opposite side of the cashbook is £26601			
	Amount	Debit	Credit
The balance on 1 August 2022 is	2,876.40	2,876.40	

2 Marks

Task 9 (20 Marks)

ALL Ltd posts its cashbook by downloading its bank statement first and posting the bank statement. All items except wages are subject to VAT @20%		
The bank statement for April is as follows:		

Bank of Norton	Debit	Credit
Balance bfwd		1231.00
Payment for purchases bought on credit	2850.00	
Wages	2270.00	
Purchase of goods for cash	879.60	
Amounts received from customers for sales on credit		2089.00
Amounts received from customers for sales on credit		2838.00
Office expenses	1716.00	
Motor vehicle running costs	1164.00	
Sale of goods for cash		1182.60
Sale of goods for cash		1179.60

(a) The total of the analysis columns in the credit side of the cashbook is

Trade Payables	VAT	Purchases	Motor expenses	Office Expenses	Wages

6 Marks

(b) The total of the analysis columns in the debit side of the cashbook is

Sales	VAT	Trade receivables

3 Marks

(c)

What are the balances at	Debit	Credit
30/April		
01/May		

2 Marks

(d) The balance before the transactions are provided. Determine the closing balances

	Balance before transactions		Balances after transactions	
	Debit	Credit	Debit	Credit
Trade Payables		5834.00		
VAT		672.50		
Purchases	1751.00			
Motor running costs	271.40			
Office Expenses	1867.00			
Wages	2625.00			
Sales		13895.00		
Trade receivables	7380.00			
Bank	1231.00			
Shareholders funds	5276.10			
	20401.50	20401.50		

9 Marks

Page 56

Answers

Task 1 (10 marks)

(a)

Detailing the goods supplied to credit customers and the amount to be paid	Invoice
Details an offer for goods and services including quantities, price and terms of payment	Quotation
Document prepared by the buyer of the amounts delivered and the person checking the quality of delivery	Goods inwards note
Reminder from the supplier of amounts due	Supplier statement

(b)

Product	Code
Copper wire 5mm	Wi-107
Copper wire 7mm	Wi-108
Wooden pegs 10mm	Wo-42
Wooden pegs 12mm	Wo-43

c)

	Which code?
Block	Block
Alphanumeric	
Hierarchical	

(d)

	True/False
Digital systems automatically balances	True
Digital systems eliminate the possibility of error	False

(e) A company does not use goods inwards notes. What possible outcome could occur from not using this control

The quality of goods received may not be checked	The goods inwards note checks the quality of goods received

Task 2 (10 marks)

a)	Amount £
Net amount before discount	420.00
Net amount after discount	420.00
VAT	84.00
Gross amount	504.00

Note prompt payments are not deducted from the Net amount. This is a trick question.

b) Date	Details	Invoice number	Total	VAT	Net
30 May 20XX	HABNY Ltd	1536538	504.00	84.00	420.00

c)

Circle omitted	
Balance bfwd	
Invoice 425	Credit note 88806
Invoice 470	Payment
Invoice 499	Credit note 81676
Invoice 565	**Credit note 65100**

Task 3 (10 Marks)

(a) identify any discrepancies on the invoice by selecting the correct option in the table below

	Not shown on invoice	Correctly shown on invoice	Incorrectly shown on invoice
Terms of payment	answer		
Quantity		answer	
Price			answer
Discounts		answer	

4 Marks

(b)	Debit	Credit
Amount	371,939	137,651
Bank	16,612	
VAT owed from HMRC	19,817	
Shareholders funds		270,717
Total	408,368	408,368

5 marks

Supplies to customers for cash are posted to which daybook:

(c) Daybook	Cashbook

Task 4 (10 Marks)

At 30 July the balance on the cashbook is £5869 credit

Code the following transactions have been downloaded from the bank account.	Amount £	Code
Payment to suppliers for purchases on credit	945	1201
Income from customers for sales on credit	966	1101
Cash sales	290	2101
Repairs to office	925	3151

2 Marks

(b) What are the cashbook balances on the following dates	Debit £	Credit £
Balance on 31 July	6,483	
Balance on 1 August		6,483

4 Marks

Date	Detail	Amount	Date	Detail	Amount
			30 Jul	bfwd	5869
			31 Jul	Trade payables	945
31 Jul	Trade receivables	966			
31 Jul	Sales	290			
			31 Jul	Repairs expense	925
31 Jul	cfwd	6483			
	Total	7739			7739
			1 Aug	bfwd	6483

(c) The following daybooks have been totalled. What is a correct entry to the ledgers

Daybook	Choice
Purchases	Credit to the trade payables ledger
Purchases returns	Debit to the trade payables ledger
Sales	Debit to the trade receivables ledger
Discounts allowed	Credit to the trade receivables ledger

2 Marks

Task 5 (10 Marks)

	Amount £		Select Option
Invoice 165733	2,158.63		Underpaid - follow up
Invoice 165743	3,094.33		Paid in full
Invoice 165748	2,456.78		Paid in full
Invoice 165750	4,860.84		Underpaid - follow up
Credit note re 165743	-649.81		Paid in full
Invoice 165756	5,000.76		Underpaid - follow up
Invoice 165759	4,795.99		Overpaid - Query

(b) The amounts owed to ABC Ltd are set out below. Determine any amounts remaining due

	Invoice date	Amounts invoiced	Prompt payment terms	Date Paid	Amount paid	Discount due	Amount due
XYZ Ltd	05/04/2022	67,644.00	5% Net monthly	24/04/2022	62,908.92	5%	1352.88
UTD Plc	10/04/2022	37,399.00	10% within 7 days	17/04/2022	31,789.15	10%	1869.95
OBO LLP	15/04/2022	96,053.00	5% Net monthly	08/06/2022	96,053.00	0%	0.00
PERDY Ltd	17/04/2022	42,252.00	10% within 7 days	24/04/2022	35,914.20	10%	2112.60

4 Marks

Task 6 (10 Marks)

Jones Plumbers would post this invoice to which daybook

Sales

1 Mark

Complete the relevant daybook

Detail	Date	Invoice number	Total	VAT	Net
Fred Ltd	18/03/2022	1771417	120	20	100
Scoob Plc	21/03/2022	1771418	174	29	145
Velma LLP	24/03/2022	1771419	216	36	180
Daphnie	27/03/2022	1771420	216	36	180
Jones Plumbers	30/03/2022	1771421	132	22	110
Total			858	143	715

6 Marks

The journal to the general ledger will be	Debit	Credit
Trade Receivables	858	
Sales		715
VAT		143

Task 7

The following balances have been extracted from the general ledger. Determine the debit and credit values

	Amount £	Asset	Liability	Capital	Debit	Credit
Van at cost	4,799	4,799			4,799	
Fixtures and fittings	5,350	5,350			5,350	
Trade receivables	extracted above	8,916			8,916	
Trade payables	5,682		5,682			5,682
Bank	3,154	3,154			3,154	
Purchases expense	5,302			-5,302	5,302	
Wages	3,422			-3,422	3,422	
Sales	4,499			4,499		4,499
Sales returns	5,668			-5,668	5,668	
Discounts allowed	5,121			-5,121	5,121	
Shareholders funds				31,551		31,551
		22,219	5,682	16,537	41,732	41,732

The totals of assets, liability and capital are:		
Assets	Liability	Capital
22,219	5,682	16,537

Task 8 (10 Marks)

Date	Detail	Trade receivables	Sales	VAT	Total
30-Jul-22	Balances to date	8,348.00	4,977.50	995.50	14,321.00
31-Jul-22	Harry Rico		7,747.00	1,549.40	9,296.40
31-Jul-22	Phillip Leon	5,860.00			5,860.00
	Total	14,208.00	12,724.50	2,544.90	29,477.40

4 Marks

The above entries will be posted to which side of the cashbook	Debit

1 Mark

The amounts to be posted to the general ledger are:			
	Amount	Debit	Credit
Trade receivables	14,208.00		14,208.00
Sales	12,724.50		12,724.50
VAT	2,544.90		2,544.90

Note the cashbook also forms part of the general ledger such that the debit part of this journal has already been posted through preparing the cashbook.

3 Marks

The total on the opposite side of the cashbook is £26601			
	Amount	Debit	Credit
The balance on 1 August 2022 is	2876.40	2876.40	

2 Marks

Task 9 (20 Marks)

The total of the analysis columns in the credit side of the cashbook is					
Trade Payables	VAT	Purchases	Motor running costs	Office Expenses	Wages
2850.00	626.60	733.00	970.00	1430.00	2270.00

6 Marks

The total of the analysis columns in the debit side of the cashbook is		
Sales	VAT	Trade receivables
1968.50	393.70	4927.00

3 Marks

What are the balances at	Debit	Credit
30/April	359.40	
01/May		359.40

Note that the examiner calls the carried forward balancing figure in the T account a "balance" such that this is the end of month balance. The actual balance to be used for the trial balance is the bfwd figure on the 1st day of the following month. You will not see this approach in the workplace.

2 Marks

The balance before these transactions are shown below. Determine the closing balances				
	Balance before transactions		Balances after transactions	
	Debit	Credit	Debit	Credit
Trade Payables		5834.00		2984.00
VAT		672.50		439.60
Purchases	1751.00		2484.00	
Motor running costs	271.40		1241.40	
Office Expenses	1867.00		3297.00	
Wages	2625.00		4895.00	
Sales		13895.00		15863.50
Trade receivables	7380.00		2453.00	
Bank	1231.00			359.40
Shareholders funds	5276.10		5276.10	
	20401.50	20401.50	19646.50	19646.50

9 Marks

aat

Practice Assessment

Introduction to Bookkeeping

Practice Assessment 4

Task 1 (10 Marks)

ABC Ltd has received two remittance advices and cheques from XYZ Ltd totalling £ 13501.91

XYZ Ltd	
Remittance Advice 223668	
	Amount £
Invoice 428156	3,354.69
Invoice 428158	3,906.57
Invoice 428161	3,189.46
Invoice 428170	1,128.40
Amount paid	7,033.07

XYZ Ltd	
Remittance Advice 223704	
	Amount £
Invoice 428175	4,050.69
Invoice 428184	3,965.99
Amount paid	8,016.68

There are no prompt payment discounts

ABC has a policy of allocating all payments received against individual invoices/credit notes

(a) The balances on the sales ledger before the payments are below. Allocate the payments

	Amount £	Select Option
Invoice 428156	3,453.69	
Invoice 428158	3,905.57	
Invoice 428161	3,889.59	
Invoice 428170	1,128.40	
Credit note re 428161	-700.13	
Invoice 428175	4,049.69	
Invoice 428184	3,965.99	

6 Marks

	Paid in full
	Underpaid - follow up
Options	Overpaid - Query

(b) The amounts owed to ABC Ltd are set out below. Determine any amounts remaining due

	Invoice date	Amounts invoiced	Prompt payment terms	Date Paid	Amount paid	Discount due	Amount due
XYZ Ltd	05/04/2022	61,799.00	5% by end of month	15/04/2022	55,619.10		
UTD Plc	07/04/2022	14,256.00	5% Net monthly	17/04/2022	13,543.20		
OBO LLP	11/04/2022	94,924.00	10% within 7 days	20/04/2022	85,431.60		
PERDY Ltd	13/04/2022	81,819.00	5% Net monthly	13/05/2022	77,728.05		

4 Marks

Task 2 (10 Marks)

ABC Ltd receives a credit note in full for the following invoice generated incorrectly

Jones Plumbers	
Date	30/01/2022
Invoice number	2543622
	£
Services rendered	220
VAT	44
Total due	264
Prompt payment discount of 2% if paid within 7 days	

(a) Jones Plumbers would post the credit note to which daybook

Purchase Returns	
Sales	
Purchases	
Sales returns	

1 Mark

Complete the relevant daybook

Detail	Date	Invoice number	Total	VAT	Net
Fred Ltd	18/01/2022	2543602	240.00	40.00	200.00
Scoob Plc	21/01/2022	2543607	270.00	45.00	225.00
Velma LLP	24/01/2022	2543612	198.00	33.00	165.00
Daphnie	27/01/2022	2543617	228.00	38.00	190.00
Jones Plumbers	30/01/2022	2543622			
Total					

6·Marks

The journal to the general ledger will be	Debit	Credit
Options		
Options		
Options		

3 Marks

Options		
Trade Payables	Purchases	Sales
Trade Receivables	Purchases Returns	Sales Returns
VAT	Discount Received	Discount Allowed

Task 3 (10 Marks)

The following accounts have been extracted from the Purchase ledger

b/d	4,843	c/d		b/d	3,862

b/d	3,472	b/d	5,125	

	Amount £	Debit	Credit
Office Furniture	3,512		
Bank	5,011		
Trade receivables	5,819		
Trade payables	extracted above		
Bank loan	3,539		
Purchases expense	3,026		
Drawings	3,827		
Sales	3,214		
VAT from HMRC	3,369		
Discounts received	4,661		
Shareholders funds			
Total			

7 Marks

The totals of assets, liability and capital are:		
Assets	Liability	Capital

3 Marks

Task 4 (10 Marks)

(a) ABC Ltd prepares its payment run for suppliers monthly on the day before the end of each month. What is the amount of prompt payment discount it will lose from the paying in this way in April rather than reviewing individually to take full advantage of discounts?

	Invoice date	Amounts invoiced	Prompt payment discount terms	Date Paid	Discount due	Amount missed
XYZ Ltd	17/04/2022	56,879.00	10% within 7 days	30/04/2022		
UTD Plc	22/04/2022	74,708.00	5% Net monthly	30/04/2022		
OBO LLP	26/04/2022	96,583.00	5% by end of month	30/04/2022		
PERDY Ltd	31/03/2022	65,211.00	5% by end of month	30/04/2022		

4 Marks

(b) James Smith starts up his own plumbing business. Set up the opening journal

	Amount	Debit	Credit
Provides own van	9338.00		
Puts amount into business account	1315.00		
Provides laptop for quotes	396.80		
Provides own tools and ladder	333.80		
Debt to supplier transferred to business	5067.00		
Shareholder capital			
Total			

6 Marks

Task 5 (10 Marks)

(a) When the cashbook is the book of prime entry and the ledger account what is the journal from the cashbook to the general ledger:

Option	Choose option
Post the totals column to the bank account and analysis columns to the other accounts	
Post the totals column only to the bank account and not the analysis columns	
Post the analysis columns only to the other accounts and not the totals column to the bank account	
Make no entries into the general ledger accounts	

2 Marks

(b) Post the following petty cash vouchers to the cashbook and return the cashbook to the imprest amount

Petty cash voucher				Petty cash voucher		
Detail	Amount Claimed	VAT		Detail	Amount Claimed	VAT
Fuel for van	10.50	2.10		Pens and notepads	10.50	2.10
Total	10.50			Total	10.50	
Dated	03/04/2022			Dated	13/04/2022	

					Petty Cashbook					
Date	Detail	Other	VAT	Amount	Amount	VAT	Fuel	Office stationery	Meeting expense
01/04/2022	bfwd			150.00					
03/04/2022	Fuel for van								
06/04/2022	Xmas Party	15.00		15.00					
11/04/2022	Xmas Party	15.00		15.00					
13/04/2022	Pens and notepads								
18/04/2022	Xmas Party	15.00		15.00					
30/04/2022	From/ To bank								
	cfwd								
	Totals								

8 Marks

Task 6 (10 Marks)

(a) Prepare journals for the following transactions for Yousef Groceries:

	Debit account	Debit amount £'s	Credit account	Credit Amount £'s
Pays wages paid from Bank of £7672	Options		Options	
Makes purchases paid for immediately of £5710	Options		Options	
Makes sales paid into the bank immediately of £37585	Options		Options	
Pays wages paid from Bank of £7672	Options		Options	
A customer pays into the bank account for purchase on credit of £12834	Options		Options	

10 Marks

Options

Wages expense	Bank	Trade receivables control account
Purchase expense	Sales	Trade payables control account

Task 7 (10 Marks)

Yousef Groceries provides a cheque for £7276 stated as Amount paid in full on Remittance Advice. Their sales ledger account states

Yousef Groceries

Balance Bfwd	6397		
		Credit Note 781701	786
Invoice Number 781801	1404		
Invoice Number 781901	1548		
		Credit Note 782001	525
		Balance c/d	8038

(a) Determine which amounts are included in the payment and which are missing:

Item	Included/Missing
Balance Bfwd	
Credit Note 781701	
Invoice Number 781801	
Invoice Number 781901	
Credit Note 782001	

4 Marks

(b) Determine the daybook from the following description

Description	Daybook	Options
Collates reductions in amounts owed to suppliers due to prompt payment		Sales daybook
Collates goods and services provided to customers on credit		Discounts received daybook
Collates goods and services acquired by the business on credit		Cashbook
Collates payments into and out of the bank account		Discounts allowed daybook
Collates reductions in amounts owed by customers because of their prompt payment		Purchase returns daybook
Collates credit notes provided by suppliers for goods and services		Purchases daybook

6 Marks

Task 8 (20 Marks)

ALL Ltd posts its cashbook by downloading its bank statement first and posting the bank statement. All items except wages are subject to VAT @20%

The bank statement for April is as follows:

Bank of Norton	Debit	Credit
Balance bfwd		1658.00
Payment for purchases bought on credit	2119.00	
Wages	2176.00	
Purchase of goods for cash	1085.40	
Amounts received from customers for sales on credit		2757.00
Amounts received from customers for sales on credit		5446.00
Office expenses	1599.00	
Motor vehicle running costs	1458.60	
Sale of goods for cash		1387.80
Sale of goods for cash		1192.20

(a) The total of the analysis columns in the credit side of the cashbook is

Trade Payables	VAT	Purchases	Motor Expenses	Office Expenses	Wages

6 Marks

(b) The total of the analysis columns in the debit side of the cashbook is

Sales	VAT	Trade receivables

3 Marks

(c) What are the balances at	Debit	Credit
30/April		
01/May		

2 Marks

(d) The balance before these transactions are shown below. Determine the closing balances

	Balance before transactions		Balances after transactions	
	Debit	Credit	Debit	Credit
Trade Payables		3579.00		
VAT		1337.00		
Purchases	2815.00			
Motor running costs	234.90			
Office Expenses	2142.00			
Wages	2693.00			
Sales		10170.00		
Trade receivables	7230.00			
Bank	1658.00			
Shareholders funds		1686.90		
Total	16772.90	16772.90		

9 Marks

Task 9 (10 Marks)

(a) ABC Ltd has undertaken a new photocopying lease contract that runs for 36 months. After every 12 months the monthly lease is increased by RPI. What is the maximum length a recurring journal can be created for the lease costs?

Answer	Options

2 Marks

Options	1 Month	12 Months	36 Months

(b) The amount is £120.00 per month including VAT at 20% which will be paid via direct debit from the bank account. Prepare the recurring journal for this transaction:

Supplier	Supplier code	Dr Account Code	Cr Account Code	Net Amount	VAT code
Norton's Copiers	Nor-101	Option 1	Option 1	100.00	Option 2

4 Marks

Option 1 Account Codes

Trade Payables	2001
VAT	2002
Bank	1001
Cash	1001
Photocopier expenses	5062
Petty cash sundries	5064

Option 2 VAT Codes

V-1	0% exempt
V-2	0% zero rated
V-3	5%
V-4	20%

(c) The supplier code is an example of which type of code:

Numeric	
Alphabetic	
Alphanumeric	

1 Mark

(d) Which of the following is a risk associated with using recurring journals over normal journals

	Risk Yes/No
That the initial journal may be less accurate than several journals	
That the circumstances of the transaction may change over time	
That the transaction may be paid twice	

3 Marks

ANSWERS

Task 1 (10 Marks)

	Amount £		Select Option
Invoice 428156	3,453.69		Underpaid - follow up
Invoice 428158	3,905.57		Overpaid - Query
Invoice 428161	3,889.59		Paid in full
Invoice 428170	1,128.40		Paid in full
Credit note re 428161	-700.13		Paid in full
Invoice 428175	4,049.69		Overpaid - Query
Invoice 428184	3,965.99		Paid in full

6 Marks

(b) The amounts owed to ABC Ltd are set out below. Determine any amounts remaining due

	Invoice date	Amounts invoiced	Prompt payment terms	Date Paid	Amount paid	Discount due	Amount due
XYZ Ltd	05/04/2022	61,799.00	5% by end of month	15/04/2022	55,619.10	5%	3089.95
UTD Plc	07/04/2022	14,256.00	5% Net monthly	17/04/2022	13,543.20	5%	0.00
OBO LLP	11/04/2022	94,924.00	10% within 7 days	20/04/2022	85,431.60	0%	9492.40
PERDY Ltd	13/04/2022	81,819.00	5% Net monthly	13/05/2022	77,728.05	5%	0.00

Task 2 (10 Marks)

Jones Plumbers would post the credit note to which daybook

Sales returns – Jones plumbers is the seller despite the wording stating ABC Ltd – this is a trick

1 Mark

Complete the relevant daybook

Detail	Date	Invoice number	Total	VAT	Net
Fred Ltd	18/01/2022	2543602	240.00	40.00	200.00
Scoob Plc	21/01/2022	2543607	270.00	45.00	225.00
Velma LLP	24/01/2022	2543612	198.00	33.00	165.00
Daphnie	27/01/2022	2543617	228.00	38.00	190.00
Jones Plumbers	30/01/2022	2543622	264.00	44.00	220.00
Total			1200.00	200.00	1000.00

6 Marks

The journal to the general ledger will be	Debit	Credit
Sales Returns	1000.00	
VAT	200.00	
Trade Receivables		1200.00

3 Marks

Task 3 (10 Marks)

	Amount £	Asset	Liability	Capital	Debit	Credit
Office Furniture	3,512	3,512			3,512	
Bank	5,011	5,011			5,011	
Trade receivables	5,819	5,819			5,819	
Trade payables	extracted above		7,052			7,052
Bank loan	3,539		3,539			3,539
Purchases expense	3,026			-3,026	3,026	
Drawings	3,827			-3,827	3,827	
Sales	3,214			3,214		3,214
VAT from HMRC	3,369	3,369			3,369	
Discounts received	4,661			4,661		4,661
Shareholders funds				6,098		6,098
		17,711	10,591	7,120	24,564	24,564

Note VAT is stated as from HMRC to see if double entry is understood instead of students simply using DEAD CLIC (which has VAT memorised as a credit where here it is positive money in the future and a debit).

The totals of assets, liability and capital are:		
Assets	Liability	Capital
17,711	10,591	7,120

Task 4 (10 Marks)

	Invoice date	Amounts invoiced	Prompt payment discount terms	Date Paid	Discount due	Amount missed
XYZ Ltd	17/04/2022	56,879.00	10% within 7 days	30/04/2022	0%	5687.90
UTD Plc	22/04/2022	74,708.00	5% Net monthly	30/04/2022	5%	0.00
OBO LLP	26/04/2022	96,583.00	5% by end of month	30/04/2022	5%	0.00
PERDY Ltd	31/03/2022	65,211.00	5% by end of month	30/04/2022	0%	3260.55

4 Marks

	Amount	Debit	Credit
Provides own van	9338.00	9338.00	
Puts amount into business account	1315.00	1315.00	
Provides laptop for quotes	396.80	396.80	
Provides own tools and ladder	333.80	333.80	
Debt to supplier transferred to business	5067.00		5067.00
Shareholder capital			6316.60
Total		11383.60	11383.60

6 Marks

Task 5 (10 Marks)

Post the analysis columns only to the other accounts and not the totals column to the bank account

2 Marks

Petty Cashbook									
Date	Detail	Other	VAT	Amount	Amount	VAT	Fuel	Office stationery	Meeting expense
01/04/2022	bfwd			150.00					
03/04/2022	Fuel for van				10.50	2.10	8.40		
06/04/2022	Xmas Party	15.00		15.00					
11/04/2022	Xmas Party	15.00		15.00					
13/04/2022	Pens and notepads				10.50	2.10		8.40	
18/04/2022	Xmas Party	15.00		15.00					
30/04/2022	From/ To bank				24.00				
	cfwd				150.00				
	Totals	45.00	0.00	195.00	195.00	4.20	8.40	8.40	0.00

8 Marks

Task 6 (10 Marks)

	Debit account	Debit amount £'s	Credit account	Credit Amount £'s
Pays wages paid from Bank of £7672	Wages expense	7,672	Bank	7,672
Makes purchases paid for immediately of £5710	Purchase expense	5,710	Bank	5,710
Makes sales paid into the bank immediately of £37585	Bank	37,585	Sales	37,585
Pays wages paid from Bank of £7672	Wages expense	7,672	Bank	7,672
A customer pays into the bank account for purchase on credit of £12834	Bank	12,834	Trade receivables control account	12,834

10 Marks

Task 7 (10 Marks)

Balance Bfwd	Included
Credit Note 781701	Missing
Invoice Number 781801	Included
Invoice Number 781901	Missing
Credit Note 782001	Included

4 Marks

Determine the daybook from the following description

Description	Daybook
Collates reductions in amounts owed to suppliers due to prompt payment	Discounts received daybook
Collates goods and services provided to customers on credit	Sales daybook
Collates goods and services acquired by the business on credit	Purchases daybook
Collates payments into and out of the bank account	Cashbook
Collates reductions in amounts owed by customers because of their prompt payment	Discounts allowed daybook
Collates credit notes provided by suppliers for goods and services	Purchase returns daybook

6 Marks

Task 8 (20 Marks)

The total of the analysis columns in the credit side of the cashbook is					
Trade Payables	VAT	Purchases	Motor Expenses	Office Expenses	Wages
2119.00	690.50	904.50	1215.50	1332.50	2176.00

6 Marks

The total of the analysis columns in the debit side of the cashbook is		
Sales	VAT	Trade receivables
2150.00	430.00	8203.00

3 Marks

What are the balances at	Debit	Credit
30/April		4003.00
01/May	4003.00	

Note the balance on the account for the trial balance is the bfwd figure. The cfwd amount is stated as a balance. In the workplace it is never referred to as a balance and this is an examiners quirk only

2 Marks

The balance before these transactions are shown below. Determine the closing balances				
	Balance before transactions		Balances after transactions	
	Debit	Credit	Debit	Credit
Trade Payables		3579.00		1460.00
VAT		1337.00		1076.50
Purchases	2815.00		3719.50	
Motor running costs	234.90		1450.40	
Office Expenses	2142.00		3474.50	
Wages	2693.00		4869.00	
Sales		10170.00		12320.00
Trade receivables	7230.00		-973.00	
Bank	1658.00		4003.00	
Shareholders funds		1686.90		1686.90
Total	16772.90	16772.90	16543.40	16543.40

9 Marks

Task 9 (10 Marks)

(a) Answer	12 Months – after this time period the amounts change

2 Marks

Supplier	Supplier code	Dr Account Code	Cr Account Code	Net Amount	VAT code
Norton's Copiers	Nor-101	5062	1001	100.00	V-4

4 Marks

(c) Alphanumeric

1 Mark

(d)	Risk Yes/No
That the initial journal may be less accurate than several journals	No
That the circumstances of the transaction may change over time	Yes – the values may change or even cancelled yet the recurring journal will continue to post in error
That the transaction may be paid twice	Yes – the recurring journal may make a payment and we may process the invoice again making an additional payment

3 Marks

aat

Practice Assessment

Introduction to Bookkeeping

Practice Assessment 5

Task 1 (10 marks)

This task is about manual and digital bookkeeping systems

(a) Identify which document would be used for each of the purposes below:

Identifying transactions that have been received into or paid out of the bank account	
Details an offer for goods and services including quantities, price and terms of payment	
Requests goods or services from a supplier and provides an authorised number from the buyer	
Corrects an error in an invoice changing the amounts due	

4 marks

(b) Supplier accounts are made up of the first four letters of their name and a sequential number separated by a /. The next available number is 106. Assign the supplier codes to the following two new suppliers:

Supplier	Code to be assigned
Freedy Ltd	
Jones llp	

2 Marks

(c) A code is made up of a combination of numbers separated by a -. This type of code is:

	Which code?
Alphabetic	
Alphanumeric	
Numeric	

1 Mark

(d) Identify whether the following statements about digital bookkeeping systems are true or false:

	True/False
Digital systems allow for electronic extract of data	
Digital systems automatically extract the trial balance	

2 Marks

(e) A purchase invoice has been omitted from the purchases day book. Identify one possible consequence of this error:

	Pick correct option
Purchases will be overstated	
The amounts available for shareholders will be understated	
A prompt payment discount may be missed	
VAT payable to HMRC will be understated	

1 Mark

Task 2 (10 Marks)

This task is about principles of double-entry bookkeeping.

(a) At the end of July a business had the following assets and liabilities

Assets and liabilities	£
Property	6,821.38
Fixtures and Fittings	6,566.44
Cash at bank	6,105.14
Trade receivables	3,355.18
Trade payables	1,829.91
Bank loan	4,999.71

What is the total of the following:

Assets	Liabilities	Capital
£	£	£

3 Marks

(b) The first transaction recorded in August related to the payment of a supplier debt. The effect of this transaction:

Effect	Pick option
Increase assets and reduce liabilities	
Both increase and reduce liabilities	
Both increase and reduce assets	
Reduce assets and reduce liabilities	

1 Mark

(c) Identify the opposite effect of each bank trasaction. You should ignore VAT

Bank transaction	Opposite effect	Options
Make a dividend payment to shareholders from bank		Drawings
Payment made to supplier for goods bought on credit		Purchases
Payment of rent due on office		Dividends
Owner takes money from till for personal expenses		Trade payables
Transfer of money to imprest account for small expenses		Rent
Goods bought from supplier for cash		Petty Cash

6 Marks

Page 81

Task 3 (10 marks)

A sales invoice is being prepared for goods supplied, as shown in the customer order below:

HABNY Ltd	
order 348990	
Please supply	30 May 20XX
200 Toy cars	
@ 7.65 each less 5% Prompt payment	

a)   Calculate the amounts to be included on the invoice 3 Marks

	Amount £
Net amount before discount	
Net amount after discount	
VAT	
Gross amount	

b) what will be the amount entered into the sales daybook when the invoice in a) has been processed? 3 Marks

Date	Details	Invoice number	Total	VAT	Net
30 May 20XX	HABNY Ltd	738699			

c) a cheque has been received from HABNY Ltd for £5567.19 which they incorrectly state as being in full payment of any amounts due. The customer's account from the sales ledger is shown below. Which three items are outstanding? 4 Marks

Customer account

Date	Details	Amount	Date	Details	Amount
	Balance bfwd	5734.60			
1 July 20XX	Invoice 425	4145.00	6 July 20XX	Credit note 10587	908.61
3 July 20XX	Invoice 470	6475.80	4 July 20XX	Payment	6897.90
13 July 20XX	Invoice 499	2032.30	15 July 20XX	Credit note 82312	869.00
14 July 20XX	Invoice 565	7316.80	18 July 20XX	Credit note 22444	425.16

Circle omitted	
Balance bfwd	
Invoice 425	Credit note 10587
Invoice 470	Payment
Invoice 499	Credit note 82312
Invoice 565	Credit note 22444

Task 4 (10 Marks)

The invoice and purchase order below relate to goods from XYZ LLP

Invoice	
XYZ LLP	
VAT Reg no 9323642	
invoice number 5597	
To ABC Ltd Date 12/03/2022	
	£
242 FF06 @ each	6.00
Less trade discounts	-0.18
VAT @ 20%	1.24
Total	7.24

Purchase Order	
ABC Ltd	
Purchase order 5349	
To XYZ LLP Date 08/03/2022	
Please supply	
Product FF06 @ each	
223 code: £	6.00
Less 3% bulk discount	
As agreed, terms 0.02 discount for payment by the end of the month	

(a) identify any discrepancies on the invoice by selecting the correct option in the table below

	Not shown on invoice	Correctly shown on invoice	Incorrectly shown on invoice
Terms of payment	✔		
Quantity			✔
Price		✔	
Discounts			✔

4 Marks

The balances on GHER's sales and purchase ledger are as follows

Sales ledger (owed from customers)	71,672
Purchase ledger (owed to suppliers)	9,112

Complete the partially completed trial balance extracted below.

Amount	Debit	Credit
Balances extracted to date	200,468	119,233
Trade receivables control account		
Trade payables control account		
Shareholders funds		
Total		

5 marks

(c) Payments of small denominations in physical cash are posted to which daybook:

Daybook	Choice
Cashbook	
Purchases	
Sales returns	
Petty cashbook	
Purchase returns	
The Journal	

1 mark

Task 5 (10 Marks)

(a) At 30 July the balance on the cashbook is £7600 debit

Code the following transactions have been downloaded from the bank account.	Amount £	Code
Income from customers for sales on credit	207	
Cash sales	457	
Cash purchase	119	
Income from customers for sales on credit	347	

2 Marks

General ledger codes	Code
Van at cost	1001
Computers at cost	1010
Trade receivables	1101
Trade payables	1201
Cash	1301
Sales	2101
Interest received	2302
Wages expense	3101
Repairs expense	3151
Purchases	3201
Interest paid	3305

(b) What are the cashbook balances on the following dates	Debit £	Credit £
Balance on 31 July		
Balance on 1 August		

4 Marks

(c) How would the following daybooks be posted to the relevant ledger?

Daybook	Choice	Options
Discounts allowed		Debit to the trade receivables ledger
Purchases returns		Credit to the trade receivables ledger
Purchases		Debit to the trade payables ledger
Sales		Credit to the trade payables ledger

4 Marks

Task 6 (10 Marks)

ABC Ltd takes advantage of the prompt payment discount on the following invoice

Jones Plumbers	
Date	10/10/2021
Invoice number	8491778
	£
Services rendered	195
VAT	39
Total due	234
Prompt payment discount of 2% if paid within 7 days	

(a) Jones Plumbers would post the discount to which daybook

Discounts allowed	
Sales	
Purchases	
Discounts received	

1 Mark

(b) Complete the relevant daybook

Detail	Date	Invoice number	Total	VAT	Net
Fred Ltd	28/09/2021	8491758	18.00	3.00	15.00
Scoob Plc	01/10/2021	8491763	22.20	3.70	18.50
Velma LLP	04/10/2021	8491768	25.80	4.30	21.50
Daphnie	07/10/2021	8491773	19.20	3.20	16.00
ABC Ltd	10/10/2021	8491778			
Total					

6 Marks

(c) The journal to the general ledger will be	Debit	Credit
Options		
Options		
Options		

3 Marks

Options			
Trade Payables	Purchases		Sales
Trade Receivables	Purchases Returns		Sales Returns
VAT	Discount Received		Discount Allowed

Task 7 (10 Marks)

The following accounts have been extracted from the sales ledger

	c/d	4,093			c/d	3,295

	c/d	5,657	c/d	4,166	

(a) Determine the trial balance from the amounts below

	Amount £	Debit	Credit
Office Furniture	4,721		
Cash in safe	5,273		
Trade receivables	extracted above		
Trade payables	5,349		
Bank (overdraft)	5,008		
Purchases expense	3,855		
Wages	3,318		
Sales	5,754		
VAT from HMRC	5,430		
Discounts received	4,910		
Shareholders funds			

7 Marks

(b) The totals of assets, liability and capital are:		
Assets	Liability	Capital

3 Marks

Task 8 (10 Marks)

(a) The following is to be posted into the cashbook for the month of July:					
Cash purchase to James Bucko (subject to VAT) amount including VAT is £8510.4					
Amount paid to Bill Hat to pay for purchase on credit (that included VAT) £8323					
Date	Detail	Trade payables	Purchases	VAT	Total
30-Jul-22	Balances to date	1,143.00	3,709.50	741.90	5,594.40
31-Jul-22	James Bucko				
31-Jul-22	Bill Hat				
	Total				

4 Marks

(b) The above entries will be posted to which side of the cashbook	Debit/Credit

1 Mark

(c) The amounts to be posted to the general ledger are:			
	Amount	Debit	Credit
Options			
Options			
Options			

3 Marks

Options		
Bank	VAT	Sales
Trade receivables	Trade payables	Purchases

(d) The total on the opposite side of the cashbook is £6786			
	Amount	Debit	Credit
The balance c/d on 31 July 2022 is			

2 Marks

Task 9 (10 Marks)

(a) A cashbook has been prepared from the following bank statement. Post the remaining highlighted item to the cashbook as well as a purchase for cash of £120.00 including VAT and determine the balances carried forward.

The bank statement for April is as follows:		
Bank of Norton	Debit	Credit
Balance bfwd		118.00
Sale of goods for immediate payment		1005.00
Amounts received from customers for sales on credit		3664.00
Wages	2834.00	
Purchase of goods for immediate payment	999.00	

Debit Side						
Date	Detail	Sales	VAT	Trade receivables	Cash	Bank
01/04/2022	Balance bfwd				300.00	118.00
04/04/2022	Amounts received from customers for sales on credit			1005.00		1005.00
07/04/2022	Amounts received from customers for sales on credit			3664.00		3664.00
	Balance cfwd					
	Total					

Credit side						
Date	Detail	Bank	Cash	VAT	Purchases	Wages
01/04/2022	Balance bfwd					
10/04/2022	Wages	2834.00				2834.00
	Balance cfwd					
	Total					

8 Marks

(b) On the first of every month the first journal is to return cash holdings to £300. What journal would be posted on 1 May 2022?

	Debit	Credit
Bank		
Cash		

2 Marks

Task 10 (10 Marks)

In the first month of trading James Builders merchant has the following sales on credit in the sales ledger.

Phion's Plumbers

invoice 24993	1,867.00
invoice 24996	3,554.00

Khalid Ltd

invoice 24988	4,986.00
invoice 24994	1,487.00
invoice 24997	4,924.00

LLOP LLP

invoice 24989	4,968.00
invoice 24991	2,370.00

The Hope Factory

invoice 24990	2,210.00
invoice 24992	4,175.00
invoice 24995	4,291.00

James downloads the bank statement and posts it to the cashbook. Customers quote their invoice numbers on payments

The bank statement for the first month of trading is as follows:

Bank of Norton	Debit	Credit
Balance bfwd		0.00
inv 24989		4,968.00
Building supplies	3,600.00	
invoice 24991		2,370.00
24,992.00		4,175.00
Building supplies	2,284.00	
invoice 24995		4,291.00
24,996.00		3,554.00
inv 24997		4,924.00
Wages	3,236.00	
Rent	4,118.00	

(a) Determine the following balances	Debit	Credit
Phion's Plumbers		
Khalid Ltd		
LLOP LLP		
The Hope Factory		

8 Marks

(b) The closing bank balance is:

	Debit	Credit
Bank		

2 Marks

ANSWERS

Task 1 (10 marks)

(a) Identify which document would be used for each of the purposes below:

Identifying transactions that have been received into or paid out of the bank account	Bank statement
Details an offer for goods and services including quantities, price and terms of payment	Quotation
Requests goods or services from a supplier and provides an authorised number from the buyer	Purchase order
Corrects an error in an invoice changing the amounts due	Credit note

b)

Supplier	Code to be assigned
Freedy Ltd	Free/106
Jones llp	Jone/107

(c) A code is made up of a combination of numbers separated by a -. This type of code is:

Numeric

(d) Identify whether the following statements about digital bookkeeping systems are true or false:

	True/False
Digital systems allow for electronic extract of data	True
Digital systems automatically extract the trial balance	True

(e) A purchase invoice has been omitted from the purchases day book. Identify one possible consequence of this error:

A prompt payment discount may be missed

Task 2 (10 Marks)

(a) What is the total of the following:

Assets	Liabilities	Capital
£	£	£
22,848.14	6,829.62	16,018.52

(b) The first transaction recorded in August related to the payment of a supplier debt. The effect of this transaction:

Reduce assets and reduce liabilities

(c) Identify the opposite effect of each bank trasaction. You should ignore VAT

Bank transaction	Opposite effect
Make a dividend payment to shareholders from bank	Dividents
Payment made to supplier for goods bought on credit	Trade payables
Payment of rent due on office	Rent
Owner takes money from till for personal expenses	Drawings
Transfer of money to imprest account for small expenses	Petty Cash
Goods bought from supplier for cash	Purchases

Task 3 (10 marks)

a)

	Amount £
Net amount before discount	1530.00
Net amount after discount	1530.00
VAT	306.00
Gross amount	1836.00

Note the prompt payment discount does not affect the net amount due

b)

Date	Details	Invoice number	Total	VAT	Net
30 May 20XX	HABNY Ltd	738699	1836.00	306.00	1530.00

c) Circle omitted	
Balance bfwd	
Invoice 425	Credit note 10587
Invoice 470	Payment
Invoice 499	Credit note 82312
Invoice 565	**Credit note 22444**

Task 4 (10 Marks)

(a) identify any discrepancies on the invoice by selecting the correct option in the table below

	Not shown on invoice	Correctly shown on invoice	Incorrectly shown on invoice
Terms of payment	answer		
Quantity			answer
Price		answer	
Discounts		answer	

4 Marks

(b)

Amount	Debit	Credit
Balances extracted to date	200,468	1192,33
Trade receivables control account	71,672	
Trade payables control account		9,112
Shareholders funds		143,795
Total	272,140	272,140

5 marks

(c) Payments of small denominations in physical cash are posted to which daybook:

Petty cashbook

1 mark

Task 5 (10 Marks)

Code the following transactions have been downloaded from the bank account.	Amount £	Code
Income from customers for sales on credit	207	1101
Cash sales	457	2101
Cash purchase	119	3201
Income from customers for sales on credit	347	1101

2 Marks

(b) What are the cashbook balances on the following dates	Debit £	Credit £
Balance on 31 July		8492
Balance on 1 August	8492	.

4 Marks

Date	Detail	Amount	Date	Detail	Amount
30 Jul	bfwd	7600			
31 Jul	Trade receivables	207			
31 Jul	Sales	457			
			31 Jul	Purchases	119
31 Jul	Trade receivables	347			
			31 Jul	cfwd	8492
	Total	8611		Total	8611
1 Aug	bfwd	8492			

Daybook	Choice
Discounts allowed	Credit to the trade receivables ledger
Purchases returns	Debit to the trade payables ledger
Purchases	Credit to the trade payables ledger
Sales	Debit to the trade receivables ledger

Task 6 (10 Marks)

Jones Plumbers would post the discount to which daybook

(a)Discounts allowed	1 Mark

(b)Detail	Date	Invoice number	Total	VAT	Net
Fred Ltd	28/09/2021	8491758	18.00	3.00	15.00
Scoob Plc	01/10/2021	8491763	22.20	3.70	18.50
Velma LLP	04/10/2021	8491768	25.80	4.30	21.50
Daphnie	07/10/2021	8491773	19.20	3.20	16.00
ABC Ltd	10/10/2021	8491778	4.68	0.78	3.90
Total			89.88	14.98	74.90

6 Marks

(c)The journal to the general ledger will be	Debit	Credit
Discount Allowed	74.90	
VAT	14.98	
Trade Receivables		89.88

3 Marks

Task 7 Note in this task the ledger was given as carried down figures. The trial balance would be the brought down figures on the following day (this is a trick that could be played in an exam).

	Amount £	Asset	Liability	Capital	Debit	Credit
Office Furniture	4,721	4,721			4,721	
Cash in safe	5,273	5,273			5,273	
Trade receivables	extracted above	8,879			8,879	
Trade payables	5,349		5,349			5,349
Bank (overdraft)	5,008		5,008			5,008
Purchases expense	3,855			-3,855	3,855	
Wages	3,318			-3,318	3,318	
Sales	5,754			5,754		5,754
VAT from HMRC	5,430	5,430			5,430	
Discounts received	4,910			4,910		4,910
Shareholders funds				10,455		10,455
		24,303	10,357	13,946	31,476	31,476

The totals of assets, liability and capital are:		
Assets	Liability	Capital
24,303	10,357	13,946

Task 8 (10 Marks)

Date	Detail	Trade payables	Purchases	VAT	Total
30-Jul-22	Balances to date	1,143.00	3,709.50	741.90	5,594.40
31-Jul-22	James Bucko		7,092.00	1,418.40	8,510.40
31-Jul-22	Bill Hat	8,323.00			8,323.00
	Total	9,466.00	10,801.50	2,160.30	22,427.80

4 Marks

The above entries will be posted to which side of the cashbook	Credit

1 Mark

The amounts to be posted to the general ledger are:			
	Amount	Debit	Credit
Trade payables	9,466.00	9,466.00	
Purchases	10,801.50	10,801.50	
VAT	2,160.30	2,160.30	

3 Marks

The total on the opposite side of the cashbook is £6786			
	Amount	Debit	Credit
The balance c/d on 31 July 2022 is	15641.80	15641.80	

2 Marks

Task 9 (10 Marks)

Debit Side						
Date	Detail	Sales	VAT	Trade receivables	Cash	Bank
01/04/2022	Balance bfwd				300.00	118.00
04/04/2022	Amounts received from customers for sales on credit			1005.00		1005.00
07/04/2022	Amounts received from customers for sales on credit			3664.00		3664.00
	Balance cfwd					
	Total			4669.00	300.00	4787.00

Credit side						
Date	Detail	Bank	Cash	VAT	Purchases	Wages
01/04/2022	Balance bfwd					
10/04/2022	Wages	2834.00				2834.00
13/04/2022	Purchase of goods for immediate payment	999.00		166.50	832.5	
	Cash Purchase		120.00	20.00	100	
	Balance cfwd	954.00	180.00			
	Total	4787.00	300.00	186.50	932.50	2834.00

8 Marks

	Debit	Credit
Bank		120.00
Cash	120.00	

2 Marks

Task 10 (10 Marks)

Phion's Plumbers

invoice 24993	1,867.00			
invoice 24996	3,554.00			3,554.00
		Cfwd	1,867.00	
	5,421.00			5,421.00
bfwd	1,867.00			

Khalid Ltd

invoice 24988	4,986.00			
invoice 24994	1,487.00			
invoice 24997	4,924.00			4,924.00
		cfwd	6,473.00	
	11,397.00			11,397.00
bfwd	6,473.00			

LLOP LLP

invoice 24989	4,968.00	Bank	4,968.00
invoice 24991	2,370.00	Bank	2,370.00
		cfwd	0.00
	7,338.00		7,338.00
bfwd	0.00		

The Hope Factory

invoice 24990	2,210.00		
invoice 24992	4,175.00		4,175.00
invoice 24995	4,291.00		4,291.00
		cfwd	2,210.00
	10,676.00		10,676.00
bfwd	2,210.00		

The closing bank balance is

	Debit	Credit
Bank	11,044.00	

2 Marks

Printed in Great Britain
by Amazon